THIRD EDITION

Classroom Discipline and Management

Clifford H. Edwards

Brigham Young University

JOHN WILEY & SONS, INC.

New York • Chichester • Weinheim • Brisbane • Singapore • Toronto

Library of Congress Cataloging-in-Publication Data
Edwards, Clifford H.
    Classroom discipline & management / Clifford H. Edwards.—3rd ed.
      p. cm.
    Rev. ed. of : Classroom discipline and management. ©1997. Includes biblio-graphical references (p.) and index.
    ISBN 0-471-36522-X (paper : alk. paper)
    1. School discipline—United States. 2. Classroom management—United States. I. Edwards, Clifford H. Classroom discipline and management. II. Title. III. Title: Classroom discipline and management.
  LB3011.E34   2000
  371.102′4—dc21   99-38840
                                              CIP

Cover photo: ©SuperStock, Inc.

Photo Credits: All photographs supplied by Clifford H. Edwards.

Printed in the United States of America

10 9 8 7 6 5 4 3 2 1

ISBN: 0-471-36522-X

For Deanna, Shon, Steve, Jeff, and Eric

Preface

Discipline, along with drug abuse, remains the single most common and pernicious problem educators face in their day-to-day teaching. Because discipline problems are so prevalent and difficult to solve, many educators and specialists in related fields have attempted to provide help for teachers. Their suggestions come from a variety of perspectives and are based on different assumptions about the purposes of schooling and the capabilities of students. Teachers often fail to scrutinize the assumptions on which these discipline approaches are based or to measure them against their own values and educational philosophy. Some teachers use a procedure simply if it "works." The extent to which a discipline approach works is, of course, a critical concern. However, there are other considerations, such as the assumptions upon which the approach is based and the teacher's own philosophy, that must be included in decisions about discipline.

Knowing a successful method of discipline is essential to teaching; so are a teacher's own values and beliefs about discipline. This book is designed to help teachers thoughtfully examine various approaches to discipline along with their personal philosophy and then either choose an existing approach or create one. To make decisions about discipline, teachers must have a thorough understanding of the assumptions that undergird various discipline approaches in addition to knowledge of theory and practical applications. Otherwise, informed choice is impossible.

Identifying basic assumptions is important for two reasons. First, teachers need to follow consistently their own educational philosophy, not only in matters of discipline but in the overall instructional program as well. Teachers who are guided by consistent philosophy are able to teach with integrity and authenticity. Second, teachers who carefully examine their educational policies in terms of personal philosophy are able to achieve a level of commitment unattainable by those who are less systematic in examining their personal values and teaching practices. Committed teachers are more inclined to devote themselves to the profession and achieve success.

One aspect of discipline often ignored is the extent to which a particular theory or approach is designed to prevent or correct discipline problems. Most models claim to correct discipline problems. Few are deliberately designed to prevent them. This important consideration is raised for each discipline approach presented. Another important topic covered is the question of whether a particular discipline model is appropriate for schoolwide application or is limited to classroom use.

Successful discipline also depends on how well teachers manage various classroom routines as well as their ability to establish positive relationships with their students. Positive student–teacher interactions depend appreciably on how well teachers can relate to a diverse student population. Teachers commonly need to deal with issues regarding race, culture, gender, and exceptionality. These considerations are a basic focus of this book.

ORGANIZATION

The sequence of chapters is arranged to help teachers make consistent, rational decisions about discipline. Chapter 1 is an introduction to the effects as well as the sources of discipline problems in the schools. Chapter 2 provides a model for determining a personal discipline approach. In Chapters 3 through 10 various discipline models are described in terms of basic principles and procedures. The models selected cover a wide spectrum of possible approaches.

In Chapters 11 and 12 the various models are considered for inclusion in a comprehensive discipline program. Chapter 11 shows how to compare various discipline approaches with one another and to select the one that most closely corresponds to one's personal philosophy. Chapter 12 provides an example to illustrate the development of a comprehensive, personal approach to discipline that is consistent with specified criteria and is based on verifiable assumptions.

The focus in Chapters 13, 14, and 15 is on classroom management. Chapter 13 is designed to help teachers ensure that their discipline approach is consistent with their overall instructional program. Emphasis is placed on cooperative learning as an option to traditional instruction. Chapter 14 demonstrates the importance of having good student–teacher relationships, particularly as they relate to self-concept development and multicultural experiences. Chapter 15 shows teachers how to properly manage the various aspects of the classroom—teacher–student relationships, time, the physical environment—so that students will stay on-task and maintain their interest in learning.

Acknowledgments

The following professors provided timely and helpful reviews of the manuscript, for which I am grateful: Sue R. Abegglen, Culver-Stockton College; Karen J. Agne, Plattsburgh State University of New York; Karen A. Bosch, Virginia Wesleyan College; Sandra L. DiGiaimo, University of Scranton; George M. Rawlins, Austin Peay State University; and M. Kayt Sunwood, Iowa State University.

Brief Contents

Contents

UNIT 2
Discipline Models   43

CHAPTER 3
Behavior Modification: B. F. Skinner   44

CHAPTER 4
Assertive Discipline: Lee Canter   68

CHAPTER 7
Teacher Effectiveness Training: Thomas Gordon   147

CHAPTER 10
The Jones Model: Fredric H. Jones   234

UNIT 3
Creating a Comprehensive Discipline Program   259

CHAPTER 11
Choosing a Discipline Approach   260

CHAPTER 12
Creating a Personal Theory of Discipline   279

UNIT 4
Classroom Management Approaches and Procedures   297

CHAPTER 13
Classroom Management and Instruction   298

UNIT

1

Problems and Issues
in Discipline

The sources of school discipline problems are many and varied. Home, society, and school all play a role. Educators often contend that problems in school stem from children's experiences at home or in society at large. Schools, however, must take responsibility for some of these problems. Some home and social problems do carry over into the schools, but many difficulties are created through various school practices and conditions.

For schools, creating an appropriate learning environment is critical. Learning is what schools are about. An improper learning environment strikes at the very heart of the school's purpose. Because good learning conditions are critical and because discipline problems are a constant threat to learning, classroom discipline is very important. The need for good discipline has stimulated educators and others to create and promote a variety of approaches to ensure that a proper learning environment is maintained. These different approaches are based on various assumptions about human beings and how they should be treated in the schools. These approaches also produce different outcomes.

Because many different discipline options are available to teachers and because there is no one generally accepted theory of discipline, individual teachers must decide for themselves which discipline approach to use. This decision requires teachers to examine the various assumptions on which each discipline theory is built, as well as its principles and practices, and compare them with their own personal values and beliefs. The purpose of Unit 1 is to help readers to begin this important process.

1

Discipline Problems and Their Causes

OBJECTIVES

This chapter is designed to help you
1. Understand the nature of discipline problems and their causes.
2. Recognize the roles of home, society, and school in creating discipline problems.
3. Identify some common mistakes teachers make when they discipline their classes.

Introduction

Children often bring problems to school that originate in other areas of their lives. Teachers must learn to recognize these problems and deal with them effectively rather than contributing to them. Some of the more serious problems involve divorce, abandonment, death, and various forms of abuse. Sometimes school personnel or students' peers aggravate conditions by reacting in ways that exacerbate the situation. Teachers need to discern the nature of problems children bring to school but also need to recognize problems that are the result of how schools operate. School problems include those that relate to academics as well as extracurricular activities, school rules and procedures, and personal relationships. The frustrations encountered by some students regarding these matters may result in extreme reactions. For example, children who are excluded from belonging to a particular clique or who are ridiculed as outsiders may sometimes take extreme measures against those who reject them. Sometimes devastating confrontations and loss of life are the results. Educators must be able not only to skillfully deal with these problems but also to recognize the conditions that promote these reactions and take steps to prevent them.

▼ Mr. Haskell looked up as Marcia sauntered into the room. He watched out of the corner of his eye as Marcia swaggered down the aisle between the first two rows of desks and took a seat in the back of the room. After a similar incident the day before, Mr. Haskell had appealed to the class to help him solve the problem. Earlier in the year the class had agreed to rules and consequences regarding misbehavior in class. They had decided then that students who disrupted class had to forfeit their right to sit where they wanted and instead be placed in a designated seat near the front of the room. Confronted with Marcia's recent disruptiveness, they had together agreed that she should sit in the front row seat next to Mr. Haskell's desk until further notice. Obviously, Marcia was ignoring these directions and provoking a confrontation. Mr. Haskell shuddered as he contemplated the scene that would probably result if he tried to get Marcia to cooperate. Marcia was always picking fights with other students and routinely threw spit wads and paper airplanes around the room. Mr. Haskell could not remember the last time Marcia had not disrupted the class by talking loudly to other class members. Then there was that arrogant smirk whenever she misbehaved. It was easy to see that she was just issuing a challenge. Mr. Haskell hated to confront Marcia because she always seemed to prevail. Most of the class was assembled now. Mr. Haskell knew that the bell was going to ring any minute, and he still had not decided how to deal with the situation. Marcia was looking at him with a big smile on her face. The other students were looking on expectantly, wondering how their teacher would handle Marcia this time. Mr. Haskell stepped reluctantly to the front of the room and, looking at Marcia, asked, "Class, what did you decide the consequences should be for anyone who disrupts class?"

Amanda quickly replied for the class, "They were to be moved to the front of the class."

Looking directly at Marcia, Mr. Haskell said, "Marcia, you can either take your seat here near my desk or be excused to talk to Mr. Pugmire in the counseling department about finding a new English class."

The entire class was now looking at Marcia. She slowly rose to her feet and, making her way to the front of the class, picked up the hall pass and defiantly walked through the classroom door. Mr. Haskell was suddenly aware that he had been holding his breath. He silently exhaled and filled his lungs again. "Thank heavens she's gone," he thought. "I wonder what she will do now?" Coupled with his desire to get Marcia out of his class was a tinge of regret that he had been unable to reach her. He knew of Marcia's family situation—that her father had been convicted of drug possession and was currently serving a prison term. He knew also that Marcia was actively involved in one of the local street gangs.

Forcing these thoughts from his mind, Mr. Haskell turned to the class and said, "All right, class, let's get started with our lesson for the day." For about 30 minutes Mr. Haskell involved the class in a spirited discussion. Just before he was about to close the discussion and give the class a few minutes to start their homework assignment, the classroom door opened and in walked Mr. Pugmire, directing Marcia ahead of him. Walking straight up to Mr. Haskell he said, in a voice the entire class could hear, "Mr. Haskell, you're just going to have to take Marcia back in your class. The other 11th-grade English classes are filled. There is nowhere else she can be placed." Mr. Haskell looked at Mr. Pugmire's determined face and then back at Marcia. He anticipated what he would see—the telltale smirk was slowly forming on Marcia's lips. Without waiting for further direction, Marcia boldly turned and strutted to the back of the room, where she defiantly took her seat.

Causes of Discipline Problems

Teachers can often be overwhelmed by the discipline problems with which they have to deal. They cause some of these problems themselves, of course. However, many of the problems they face are an outgrowth of problems at home and in society or of conditions and administrative procedures in the school. As illustrated in the story about Mr. Haskell and Marcia, teachers can sometimes be confronted with a combination of these problems all at once. Their combined effects may sometimes make it nearly impossible to handle disruptive students effectively. When these difficulties persist despite one's best efforts to solve them, it is common for a teacher to blame other contributing factors. Mr. Haskell could well have blamed parents, the society at large, or the ineffective performance of counselors and administrators. Such recrimination, of course, does little to change conditions and solve problems. Certainly, teachers can work with administrators and counselors in an attempt to alter school policies and procedures that impede effective discipline. They can do little, however, to change influences outside the school that promote children's misbehavior. But, by understanding these outside influences, they can be better prepared to manage the discipline problems that result.

THE ROLE OF THE HOME

Various home experiences have an influence on children's behavior. If parents spend little time at home, children may seek unsuitable social experiences elsewhere, experiences that sometimes have devastating consequences. Even when parents are at home, parent–child interactions may be laced with conflicts. Factors such as divorce and poverty, as well as physical and mental abuse, can adversely affect children's ability to function properly. Children from severely dysfunctional families in particular face enormous adjustment problems at school.

Four aspects of dysfunctional families will be discussed briefly in this section:

- Damage to self-concept
- Attention deprivation
- Love deprivation
- Excessive control

Damage to Self-Concept. The development of self-concept in children begins long before they start attending school. The confidence with which children enter school will have been either enhanced or diminished by various home experiences. Children are able, at an early age, to perceive their own helplessness when compared with larger and more capable adults (Harris, 1967). This perception is perhaps the reason why children so readily seek adult approval. Children's outlook on life depends generally on how successful parents are in helping them shift from feeling helpless to feeling confident about themselves. The very foundation of children's growth depends on their achieving a positive image of themselves as they form a personal identity. Achieving this image involves developing a sense of personal control over their lives.

Dysfunctional families provide little or none of the emotional support children need to develop this control, and children from such families experience extreme personal problems (Biehler & Snowman, 1982). The success in school of children from dysfunctional homes is greatly limited (Purkey, 1970). One problem promoting dysfunctional family life is divorce. Divorce can be an especially difficult problem for children, putting pressure on them in several ways. For example, some children feel personally responsible for the breakup of their parents. Loss of love and support from one or both parents is a common result of divorce simply from the increased absence of one or both parents. Often, parents engage in postdivorce battles that undermine children's confidence in their parents and promote an atmosphere of conflict. Such conditions stimulate a good deal of insecurity and trauma. In addition, financial problems obviously increase. Sometimes the accustomed lifestyle can be catastrophically disrupted. Adult supervision can also be greatly reduced, predisposing children to spend more time with peers in unsupervised settings where there is greater potential for crime and other problems. If the single parent must work to provide for the family, there may be even less supervision. This may pose a problem for children in some neighborhoods where it is unsafe for them to be home alone. Under these circumstances, children commonly become preoccupied with things other than their schoolwork. Not only do they tend to devote less time and energy to school, they also fail to get the help and encouragement from parents they need to do well in their studies. They also may not receive sufficient attention from parents to enable them to develop a positive image of themselves.

Attention Deprivation.   Children who do not get enough attention at home often compensate by seeking attention from their teachers. Unfortunately, many children receive their parents' attention only when they misbehave. If they do not disturb parents unduly, they are ignored. These conditions encourage unacceptable behavior and discourage acceptable behavior. Children from such homes discover that their bad behavior is a sure way to get the attention they crave. When children learn these behavior patterns at home, they tend to repeat them in school. If teachers of these

Problems at home or at school can significantly interfere with students' inclination to learn.

children do not recognize these patterns, they can fall into the same trap of attending only to the children's misbehavior.

Love Deprivation.   Love deprivation is similar to attention deprivation. In fact, children usually consider attention to be an indication of how much they are loved. They feel unloved when parents are too preoccupied to give them sufficient attention. Some parents have the mistaken idea that the *quality* of time spent with children can make up for the lack of *quantity*. Quality time is obviously critical. However, children often interpret the lack of time spent as lack of caring. Children deprived of love often cause discipline problems as they try to satisfy this need. They may become so preoccupied in their quest that they gain very little from school.

Excessive Control.   A history of excessive control at home may also create discipline problems in the school, particularly when the level of control has been extreme. Human beings need freedom; they want to control their own lives. They also want to control others (Glasser, 1984). This conflict is particularly challenging in the rearing and teaching of children. As children mature, they increasingly seek freedom from adult control. Conscientious parents ordinarily allow and even encourage their children to assert their independence as the children demonstrate an ability to use it wisely. However, some parents not only fail to teach their children to act independently in appropriate situations; they actively try to stifle all independent thought or action in their children, which they regard as signs of rebellion. The conflict between the children's desire for freedom and the parents' unwillingness to allow it may actually encourage the children to rebel. Rebellion at home may extend to the school and other areas of society. In dysfunctional homes, parental control may take the form of abuse, whose symptoms can show up in children as extreme rebellion, criminal behavior, or withdrawal.

THE ROLE OF SOCIETY

Society has a significant role in promoting school discipline problems. This role is sometimes far more influential than that of the family. Social influences may be pervasive because of parental neglect or because of the nature of the family's role in child rearing. In addition intrusions are made by various social elements over which parents may have little control.

Four areas of social influence will be referred to in this section:

- Gang activity and drugs
- Peer pressure
- Technology
- Racial and class conflicts

Gang Activity and Drugs.   Family influences and social influences on discipline problems are usually interrelated. Rejection at home, for example, may encourage children to search elsewhere for acceptance. Rejected children are often attracted to gangs, even though—or perhaps because—certain gangs flout accepted behavioral norms. A gang may satisfy a child's need for attention and for an identity. Gang members often demand and receive greater allegiance from one another than from their families. This allegiance further alienates children from their families and solidifies their gang identity. As evidence of their worthiness to join a gang, children are sometimes expected to participate in acts deplored by the rest of society—an armed robbery or a mugging, for example—and they may be periodically required to repeat such acts to confirm their commitment to the gang's value system. Such participation is designed to force members to choose between the gang and society and to reinforce loyalty within the gang. Gangs tend to be territorial, and conflict between gangs or within a gang usually revolves around turf, privilege, or property. The conflict can turn violent. When gangs become established, school officials may have considerable difficulty dislodging them.

A problem often associated with gangs, but certainly not limited to them, is drug abuse. Using or selling illegal drugs not only influences students' behavior directly but also alters the general atmosphere of the school. Drug abuse and its associated violence have become so severe in many schools that school officials must enlist the help of law enforcement personnel to maintain order.

Peer Pressure.   Peer pressure, which is part of everyday life at school, contributes significantly to shaping students' behavior. If their peer group considers school a joke, students may go along with the crowd and put little effort into their studies; nearly every large high school has such a group, universally recognized but rarely acknowledged.

If students place great value on conspicuous consumption, they may feel compelled to keep up with the latest styles. An increasing number of students carry and listen to portable CD players, which often interfere with their attentiveness in class.

Technology.   Even the kind of music children play may be a source of conflict between them and their teachers. Rap music is sometimes identified as being connected to various specific crimes committed by youth. Rap music is often confrontational and violent in its orientation. Sometimes it suggests that violence be aimed at a particular segment of the population, like police officers. Rap music is readily available to youth not only on tapes and compact discs but also through music video channels on television.

In addition, there has been an enormously rapid growth in the availability of videocassettes, either for rental or purchase, containing programming that is violent and/or pornographic. There is evidence that this kind of programming has a negative impact on children's behavior and may, in part, be responsible for specific criminal behavior (Paik & Comstock, 1994). Currently, there is also a controversy surrounding the availability of pornography via computer networks. Even very young children have access to these materials through the Internet. Schools have tried to block access to offensive materials, but this may not have taken place in some homes.

Furthermore, students' schoolwork—and their attitudes—may suffer if they work long hours at part-time jobs to earn money for clothes, music, or electronic equipment. (Some students, of course, have to work because their families need the money.) If students feel that their interests lie elsewhere, they may drop out of school.

Racial and Class Conflicts.   Racial problems also contribute to the growing unrest and conflict in society. In many larger cities, civil unrest along with forced integration and other factors stimulated "white flight" (the white population leaving urban areas). This created central city areas populated by the black poor and other disadvantaged racial groups. These pockets of poverty along with racial tensions have promoted riots accompanied by burning and looting of a magnitude that is truly frightening. These shifting demographics and racial tensions along with changing economic conditions and unemployment create a climate that is like a powder keg waiting for the fuse to be lit. On April 29, 1992, in Los Angeles, when the defendants in the Rodney King case were acquitted of police brutality, the fuse was lit, and the resultant riot escalated into a horrifying display of violence. Episodes of this kind are more likely to polarize races than stimulate unity.

The hoped for "melting pot" of various races coming to America and creating a new "American race" has never become a reality. Different races have settled in their own enclaves, trying to maintain a sense of racial identity while at the same time trying to participate in the American Dream of wealth and prosperity. However, many find it difficult even to sustain themselves, which is due to the unemployment and poverty that surround them. In some areas, particularly in those states bordering Mexico and the Pacific Ocean, immigration, both legal and illegal, has created extreme economic pressures. Current law provides for even illegal aliens to receive welfare assistance and other benefits. In California this has reached crisis proportions, precipitating the passage of a referendum that limits benefits to illegal aliens. Because the bulk of the illegal aliens are Hispanics, and because they make up an enormous percentage of the poor as well as an increasing proportion of the total population in California, conditions are ripening for additional rioting and violence. Active drug trafficking and other criminal activity exacerbate the situation.

Children who grow up in such environments will experience a far less productive education. Problems they encounter in society find their way into the school in the form of less learning, poor emotional adjustment, violence, and discipline problems. Children, of course, benefit less in schools with extreme discipline problems. This unfortunately undermines their capacity to escape from the conditions that keep them bound to poverty generation after generation.

THE ROLE OF THE SCHOOL

Teachers usually consider students to be the source of school discipline problems. However, many behaviors should be looked on as normal reactions by children to deficiencies in the school as an institution and to teachers and administrators as directors of the educational enterprise. In fact, the school not only may promote misbehavior in students; it may also help create conditions that put children at risk generally. Teachers and administrators can invite discipline problems if they

1. Misunderstand learning conditions and require students to learn information that is not meaningful to them
2. Fail to encourage the development of independent thinking patterns in students

3. Establish rigid conditions for students to meet in order to feel accepted
4. Sponsor a competitive grading system that prohibits success for the majority of the students and erodes their self-concepts
5. Exercise excessive control over students and fail to provide an environment in which children can become autonomous and independent
6. Use discipline procedures that promote misbehavior (Edwards, 1989)

Each of these problem-promoting practices will be discussed in detail in this section.

Instruction Without Context.   Educators may fail their students if they teach concepts as though they were abstract, self-contained entities. Outside the school, children learn by acquiring information in a real-life context and applying it to new situations and experiences. In school, however, students may be expected to manipulate symbolic information and to apply it in ways that are detached from the real world. Under such conditions, children fail to make proper associations and are unable to apply what they learn to the problems they face each day (Resnick, 1987). Because they are unable to readily comprehend the usefulness of what they are taught in school, they are frustrated. They see school as unrelated to real life. They are required to attend, but they find no meaning there. They repeatedly ask why they have to learn what teachers offer and often sabotage the learning of classmates.

A number of things can be done to alleviate this problem. Considerable emphasis is currently being placed on school reform in America. One of these reform movements is an effort to involve students in community service. These service experiences, designed as outgrowths of academic programs, are intended to give students an opportunity to learn in practical settings. Commonly, these service experiences help students learn civic responsibility, but they also provide a means of acquiring important social, scientific, and communication skills.

For example, students in Salt Lake City have been responsible for the cleanup of a hazardous waste site, the passage of two crucial environmental laws, the planting of hundreds of trees, and the completion of several neighborhood improvement projects (Lewis, 1991). In the south Bronx, students have been involved in the restoration of a building to be used for homeless people. In Chicopee, Massachusetts, middle schools have saved the city $119,500 by helping to solve sewage problems. Students in Brooks County, Georgia, were responsible for establishing a day care center that has been in operation since 1981 (Nathan & Kielsmeier, 1991). Researchers have concluded that these activities not only have enhanced and broadened students' academic performance but have contributed greatly to the social and psychological development of participants (Conrad & Hedin, 1991).

In science education, a similar new approach has been advanced in a program called Science Technology Society (STS). In this program, students identify a social problem that can be studied both scientifically and technologically. They may, for example, choose to work on a specific pollution problem, using their science skills to take measurements of various pollutants and track their effects. When the problem has been carefully studied, the students make their recommendations to appropriate community groups. In some cases, when they have received little or no response, groups of students have been given free legal services to initiate litigation to correct the problem (Bybee, 1985).

Students can also gain academic experience that is less abstract through work–study programs in which they spend part of the school day working for various community agencies. Each student may work in a doctor's office, insurance company, factory, or other location to learn how school is related to the world of work and to explore various career opportunities. When students are involved in service- and project-based curricula, far fewer discipline and personal problems can be anticipated.

Failure to Teach Thinking Skills.   When children are consistently unable to solve their problems, they often seek to escape them through alcohol or other drugs or various thrill-seeking activities. Some drop out of school or even commit suicide (Frymier, 1988). Some children fail to find satisfactory solutions to their problems because they have difficulty thinking through them. Some have trouble organizing their lives and responding appropriately to life's demands. Others are unable to set priorities for themselves. If higher-order thinking skills were regularly taught in the schools, a good deal of frustration and failure, as well as behavioral problems, could be avoided. Learning these skills would also help children deal with conflicts at home and elsewhere.

Traditional methods of teaching make learning a passive endeavor. Students are just expected to assimilate information. Recently, cognitive psychologists have proposed that learners be allowed to generate their own conceptual structures (Jones, 1988). Children actually resist knowledge assimilation; instead, they insist on adding to their present conceptual structures only the knowledge that makes sense to them personally (Osborne & Wittrock, 1983). In other words, they tend to learn only what fits in with what they already know. Teachers must introduce children to higher-order thinking so that they can make more valid conceptual structures of the world. Failure to do so dooms children to the frustration of taking simplistic lessons memorized in school and trying to apply them to the complex problems of the modern world. It is unfortunate, and ironic, that the children who most lack advanced thinking skills are considered at risk because they also lack basic skills. They are assigned remedial work, while their more advanced counterparts are given more meaningful and integrated learning experiences (Shavelson, 1985), experiences from which they too might greatly benefit.

A number of excellent programs are currently available for teaching children how to think and make valid decisions. Most have sets of materials that can be used as supplementary lessons in nearly every classroom. Chance (1986) has reviewed eight different programs and compared their characteristics, goals, methods, underlying philosophy, and target audiences. The eight programs include sample exercises, along with research data and staff development requirements. These programs are

- Cognitive Research Trust (CoRT) Thinking Lessons
- Productive Thinking Program
- Philosophy for Children
- Odyssey
- Instrumental Enrichment
- Problem Solving and Comprehension

- Techniques of Learning
- Thoughtful Teaching

Teaching thinking skills can provide a means of improving students' motivation and help solve the perennial problems of failure, disillusionment, and unmet potential in students. In the process, many discipline problems can be avoided (Marzano et al., 1988).

Nonacceptance.   Without realizing it, many teachers convey nonacceptance to some of their students. For example, when teachers force students to do a task in a prescribed way, they implicitly show a lack of confidence in the students' ability to make decisions about their own work. In an attempt to show approval, a teacher may say to a student, "You have done good work, but I know you can do better" or "It really helps a lot when you clean up your work area." Such praise carries with it implied criticism; it rewards students for conformity but leaves their need for acceptance unfulfilled. Children do need to grow and therefore to change. However, they also need to feel that they are acceptable as they are.

The simplest way to avoid conveying nonacceptance is to permit students to evaluate themselves more and to establish their own directions and expectations. Allowing self-evaluation does not mean simply letting students give themselves a grade. Children must compare their own performances over time to achieve a sense of their own growth and to learn and accept the true value of their efforts.

Competitive Grading.   Many schools foster competition between children through the use of grades. Only a few students, however, are consistently good at taking tests. The rest must find other means of bolstering their sense of worth. Unfortunately, many of them conclude that they are less able—they would say "dumber"—than more successful classmates and are therefore less valuable.

Thus, in an effort to motivate them, schools can demoralize students with the implicit threat of possible failure. They virtually ensure that many students will fail and feel the sense of incompetence that comes with failure (Englander, 1986).

Some teachers make sincere efforts to reduce the impact of school competition by giving more high grades or refusing to give students failing grades. Many teachers realize the detrimental effects of grading on their students but feel powerless to change the system. Some school districts actually impose grade quotas on teachers, who are not allowed to give too many high grades for fear that grade inflation will erode academic standards.

Making evaluation less traumatic for students may be one of the most difficult problems teachers have to face. The system of norm-based grades, in which the performance of each student is compared with that of others, may have to be set aside in favor of other systems. Such changes certainly merit consideration. Many teachers who recognize the negative effects of grades have already made some adjustments to lessen their impact. Nevertheless, competition for grades, with all its attendant problems, continues.

One adjustment some teachers have made is to evaluate students' progress individually and grade them accordingly. Others have involved their students in the evaluation process. This practice has the added advantage of helping students become more self-directed. The problem with most of these adjustments is that letter grades are given as a consequence of the evaluations. These grades, which still carry the connotation that students are being compared with one another academically, are likely to promote some of the same problems as grades given in the regular norm-based system. This problem will continue until universities and employers begin to accept forms of evaluation other than comparative grading and school professionals and parents begin to recognize fully the negative impact of grades and make appropriate changes.

Excessive Coercion.   Much is said by teachers and school administrators about teaching children to be more responsible. This "responsibility" often consists of completing assignments on time and accomplishing other tasks as directed. Students judged to be the most responsible and mature are those who comply exactly with expectations. Responsibility, however, requires the exercise of free will and the opportunity to make choices. Ironically, a common assumption behind many school practices is that children are unable to govern themselves or even to learn how to be self-regulating. Students, therefore, are given few opportunities to make decisions. Teachers fear that students will behave improperly—get "out of control"—if they are allowed "too much" freedom. Undoubtedly, some children appear to have little ability to direct their own lives. This apparent inability prompts teachers to give them excessive guidance and to exercise too much coercive control. The result is increased rebellion by students. When children rebel, teachers believe that they have made correct assumptions about the students' irresponsibility. More control is the usual remedy. Unfortunately, rebellion cannot be subdued by coercion and control. Perhaps some children can be broken in this process, but many others rebel all the more. These "incorrigible" children usually end up being expelled.

Children who are coerced commonly develop a sense of personal powerlessness. They feel like second-class citizens and justifiably so. They are, in fact, second-class citizens because they may be subject to the wishes and whims of teachers and school administrators without recourse. Sometimes students are given quasi-authority when elected to the student council or other student governing bodies. Their decisions and actions are always subject to veto by those who have the real authority. Under these conditions students are prone to put their authority to the test only to have their suspicions confirmed that they have none at all. They are left with no way to appeal their powerlessness but to rebel.

Happily, responsibility can be taught by providing children with more real opportunities to make decisions. Responsible actions will replace rebellious ones when children are taught to make valid decisions within a context of free choice and when they are held personally accountable for the decisions they make. This is how true responsibility is fostered. A balance must be struck between the teacher's control and students' self-determination. Students should not simply be turned loose to do as they wish. They must be involved with the teacher in responsible decision making.

Punishment.   The method of discipline used by teachers and administrators may itself contribute to discipline problems. Historically, punishment is how society has dealt with infractions. It is still the most common way to deal with discipline problems in school. From 80% to 90% of the rule violations in schools are dealt with punitively

(Englander, 1986). The long tradition of punishment in schools has been supported by general child-rearing practices, court decisions, and public opinion. Part of this tradition includes corporal punishment. The use of corporal punishment has been upheld by the U.S. Supreme Court, but by 1996 23 states had forbidden its use in the schools (Hyman, 1996). Despite the fact that corporal punishment is increasingly being abolished by state laws, Chase (1975) reports that the majority of teachers and parents believe in its use. Perhaps in time it will be universally considered unacceptable for use in schools.

Although punishment is still the most prevalent means of dealing with problems in the schools, most of the research on punishment is dated. There seems to be little current interest in the subject. In addition, most of the research that is done in this area focuses on the extent to which punishment can be successfully used to enforce students' compliance. Little attention has been given to other effects of punishment. The research on punishment and its effects is explored more fully in Chapter 4.

If punishment tends to be ineffective and produces unexpected negative results, what can be done to replace it? Most of the discipline approaches outlined in this book are punishment-free. Among them, teachers will find a number of ways to deal with misbehavior in nonpunitive ways.

▼ SUMMARY

Discipline problems experienced in school may originate in the family or in society at large, but many problems are aggravated and sometimes caused by school policies and procedures as well as by teachers and other school personnel. To reduce the number of discipline problems, teachers need to make learning more relevant and meaningful, foster independent thinking, show greater acceptance of diversity, encourage cooperative learning, avoid excessive control, and discontinue the use of punishment to discipline children.

CENTRAL IDEAS

1. School discipline problems can be created at home if parents do not provide their children
   a. family unity
   b. the support they need to develop a healthy self-concept
   c. adequate attention
   d. unconditional love
   e. an opportunity to develop responsible independence
2. Certain aspects of society can cause discipline problems in the school. The following social phenomena are particularly important:
   a. Peer pressure plays a strong role in shaping children's behavior.
   b. Gangs in particular often recruit members from among children who have experienced adjustment problems at school and at home. Gangs often create problems for schools by pushing drugs and encouraging

delinquency and violence in their members, especially participation in illegal acts as a sign of their allegiance to the gang.
c.   Factors such as the drive to earn money to buy the latest styles of clothing can also affect students' participation in and attitudes toward school.
3.   Schools create their own discipline problems by
a.   failing to provide children relevant, meaningful learning
b.   failing to help children learn to think independently
c.   failing to show children they are accepted
d.   exercising too much coercion
e.   forcing children to compete with one another and thereby limiting the number who can be successful
f.   disciplining with punishment

REFERENCES

Biehler, R., & Snowman, J. (1982). *Psychology applied to teaching.* Boston: Houghton Mifflin.
Bybee, R. (Ed.). (1985). *Science Technology Society: 1985 yearbook of the National Science Teacher's Association.* Washington, DC: National Science Teacher's Association.
Chance, P. (1986). *Thinking in the classroom: A survey of programs.* New York: Teacher's College Press.
Chase, N. F. (1975). *A child is being beaten: Violence against children, an American tragedy.* New York: Holt, Rinehart & Winston.
Conrad, D., & Hedin, D. (1991). School-based community service: What we know from research and theory. *Phi Delta Kappan, 72,* 543–549.
Edwards, C. H. (1989). Self-regulation: The key to motivating at-risk children. *The Clearing House, 63*(2), 59–62.
Englander, M. E. (1986). *Strategies for classroom discipline.* New York: Praeger.
Frymier, J. (1988). Understanding and preventing teen suicide: An interview with Barry Garfinkel. *Phi Delta Kappan, 69,* 290–293.
Glasser, W. (1984). *Control theory: A new explanation of how we control our lives.* New York: Harper & Row.
Harris, T. A. (1967). *I'm OK—You're OK.* New York: Avon Books.
Hyman, I. A. (1996, March). *The enemy within: Tales of punishment, politics, and prevention.* Paper presented at the annual meeting of the School of Psychologists, Atlanta, GA.
Jones, B. F. (1988). Toward redefining models of curriculum and instruction for students at risk. In B. Z. Presseisen (Ed.), *At-risk students and thinking: Perspectives from research* (pp. 76–103). Washington, DC: National Education Association and Research for Better Schools.
Lewis, B. (1991). *The kids' guide to social action.* Minneapolis, MN: Free Spirit.
Marzano, R. J., Brandt, R. S., Hughes, C. S., Jones, B. F., Presseisen, B. Z., Rankin, S. C., & Suhor, C. (1988). *Dimensions of thinking: A framework for curriculum and instruction.* Alexandria, VA: The Association for Supervision and Curriculum Development.
Nathan, J., & Kielsmeier, J. (1991). The sleeping giant of school reform. *Phi Delta Kappan, 72,* 729–742.

Osborne, R. J., & Wittrock, M. C. (1983). Learning science: A generative process. *Science Education, 67,* 489–508.

Paik, H., & Comstock, G. (1994). The effects of television violence on antisocial behavior: A meta-analysis. *Communication Research, 21*(4), 516–546.

Purkey, W. W. (1970). *Self-concept and school achievement.* Englewood Cliffs, NJ: Prentice-Hall.

Resnick, L. B. (1987). Learning in school and out. *Educational Researcher, 16,* 13–20.

Shavelson, R. J. (1985). *Schemata and teaching routines.* Paper presented at the annual meeting of the American Educational Research Association, Chicago.

2

Making Decisions About Discipline

OBJECTIVES

This chapter is designed to help you

1. Understand the value of theory in school discipline.
2. Recognize the fundamental emphasis that different approaches to discipline place on the amount of control the teacher exercises or the amount of autonomy students have.
3. Use criteria to evaluate different discipline approaches.
4. Identify and validate assumptions on which discipline approaches are based.
5. Learn how to select or create a discipline approach that is most appropriate for you.
6. Determine not only whether a discipline approach corrects and prevents discipline problems in the classroom but also whether it can be applied to schoolwide discipline.
7. Develop reflective thinking skill to use in making decisions about teaching and discipline.

Introduction

To be successful in the classroom, teachers need a well-planned, individual approach to discipline. They must understand various psychological theories of discipline and the assumptions on which they are based, they must understand their own values and educational philosophy, and they must take an approach to discipline that is in harmony with their convictions. Unfortunately, some teachers unwittingly discipline their students in ways contrary to their own beliefs without considering the inherent conflicts. When teachers' behavior is incompatible with their beliefs, they not only experience personal conflict but confuse their students as well. Teachers must clarify objectives, both for themselves and for their students, and then ensure that learning experiences and discipline procedures are consistent with these objectives.

Educational Philosophies and Child Development Theories

Different educational philosophies dictate different school purposes, and within these different philosophies are a number of child development theories designed to achieve these purposes. Educational philosophies have been variously categorized, mostly according to the relative amount of freedom or control to be exercised by teachers and students. These philosophies emphasize the role either of the teacher in transmitting knowledge and culture to students in an orderly and controlled manner or of students in determining for themselves what is important to learn from the teacher. Theories of child development and discipline follow a similar pattern (see Figure 2.1). Generally, these theories can be arranged into three categories:

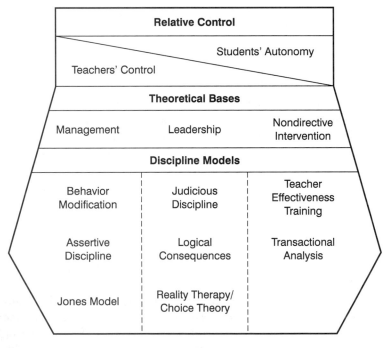

FIGURE 2.1
Theoretical bases for eight models of discipline.

- Management theories
- Nondirective intervention theories
- Leadership theories

MANAGEMENT THEORIES

Management theories assume that children's growth and development are consequences of external conditions over which they may have little control. Children, according to this point of view, are born as "blank slates" and are "written upon" by the environment. These theories hold that human development can be explained essentially in terms of observable human behaviors and the environmental stimuli that promote or reinforce these behaviors. Changing children's behavior is simply a matter of arranging environmental conditions (e.g., giving rewards) to influence desired responses.

The leading proponent of management theories is B. F. Skinner. His work has become very popular and enjoys considerable support in the schools and in other institutions. Teachers who use management theories believe that the behavior of children must be controlled because, they assume, children are unable to adequately monitor and control themselves and because without supervision their behavior will be erratic and potentially destructive. Therefore, teachers must control the students' environment to elicit only desirable behaviors (Martin & Pear, 1992).

NONDIRECTIVE INTERVENTION THEORIES

Nondirective intervention theories are based on the assumption that children develop from an inner unfolding. Children contain within themselves the necessary "blueprint" for complete rational self-determination. Intervention in the form of control or directed interaction is unnecessary for children to reach their fullest potential. Children achieve the best possible growth only if they are allowed to direct themselves. From this perspective, children have a natural inclination to learn and become self-directed and self-actualized. Actualization is a process of personal growth that only the individual can properly direct and achieve.

The role of the teacher in this process is to provide conditions that promote self-growth and help to clarify life experiences for the individual. Carl Rogers is the most popular proponent of this child development approach. In the school setting, he advocates considerable freedom for children. So long as children are able to direct their own school experiences, Rogers argues, there is little cause to fear that they will make inappropriate choices (Rogers & Freiberg, 1994).

LEADERSHIP THEORIES

Leadership theories are based on the assumption that children develop from an interaction of both inner and outer influences. From this viewpoint, behavior is the product of a multitude of factors, each of which is vital. Children can be understood only insofar as all these factors and their relationships are properly taken into account.

Growth is believed to come from a constant interplay between children and their social experiences.

The role of teachers from this perspective is one of leadership. It is assumed that children can achieve a state of responsible self-determination if the teacher uses appropriate intervention strategies. Children, it is believed, want to control their own lives and can eventually do so responsibly if teachers and other adults teach them how. Children continually try to gain greater competence and achieve more control over their lives, but they often fail to understand that their behavior is a hindrance to their own growth and development. They need to recognize the consequences of their behavior and make adjustments to achieve more favorable consequences. William Glasser is a leading proponent of leadership-oriented discipline. He believes that teachers can provide valuable assistance to children as they learn to assume greater responsibility for themselves and gain more control over their behavior (Glasser, 1984).

Developing a Personal Theory of Discipline

One's personal "theory" or model of discipline should be developed around a consistently formulated and carefully articulated personal philosophy of education. All that teachers do in the classroom should be a reflection of their personal philosophy. Otherwise, contradictions of various kinds can be anticipated in day-to-day teaching. A philosophy serves as a guide and helps eliminate problems that stem from having to make decisions without the benefit of a firm set of principles. Without a consistent, well-understood system of beliefs and associated theories, teachers have little guidance in dealing with the complexity of the classroom. Certainly, most classrooms present teachers with a plethora of problems and procedures that can be dealt with most efficiently and effectively by using a single set of principles rather than managing each new happening as though it were different from any other. Most efforts by scholars to understand the world and how best to handle its complexity are a matter of developing theories to simplify both the basic knowledge in the field as well as associated applications and procedures. Similar efforts have been undertaken by educational scholars. Teachers need to search out these theories and compare them with their personal philosophy, thereby increasing their effectiveness in the classroom.

An educational philosophy first and foremost includes explanations regarding how children learn and why they behave as they do. It also outlines appropriate information regarding teacher–student interactions that best promote learning and proper decorum in the classroom. Teachers' beliefs about how children learn and why they behave as they do have a direct bearing on how the curriculum is formulated and delivered in the classroom and how children's behavior can best be regulated.

One of the most critical determinations that must be made is whether children by nature have a will and are inherently self-regulating or if they respond primarily to need-satisfying stimuli and are exclusively conditioned by the environment. Behaviorists believe that children are born with no inherent will. Without the benefit of need-satisfying environmental stimuli, they would not respond. They would not, for example, go in search of meaningful experiences. They would not direct their activity toward understanding what is going on around them with an attitude of learning how to cope with the environment and master it. They would not have an inherent curiosity and be self-directed explorers of their world with an intrinsic need to know how things work and to regulate the world to their own desires.

Cognitive psychologists, on the other hand, see children as primarily self-regulating. Even the knowledge that eventually constitutes the conceptual structures in a person's brain is believed to come from the individual's own efforts to formulate it. In other words, we each construct for ourselves what we store in our brains. Research has shown that children's pre-existing knowledge is very resistant to change by additional instruction, even when their prior knowledge is in error and painstaking efforts are undertaken to correct their misunderstandings (Osborne & Wittrock, 1983). Behaviorists, however, believe that knowledge is simply absorbed in the form in which it is given.

Cognitive psychologists believe generally that human beings purposefully confront their environment in an effort to satisfy their personal intentions. They are not molded by the environment. They may be influenced by the environment regarding how they behave, but in the final analysis, they make decisions about how they behave. For example, a distraught parent who is rushing to the hospital with an injured child does not simply respond to a red light by stopping and waiting for it to turn green. Instead, she goes right through the red light if possible, pausing only to decide if she can make her move safely (Glasser, 1984).

Obviously, if humans are exclusively shaped by their environment, as behaviorists claim, responsible self-regulation is impossible. It is thought that environmental influences are so diverse that some kind of supervision is necessary to avoid the chaotic and catastrophic results that can be anticipated with self-management. Behaviorists believe that left to their own devices humans will suffer poverty, war, and other calamities. In their view, human behavior, therefore, needs to be regulated.

Cognitive psychologists do not believe humans are able at birth to regulate themselves responsibly. This is something that needs to be taught. However, humans are believed to desire self-determination and to exert themselves to regulate their own lives. Evidence for this is shown in the efforts by people all over the world to throw off the yoke of bondage in dictatorial societies and by the rebellion commonly exhibited by children in homes and schools when they are excessively restricted.

Behaviorists believe that children should be managed by reinforcing their appropriate behavior. Their research shows that children's behavior can be shaped through systematic reinforcement programs. Research also shows that these extrinsic reinforcers can significantly undermine intrinsic motivation. For example, when children are given rewards for learning, they become conditioned to the reward and refuse to learn without being rewarded. Intrinsic interest in learning is forfeited for rewards. In addition, the more you learn to like the rewards given, the more you dislike whatever you have to do to get them (Kohn, 1993). Some psychologists believe that students are influenced to dislike learning through the rewards ordinarily supplied in the schools.

There is no question that children respond to reinforcement. However, teachers must ask themselves two important questions regarding this practice. First, are children exclusively controlled through the external environment? When children are confronted with enticing reinforcers, do they make choices about whether to respond, or do sufficiently powerful reinforcers attain control regardless? The second question is whether or not proposed negative side effects of external reinforcers constitute a valid criticism, and whether or not their influence is sufficiently detrimental. How teachers discipline depends on how these questions are answered and constitutes a major component of one's educational philosophy.

In selecting an approach to discipline, teachers first need to determine which of the general views of child development is most consistent with their personal values and educational philosophy. Then they can examine various theories and discipline models more carefully to determine which would be most appropriate to use; they may even combine features of several models to create a discipline model of their own. Child development theories and discipline models are usually categorized according to the relative amounts of freedom they give to children and the control they give to teachers or parents:

- Management theories allow children very little autonomy and depend on teachers to carefully monitor students' behavior and control its expression.
- Nondirective intervention theories favor almost unlimited freedom for children.
- Leadership theories advocate considerable freedom for children, but only as they become able to use it responsibly.

Before choosing an approach to discipline—or designing an entire educational program—teachers should ask themselves how much freedom they believe children should have in school. The answer will make it much easier to select from among the various theories and models.

Characteristics of Theories

Choosing a discipline model also depends on which model is judged to be the most powerful. Better theories provide clearer descriptions, more insightful explanations, and more valid predictions (Beauchamp, 1968). These three components of good theories are elaborated next to show the usefulness of theory in educational practice.

DESCRIPTION

Description consists of ordering and organizing a jumble of facts and observations and unifying them into some scheme that makes the assembled material comprehensible. Ideas and phenomena that at first may appear unrelated are arranged in such a way that the scope and the internal relationships of the total body of information become visible. Without theory, masses of data and their complex interrelationships would be difficult if not impossible to comprehend. Choice theory, for example, explains a wide variety of human activity, such as efforts on the part of individuals to achieve better control of their lives and satisfy their needs in a way they find personally gratifying. From this theoretical perspective, political activity as well as rebelliousness and a host of other behaviors can be better understood.

EXPLANATION

Theories also account for phenomena. They can trace cause and effect, show correlations, and explain how things work. A theory of discipline may, for example, show that reinforcement increases the frequency of the behavior with which it is associated and also explain how it does so. Theory not only can clarify meaningful relationships between areas of knowledge; it can show how various areas of knowledge can be applied in the practical world. Theory makes the connection between abstract concept and concrete act; good theories provide clear explanations and produce explicit applications. In the logical consequences approach to discipline, for example, misbehavior is believed to be misdirected effort to satisfy specified needs. The practical application involves helping individuals understand the motives behind their misbehavior and helping them change their behaviors so they are more personally satisfying and socially acceptable.

PREDICTION

Finally, theory has the quality of predictability, which is perhaps its most powerful feature. Prediction in the area of discipline helps teachers anticipate the effects of their strategies on the behavior of their students. Some theories also predict behavior in a more general sense. For example, William Glasser's (1984) reality therapy/choice theory may be used to predict not only the effects of interpersonal and intrapersonal relationships but also what can be expected from different family interactions, social relations, conflicts at school, political behavior, and so on. Teachers who apply theory appropriately in their classrooms can predict outcomes in advance with some assurance that their predictions will be correct. The frequency of classroom disruptions, for example, can be reduced by not paying attention to them.

THEORETICAL BASIS

The ability of theories to provide comprehensible descriptions, clear explanations, and valid predictions is a critical aspect of theory building. These attributes also make theories very useful. Discipline theories help teachers conceptualize the field of discipline so that adequate comparisons can be made. Otherwise, there would be a good deal of confusion in trying to decide which models are more consistent with one's educational philosophy.

Each of the three general approaches to child development—management, nondirective intervention, and leadership—has a number of discipline theories or models. Eight of these discipline theories and models are presented in detail in the next eight chapters: behavior modification, assertive discipline, logical consequences, transactional analysis, teacher effectiveness training, reality therapy/choice theory, judicious discipline, and the Jones model.

Behavior modification, assertive discipline, and the Jones model are based on management theories. The logical consequences model, judicious discipline, and reality therapy/choice theory are based on leadership theories. Teacher effectiveness training and transactional analysis are based on nondirective intervention theories (see Figure 2.1).

Comparing Four Approaches to Discipline

The discussion of a single discipline problem can illustrate the distinctive characteristics of four of the discipline models:

- Behavior modification
- Assertive discipline
- Logical consequences
- Reality therapy/choice theory

You can then see how these theories differ from or coincide with your own educational philosophy.

▼ *The Problem:*   Clair and Jo continually disrupt classes by talking to neighbors, yelling across the room, and throwing objects at other students.

BEHAVIOR MODIFICATION

When Mr. Condie observed Jo talking and throwing objects in class, he decided to set up a token economy to help Jo improve her behavior. Mr. Condie explained to Jo the behavior he expected of her and the rewards she could receive for demonstrating them. He gave her a folder, inside of which were listed the various expected behaviors. Next to this list were boxes in which Mr. Condie could mark the points Jo received for each appropriate behavior. Mr. Condie would ignore all of Jo's inappropriate behavior. A second list in the folder contained the rewards possible for behaving appropriately and the number of points needed to receive each of these rewards. Jo was allowed to decide which of the rewards she wished to receive and when she wanted to earn them.

ASSERTIVE DISCIPLINE

When Clair yelled across the room, Ms. Adams, his teacher, wrote his name on the board as a warning for Clair to refrain from any further misbehavior. Later, when Clair threw his pencil at James, Ms. Adams put a check mark by his name. Before the end of the class period, Clair's name had three check marks by it. The rules as well as punishments for misbehavior had been given to the class at the beginning of the year; a poster outlining this information hung in the front of the room for ready reference. The punishment to be received for each check mark was carefully explained. Clair's punishment for getting three check marks was to be sent to the principal's office and to have a conference with his parents and the principal. He could not return to class until this conference had been held and appropriate action taken.

LOGICAL CONSEQUENCES

After Ms. Taggert had observed Jo's habitual misbehavior, she tried to decide what her motives were. She realized that Jo's misbehavior was primarily an attempt to satisfy her needs, an attempt based on mistaken goals: Jo was either seeking attention, power, or revenge or struggling with feelings of inadequacy. Unable to determine Jo's exact motives herself, Ms. Taggert decided to talk directly to Jo. She first asked Jo whether she thought that her talking and throwing objects were related to a need for attention. Jo replied that she did not know why she had talked out in class. Ms. Taggert then asked whether Jo felt anger toward her. She said that, no, she just liked to talk with friends. Ms. Taggert concluded that Jo talked out in class for the attention she received. She explained this conclusion to Jo and told her that she could better satisfy this need for attention by assuming a leadership position in class. Ms. Taggert asked Jo whether she would like to be the class president for the next month. Jo agreed. Ms. Taggert explained that one of Jo's responsibilities would be to help ensure that the classroom was quiet.

REALITY THERAPY/CHOICE THEORY

When Mr. Ronowski observed Clair disturbing the class by talking excessively and throwing objects, he motioned him up to his desk and, out of earshot of the rest of the class, engaged him in the following conversation:

Mr. Ronowski	Clair, what were you doing during class discussion today that disturbed others around you?
Clair	I was just talking to Owen.
Mr. Ronowski	What did you along with the rest of the class decide would happen to anyone who disturbed the class by talking?
Clair	We decided we would be kicked out of class and not be allowed back until we made a written plan about how we planned to avoid these problems.
Mr. Ronowski	When will you get your plan to me?
Clair	I'll try to get it by tomorrow.
Mr. Ronowski	Where must you go until you have your written plan prepared?
Clair	The counselor's office.
Mr. Ronowski	I will anticipate hearing from you tomorrow before class, then.

Deciding on a Personal Approach to Discipline

How does one decide what discipline approach to use, given the various options available? A number of considerations must be taken into account in this process. The following steps are useful in making this determination (see Figure 2.2):

1. Make a thoughtful examination of your personal philosophy of education. Decide how much emphasis you feel is appropriate to place on the teacher's control or students' autonomy. Examine the various discipline models to see which one most closely fits your philosophy.
2. Establish a set of criteria, and use them to evaluate each discipline model.
3. Identify the assumptions on which each discipline model is based, and determine their validity. The validity of assumptions can be determined by using
   a. Personal experience
   b. Empirical evidence
   c. Logical exposition
4. From the various discipline options you examine,

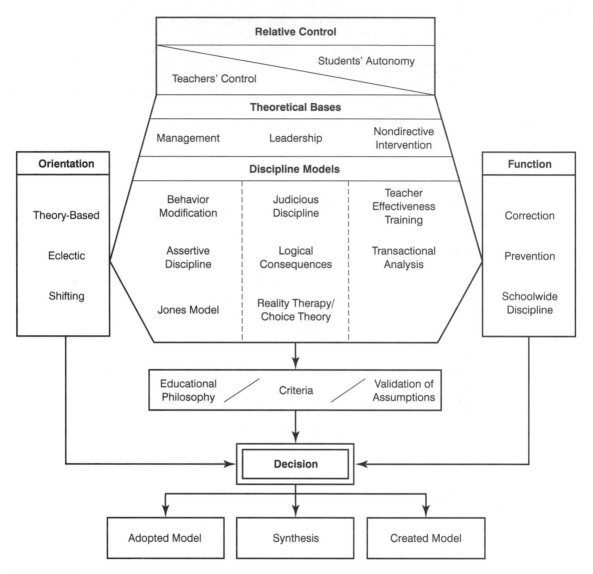

FIGURE 2.2
Deciding on a discipline approach.

        a. Select an existing option that meets the bulk of your expectations.
        b. Synthesize components of two or more options.
        c. Create your own discipline model.
    5. Consider also the extent to which the discipline approach you plan to use provides adequately for the functions of
        a. Correction of discipline problems
        b. Prevention of discipline problems
        c. Schoolwide discipline

6. Determine the orientation you prefer:
   a. A theory-based approach
   b. An eclectic approach
   c. A shifting approach
7. Keeping all these factors in mind—your personal values, the criteria you used, their relative strengths and weaknesses, the assumptions on which various approaches to discipline are based, their functions, and your preferred orientation—make a decision about your approach to discipline.

Now let's go through the process of choosing a discipline approach one step at a time, illustrating what must be done to make wise choices.

EXAMINING ONE'S PERSONAL PHILOSOPHY

In deciding on a discipline approach, teachers not only must understand the underlying psychological and philosophical consequences of that choice but also must ensure that what they decide is consistent with their own beliefs and values. As Wolfgang and Glickman (1980) indicate,

> All too often, we unwittingly practice behaviors that are contrary to our own beliefs. Unless we behave towards children in ways that are reasonably compatible with our own values and ideals, we find ourselves working at cross purposes with our inner selves. In other words, what we desire in students' behavior will not materialize until we choose those strategies that are most consistent with our own beliefs in achieving those ends. We cannot possibly know what is most congruent in these contexts until we understand the psychological basis for each of our actions. (p. 9)

When you choose an approach to discipline, the most important philosophical consideration is the relative importance you give to teachers' control and students' autonomy. You must decide whether or not children can learn to be responsibly

Without a well-organized discipline program, teachers sometimes react inappropriately to discipline problems.

self-determined, that is, whether you believe that children assert themselves as persons having a will of their own or are essentially controlled by the environment. Theorists who believe in human self-determination conclude that children can be controlled only to the extent they allow themselves to be. Theorists who discount human will believe that controlling others simply involves finding a compelling reinforcer or exerting enough force. They believe that systematic control is necessary to help children behave appropriately. If these outside controls are neglected, children will be adversely affected by the indiscriminate influences of the environment. Clarifying your attitudes about students' autonomy helps determine which general theory of child development most closely reflects your own views: (1) Development is completely determined by external conditions; (2) development is an inner unfolding of potential, as some developmental psychologists believe; or (3) development is a consequence of an interaction of both internal and external forces.

Another important philosophical consideration is the role motives are believed to play in human behavior. Behaviorists, for example, believe that children are motivated by external rewards. In the logical consequences approach, children are thought to seek attention in an effort to determine how well they are accepted by others. In choice theory, children seek not only to obtain acceptance and affection but also to satisfy their needs for control.

The philosophical considerations identified here will be elaborated in subsequent chapters in connection with the various discipline approaches with which they are associated. As you explore your own beliefs about these critical matters, you should begin to formulate your own personal views.

ESTABLISHING CRITERIA FOR MAKING DECISIONS

Criteria provide the basis on which decisions are made. They are standards of judgment, crystallized from one's educational philosophy. The following list is an example of criteria a teacher could use to decide among a number of discipline models. You, of course, will want to construct your own list. The particular criteria used have an enormous bearing on the decisions made.

Which of the discipline approaches

1. Is most likely to help children become more self-disciplined and responsible?
2. Is consistent with the view that children's motives are based on a self-directed effort to achieve autonomy, gain control of themselves and their environment, and achieve a high level of acceptance by others?
3. Can be most easily implemented?
4. Can be readily learned?
5. Is most consistent with an instructional program involving self-determined learning projects?
6. Is most effective in achieving good classroom behavior?
7. Will help promote good self-concept in students?
8. Is most likely to help prevent discipline problems?
9. Can be applied in a schoolwide discipline program?

Now let's see how you could apply some of these criteria in deciding between several possible approaches to discipline. For convenience, use the models discussed in the section of this chapter entitled "Comparing Four Approaches to Discipline." The teacher who uses behavior modification monitors Jo's behavior and rewards her when she behaves appropriately. Behavior modification obviously does not contribute toward the development of self-discipline. A similar conclusion may be drawn about assertive discipline. In this case, Clair is not consulted regarding the rules in the class or the punishment he can expect. When the logical consequences approach is used, Jo is consulted about her behavior. Her teacher tries to help Jo analyze her misbehavior and make appropriate changes. In the reality therapy/choice theory approach, Clair has already been involved with his classmates in making decisions about classroom conduct and the consequences of misbehavior; students also have the right to decide how to correct their own misbehavior. Obviously, reality therapy/choice theory promotes more self-discipline in students.

Reality therapy/choice theory also more readily satisfies criterion 8: It has a better prevention component not only because it defines behaviors and consequences in advance but also because it involves students in making this determination. Both assertive discipline and behavior modification have limited preventive elements. In assertive discipline, the teacher determines rules and punishments in advance. Because students are not involved in their determination, these rules and punishments have less preventive power. In behavior modification, the teacher may reward students for appropriate behavior as a deterrent to misbehavior. Behavior modification may prevent problems to some extent; students may anticipate receiving rewards and behave appropriately. However, just as with assertive discipline, students are not directly involved in the process, and consequently the prevention aspect is not as strong.

IDENTIFYING AND VALIDATING ASSUMPTIONS

When making decisions, you should examine the assumptions on which your options are based and attempt to judge their validity. Teachers often make decisions without identifying the assumptions behind the alternatives being considered. More often, the assumptions are recognized, but their validity goes unquestioned. Nearly everyone has failed to identify and validate assumptions in daily living. Many people lock themselves out of their car or house, confidently assuming that they took their keys with them. When common, everyday assumptions are checked, fewer problems can be anticipated in life. When the assumptions behind the various discipline options are carefully identified and validated, better decisions can be expected.

What are the assumptions for the different discipline models, and how can they be validated? Lists of assumptions will be provided for your consideration at the beginning of each of the chapters dealing with models (Chapters 3 through 10). In Chapter 11 you will be given an example of how to compare these assumptions and determine their validity. At this point, however, attention will be focused on the basic process of identifying assumptions and determining their soundness. A few assumptions from several of the discipline theories will be used as illustrations.

Sometimes, in the writings of discipline theorists, assumptions are explicitly stated and defended. More often, you must sift through what is written and discover them for yourself. You will occasionally find inconsistencies between the assumptions of a particular theory and the way in which it is actually put into operation. For example, responsibility is presented as a necessary component of the Jones model. You might expect, then, that the model would help students become more responsible. However, it is almost entirely teacher-directed, with little opportunity for students to achieve responsibility. Another application of the Jones model intended to help students become more responsible is preferred activity time. In reality, preferred activities are allotted through a program of negative reinforcement, an aspect of the Jones model that also fails to promote responsible behavior in students. These inconsistencies must be identified, for often they make a great deal of difference in a model's attractiveness.

The best way to identify assumptions about various discipline theories is to look for statements about

- The nature of children
- How children grow
- How children learn
- Whether children are capable of self-control or need to be directed
- How children react to different situations and treatments
- How children interact with others
- What children's needs are

Reference has already been made to what different theories say about children's needs and their ability to be self-directed. Remember that leadership theories and nondirective intervention theories believe in self-direction; management theories do not. Each type of theory focuses on a significantly different set of needs.

Let's look now at different sets of assumptions. If we compare what the various discipline models say about children's reactions to their teachers, we see a marked contrast:

1. In assertive discipline, it is assumed that children like to be in classrooms where the teacher controls their behavior rigidly. Students supposedly realize the necessity of teachers' punishment as a deterrent to bad behavior and think positively of their teachers when they punish misbehaving students.
2. However, according to reality therapy/choice theory, punishment will only create rebellion. From the reality therapy/choice theory perspective, it is assumed that children want to control the various situations in which they find themselves and to be free from the control of others.
3. The assumptions of transactional analysis are similar to those of reality therapy/choice theory: The influence of the teacher is more positive when control by the teacher is absent.
4. The Jones model relies on nonverbal techniques to control children's behavior. Teachers use their imposing physical presence to encourage children to behave.
5. In the logical consequences approach, it is assumed that children will react positively toward their teachers only when a democratic environment is provided. The consequences for misbehavior are spelled out in advance in consultation with students.
6. In the behavior modification model, it is assumed that if teachers provide desirable reinforcers, then students not only will reach a higher level of academic achievement but will also have higher regard for the classroom.

7. With teacher effectiveness training, it is assumed that children inherently rebel when others attempt to regulate them. It is also assumed that they can learn to effectively regulate their own behavior if their teachers practice active listening and send properly constructed I-messages.

8. With judicious discipline, it is assumed that through application of democratic principles, students can learn to regulate their personal and social behavior so as not to violate compelling school interests. It is also assumed that students can learn to responsibly use their personal freedoms as guaranteed by the U.S. Constitution.

The assumptions of different discipline models exhibit obvious differences regarding the effects of student–teacher interactions. Once teachers have identified these differences, they must examine them and determine which they believe to be most valid or true. The validity of assumptions can be checked by evidence gained in any of at least three ways; that is, assumptions can be validated from at least three evidence bases:

- Experience
- Empirical research
- Logical exposition

Greater assurance of validity is possible when all three types of evidence are examined. Perhaps the type least used by teachers is empirical research (Darling-Hammond, 1997).

Experience.   You can validate assumptions from an experience base, that is, check them against your own experience and that of others. If, for example, you wanted to examine assumptions about the effect of teachers' control on student–teacher relationships, you could simply try out all the techniques from various models over a period of time to see what happens. You could also share in the experiences of other individuals by talking to them, corresponding with them, or reading their professional writings.

Empirical Research.   To validate from an empirical base, examine research. Unfortunately, most discipline models have not been studied extensively. Hardly any research is available that compares different models. More often than not, the validity of assumptions for the different models is held to be self-evident. Assumptions usually are not even explicitly stated, so readers themselves must identify them. Because it is not always possible to locate research to validate assumptions directly, interpretations may have to be made with what little information is available. Teachers may also desire to conduct their own research. This can be in the form of action research, which is generally characterized as less well controlled, or more formal studies can be conducted. Currently, research is being recommended that involves collaboration between universities and public schools. These efforts are particularly laudatory because they help increase the chances that research will find its way into school practice (Goodlad, 1990).

Logical Exposition.   Logical exposition is a method of validating assumptions perhaps more commonly used by beginning teachers, who usually do not have enough experience to validate assumptions directly or to wade through the body of research or engage in research on their own. The bulk of the data they use for validation must come from personal judgment; they make an educated guess.

ADOPTING, SYNTHESIZING, OR CREATING A MODEL

After you have examined your own educational philosophy, created a defensible set of criteria, and validated the assumptions behind the different discipline options, your next step is to use all this information to decide which of the models is most acceptable to you. In making this decision, you can go in any one of three directions (see Figure 2.2). First, you may decide that one of the models meets your expectations sufficiently to be adopted without substantial adjustment. Second, you may decide to synthesize compatible components of two or more models. Third, you may discover that none of the models is satisfactory and decide to create your own discipline approach.

What is involved with each of these courses of action? It is obviously simplest just to adopt a single existing approach to discipline. All that is necessary then is to master its use.

It is more difficult and complicated to combine components from several approaches. Each of the models has some incompatible elements. The task of synthesis is to include only compatible elements. For example, if you decided to use Glasser's (1984) reality therapy/choice theory as your basic model with the addition of some components from behavior modification, you would have to be careful to avoid those aspects that detracted from the self-determination emphasized by reality therapy/choice theory. In fact, the only aspects of behavior management likely to be compatible are the practices of ignoring bad behavior and avoiding punishment. If you considered including elements of the logical consequences approach, you would have to be sure to avoid the practice of publicly determining motives so as not to encourage students to make excuses. You would also have to decide whether you wanted to have students personally explore a wide range of possible consequences for misbehavior, as reality therapy/choice theory advocates, or just give them a choice between two designated options, as the logical consequences model requires.

Creating your own discipline model is the most difficult of these three options. You might have to construct an entirely different approach, or you might combine some components of your own creation with compatible components of other models. If you construct a personal model, the first step is to formulate basic principles. Then you would describe discipline practices. An example of how to create a personal discipline approach is discussed in Chapter 13.

CONSIDERING FUNCTIONS OF A COMPREHENSIVE DISCIPLINE PROGRAM

An adequate discipline model should include

1. Techniques for correction of misbehavior
2. Procedures for prevention of classroom discipline problems
3. Applications for a schoolwide discipline program (see Figure 2.2)

Correction.   Most discipline models are designed primarily to correct discipline problems. In fact, little is usually said about how they may be used, either to prevent problems or to create a schoolwide discipline program. Usually, the focus is on existing problems in the classroom and how to eliminate them once they appear.

Prevention.   Prevention involves steps taken in class to avoid potential discipline problems. Students are commonly involved in determining preventive discipline procedures. The logical consequences and reality therapy/choice theory models incorporate preventive discipline in this way. Teacher effectiveness training provides students an opportunity to talk about how to deal with potential problems. They talk about potential distractions and make suggestions about how to modify the classroom environment so it is more compatible with their learning needs. When the model emphasizes control by the teacher, preventive discipline usually takes the form of deterrence. For example, in assertive discipline, the threat of punishment is designed to act as a deterrent.

Schoolwide Discipline.   Schoolwide discipline is the least common discipline function to find in any particular discipline model. It involves procedures used for discipline in hallways, the library, the cafeteria, and on the school grounds. This feature has been a component of reality therapy/choice theory and has been strengthened over the years. It is highly developed in Glasser's book *The Quality School* (Glasser, 1990) and is included by Canter in the *Assertive Discipline Follow-up Guidebook* (Canter & Canter, 1981). Explicit statements about schoolwide discipline are decidedly lacking from the other approaches, although this aspect could possibly be added to any of them. Specific prevention and schoolwide discipline procedures are discussed for each model in Chapters 3 through 10.

CHOOSING A DISCIPLINE ORIENTATION

The orientation of a discipline program refers primarily to the consistency with which it is applied. Some theorists emphasize the importance of using a single set of internally consistent principles and believe that discipline practices should conform as much as possible to these principles. Others contend that teachers should be encouraged to choose freely from among a variety of techniques or discipline models as the situation dictates, despite their being based on disparate principles. There are three possible orientations for a discipline program:

- Theory-based
- Eclectic
- Shifting (see Figure 2.2)

Theory-Based Discipline Programs.   A theory-based discipline program is one in which a single theory or model is used to prevent and correct all discipline problems in the school as well as in the classroom. This theory could be one that is already in use or one that has been personally created. Any discipline procedures used must conform to the principles of the theory. Teachers who find a theory-based approach attractive usually have a well-organized and carefully articulated set of values to which they are committed. The principles they live by professionally are the same as those governing their private lives.

Eclectic Discipline Programs.   In the eclectic orientation to discipline, components of various discipline theories and models are synthesized. As Charles (1992) explains, teachers select components from various discipline models that suit them best and recombine them into an "effective approach that is satisfactory to all." Charles claims that this recombination is necessary because one approach may work well with one student whereas another approach works better with others. Combining approaches helps teachers discipline various students in different circumstances. Eclectic teachers are less concerned about possibly causing confusion to their students with a conglomeration of various theories and more concerned about maintaining the flexibility of their approach.

Shifting Discipline Programs. The shifting orientation to discipline is similar to the eclectic approach. However, instead of combining various theories or theory components, advocates of this approach favor changing from one theory to another as circumstances dictate. Wolfgang and Glickman (1980) provide an excellent example of this orientation. Instead of settling on one approach created out of various pieces, as does Charles (1992), they recommend using all the valuable elements contained in all the models.

In the discipline procedure of Wolfgang and Glickman, teachers make decisions on the spot as circumstances demand and follow one of three possible procedural pathways. These three pathways incorporate different levels of autonomy for students and control for the teacher. On one pathway, the teacher moves from discipline techniques that provide a lot of autonomy for students (such as transactional analysis or teacher effectiveness training) to those that involve more control by the teacher (such as the logical consequences approach) and then finally to even more controlling techniques (such as behavior modification) as conditions warrant. The second pathway provides for movement in the opposite direction: The teacher begins with strong control and gives up power to students as they appear more able to regulate themselves. On the third pathway, the teacher starts with a discipline model that advocates sharing power with students (such as reality therapy/choice theory) and can move toward either more autonomy for students or more control by the teacher as the situation demands.

The defense made for using the eclectic and shifting orientations is about the same. The following are the essential elements of that defense:

1.   Some theories work better than others with children of different ages, children with different personal and social aptitudes, children from different home situations or social environments or ethnic and racial groups, and children involved in different school situations. All these elements create considerable complexity and, to be properly managed, require a full range of discipline approaches. As Charles (1992) indicates, behavior modification may work better with young children and students with developmental disabilities than with older children or students with more severe behavior disorders. Assertive discipline, he claims, may control misbehavior at all levels but be too cumbersome for primary grades. It may also fail to help students gain a proper value orientation because it focuses exclusively on students' obedience.

2.   It may be difficult for some teachers to use some techniques successfully with some groups of students. For example, a teacher may be able to apply reality therapy/choice theory as long as students do not become too unruly. However, if students get too far out of control, more teacher-directed discipline may be necessary.

3.   Some groups of students may be so difficult to handle that initially they have to be controlled more vigorously by the teacher, even though the teacher wants them eventually to achieve greater self-control. The teacher must then change tactics as students become more able to govern themselves.

4.   If a discipline approach does not seem to work, for whatever reason, it makes sense to change to some other technique that holds more promise of success. If, for example, students are not achieving greater responsibility through the use of reality therapy/choice theory, a change may be appropriate.

Teachers who use one discipline approach based on a single set of principles present arguments counter to those set forth by proponents of eclecticism:

1.   Teachers who advocate changing discipline theories assume that such a change is warranted by different or changed circumstances in the classroom. These circumstances may be related to children's growth and development or to students' inclinations to be more or less disruptive. Younger children, for example, are considered less able to deal intellectually with the rational problems implied by discipline theories that emphasize self-determination. They are also thought less able to accurately express their personal thoughts and feelings and to construct the responses necessary to engage in meaningful communication. However, the level at which children of elementary school age can function has proven adequate for techniques such as reality therapy/choice theory, teacher effectiveness training, and transactional analysis. Perhaps the only exceptions are very small children or children with conditions such as autism.

2.   A second reason given to change discipline theories periodically is that the approach currently being used does not successfully limit students' misbehavior. It is assumed that changes in classroom circumstances have promoted more misbehavior and that more misbehavior dictates the use of a more control-oriented discipline theory. However, no evidence suggests which theory is best to use in any particular set of circumstances or change of circumstances. Without such evidence, it is better to select one theory and stay with it.

Some discipline theories routinely and effectively used in a wide variety of classroom situations have also been useful in a number of other settings. For example, behavior modification has been successfully applied to persons with mental illness, children with autism, individuals with social and behavioral disorders, and individuals with a host of everyday problems such as smoking and eating disorders. Reality therapy/choice theory has been used not only in teaching children but also in treating people with nearly all types of mental illness, in counseling individuals who are socially maladaptive, and in helping inmates in penal institutions regulate their behavior. Both behavior modification and reality therapy/choice theory have been applied in a variety of special schools for children who have been unsuccessful in regular school situations. The wide use of these theories in various difficult circumstances attests to their suitability for use in most situations that might be encountered in school classrooms.

3.   Another problem with using multiple discipline theories is that many teachers have difficulty learning them well enough to apply them all properly, particularly those

theories that require considerable interpersonal skill, such as reality therapy/choice theory, teacher effectiveness training, the logical consequences model, judicious discipline, and transactional analysis. In addition, most teachers have trouble switching between discipline approaches because of differences in their application, assumptions, and expected results. The educational philosophies of many teachers would also prevent them from applying such a divergent array of discipline tactics.

4.   The use of multiple theories may also be confusing for students. Because the one variable that is likely to be in a constant state of flux is autonomy, teachers may never be sure what level of autonomy is acceptable. Even if it is made clear that students' autonomy and the teacher's control depend on how responsibly students use the freedom they have, students will certainly view increased control by the teacher as undermining their desire to become more self-determined.

MAKING A DECISION

In making a decision about which discipline approach to use, it will be very helpful to follow the steps outlined earlier in this section of the chapter. The steps are not sequential, although step 1, examining your personal philosophy, should probably be done first. This examination allows you to eliminate quickly some discipline approaches that are too incompatible with your most important values. Eliminating possible models, of course, simplifies your work. You may also want to decide at this point whether or not you plan to use a theory-based, an eclectic, or a shifting orientation to discipline. You could then create and apply criteria to the remaining models and decide whether or not the assumptions for each model are valid.

When you have carefully examined the different models outlined in Chapters 3 through 10, compared them with your philosophy, and judged them in terms of your criteria, you should be prepared to make a decision about the discipline option you prefer. You should remember to examine and validate the assumptions associated with each model and then decide to what extent each of the models meets your expectations. At this point you will also need to decide (1) whether a single model satisfies your requirements, (2) whether you need to make a synthesis of two or more models, or (3) whether you need to create your own discipline approach (see Figure 2.2). Be sure that the approach you choose can be applied to preventing classroom discipline problems as well as to solving them and that your approach has potential beyond your classroom alone.

Chapter 11 gives you an example of how to use this decision-making process. As you make your decision, you should think carefully about the relative strengths and weaknesses of the models presented. A list of the strengths and weaknesses of each model may be found near the end of its chapter.

DECISION MAKING THROUGH REFLECTIVE THINKING

Teachers have to make decisions regarding not only how they plan to discipline but also how they plan to teach. This involves learning the skills of reflective thinking in their daily teaching practice. Through reflective thinking, teachers can understand how complex, situation-specific, and dilemma-ridden teaching really is and can learn to make valid decisions and take valid actions in complex ongoing classroom situations. Reflection is not a passive, unstructured sifting of information and experience. It must be approached with considerable rigor and formal structure. Through reflection, teachers are able to create a context-specific understanding of their craft and generate knowledge to inform future practice.

Reflection involves the following kinds of activities:

1. Develop your own professional position through integrating the best advice from others (research reports, others' experience, philosophical writings), your own observations, your past experience, your beliefs about teaching, and your own goals as they relate to the kind of teacher you want to be and the impact you wish to make on your students.
2. Write about an educational issue that is important to you. Think critically about the issue. Try to expand your awareness and then make a reasoned choice about the issue.
3. Examine various positions about learners, learning, curriculum, instructional techniques, management, and planning, as well as personal goals, values, beliefs, and biases. Try to identify connections and/or conflicts among components of these positions.
4. Think about what is meaningful regarding various aspects of teaching–learning and the role you wish to play in this important enterprise.

One useful format for engaging in reflective thinking is to

1. Read and study various sources about education including your own thoughts and experiences.
2. Engage in a discussion with a group of teachers or prospective teachers, and compare their thinking and judgments with your own.
3. Discuss your views in a formal class setting with a knowledgeable instructor.
4. Write your reactions and conclusions in a journal.

There are three critical components in teachers' reflective thinking (Sparks-Langer & Colton, 1991):

The cognitive element of reflection
The critical element of reflection
Teachers' narratives

The cognitive element of teacher reflection focuses on how teachers use knowledge in their planning and decision making. According to Shulman (1987), teachers should be concerned about six areas of knowledge:

1. Content/subject matter knowledge
2. Pedagogical methods and theory
3. Curriculum
4. Characteristics of learners
5. Teaching contexts
6. Educational purposes, ends, and aims

The first three areas Shulman identifies refer to how teachers portray important ideas to their students that are specific to their content. This involves the way teachers are able to convey complex ideas and bring meaning to their students. The next three areas include ethical and moral considerations as well as judgments that are best determined within the context of actual teaching.

It has been found that beginning teachers are less able to weigh what they perceive in their teaching against various other information and then form connections that help them to make meaningful teaching decisions. However, veteran teachers eventually achieve a level of automaticity that allows them to engage in some actions automatically while simultaneously focusing their attention on more novel and important events (Carter, Cushing, Sabers, Stein, & Berliner, 1988). Novice teachers thus experience difficulty in achieving the level of flexibility required to deal with distractions and then improvise naturally so that instruction flows without the teacher also becoming a distraction. Reflection and practice are key elements in developing these skills.

Experienced teachers are more able to deal with the complexities of the classroom, which is due to the automaticity they have acquired as well as a rich set of personal schemata they have internalized. These attributes allow them to quickly consider cues from the classroom and make judgments regarding appropriate teaching strategies. Schemata consist of stored mental constructs regarding teaching–learning. They are not arrived at automatically but appear in a teacher's mind as a consequence of experience. According to constructivist theory (Greeno, Magone, & Chaiklin, 1979), individuals are constantly creating their own meaning out of what is experienced. The experiences, values, and beliefs already stored in memory serve as a filter for new encounters. Thus, teaching–learning decisions are created through interactions between the mind and the context surrounding the problem. Teachers, therefore, use their schemata to make case-by-case responses to particular problems. Future teachers therefore need to anchor their knowledge in a variety of rich "within-context" educational experiences. These experiences need to be processed repeatedly through reflective thinking.

The second component of reflective thinking is the critical element. While the cognitive element of reflection emphasizes how teachers make decisions, the critical approach focuses on the substance that drives the thinking—experiences, beliefs, sociopolitical values, and goals—of teachers. In critical reflection, moral and ethical aspects of teaching–learning are considered, as well as the means and ends of education. Teachers reflecting in this dimension begin to clarify their own beliefs about the purposes of education and to critically examine teaching methods and materials to look for such obscure happenings as equity, power, and need fulfillment. In the process of reflecting on these issues, teachers create their own pedagogical principles.

One strategy for promoting reflective thinking in terms of critical elements is to (1) identify an educational dilemma, (2) respond to the dilemma by identifying both similarities to other situations and special qualities of the particular situation being analyzed, (3) frame and reframe the dilemma, (4) experiment with the dilemma to find out the consequences and implications of various proposed solutions, and (5) examine the intended and unintended consequences of the solution that is implemented and evaluate the solution (Ross, 1990). For example, the dilemma regarding how much autonomy students can responsibly use in the classroom may be examined. The long-term effects of limiting students' autonomy and its influence on students' values and behavior could be determined, along with possible societal effects. Once a decision is made about how best to create educational experiences conducive to how the dilemma is resolved, appropriate teaching strategies can be examined and their good and bad consequences evaluated. Reflection can be further extended through action research projects, journal writing, and self-critiques.

The third component of reflective thinking is teachers' narratives. This component focuses on teachers themselves, the questions they ask, the ways they use writing and intentional talk in their teaching, and the interpretive frames they use to understand and improve their own classroom practices (Cochran-Smith & Lytle, 1990, p. 2). Here, the emphasis is on each teachers' own interpretations of the context in which professional decision making takes place. These narratives serve powerfully to heighten teachers' awareness of their own professional reasoning. A central consideration is the acceptance of the validity of teachers' judgments that they draw from their own experience. From this perspective, teaching is essentially an art and the teacher an artist. A common theme in the narrative component of reflection is the focus on the naturalistic study of teaching. Instead of the experimental and quantitative format for the study of teaching, naturalistic studies explore meanings and personal interpretations by the teacher. Reflection through narratives provides insights into what motivates teachers, actions, and an appreciation for the complexity of teachers' everyday lives. In addition, it provides a more clear delineation of what makes up dilemmas in teaching. Finally, narratives provide invaluable insights by the teachers themselves as they engage in this self-inquiry process.

▼ SUMMARY

Deciding which discipline approach to use is an extremely important task for teachers. Many approaches are available to choose from. The best discipline theories provide the most insightful descriptions and explanations of phenomena as well as the most powerful predictions. You should carefully weigh the various choices against your own educational philosophy and personal values. The most significant aspect of your personal philosophy of discipline is the relative importance you place on the teacher's control or students' autonomy. You can make better decisions about which model of discipline to use if you first establish criteria for making these decisions and then carefully examine and validate the assumptions underlying each model.

After you have evaluated the various discipline models in this way, you can decide whether to accept a particular model, synthesize two or more models, or create your own. Whatever you choose to do, it is imperative that your model correct and prevent discipline problems and have schoolwide applications. You must also determine whether your approach to applying discipline in the classroom should be consistently based on one particular set of principles and practices, created eclectically from the components of a number of models, or allowed to change from one discipline model to another according to various circumstances and conditions.

Teachers also need to thoughtfully formulate and then carefully analyze their teaching practices. This can be accomplished through formal reflective thinking practices. Reflective thinking involves cognitive, critical, and narrative elements. These three elements allow teachers to examine cognitive aspects of teaching like the content, methods, curriculum, learners, teaching contexts, and educational goals. The critical element focuses more on the moral and ethical aspects of teaching. Finally, narrative reflection centers on the personal context of teaching. Taken together, these three elements of reflection provide teachers an excellent basis for formulating their personal teaching principles.

CENTRAL IDEAS

1. Theory provides useful descriptions of phenomena and their operations, along with predictions of what will happen when associated principles are applied in real situations.
2. Using theory simplifies and provides a more consistent approach to classroom discipline.
3. Personal values and philosophy should provide the basis for selecting or creating an approach to discipline.
4. Choosing an approach to discipline involves the application of an appropriate set of criteria.
5. Before a particular discipline model is accepted, its assumptions should be identified and validated.
6. A chosen approach to discipline should prevent as well as correct discipline problems in the classroom, and it should be applicable to schoolwide discipline.
7. The orientation of a discipline approach can be theory-based, eclectic, or shifting.
8. Teachers must decide whether to use an existing model of discipline, synthesize one from components of two or more models, or create their own.
9. Reflective thinking provides an excellent format for creating personal principles for teaching.
10. Reflective thinking has three basic elements: cognitive, critical, and narrative.

▼ QUESTIONS AND ACTIVITIES

QUESTIONS TO CONSIDER

1. What are the essential elements of an adequate theory of discipline?
2. What basic questions must a theory of discipline answer?
3. What are the considerations involved in deciding whether or not to use a particular theory of discipline?

CLASSROOM ACTIVITIES

1. Debate the issue of whether to follow a single theory or multiple theories for handling discipline problems in the schools.

2. As a class, prepare a list of concerns about discipline for which a theory should provide explanations and procedures.
3. As a class, engage in reflective thinking about teaching practices and preferences.

EXPLORE YOUR PHILOSOPHY

The "Explore Your Philosophy" activity will be included in the "Questions and Activities" section of each of the remaining chapters in the book. If you intend to use these exercises, obtain a notebook to record your personal philosophy and your reactions to the various proposed discipline models as compared to your philosophy. You can use this journal to confront your thinking as you consider the various discipline models and instructional strategies. Your instructor may want to periodically read your journal and provide you feedback. Specific suggestions will be provided at the end of each chapter to help you focus your analysis on important factors.

1. Engage in reflective thinking about various aspects of what to include in your personal philosophy of education. Prepare a written description of your personal philosophy of education. Include reference to the nature of human beings and how they learn, and what kind of learning experiences should, therefore, be included in their educational experiences. Also provide a description of the principles on which you tentatively wish to base your discipline approach.
2. Meet with a group of your peers, and compare their educational philosophies with your own. In this process, try to determine the assumptions on which each of the philosophies of your group are based.
3. Defend your philosophy of education. To do this, provide what you feel is evidence that your philosophy is sound, given your experiences and current level of knowledge.

▼ REFERENCES

Beauchamp, G. A. (1968). *Curriculum theory* (2nd ed.). Wilmette, IL: Kagg Press.

Canter, L., & Canter, M. (1981). *Assertive discipline follow-up guidebook.* Los Angeles: Canter & Associates.

Carter, K., Cushing, K., Sabers, D., Stein, P., & Berliner, D. (1988). Expert–novice differences in perceiving and processing visual classroom information. *Journal of Teacher Education, 39*(3), 25–31.

Charles, C. M. (1992). *Building classroom discipline: From models to practice* (4th ed.). New York: Longman.

Cochran-Smith, M., & Lytle, S. L. (1990). Research on teaching and teacher research: The issues that divide. *Educational Researcher, 19*(2), 2–11.

Darling-Hammond, L. (1997). *The right to learn: A blueprint for creating schools that work.* San Francisco: Jossey-Bass.

Glasser, W. (1984). *Control theory: A new explanation of how we control our lives.* New York: Harper & Row.

Glasser, W. (1990). *The quality school.* New York: Harper & Row.

Goodlad, J. I. (1990). *Teachers for our nation's schools.* San Francisco: Jossey-Bass.

Greeno, J. G., Magone, M., & Chaiklin, D. (1979). Theory of constructions and set in problem solving. *Memory and Cognition, 7*(6), 445–461.

Kohn, A. (1993). *Punished by rewards.* Boston: Houghton Mifflin.

Martin, G., & Pear, J. (1992). *Behavior modification* (4th ed.). Upper Saddle River, NJ: Prentice Hall.

Osborne, R. J., & Wittrock, M. C. (1983). Learning science: A generative process. *Science Education, 67,* 489–508.

Rogers, C. R., & Freiberg, H. J. (1994). *Freedom to learn* (3rd ed.). Upper Saddle River, NJ: Merrill/Prentice Hall.

Ross, D. D. (1990). Programmatic structures for the preparation of reflective teachers. In Clift, R., Houston, W. R., & Pugach, M. D. (Eds.), *Encouraging reflective practice in education* (pp. 97–118). New York: Teachers College Press.

Shulman, L. S. (1987). Knowledge and teaching: Foundations of the new reform. *Harvard Educational Review, 57*(1), 31.

Sparks-Langer, G. M., & Colton A. B. (1991). Synthesis of research on teachers' reflective thinking. *Educational Leadership, 48*(6), 37–44.

Wolfgang, C. H., & Glickman, C. D. (1980). *Solving discipline problems: Strategies for classroom teachers.* Boston: Allyn & Bacon.

UNIT

2

Discipline Models

A number of classroom discipline options are available for teachers. In Unit 2 you will learn about several discipline theories or models that have been created for classroom use. These theories have been selected to cover a broad spectrum of values and educational philosophy so that you can compare divergent discipline approaches and the assumptions on which they are based. The underlying principles of each model are presented, along with an explanation of how the model is applied in the classroom. The extent to which each theory can be used to prevent as well as correct discipline problems is discussed. The model's usefulness for a schoolwide discipline program is considered, and its strengths and weaknesses are identified.

3

Behavior Modification: B. F. Skinner

OBJECTIVES

This chapter is designed to help you

1. Understand the difference between positive and negative reinforcement.
2. Explain the mistake teachers make of reinforcing students they intend to punish.
3. Discover the applications of behavior modification in the classroom.
4. Understand the technique of extinction.
5. Explain the procedures and purpose of providing students time-out.
6. Identify the negative effects of punishment.
7. Describe the effects of using different schedules of reinforcement.
8. Explain the role of conditioned reinforcers in the classroom.
9. Recognize the various kinds of reinforcers that may be used in the classroom.
10. Explain the use of a token economy.
11. Understand the negative effects rewards may have on intrinsic motivation.
12. Understand how children's academic behavior may become dependent on rewards.

ASSUMPTIONS

1. Human beings have no will. They simply respond to environmental stimuli.
2. Human beings are essentially responders to external stimuli. They are regulated by environmental influences that satisfy basic needs.
3. For students to behave appropriately, they must receive guidance from their teachers.
4. Students cannot learn to be responsibly self-governing. They must be managed by someone who can arrange reinforcers appropriately.
5. If the behavior of humans is not managed, we can expect an increase of discipline problems, crime, poverty, war, and other social ills.

Introduction

Behavior modification has had broad application in American society. Not only has it had extensive school use, it has also been implemented in a variety of situations either to help people eliminate such behaviors as smoking and excessive TV watching or to encourage such actions as cleaning one's room and increasing productivity on factory assembly lines. It has been implemented in mental hospitals, in schools for the incorrigible, and in prisons, as well as in business and industry. Its school uses have been extensive. It has been applied both to encourage learning as well as to eliminate various inappropriate behaviors. Of all the discipline approaches, it is the most carefully researched. Teachers have used behavior modification techniques to shape student behavior, to encourage more sustained study, to increase excellence of student performances, and to discourage behaviors that interfere with productive schoolwork.

B. F. Skinner, the most prominent behaviorist of our day, was born in Susquehanna, Pennsylvania, in 1904. He died in 1990. He trained and spent his professional career at Harvard University, where he worked extensively with animals, particularly rats and pigeons. But he is perhaps most widely known for his studies of human babies who were cared for inside glass enclosures called air cribs. In this environment, children were kept dry, warm, and comfortable, and all their needs were satisfied. He even raised his own daughter in an air crib. His purpose, of course, was to create an environment that could be more completely controlled.

Skinner received considerable attention after the publication of his novel, *Walden Two,* in which he envisioned a utopia brought about by social engineering (Skinner, 1948). He believed that war, poverty, and other social ills could be eliminated through the application of the principles of reinforcement he had carefully researched. Increased attention came with the publication of *Beyond Freedom and Dignity* (Skinner, 1971). In this book he rejected freedom and dignity as viable concepts for society. Instead, he claimed that our choices are determined by the environmental conditions under which we live.

From his research, Skinner formulated reinforcement strategies to be used by teachers in the classroom. He found that students' behavior could be controlled through a program of reinforcement. Many teachers now use reinforcement principles and procedures to discipline their students and manage learning in their classrooms.

▼ Jimmy Carington came into the school building after lunch and walked quickly down the hall toward Mr. Johnson's social studies room. He was followed by an entourage of seventh- and eighth-grade students who had accepted him as their leader. A ninth grader, Jimmy was taller and more powerfully built than the rest. As he strode down the hall, determination showed in his face. The younger children chattered noisily as they hurried to keep up with Jimmy's rapid pace. Jimmy was their hero. His heroics

Jimmy Carington's disruptive behavior had mistakenly been reinforced until he was bold enough to attack his teacher.

thus far consisted of nine infractions, nine appearances before the juvenile judge, and avoidance in each case of any punishment. He always succeeded in being released and returned to school, where he continued to ignore the same old warnings. His latest offense was to break into the school several days earlier and use a hammer to smash all the typewriters in the typing classroom. All 25 machines were beyond repair.

When Jimmy and his followers reached Mr. Johnson's room, they found him standing out in the hall. Jimmy went directly up to him and said, with a sneer, "I'm not going to make up any of your stupid assignments. You'd better not send me to the principal again, either." He then punched the teacher directly in the face.

The teacher grabbed Jimmy by the arm and, twisting it behind him, marched him straight to the principal's office. Dr. Stroud, the principal, was not happy to see Jimmy again. She knew that she could not send him back to Mr. Johnson's class. And the other social studies teachers had already refused to take him.

Some will say that legal officials and school administrators indulged Jimmy until he was spoiled. From the behaviorist point of view, this explanation is too imprecise. A behaviorist would explain that school officials and others mistakenly reinforced Jimmy's bad behavior. They intended to get him to stop being destructive by punishing him, but what they did to punish him acted as a reinforcer instead. It is not uncommon for teachers, parents, and other adults to make the mistake of reinforcing bad behavior (Madsen, Becker, Thomas, Koser, & Plager, 1968).

Inadvertently reinforcing unwanted behavior is common in most situations in life. In mental hospitals, for example, it was formerly believed that inmates' inability to dress, feed, or wash themselves was a symptom of mental illness. It was discovered, however, that these and other unacceptable behaviors were actually taught to patients by the hospital staff. If the patients did not perform these functions, the staff would; patients thus had little incentive to care for themselves. To correct this problem, smoking, watching television, and other privileges were made to depend on patients' dressing, feeding, and washing themselves. Under these conditions, patients demonstrated that they could perform these tasks adequately (Ayllon & Michael, 1959).

One resident of a mental institution made a practice of stealing towels and hiding them in her room. Each time the towels were stolen, hospital workers entered her room to retrieve them. When they realized that their attention was reinforcing her towel collecting, they decided to stop retrieving stolen towels. Over a period of several days, while staff members ignored her, the towel thief accumulated more than 400 towels. She stacked them on the floor, in cupboards, under the bed, and on the bed. When there was no longer enough space for her to occupy her room comfortably, she removed all but one towel. Because stealing towels no longer brought attention, she decided to stop (Ayllon, 1963). Inadvertent attention by hospital workers helped shape the patient's inappropriate behavior, and withdrawing attention helped reverse it.

In school, students' misbehavior may be encouraged by teachers in a similar way. Educators tend to attribute bad behavior by students to poor home environment or other causes outside the school. Outside influences do affect children's behavior. Much misbehavior in school, however, may be shaped by teachers and administrators, whose attention to the misbehavior actually reinforces it. Behavioral scientists claim that habitual misbehaviors persist because they are reinforced. When children misbehave in school, it is very common for teachers to pay attention to them in some way—by scolding, shaming, insulting, or otherwise acknowledging them. Another common tactic is to formally punish students who break rules. School personnel try to stop bad behavior by creating very aversive consequences. However, these consequences usually stimulate more bad behavior, as evidenced by the fact that a very small percentage of the student body exhibit a disproportionately large number of behavior problems and receive the most administrative sanctions. If repeated punishment were effective, children would stop their unacceptable practices. The fact that they do not is an indication that the "punishment" they receive is reinforcing.

Not all misbehavior in school comes from the misapplication of reinforcement principles. Often the complexity of the school environment creates problems that teachers find difficult or impossible to counter. Teachers are frequently required to adhere to administrative directives about discipline and other policies that are contrary to their own desires and beliefs. Sometimes community expectations, financial constraints, and other factors limit the way teachers can practice their craft. Improving discipline is, therefore, not just a matter of helping teachers learn more effective methods. School practices that limit the effectiveness of teachers must also be eliminated.

Basic Principles of Behavior Modification

Behavior modification had its beginning in the work of psychologist Ivan Pavlov. He succeeded in getting dogs to salivate by ringing a bell. This bell had previously been rung whenever the dogs were fed meat powder. The salivating response was made in the absence of the meat powder because the bell had become associated with, or *conditioned to,* the food. The salivating response is called a *respondent* because it is controlled by stimuli that precede it. Other responses, called *operants,* are controlled by stimuli that follow them (Bijou & Baer, 1961).

Much of what we know about operant conditioning we owe to the work of B. F. Skinner. His work was primarily done with rats and pigeons, but it has often been applied to humans as well. Skinner believed that all human behavior could be explained as responses to environmental stimuli. He concluded that humans have no internal will to guide their behavior—that they are not directed toward goals but are instead controlled by their environment. Therefore, to behave properly, children need to have adults manage their behavior by arranging environmental consequences. If adults fail to properly reinforce desirable behavior, various rewarding factors in the environment may inadvertently influence children to behave in undesirable ways. Skinner even envisioned a utopia regulated by social engineers arranging contingencies of reinforcement and directing the behavior of inhabitants toward socially desirable ends. He believed that problems such as poverty, war, and rioting could be prevented in a properly conditioned society (Skinner, 1948).

Behaviorists do not make any attempt to explain human behavior in terms of will. Such expressions as *wish-fulfilling, pleasure-seeking,* and *pain-avoiding* imply that people actively seek or desire certain stimuli and that they choose certain behaviors that are likely to produce them. Behaviorists wish to avoid such implications. They simply state that behavior is controlled by consequences. In other words, any behavior can be reinforced if a sufficiently strong reward is provided following the behavior.

To modify behavior, behaviorists provide either reinforcement or punishment. Reinforcement increases the strength or frequency of a particular behavior; punishment reduces it. It has been noted that some teachers inadvertently reinforce bad behavior when they intend to punish. It must be concluded, therefore, that neither teachers' intentions nor the nature of their actions determines whether or not punishment has taken place. Whether an action is punitive is determined instead by the responses students make to these stimuli. It is more appropriate, then, to refer to the influence of teachers' actions by their consequences than by their intentions. It is correct to say that Stephanie found the teacher's actions to be reinforcing or that Jeff found the teacher's actions to be punishing. It is incorrect to say that the teacher reinforced Ray or that the teacher punished Jane.

Correction Strategies

▼ Ms. Ropp was a young, new teacher who had very little understanding of classroom management. The noise level in her sixth-grade classroom had become intolerable. This noise consisted mainly of visiting between children, yelling across the room, and whistling. There was also an occasional fight, and several students made a habit of throwing spit wads and paper airplanes. Sometimes children chased one another around the room and climbed over desks to catch other children or avoid being caught by their pursuers. Ms. Ropp routinely dealt with these situations by issuing threats and loudly directing students to be quiet and take their seats. These efforts usually reduced the noise level temporarily, but within minutes students' misbehavior increased. One day Ms. Ropp could take it no longer. Utterly exasperated, she fled from the room, determined never to go back again. She spent a couple of hours in the main office, resisting the principal's efforts to have her return to the classroom. She finally consented to go back to class if the principal agreed to spend a couple of hours each day in her classroom for a week or so and also to help her develop successful management techniques.

The principal taught Ms. Ropp the following three procedures:

1. *Specify rules clearly.*   Specify the desired behavior. Make your rules clear, so that children will know what is expected. Explain the rules periodically, so that they are always understood.
2. *Ignore disruptive behavior.*   Do not attend to the behavior you wish to eliminate. Call attention to the behavior of children who are following the rules. Praise behavior that is distinctly different from disruptive behavior. Ignore inappropriate behavior.
3. *Praise the children for following rules.*   Look for instances when students are following the rules, and praise them for doing so. Provide special privileges to children who are following the rules (Becker, Engelmann, & Thomas, 1971).

It was difficult at first for Ms. Ropp to resist her natural tendency to call attention to the misbehavior of her students. It seemed wrong not to inform misbehaving students that they were disrupting the class. She felt that it was her responsibility to control the class and was constantly tempted to continue with her threats and admonitions. With the principal present, however, she held her tongue and ignored the antics. After 2 or 3 days, it was agreed that the principal would no longer remain in her class. When the principal had left, the children immediately began behaving as they had before. Ms. Ropp, determined to follow through with her new management approach, continued to ignore inappropriate behavior and praise those students who were following the rules. After a week she could see a noticeable difference in her students. Encouraged, she remained faithful to the management procedures. Before long her students were reasonably well-behaved.

REINFORCEMENT

Stimuli used to reinforce behavior are called *reinforcers*. There are two kinds of reinforcement, negative and positive. Negative reinforcement is often mistakenly thought of as a negative act on the part of the teacher designed to suppress undesired behavior. Although it is often confused with punishment, negative reinforcement actually involves students' avoiding an unpleasant stimulus, not being provided negative experiences. In addition, the result of a negative reinforcer is to increase the frequency of a particular behavior, not reduce it, as is true in the case of punishment. The student wishes to avoid the withdrawal of the stimulus. For example, at the beginning of a term, students may be given 100 points that can be applied toward their citizenship grade. Points are then taken away for each previously defined inappropriate behavior. If students increase good citizenship to avoid having points taken away, they are said to have been negatively reinforced (see Table 3.1).

Positive reinforcement, on the other hand, occurs when stimuli are presented. For example, if children are given points when they display good citizenship and they then demonstrate better citizenship behavior, they have been positively reinforced.

TABLE 3.1
Reinforcement and punishment.

		Effect on Response Frequency		
		None	**Increase**	**Decrease**
Stimulus Change After Response	**None**	Neutral	Recovery after punishment	Extinction after positive reinforcement
	Presented	Neutral	Positive reinforcement	Punishment by presentation
	Removal or Avoided	Neutral	Negative reinforcement	Punishment by removal

Notice that, in these two examples, good citizenship is the object of providing reinforcement. In the case of positive reinforcement, points are given when acceptable behavior occurs. With negative reinforcement, students avoid having points taken away by behaving in a proper way. Both positive and negative reinforcement stimulate an increase in the response with which they are associated.

Another approach to reinforcement is to focus attention on academic performance. When good academic behavior is reinforced, disruptive behavior is correspondingly reduced (Edwards, 1975). Obviously, when one increases, the other must decrease.

Some research on behavior management has involved teaching students to shape the behavior of their teachers (Klein, 1971). When their teachers' behavior improved, the behavior of students also improved. Researchers trained several students with very disruptive behavior to react positively to their teachers. In the process teachers behaved better, had better attitudes, and made comments that were more supportive of students. As a result, students' disruptive behavior decreased (Sherman & Cormier, 1974).

EXTINCTION

▼ Mr. Chen made a practice of criticizing a group of students in his class for talking during quiet study time. Occasionally, he referred one or more of them to the assistant principal, Mr. Howe, for disciplinary action. However, the problem continued, and many days it seemed to be worse. One day, it occurred to Mr. Chen that the unruly students may have been reacting to the attention he gave them. He decided to ignore them while at the same time looking for opportunities to provide reinforcement when they worked quietly on classroom projects. Over a period of time, talking out in quiet study time by these students was eliminated.

When inappropriate behavior that was once reinforced is resolutely ignored, it is often extinguished, that is, weakened to the point of disappearing. Extinction is particularly effective when desired behaviors are reinforced at the same time. While teachers are ignoring disruptive students and paying attention to their well-behaved classmates, they should be on the lookout for any sign that the disruptive students are changing their behavior patterns. As soon as any appropriate behavior is noticed, it should be reinforced. When extinction is combined with reinforcement, teachers can expect significant improvement in classroom discipline (Hall et al., 1971). Inappropriate behavior will be extinguished while the good behavior increases in frequency.

For example, one kindergarten child had a habit of crying and throwing tantrums on the playground. The teacher responded by approaching the child and imploring her to stop crying and carrying on. Sometimes the teacher got angry with the child. Tantrum behavior became more pronounced and intolerable. On the advice of a knowledgeable principal, the teacher started ignoring the tantrums. She brought a book or magazine with her to the playground and pretended to read it when the child threw a tantrum. Eventually, the child no longer displayed tantrum behavior (Alberto & Troutman, 1999).

Ordinarily, it is wise to reinforce desired behavior at the same time undesired behavior is being ignored. For example, students' talking in class could be ignored while doing their schoolwork is reinforced. This process is particularly useful in cases where one kind of teacher behavior makes a student behavior less likely to occur, as is true in the example of Mr. Chen. Often, if an undesirable behavior is just ignored, it continues to occur even though it is no longer being reinforced by the teacher. It may even increase in frequency. This is because the particular behavior may be influenced by other reinforcers the teacher has little control over, like peer approval (Walker & Shea, 1999).

TIME-OUT

Sometimes no amount of praising good behavior and ignoring bad behavior reduces a student's misconduct. Reinforcement received from peers for behaving improperly may appear to be more powerful than reinforcement for good behavior offered by the teacher. In such cases, behaviorists may recommend that the student be placed in time-out, that is, removed temporarily from the environment in which the misbehavior is being reinforced. Time-out usually takes place in a small room away from the regular classroom. The room should be as nearly free of stimuli as possible so that students do not find being there preferable to being in the classroom. Students are usually required to stay in the time-out room for some designated time or until the undesirable behavior is terminated. For example, a child who cries uncontrollably in the classroom may be expected to remain in the time-out room until the crying has stopped for 5 minutes. This situation is explained as the child enters the time-out room.

It is wise to limit the use of time-out as much as possible. Students should not be traumatized by time-out experiences. For example, a child should not be imprisoned in an "isolation box" with a bolted door.

PUNISHMENT

The most common correction strategy is punishment. Sometimes teachers elect to punish children for bad behavior rather than ignore bad behavior and reinforce good behavior. Students, however, may find a teacher's actions to be reinforcing rather than punishing. When they do, their inappropriate behavior only increases. Suppose, for example, that Ralph throws spit wads at other students and that the teacher routinely lectures him in an effort to somehow get him to stop. However, if Ralph finds the increased attention reinforcing, he will not stop throwing spit wads. He gets the double pleasure of attention from peers as well as from the teacher. He may prefer more positive attention, but if his teachers have always ignored his good behavior and focused only on his misbehavior, he may find this negative attention preferable to no attention from teachers at all. Therefore, he provokes all his teachers until they react negatively.

It is very hard to predict how students will react to punishment. Some, of course, relent and behave better. Others become more disruptive. In still other cases, students may avoid a direct confrontation but still take aggressive, retaliatory actions against their teachers. They may destroy school or personal property, for example. Some students withdraw from those who punish them; these students may stop learning if they are punished. These problems with punishment are rarely encountered when acceptable behavior is reinforced and bad behavior is ignored.

Behaviorists believe that punishment may occasionally be necessary. It is recommended, however, only when a more positive approach has failed or when quick action must be taken. For example, one would not look for opportunities to use positive reinforcement during a fight. Instead, the fight would be stopped and punishment used if necessary to suppress students' inclination to continue (Charles, 1992).

Punishment is usually arbitrary. It is often given without prior notification and involves painful experiences of a nature and duration that have little to do with students' bad behavior. For example, Deanna and her friend Jasmine threw a brick through a stained glass window in a church adjacent to the school. Deanna was a star athlete in both basketball and track. Her friend did not participate in any school activities. As punishment, Deanna was forbidden to participate in basketball for the entire season. Jasmine was reprimanded. Deanna's punishment had little to do with breaking the window, and the duration of the punishment was arbitrary. Jasmine's punishment was less severe, but it also had little to do with breaking windows. It would have been better to make the two pay for replacing the window.

Schedules of Reinforcement

A schedule of reinforcement is the pattern with which the reinforcer is presented in response to a target behavior being exhibited (Walker & Shea, 1999). The schedule of reinforcement that is applied has a significant effect on behavior changes. Reinforcement can be provided on a *continuous schedule,* in which case it is given each time the target behavior is demonstrated. If an *intermittent schedule* is desired, some instances of a particular behavior are reinforced while others are not. Intermittent reinforcement can either be predictable or unpredictable. Intermittent reinforcement can be made predictable in two ways: with a *fixed interval* or with a *fixed ratio.* In a fixed interval schedule, the first response after a fixed period of time following the previous reinforcement is reinforced. After this, a new interval begins. For example, children might be given a gold star for spending 20 minutes reading. They would continue to be reinforced after each subsequent 20-minute interval of reading. With a fixed ratio schedule, reinforcement occurs each time students emit a set number of responses of a particular type. In this case, children might receive 10 minutes of free time each time they complete 20 algebra problems.

Intermittent reinforcement can be made unpredictable in two ways: a *variable ratio* and a *variable interval*. The variable ratio schedule is designed to sustain the level of response to reinforcement once an acceptable level of behavior is reached by means of a continuous or fixed ratio schedule. In this case the number of responses occurring before a reinforcer is given is varied about some mean. For example, reinforcement may be given on the average of every 20th response, but it might be given after any number of response from 1 to 40 in an unpredictable way. To illustrate, Mr. Quincy has succeeded in getting Myrna to raise her hand while participating in class discussions. This was done with a fixed ratio schedule. He now wants to employ a variable ratio schedule. Myrna could be placed on a variable ratio schedule of 5, which means that reinforcement could take place on the average of every 5 times she raises her hand. This might mean that she is reinforced the 6th, 3rd, 7th, and 4th times she raises her hand for an average of 5. The fact that Myrna doesn't know exactly when Mr. Quincy will call on her helps maintain her hand-raising behavior at a high level.

A variable interval schedule is similar to a variable ratio schedule, except that the presentation of the reinforcer is based on a behavioral response mean or average. Again, the individual receiving the reinforcer is unaware when it will occur. For example, Ms. Condie wants to use a variable interval schedule to reinforce Stan's in-seat behavior. She decides to pick an interval of 10 minutes. She may reinforce Stan the first time after 4 minutes, the second time after 9 minutes, the third time after 13 minutes, the fourth time after 15 minutes, and the fifth time after 9 minutes, for an average of 10 minutes.

The use of an intermittent schedule of reinforcement has two advantages. First, it is more economical of the teacher's time and effort. Second, the use of an intermittent schedule of reinforcement, administered in connection with appropriate behavior, is more likely to lead to more persistent behavior that is resistant to change (Martin & Pear, 1992). This persistence comes about apparently because reinforcement is unpredictable and therefore more elusive and enticing (Kazdin & Polster, 1973).

The use of intermittent reinforcement also has its drawbacks. Undesirable behavior that is intermittently reinforced will have a greater tendency to persist. As shown in the following example, if inappropriate behavior is reinforced intermittently, as it often is, greater effort will be required to eliminate it later.

▼ Mr. Forsgren had been watching K.D. and Jinyun out of the corner of his eye for some time as they talked incessantly in the back of the room. The conversation between the two had become louder and louder as time passed. Mr. Forsgren decided not to call attention to their disruption for fear of satisfying their need for attention and promoting a worse problem. However, their talking and other disruptive antics finally could no longer be ignored. A few students were peering at him with expectant looks, and others had irritated expressions on their faces. Obviously, some class members felt that he should take action. Suddenly Mr. Forsgren shouted out, "K.D.! Jinyun! I've heard about enough of your talking. If I hear any more from you, I'll send you to Ms. Brenchley's office." There was general snickering around the room. Mr. Forsgren could not decide whether they were laughing at him or the two unruly students. He hoped that the threat to send them to the principal's office would deter them. He went on grading papers at his desk but occasionally shot a dour look in the direction of K.D. and Jinyun. Not more than 5 minutes later he heard whispering coming from where the two sat. "I'll wait them out this time," he thought. "When they have gone far enough, I'll take them both to the principal." The talking reached a crescendo as several other students joined the pair. Mr. Forsgren drew in a deep breath in preparation for another verbal assault. Before he could make a sound, the bell rang, ending the class. K.D. and Jinyun were first out the door. They knew that they had just barely missed incurring the wrath of Mr. Forsgren and a possible trip to Ms. Brenchley's office.

Some teachers recognize that paying attention to students' misbehavior only increases its frequency. This knowledge encourages them to wait until students' misbehavior becomes intolerable before responding. When they finally do react, they end up reinforcing the disruptive behavior intermittently, thus ensuring its persistence and making it much harder to curtail subsequently.

Types of Reinforcers

There are several types of reinforcers. Although there is no inherent advantage in using one type of reinforcer over another, one type may be preferable depending on the resources of the school or the inclination of the teacher.

CONDITIONED REINFORCERS

Some reinforcers are convenient to use but lack sufficient power to alter students' behavior. Verbal reinforcers, for example, are sometimes rather ineffective; attention by peers may be far more powerful in promoting bad behavior than a teacher's praise is in influencing good behavior. In this case, the teacher may want to increase the power of praise by pairing it with some other, more powerful reinforcer. For instance, praise can be given at the same time the teacher rewards a student with a special privilege such as acting as a lab assistant. A reinforcer that is thus strengthened by association with some other reinforcer is said to have become conditioned. Eventually, praise, the conditioned reinforcer, may be used in place of being a lab assistant, the more powerful one.

EDIBLE REINFORCERS

Edible reinforcers, such as candy and other goodies, are commonly used with preschool and early elementary school students and some exceptional children because they have immediate reinforcement value. Edible reinforcers are usually used in conjunction with various material reinforcers, particularly where a commissary has been established.

MATERIAL REINFORCERS

Objects such as toys, games, personal items, and so forth have been widely used as reinforcers. The specific kind of items used varies with the students' age level and interests. Trinkets and toys can be used effectively with small children. Older children may want recorded music, games, or tape players.

Often, material reinforcers can be obtained quite inexpensively. For example, stores and industries in the community may furnish rejects, excess spare parts, and other odds

TABLE 3.2
Possible edible and material reinforcers.

Edible	Material	
Bakery items	Arts and craft supplies	Party items
Cookies	Building sets	Balloons
Doughnuts	Model kits	Costumes
Candy	Modeling clay	Noisemakers
Candy bars	Painting sets	Pennants
Chocolate kisses	Pliable dough	Posters
Jelly beans	Badges	Toys and games
Lemon drops	Books	Balls
Lollipops	Picture books	Bean bags
Marshmallows	Comic books	Blocks
Cereal (sweetened)	Decals	Board games
Dairy products	Entertainment	Computer games
Cheese	Radios	Flying discs
Ice cream	Recorded music	Gliders
Yogurt	Tape players	Jacks
Drinks	Figurines	Jump ropes
Fruit juice	Makeup	Kazoos
Soft drinks	Office supplies	Kites
Fruit	Colored chalk	Marbles
Apples	Coloring books	Miniature cars
Oranges	Crayons	Playing cards
Raisins	Felt-tip pens	Puzzles
Gum	Paper	Stuffed animals
Nuts	Pencils	Yo-yos
Snacks		
Caramel corn		
Popcorn		
Potato chips		
Tortilla chips		

and ends. Sometimes edibles can be obtained in the same way; some teachers have gleaned broken cookies or day-old baked goods from wholesale bakeries.

Parents and other community members can also be asked for "white elephants" such as magazines, old toys, and all sorts of objects that are of no further use to their owners. Giveaways, promotional offers, and free samples are another possible source of inexpensive reinforcers. Old special-occasion cards, playing cards, and other colorful paper items are great to use with small children. Shells, leaves, stamps, and foreign coins are available at minimal cost. Some teachers have purchased items in bulk at very low prices from companies that service vending machines. A small amount of money can go a long way in procuring such items (Sulzner-Azaroff & Mayer, 1977).

Table 3.2 lists some common edible and material reinforcers.

ACTIVITY REINFORCERS

Sometimes teachers do not wish to give students edibles or toys but prefer instead to provide special privileges or activities as reinforcers. Table 3.3 gives a list of possible activity reinforcers.

GENERAL AND BACKUP REINFORCERS

To increase the power of reinforcement, teachers may employ general reinforcers. General reinforcers are symbols that have little or no intrinsic value to students. But they are nevertheless extremely valuable, because they can be exchanged for any one of a number of backup reinforcers that are desirable to students.

TABLE 3.3
Possible activity reinforcers.

Running errands	Passing out papers
Watching a movie	Watching TV
Listening to music	Playing games
Going to lunch early	Having a party
Choosing a seat	Taking care of classroom pets
Acting as team captain	Designing a test
Assisting the teacher	Using the microscope
Going to the library	Spending a period in a commons area
Having an extra P.E. period	Reading a book during class
Attending class outdoors	Going on a field trip
Choosing a game for recess	Putting up the school flag
Supervising the playground	Acting in a skit
Leading the music	Seeing a film strip
Supervising the lab	Attending/skipping an assembly
Making puppets	Going home early
Running the projector	Playing educational games
Spending a period talking to a friend	Demonstrating a hobby to the class

TABLE 3.4
Possible tokens.

Held by the Student	Maintained by the Teacher
Pennies	Marks on the blackboard
Gold stars or other stickers	Tallies on a sheet of paper
Tickets or slips of paper	Computer entries, displayed creatively
Beads for stringing	
Poker chips	
Punches on a card	

The best example of a general reinforcer is money. The power of money is evident in the effort most people expend to obtain it. It is almost unheard of for people to rob a store at gunpoint to obtain some particular item; they take money. Money holds such power because it can indirectly satisfy almost any need. A teacher who provides general reinforcers, along with a wide variety of backup reinforcers, does not need to decide which backup reinforcers are most satisfying. Students make this decision for themselves. In school reinforcement programs, tokens instead of money are used as a medium of exchange. Tokens may be plastic money pieces, poker chips, slips of paper, or even points marked in a folder or on a chart (see Table 3.4). The common characteristic of all these variations is that they can be exchanged for some other desired reward.

TOKEN ECONOMY

When tokens are used in a system of exchange, the system is called a *token economy*. For tokens to be effective, teachers must be able to dispense them quickly and easily. For example, a teacher with a pocketful of plastic beads could readily dispense them while moving around the room teaching the whole class or working with individual students at their desks. The effectiveness of a token economy also depends on the desirability of backup reinforcers to students. If backup reinforcers have little reinforcing value, they will not motivate students. Sometimes it is surprising what some students will find desirable. A reinforcer's appeal usually depends to a large extent on students' age. Small children may work consistently for hours on schoolwork to earn tokens with which to buy some rather inexpensive trinket. Older students, of course, will not.

Until behavior improves, tokens need to be given out on a continuous schedule. As time goes by, a more convenient intermittent schedule can be established. In addition, praise may be given at the same time tokens are delivered so that it gains power as a conditioned reinforcer. If praise is then interspersed with tokens as reinforcement, it can be expected to have a positive influence on the behavior of students.

When a formal token economy is established in a school, a commissary is often created from which students can "purchase" rewards with their tokens. Depending on the age of the students involved, the commissary is usually stocked with items such as those listed in Table 3.2.

▼ Mr. Hansen was having trouble disciplining several students in each of his seventh-grade science classes. With help from one of his university professors, he created a token economy for use exclusively with these few unusually disruptive students. One thing he wanted to avoid was the practice, common in most token economy programs, of providing students with food or play materials as backup reinforcers. Instead, he wanted to provide them with special privileges, which he felt would be more in keeping with the purposes of schooling. In addition, he doubted that he could finance tangible reinforcers out of his own pocket and knew that the school budget could not accommodate this added expense. He thought that in any case parents might consider food and trinkets a bribe but that they—and others—would be less likely to object to this kind of program.

Mr. Hansen wanted to base his token economy on the curriculum used in his science classes and so sat down one day to list the things he expected of his students. In his classes, students spent most of their time working on experiments with plants. From a side desk students picked up cards that described the experiments. They took materials from the supply room as they needed them. They performed experiments at their desks. They could then put their experimental materials into grow tables and wait for results to appear. While they waited for the results of one experiment, they were encouraged to start new ones. Consequently, each student had several experiments to work on at any one time.

This is the list of behaviors Mr. Hansen decided to use as the basis of his token economy:

1. Listening during lecture or discussion portions of the class
2. Participating in class discussion
3. Reading appropriate materials
4. Working on one's own experiments
5. Carrying out timely, complete, and correct experiments
6. Answering the review questions on experiments
7. Answering extra questions on experiments
8. Doing extra experiments
9. Improving test scores

The next task was to decide what to use as backup reinforcers. He had developed a list of things he supposed students would find attractive, but he wanted to get their suggestions as well. He asked the target students what activities they would enjoy participating in during class. A caution was added that they should only include things that could legitimately be done in school. From his own ideas, as well as the students' suggestions, the following list was created:

1. Run the film projector (50 points).
2. Mark the roll for a week (50 points).
3. Be the teacher's assistant (50 points).
4. Run errands (25 points).
5. Play a board game during class (150 points).
6. Be excused 5 minutes early for lunch (25 points).
7. Spend a period visiting with a friend in the commons (150 points).
8. Spend one science period in a physical education class (150 points).
9. Spend a period in the library (75 points).
10. Prepare a special report (25 points).
11. Prepare a true–false quiz for the class (50 points).
12. Use the microscope for a period (100 points)
13. Be the supply room attendant (50 points).

To each of the disruptive students he had identified—there were three or four in each of his six classes—Mr. Hansen gave a folder. Stapled to the inside of the folders were two sheets. One sheet contained a list of the backup reinforcers along with their point values. On the other sheet, desired behaviors were listed. At the side of each desired behavior was a series of boxes in which points could be marked. Whenever Mr. Hansen observed one of the target students exhibiting acceptable behavior, he marked an appropriate number of points in one of the boxes. Mr. Hansen thought it important that his target students receive at least the minimum number of points each day to "purchase" some reward. He therefore attempted to give each student at least 25 points in each class period. Mr. Hansen tried to assign different point values to various behaviors in such a way that his students could learn to save their points and exchange them for more valuable reinforcers.

Mr. Hansen was very pleased with the effects of his token economy system. His most unruly students became the most conscientious ones almost immediately. In the process, Mr. Hansen discovered that some backup reinforcers were more popular than others. Being excused early for lunch was the most popular. Anyone who has been in a typical, crowded junior high school cafeteria can see why. Having an extra physical education period was very popular among the boys; the girls tended to prefer being the teacher's assistant and running errands. One student chose to present a special report. However, after he had received this reward once, it lost its appeal. Such experiences helped Mr. Hansen realize that he needed to maintain and from time to time revise a fairly large list of possible backup reinforcers to satisfy students more fully.

Sometimes teachers want to involve the whole class in a token economy. More efficient ways of dispensing tokens must then be used. Passing out plastic discs or poker chips usually works well. Some teachers print up paper money of different denominations to use as tokens. This practice is common among foreign language teachers and has the added advantage of teaching students the monetary system of the country whose language they are learning. If you plan to use a token economy, it is wise to consult with your principal beforehand. Consultation may help prevent some objections that might otherwise occur, and it also provides an opportunity to get clearance for such activities as being excused early for lunch or going to an extra physical education period. If you plan to have your students participate in an extra class or go to the library as part of your program, be sure to discuss the matter with the appropriate school personnel.

The Question of Bribery and Adversives

One of the criticisms often made of behavior modification is that it constitutes bribery. Sloane, Buckholdt, Jenson, and Crandall (1979) list the following responses commonly given by behaviorists to this criticism:

1. All educators hope that children will be encouraged to learn worthwhile things because of their intrinsic value. However, most worthwhile learning requires a minimum amount of skill or understanding before children really become drawn to it. Take reading, for example. For reading to be enjoyable, certain basic skills must be

learned. A poor reader could hardly be expected to be satisfied by attempting to read a difficult book such as Hamlet. In the beginning, reading must be motivated by external rewards. These external rewards, however, are only temporary. Once adequate reading skills are developed, extrinsic rewards will no longer be necessary.

2. Some individuals, such as those who have mental disabilities or psychoses, may not be motivated by the same things as most other people. They may require concrete, immediate reinforcers before they are motivated to do many of the things that make their lives more meaningful.

3. A reinforcer given to a child for schoolwork is no more a bribe than the salary earned by teachers and other adults for their services.

4. Bribery is a word used ordinarily with reference to payoffs for illegal or immoral behavior. To use it to describe tangible learning rewards is a misapplication of the true meaning of the term.

Although it is generally recommended that reinforcement be used instead of punishment or aversive stimuli, there is some advocacy for these techniques, particularly in the case of children with disabilities and extreme behavior problems. However, there are important considerations that must be addressed in making decisions about the aversive treatment of these children. The first of these is student rights. Three principles apply to both general and special education students: (1) the principle of normalization, (2) the principle of fairness, and (3) the principle of respect (Walker & Shea, 1999).

Normalization provides for students with disabilities receiving an experience in the classroom as close to normal as possible. *Fairness* involves the necessary use of due process in actions that relate to students' personal rights. It restricts any intervention taken that denies children access to what rightfully belongs to them, namely, an education in the least restrictive environment. It may be unfair, for example, to fail to use tangible rewards when a child is found to respond exclusively to them.

The principle of *respect* is one's right to be treated as a human being. For example, it would likely restrict (1) punishing children physically or psychologically, (2) depriving them of opportunities for success, (3) segregating them from their peers, (4) isolating them in an extended time-out situation, (5) medicating them, or (6) using restraints or electric shockers.

Behavior management should be approached with great caution, particularly the use of aversives. In summarizing the research, the following conclusions can be made: (1) Aversives demonstrated only short-term improvement. (2) Much of the research has involved children with severe disabilities. Little long-term improvement and little generalizable data have been reported. (3) Little or no research has been completed regarding the comparative effects of aversives and alternative nonaversive procedures (Walker & Shea, 1999).

Some Problems With Rewards

The efficacy and appropriateness of providing children rewards for achievement and other desirable behavior are rarely questioned. It is assumed that rewards will increase the quality and quantity of children's schoolwork, in addition to eliminating discipline problems, without doing any harm. Some research does support this contention. However, numerous research findings show a dark side to the practice of rewarding children's school performance.

The more rewards are used, the more they seem to be needed (Kohn, 1993). Whereas children may be inclined to learn without being rewarded before rewards are instituted, afterward they may refuse to learn without them. Extrinsic rewards thereby replace intrinsic motivation. Intrinsically motivated people pursue optimal challenges, display greater innovativeness, and tend to perform better under challenging conditions (Koestner, Zuckerman, & Koestner, 1987). However, once rewards are provided, people become less interested in the task for which they were rewarded (Deci, 1981; Lepper, 1983). Rewards are devastatingly effective in smothering enthusiasm for activities children might otherwise enjoy (Kohn, 1993). It has also been shown that highly controlled instruction on one task reduced students' interest in a second, entirely different task. In other words, the motivation-killing features of control can spill over to poison the attitudes about new learning activities (Enzle & Wright, 1992). More than 100 studies verify the fact that extrinsic rewards reduce intrinsic motivation (Ryan & Stiller, 1991).

When studying the magnitude of rewards, Freedman, Cunningham, and Krismer (1992) found that the greater the incentive offered, the more negatively the activities for which it was received were viewed. The more you encounter what you want, dangled in front of you as a reward, the more you come to dislike whatever you have to do to get it (Kohn, 1993). It seems logical that greater rewards carry greater incentives. However, little is gained if students come to loath the activities for which they are being rewarded. It isn't even necessary to receive the rewards yourself to be turned off. Merely watching someone else get a reward can have a temporary motivation-killing effect (Morgan, 1983).

Rewards also affect the quality of the work people do. Professional artists do less creative work when their work is commissioned than when they have contracted for their work in advance for a specified reward (Amabile, 1992). Students who are rewarded use less sophisticated learning strategies and score lower on standardized achievement tests. In addition, rewards improve performance only at extremely simple—indeed, mindless—tasks, and even then the improvement is quantitative (Kohn, 1993).

People who are given rewards choose easier tasks, are less efficient in using the information available to solve novel problems, and tend to be answer oriented and more illogical in their problem-solving strategies than intrinsically motivated people (Condry, 1977).

Reward systems usually entail careful monitoring. When children are monitored as they work on a task, they tend to lose interest in it. This is likely because the surveillance is perceived as controlling. When people think they are being monitored and evaluated, their intrinsic motivation suffers, even if no reward is offered for doing something well, and even if the evaluation turns out to be positive (Harackiewicz & Manderlink, 1984). The use of surveillance and rewards comprises a double dose of control, and together they accelerate the loss of self-determination and interest in accomplishing the task being rewarded. Research shows that the practice of using surveillance in conjunction with rewards is worse than either by itself (Lepper & Greene, 1975).

Control may promote rebellion, or it may stimulate compliance if students see no way to achieve what they find is necessary or desirable (like completing school) unless they do what they are told. Some children may accept being controlled. They may be willing to forfeit their autonomy when no other alternative seems possible. This creates an interesting problem for teachers who try to get such students to think. Doyle (1983) found that high school students who were accustomed to a highly directive style of instruction and were suddenly asked to think for themselves commonly exclaimed that they had "a right to be told what to do."

Of all the ways by which people are led to seek rewards, Kohn (1993) believes that the most destructive possible arrangement is to limit the number of rewards available. In the schools, grades fit this arrangement well. As can be expected, grades eventually replace learning as the primary purpose of schooling, as far as students are concerned. In the process, the pleasure students may have experienced intrinsically is diluted. In addition, grades encourage cheating and strain the relationship between teachers and students. They reduce students' sense of control over their own fate and may induce blind conformity and alienation from their own preferences. Though the exact outcome may be different for those punished by *F*s or rewarded with *A*s, the final result of grading is anything but positive (Kohn, 1993).

Preventing Discipline Problems

Behavior modification has no explicitly stated strategies for the prevention of discipline problems. Correcting problems is emphasized exclusively. However, discipline problems are prevented to some extent when behavior modification principles are implemented. When desired behavior is reinforced, it increases in frequency. There is usually a corresponding decrease in undesirable behavior.

Schoolwide Discipline

When behavior modification is used on a schoolwide basis, it often involves a commissary from which a wide variety of backup reinforcers are dispensed. Teachers and other school personnel provide tokens to use as a medium of exchange. Usually, the commissary is open only at predetermined times such as during lunch periods and before and after school. It is ordinarily staffed by students, under the direction of a faculty member.

Usually, little if any punishment is imposed on students in a behavior modification approach to discipline. Various reinforcement programs are preferred, which sometimes take the form of incentive programs. For example, students may be occupied with advancing their reading skills to obtain rewards. Charts hung in prominent places in the school often track the progress of students in such programs. Sometimes individual students are rewarded for reading achievement. At other times the school as a whole receives a reward for cumulative reading achievement. The whole school may take a special field trip, throw a party, or sponsor a dance. In some schools, the principal or teachers promise to do certain things if students achieve specified reading goals. For example, beards may be shaved, hair may be cut short, or the principal may spend the entire day sitting on top of the school building as a reward for students' achievement. Similar rewards have been given in secondary schools that remain drug-free for a year. Schoolwide incentive programs are designed to promote good behavior and have the effect of reducing negative behavior in the process.

Strengths and Weaknesses of Behavior Modification

STRENGTHS

1. It is simple to use.
2. Results are immediate.
3. It accommodates most teachers' desire to maintain control.
4. Students can feel successful while they obtain rewards.
5. Standards of behavior are uniform, consistent, and clear to all students.
6. Time does not have to be spent in class discussing rules and students' conduct.
7. It can be readily employed with all students regardless of age.
8. The procedure has been well researched and found to work consistently.

WEAKNESSES

1. The results may not last long.
2. Students may not perform as desired when rewards are terminated.
3. Students may not learn how to govern their own behavior.
4. To some teachers, this approach seems too much like bribery.
5. It ignores any underlying problems caused by influences at home, in society, or at school.
6. To use so much control in a democratic society may be unethical.
7. Students do not get an opportunity to clarify emotions, weigh alternatives, decide on solutions, or develop their intellect.
8. Rewards undermine intrinsic motivation.
9. Rewards may promote a loss of interest in learning.
10. Rewards may reduce the quality of the work children do in school.

▼ SUMMARY

Teachers who intend to reduce students' misbehavior by punishing them often discover that their efforts produce an increase in bad behavior instead. This unintended result occurs because some students find the teachers' attempts to punish them reinforcing. The result of teachers' actions, not their intentions, determines whether their students have been punished or reinforced. Teachers may also confuse negative reinforcement and punishment, believing them to be one and the same thing. Actually, negative reinforcement is given to increase some behavior, whereas punishment is implemented to terminate a behavior. Students have been negatively reinforced when they show an increase in a behavior in an effort to avoid something or to eliminate some aversive stimulus. A stimulus is punishing, on the other hand, when students reduce the incidence of unwanted behavior rather than suffer their effects.

Teachers who want to eliminate undesirable behavior in students may elect to ignore the behavior and reinforce competing behavior. In this way the unacceptable behavior is likely to become extinguished while desirable behaviors increase in frequency.

Teachers can economize their efforts by reducing the amount of reinforcement they provide after the desired behaviors become established. This reduction usually involves shifting from a continuous schedule of reinforcement to an intermittent one. An intermittent schedule of reinforcement has the advantage of providing a stronger conditioning influence than a continuous schedule—which can also be a disadvantage if the behavior that has been conditioned intermittently is an undesirable one. Such behavior will ultimately be much more difficult to eliminate. Greater economy can also be achieved by incorporating conditioned reinforcers, that is, by pairing a reinforcer that is powerful enough to elicit a desired response with one that is less powerful but easier and more convenient to use. After the conditioning has taken place, the less powerful but more convenient reinforcer can take the place of the more powerful one.

If still more powerful reinforcement is needed to influence appropriate behavior, general reinforcers can be employed. A generalized reinforcer is one that can be exchanged for a wide variety of backup reinforcers. When general reinforcers are used in a token economy, a commissary is often established from which students can make purchases with the tokens they have earned.

External rewards may create some unexpected problems in the classroom. They may undermine intrinsic motivation and cause children to lose interest in learning without rewards being supplied. They may also reduce the quality of the work children do.

CENTRAL IDEAS

1. Many teachers believe that they are punishing students only to discover that their actions promote the behavior they are trying to eliminate. They thereby reinforce rather than punish.
2. Students are negatively reinforced when they behave in a desired way to avoid an unpleasant stimulus.
3. To eliminate undesirable behaviors, teachers should stop reinforcing them (thus causing their extinction) and should reinforce acceptable behavior.
4. An intermittent schedule of reinforcement strengthens the effect of the reinforcer.
5. The time and expense involved in reinforcement programs may be reduced by using praise and attention as conditioned reinforcers.

6. Token economies increase the power of a reinforcement program by providing a greater range of reinforcers to satisfy the diverse desires of students.
7. External rewards can undermine intrinsic motivation. This causes children to lose interest in learning and reduces the quality of the work they do.

▼ QUESTIONS AND ACTIVITIES

QUESTIONS TO CONSIDER

1. How can you determine what students find to be reinforcing?
2. What do you consider to be the strengths and weaknesses of behavior modification?
3. What differences would there be in applying behavior modification techniques in elementary schools and secondary schools?

CLASSROOM ACTIVITIES

1. As a class, create a token economy for yourselves. Outline which behaviors you would provide tokens for and what you would use as backup reinforcers. In determining what reinforcers to use, consider the different values of the group. Try to reach a consensus about which reinforcers are mutually acceptable.
2. Create a reinforcement program for someone you know who has a problem that needs to be overcome. For example, the person may be tardy frequently. Apply this program, and evaluate the results.

STUDENT APPLICATIONS

1. Dan sits in his seat and sleeps most of the time. When he is awake, he spends his time talking with his friends or reading comic books he brings to class. He never does any work in class and has not turned in a homework assignment since the beginning of the year. Using behavior modification principles, describe what you would do to help Dan to become more involved in class and complete his homework.
2. Bianca annoys other members of the class by knocking their books on the floor and throwing paper airplanes around the room. In addition, she often talks loudly during quiet study time as well as during lectures and discussions. How could you solve these problems using behavior modification principles?

EXPLORE YOUR PHILOSOPHY

1. Decide whether you believe children are exclusively responders to environmental stimuli or whether they respond purposefully to their environment. Record the specific evidence and arguments you use to either support or refute this assumption.

2. Record evidence that may be used to support or refute the assumptions regarding whether or not children are born as blank slates.
3. Defend or refute the assumption that children are incapable of self-government.
4. Defend or refute the practice of providing students with rewards to shape their behavior.
5. Compare the principles contained in your educational philosophy with those of behavior modification. Determine consistencies and inconsistencies. Make adjustments in your philosophy as you believe appropriate.

▼ **REFERENCES**

Alberto, P. A., & Troutman, A. C. (1999). *Applied behavior analysis for teachers* (5th ed.). Upper Saddle River, NJ: Merrill/Prentice Hall.

Amabile, T. (1992). *A study of effects on creativity of commissioned and uncommissioned art works.* Unpublished manuscript, Brandeis University.

Ayllon, T. (1963). Intensive treatment of psychotic behavior by satiation and food reinforcement. *Behavior Research and Therapy, 1,* 53–61.

Ayllon, T., & Michael, J. (1959). The psychiatric nurse as a behavioral engineer. *Journal of the Experimental Analysis of Behavior, 3,* 323–334.

Becker, W. C., Engelmann, S., & Thomas, D. R. (1971). *Teaching: A course in applied psychology.* Chicago: Science Research Associates, Inc.

Bijou, S. W., & Baer, D. M. (1961). *Child development I: A systematic and empirical theory.* New York: Appleton-Century-Crofts.

Charles, C. M. (1992). *Building classroom discipline: From models to practice* (4th ed.). New York: Longman.

Condry, J. (1977). Self initiated versus other initiated learning. *Journal of Personality and Social Psychology, 35,* 459–477.

Deci, E. L. (1981). Effects of externally mediated rewards on intrinsic motivation. *Journal of Personality and Social Psychology, 18,* 105–115.

Doyle, W. (1983). Academic work. *Review of Educational Research, 53,* 159–199.

Edwards, C. H. (1975). Variable delivery systems for peer associated token reinforcement. *Illinois School Research, 12,* 19–28.

Enzle, M. E., & Wright, E. F. (1992). *The origin-pawn distinction and intrinsic motivation.* Unpublished manuscript.

Freedman, J. L., Cunningham, J. A., & Krismer, K. (1992). Inferred values and the reverse-incentive effect in induced compliance. *Journal of Personality and Social Psychology, 62,* 357–368.

Hall, R. V., Fox, R., Willard, D., Goldsmith, L., Emerson, M., Owen, M., Davis, F., & Porcia, E. (1971). The teacher as observer and experimenter in the modification of disputing and talking-out behavior. *Journal of Applied Behavior Analysis, 4,* 141–149.

Harackiewicz, J. M., & Manderlink, G. (1984). A process analysis of the effects of performance-contingent rewards on intrinsic motivation. *Journal of Experimental Social Psychology, 20,* 531–551.

Kazdin, A. E., & Polster, R. (1973). Intermittent token reinforcement and response maintenance in extinction. *Behavior Therapy, 4,* 386–391.

Klein, S. S. (1971). Student influence on teacher behavior. *American Educational Research Journal, 8,* 403–421.

Koestner, R., Zuckerman, M., & Koestner, J. (1987). Praise, involvement, and intrinsic motivation. *Journal of Personality and Social Psychology, 53,* 383–390.

Kohn, A. (1993). *Punished by rewards.* Boston: Houghton Mifflin Company.

Lepper, M. R. (1983). Extrinsic reward and intrinsic motivation. In Levine, J. M., & Wang, M. C. (Eds.), *Teacher and student perceptions: Implications for learning* (pp. 308–309). Hillsdale, NJ: Earlbaum.

Lepper, M. R., & Greene, D. (1975). Turning play into work: Effects of adult surveillance and extrinsic rewards on children's intrinsic motivation. *Journal of Personality and Social Psychology, 31,* 479–486.

Madsen, C. H., Becker, W. C., Thomas, D. R., Koser, L., & Plager, E. (1968). An analysis of the reinforcing function of "sit down" commands. In R. K. Parker (Ed.), *Readings in educational psychology* (pp. 265–278). Boston: Allyn & Bacon.

Martin, G., & Pear, J. (1992). *Behavior modification: What it is and how to do it* (4th ed.). Upper Saddle River, NJ: Prentice Hall.

Morgan, M. (1983). Decrements in intrinsic motivation among rewarded and observer subjects. *Child Development, 54,* 636–644.

Ryan, R. M., & Stiller, J. (1991). The social contexts of internalization: Parent and teacher influences on autonomy, motivation and learning. *Advances on Motivation and Achievement, 7,* 115–149.

Sherman, T. M., & Cormier, W. H. (1974). An investigation of the influence of student behavior on teacher behavior. *Journal of Applied Behavior Analysis, 7,* 11–21.

Skinner, B. F. (1948). *Walden two.* New York: Macmillan.

Skinner, B. F. (1971). *Beyond freedom and dignity.* New York: Knopf.

Sloane, H. N., Buckholdt, D. R., Jenson, W. R., & Crandall, J. A. (1979). *Structured teaching: A design for classroom management and instruction.* Champaign, IL: Research Press.

Sulzner-Azaroff, B., & Mayer, G. R. (1977). *Applying behavior-analysis procedures with children and youth.* New York: Holt, Rinehart & Winston.

Walker, J. E., & Shea, T. M. (1999). *Behavior management: A practical approach for educators* (7th ed.). Upper Saddle River, NJ: Merrill/Prentice Hall.

4

Assertive Discipline: Lee Canter

OBJECTIVES

This chapter is designed to help you
1. Learn what it means to be assertive.
2. Accurately apply Canter's steps of assertive discipline in the classroom.
3. Explain the communications skills needed to apply assertive discipline effectively.
4. List the various kinds of punishment that may be used with assertive discipline.
5. Identify the positive consequences that may be provided for good behavior.
6. Understand the role of assertive discipline in preventing discipline problems.
7. Understand the potential negative effects of punishment on children.

ASSUMPTIONS

1. Students must be forced to comply with rules.
2. Students cannot be expected to determine appropriate classroom rules and follow them.
3. Punishment will cause students to avoid bad behavior and engage in good classroom behavior.
4. Good behavior can also be encouraged by positive reinforcement.
5. For proper classroom management, parents and school administrators must help to enforce rules.

Introduction

Lee Canter is a child guidance specialist who has turned his entire attention to discipline in the schools. He has established an organization in California called Canter and Associates, through which he provides training for teachers who want to become more assertive in their teaching. His wife, Marlene, who teaches people with learning disabilities, also participates actively in this endeavor. Together they lead workshops all over the country. Many school districts have accepted the Canter model and adopted it for use by their teachers. Hundreds of thousands of teachers currently use Canter's assertive discipline.

The assertive discipline approach of Lee Canter has certain similarities to behavior modification strategies, but it also differs from them in significant ways. Whereas behavior modification emphasizes reinforcing appropriate behaviors and ignoring inappropriate ones, assertive discipline emphasizes punishing unacceptable behaviors and providing reinforcement for behaviors that are acceptable to teachers. The following exchange illustrates how assertive discipline would be applied in the case of an elementary school student who refuses to work in class and walks around the room instead:

Teacher	Chris, I want you to take your seat now and do your work!
Chris	I'm going to start in a minute. Just let me get my pencil sharpened.
Teacher	I want you to go to your seat now and start your work!
Chris	I'm going to. You don't make other students work like you do me.
Teacher	Chris, you must go to your seat immediately and start working on your assignment!
Chris	Just a minute, I have to get some paper from Jess.
Teacher	Chris, you must take your seat and go to work right now or you must come in after school and do it!

Canter believes that teachers have traditionally ignored their own needs in the classroom in favor of satisfying students' needs, assuming that as professional teachers they are expected to behave in this way. This misconception, however, contributes to many of the discipline problems teachers experience. Teachers have needs, wants, and feelings just as their students do. Teachers labor under other misconceptions as well:

- Good teachers should be able to handle discipline problems without any help from administrators or parents.
- Firm discipline may cause children psychological harm.
- Discipline problems do not persist when students are provided with activities that satisfy their needs.
- Misbehavior has deep-seated causes on which teachers can have no influence.

These misconceptions—which are promoted by such authorities as Sigmund Freud, B. F. Skinner, William Glasser, and M. M. Gordon—encourage teachers to discipline their students in wishy-washy ways that lead to additional problems (Canter & Canter, 1976).

Teachers, according to Canter, need to change their indecisive approaches to discipline. First and foremost, they must insist that their own rights as teachers are met. These rights include

- The right to establish classroom rules and procedures that produce the optimum learning environment
- The right to insist on behavior from students that meets teachers' needs and that encourages the positive social and educational development of students
- The right to receive help in disciplining from both parents and school administrators

Students also have rights. They have the right to have teachers who will limit inappropriate behavior, who will provide positive support for appropriate behavior, and who will communicate how students should behave and what will happen if they do not.

To make sure that the needs of both teachers and students are met, teachers must learn to assert themselves. Assertive teachers clearly and firmly communicate personal wants and needs to students and are prepared to enforce their words with appropriate actions. They attempt to get their own needs met and still take into account the capabilities of their students. Teachers need to communicate the idea that they care too much about themselves to allow students to take advantage of them. They also need to show students that they care too much about them to allow their inappropriate behavior to go unnoticed. In simple terms, assertive teachers let students know that they mean what they say and say what they mean.

Becoming an assertive teacher involves becoming forceful and self-assured with students. The assertive teacher is able to

1. Identify wants and feelings in interpersonal situations.
2. Verbalize wants and feelings in a straightforward way.
3. Persist in stating wants and feelings.
4. Use a firm tone of voice.
5. Maintain eye contact when speaking.
6. Reinforce verbal statements with congruent nonverbal gestures.

Responses to Misbehavior

Teachers may respond to students' actions in one of three ways. They may be nonassertive, hostile, or assertive.

THE NONASSERTIVE STYLE

Nonassertive teachers fail to let their students clearly know what they want and what they will not accept. They also fail to back up their words with appropriate, decisive actions. Commonly, they threaten the misbehaving student but stop short of implementing their threats. Sometimes they even ignore the unacceptable behavior. The following example shows a teacher using a nonassertive response style:

▼ Ms. Tew had a particularly difficult time getting three of the students in her biology class to stop talking during quiet study time. They sat and talked and often roamed around the room playing in the aquaria and making noises with the other science equipment. One day Eric, the leader of the three, encouraged the other two, Alma and

With her nonassertive style, Ms. Tew found it difficult to control her class.

David, to accompany him to the back of the room during quiet study time, where they immediately began trying to catch the guppies in one of the fish tanks. In the beginning, Ms. Tew did not even look at them. She had long ago tired of the misbehavior of these three and tried her best not to pay any attention to them. Finally, however, their rowdy, noisy antics caused other students in the class to implore her to do something about the situation. Finally, in desperation, Ms. Tew called out to the three, "Please try to sit down and do your work. I'll bet none of you has your assignment ready to turn in."

The students looked up from what they were doing and, as though challenging Ms. Tow, just ignored the request and went back to what they were doing. Five minutes later the noise level had again reached an unacceptable level. "Look, you three," pleaded Ms. Tew, "I don't know what I'm going to do with you. You're going to have to learn to sit in your seats and do your work. You're disturbing other students. We just can't put up with this any longer." Eric made a snide remark, which most members of the class heard but which Ms. Tew could not understand. The whole class burst into laughter. Red-faced, Ms. Tew retorted, "I don't have to stand for this. You are going to get into real trouble if you don't watch it."

THE HOSTILE STYLE

Teachers who use a hostile response style address students in an abusive way. They make derogatory remarks and often lose their temper. Hostile teachers commonly "put down" their students. For example, they may tell children that they never act their age or that they are stupid. Sometimes they make overt or implied threats of violence: "I'll get you for what you did." Their mean-spiritedness violates the rights and feelings of their students. A hostile response style is illustrated in the following example:

▼   Mr. Applegate ruled his class with an iron fist. He felt that students should learn to be more responsible by strictly complying with his expectations. Several students in his third-period class routinely defied him, however. They never turned in their home-work on time, rarely worked on in-class assignments, and spent most of the class period disturbing students around them. One day when they were particularly rowdy, Mr. Applegate walked over to the loudest of the group and yelled, "I've taken all of the insulting behavior from you I intend! If I catch you doing just one more thing to disturb this class, you're going to be very sorry!"

THE ASSERTIVE STYLE

When teachers respond assertively, they clearly communicate their wants and feelings to their students and indicate a willingness to back up their words with actions if neces-sary. This approach ensures greater compliance with their demands and expectations, so long as those demands and expectations are not unreasonable. Assertive teachers establish limits for their students and enforce them. They give explicit directions to a child, such as "Stop running in the halls and walk" or "Stop writing on your desk or you will have to sand and refinish it." In the following example the teacher uses an assertive response style:

▼ Ms. Romero had a student named Fred in her fifth-grade class who habitually picked on the other students and was involved in fighting almost every day. One after-noon Fred hit Roy and then sat back in his seat and laughed out loud. Roy was about 6 inches shorter than Fred and weighed at least 60 pounds less. Fred usually picked on smaller children. Ms. Romero observed Fred and firmly said, "Fred, stop fighting!" She added, "Fred, I will not tolerate your fighting in class. You have a choice: Either stop fighting or go to the principal's office." Fred said, "I don't want to be sent to see the principal. I've heard she is really tough." "The next time you fight," replied Ms. Romero, "you will have to go there."

Roadblocks to Becoming More Assertive

For most teachers, the most common roadblock to becoming more assertive is their own doubt about their ability to deal with students' behavior problems. Some students, they feel, misbehave because of emotional illness, heredity, brain damage, ignorance, peer pressure, inadequate parenting, lower socioeconomic background, or other influ-ences. Children with these problems can create difficulties for teachers, but the prob-lems can be managed if the teachers are assertive. First, teachers must realize that such children can be handled in the regular classroom. They then must learn to implement assertive discipline techniques consistently. Ordinary discipline procedures will not work with such children. With some of these children teachers will have to be firmer; other children will require more lenient treatment. Teachers must realize that they have the right to set limits and to ensure that children do not exceed them. They must get over the fear that children will develop an aversion to education if teachers set strict limits. Indeed, too many children come to school burdened by emotionally and educationally crippling problems such as parental neglect, inadequate home life, poverty, and racism. However, teachers who allow such children to go undisciplined or allow them to act inappropriately without responding firmly to them run the risk of doing additional harm.

When students have severe behavioral problems, teachers have the right and responsibility to ask for help from school administrators and other teachers. Some teachers fear that they will be considered weak if they ask for assistance with particularly difficult children. If they do not ask for assistance, they may avoid dealing with students who are out of control. Ultimately, they may have no choice but to involve others. However, it is better to seek help from other professionals sooner than later. Students should know that their teachers will act decisively to bring in other school personnel if they behave inappropriately. The assistance of parents should also be sought. Many children with behavior problems will respond more readily when parents are involved.

Applying Assertive Discipline

There are six steps to follow in applying assertive discipline:

1. Create positive student–teacher relationships.
2. Establish rules or expectations.
3. Track misbehavior.
4. Use punishments to enforce limits.
5. Implement a system of positive consequences.
6. Establish strong parent support.

Each of these steps has important aspects that must be kept in mind. In addition, it is critical that assertiveness be implemented consistently.

STEP 1: CREATE POSITIVE STUDENT–TEACHER RELATIONSHIPS

More and harsher rules won't affect students who see the teacher's rules as meaningless, who aren't afraid of negative consequences, and who are not motivated by the rewards offered. Consequently, discipline must be based on a foundation of mutual trust and respect. Before rules, rewards, and consequences can be effective, teachers have to build positive relationships with students and earn their respect. To establish trust between teachers and students, teachers must show what trust and respect look like. They must model it themselves. To do this, they must learn to give their undivided attention as they listen to their students, speak to students with respect, and become aware of what actions students consider disrespectful. Discipline procedures should be applied fairly to everyone.

Teachers need to become better acquainted with their students as individuals. One way to do this is to acknowledge students' birthdays and other important events. They also need to find out what students are interested in and what motivates them. Their attendance at sports events, dance recitals, band concerts, and other student activities, as well as complementing students on their success in these activities, will also promote better relationships.

Students should learn from their teachers the behaviors expected of them. Teachers should not assume their students know how to listen, follow directions, cooperate, or solve problems. Teachers should periodically review the conduct they expect of their students in various classroom contexts: group work, class discussions, laboratory work, and independent study. In addition, students need to be motivated to learn. Teachers need to excite them to become involved in a variety of classroom learning activities. The curriculum should be made to relate to students' needs (Canter, 1996).

STEP 2: ESTABLISH RULES OR EXPECTATIONS

Rules in the classroom should be based on the needs of teachers. Teachers need to specify exactly what behaviors they expect of children. These behaviors may be specified in a list such as

1. Complete all assignments on time.
2. Do your own work.
3. Don't talk without receiving permission.
4. Follow directions.
5. Don't leave the classroom without permission.
6. Don't make any unnecessary noise in class.
7. Don't fight.
8. Don't swear.
9. Sit up straight in your seat.
10. Keep hands, feet, and objects to yourself.
11. Come to class on time.
12. Don't steal.
13. Bring books and writing materials to class each day.
14. Don't walk around the class without permission.
15. Don't be tardy.

A longer list of rules can be made, but it is wise to limit it to perhaps only five or six rules. For example, the preceding list of rules could well be consolidated into the following:

1. Sit up straight in your seat and do your own work in a timely way as directed. (Compiled from behaviors 1, 2, 4, and 9.)
2. Don't disturb the class by talking, making unnecessary noises, stealing, fighting, swearing, hitting, shoving, or throwing objects. (Compiled from behaviors 6 to 8, 10, and 12.)
3. Come to class on time with the necessary books and writing materials and having completed all assignments. (Compiled from 11, 13, and 15.)
4. Don't talk, move around the class, or leave the class without permission. (Compiled from 3, 5, and 14.)

The rules created should satisfy the teacher's needs but not make unreasonable demands on students. For example, very young children should not be expected to sit for long periods of time without moving.

Putting the names of disruptive students on the board followed by check marks allows the teacher to continue with instruction while at the same time showing students the negative consequences of misbehavior.

Once teachers have determined the behaviors expected, they must communicate them effectively to students, either verbally or with written instructions. A poster is ordinarily prepared and placed in a prominent place in the classroom. When teachers explain rules to students, they should do so clearly and assertively. Instructions can be given in a straightforward manner:

▼ As your teacher, I insist that you follow certain rules so that I can do the best possible job. I expect the following behavior from each of you during the class period: One, do not talk in class without permission. Two, do not leave the room without permission. Three, turn in all assignments on time to receive credit. Four, do your own work. Five, stay in your seat and sit facing the front of the room. Six, follow all directions. Seven, keep your hands and feet to yourself. Eight, listen when the teacher is talking. I will let you know when you are and when you are not doing as I have directed. If you disobey the rules, I will first write your name on the board as a warning. If you continue, I will place a check mark by your name. This check mark means that you must stay after school for 10 minutes. If you get a second check mark, you must stay after school for 30 minutes. A third check mark means that you must stay after school for 30 minutes, and your parents will be called. If you get a fourth check mark, you will be sent to the principal for possible expulsion from school. Now I suggest that you follow these rules. They are for your good and the good of the class.

The procedure of putting names and check marks on the board is considered by some to be an essential part of assertive discipline. Canter says that they are not (Canter, 1989). Their use is a convenience for teachers that allows them to discipline their students with limited disruptions. They can write names and check marks on the board without missing a beat in the presentation of their lessons. Then, at the conclusion of instruction, they can affirm their intentions to follow through on merited negative consequences or punishments. A negative consequence or punishment is designed to be a deterrent to misbehavior, and its intensity should fit the frequency of and seriousness of the misbehavior. However, punishment should never be psychologically or physically harmful to students. Corporal punishment should never be administered (Canter, 1989). Canter believes that tracking misbehavior should be as private as possible. Writing names on the board may humiliate some students and promote more misbehavior in others. Teachers may wish to maintain a record book or a list on a clipboard so that tracking is private (Canter, 1996).

Canter recommends that different types of activity periods be identified for use during the day (Canter & Canter, 1976). An elementary classroom, for example, may have quiet study time, discussion time, transition periods, independent work time, free time, rest periods, physical education or recess, art, music, and library time. During each of these times, teachers may have different needs that students must meet. For example, during quiet study time, there may be rules that require students to work on assignments, stay in assigned seats, and refrain from talking. During free time, quiet talking may be appropriate as long as students work on their projects. It may be useful to make different signs to use during different periods. During quiet study time, a sign saying "QUIET WORK" could be posted. During discussions, a sign might be posted informing students to raise their hands for permission to talk. Initially, teachers must inform their students of the specific expectations for each type of activity.

STEP 3: TRACK MISBEHAVIOR

Once students have been informed of teachers' expectations, teachers must follow through to ensure that their demands are met. Student misbehavior must then be carefully tracked so that students are aware their misbehavior is being monitored and that negative consequences will be provided according to the discipline system that has been established. Negative consequences should be supplied strictly according to a predetermined plan. These punishments may vary depending on local conditions and policies, grade level, and perhaps even the nature of the class or the particular rule infraction. In school districts where many students ride buses, for instance, teachers may not be allowed to keep children after school. Sometimes an entire school has the same set of punishments prescribed. Sometimes each teacher establishes his or her own rules. Canter gives the following examples (Canter & Canter, 1981) that show various discipline plans:

When a student at the primary level breaks a rule:

1st Instance: Name on the board—You receive a warning.
2nd Instance: One check mark—You lose 10 minutes of free time.
3rd Instance: Two check marks—You lose 20 minutes of free time.
4th Instance: Three check marks—You lose 30 minutes of free time, and your parents are called.
5th Instance: Four check marks—You lose 45 minutes of free time, your parents are called, and you are referred to the principal.

When a student at the primary level breaks a rule:

1st Instance: Name on the board—You receive a warning.

2nd Instance: One check mark   You are let out for recess 5 minutes late.

3rd Instance: Two check marks—You lose one recess.

4th Instance: Three check marks—You lose two recesses, and your parents are called.

5th Instance: Four check marks—You lose recess for a week, your parents are called, and you are referred to the principal.

When a student at the upper elementary school level breaks a rule:

1st Instance: Name on the board—You receive a warning.

2nd Instance: One check mark—You copy out 25 times the rule that was broken.

3rd Instance: Two check marks—You copy out 50 times the rule that was broken.

4th Instance: Three check marks—You copy out 50 times the rule that was broken and take the paper home for your parents to sign.

5th Instance: Four check marks—You are referred to the principal, and your parents are called in for a conference.

When a student at the upper elementary school level breaks a rule:

1st Instance: Name on the board—You receive a warning.

2nd Instance: One check mark—You spend 10 minutes cleaning up the playground.

3rd Instance: Two check marks—You spend 20 minutes cleaning up the playground.

4th Instance: Three check marks—You spend 30 minutes cleaning up the playground, and your parents are called.

5th Instance: Four check marks—You spend 30 minutes cleaning up the playground, your parents are called, and you are sent to another classroom for 1 hour.

When a student in junior or senior high school breaks a rule:

1st Instance: Name on the board—You receive a warning.

2nd Instance: One check mark—You receive a citation and 45 minutes of detention.

3rd Instance: Two check marks—You receive a citation and detention, and your parents are called.

4th Instance: Three check marks—You receive a citation and detention, your parents are called, and you are referred to the principal.

5th Instance: Four check marks—You receive an in-school suspension.

When a student in junior or senior high school breaks a rule:

1st Instance: Name on the board—You receive a warning.

2nd Instance: One check mark—You perform 30 minutes of campus cleanup.

3rd Instance: Two check marks—You perform 1 hour of campus cleanup.

4th Instance: Three check marks—You perform 2 hours of campus cleanup, and your parents are called.

5th Instance: Four check marks—You perform 2 hours of campus cleanup, your parents are called, and you are sent to the counselor.

Sometimes teachers end up putting many names on the board and adding check marks. This result can be expected when students are reinforced by their peers for daring to challenge class rules. Obviously, these students are not influenced by the threat of punishment. In this case, Canter believes that tougher punishments must be applied. Teachers may have to tell their students that the first time they disobey a rule they will get their name on the board with two check marks. The severity of negative consequences may also have to be increased. For example, detention may be increased from 30 minutes to 2 hours. Teachers may have to call parents or refer students to the principal earlier if applying milder punishments first does not produce adequate results (Canter & Canter, 1981).

Teachers not only must competently employ discipline plans such as names and check marks; they must also effectively employ proper assertive language with their students. Four different methods are used to request compliance:

- Statements such as "Everyone should be working" are hints.
- "Would you please get to work?" has a question format.
- "I want you to open your books and get to work" is an I-message.
- "Get to work now!" is an example of a demand.

Whenever possible, it is best to use hints, questions, and I-messages to request desired behavior. These three methods will work with most children most of the time. When a stronger request is needed, use a demand. Demands imply that a punishment will follow noncompliance. Remember, you should make no demands on which you are unprepared to follow through. You may, for example, demand that students stop talking and get to work. You may repeat this demand several times and indicate that if they do not quit talking immediately and get to work, they will be in big trouble. This approach is unlikely to alter the situation. The students will probably ignore you and go on with what they are doing. It is better simply to demand that students comply and tell them exactly what will happen if they do not.

Teachers can do several things to increase their effectiveness in requesting compliance with rules. The first is to use a tone of voice that is firm but not abusive. The tone of voice should never be harsh, sarcastic, or intimidating. It should, however, carry the message that you mean what you say and that you will carry out proper punishments if necessary.

Eye contact is also important in delivering requests to students. One's true intentions are often revealed more through the eyes than in any other way. Children often depend on this form of communication because they distrust verbal language. Some students may have difficulty understanding some words used by adults. Teachers can also learn how their students respond by watching their eyes.

Messages can be enhanced by hand gestures. Gesturing with the hands emphasizes the spoken word. When properly employed, gestures act as an affirmation: "I mean what I say." Teachers must, however, refrain from using gestures that are threatening or intimidating to children. For example, you should avoid shaking your finger in children's faces as you speak to them.

Using children's names as you make your requests also increases the impact of your message. It helps as well to direct what you have to say to the individual for whom it is intended. If, for example, a group of children across the room is disturbing the class, rather than giving a general directive—"You kids over there, stop talking!"—you would be better off singling out the noisy students: "Ruth, Larry, Cheryl, stop talking so loudly."

Finally, physical touch can be used to emphasize your verbal requests. Touching can also establish physical limits for students. If you want a child to turn around in his seat, a gentle nudge may be helpful. Placing your hand on a child while you speak to her adds forcefulness to your message. It indicates that you really do mean what you are saying and intend to enforce it. Touching students in ways that might be misconstrued as improper or abusive should, of course, be avoided. Any school district rules or guidelines about touching should be adhered to.

As you apply the skills of assertiveness, it is helpful to employ the broken record technique: Repeat your demands several times when children either ignore you or object to your request. For example:

Teacher	Bret, I want you to go to work on your project now.
Bret	No one else has started. Why are you picking on me?
Teacher	That's not the point. I want you to begin working on your project now.
Bret	I will in just a minute.
Teacher	You are not to wait a minute. Start working on your project now.
Bret	OK, I will.

Remember as you employ this technique that you should maintain eye contact and use gestures and a suitable tone of voice. Using the child's name and touching will also emphasize your requests. In repeating your request, it is wise to limit yourself to three repetitions. You should then be prepared to tell the student what punishment will be applied if she or he does not comply. For example, Bret may be told that unless he starts his project immediately, he will have to sit in the time-out area for the rest of the period and stay in class after school until he completes it.

STEP 4: USE NEGATIVE CONSEQUENCES TO ENFORCE LIMITS

It is important to follow through on demands. When telling students what will happen if they do not comply with a demand, teachers should make promises, not issue threats. A promise is a vow to take appropriate actions when necessary. A threat is a statement of proposed punishment that does not have to be taken seriously, because it often is more extreme than anything children have learned to expect. For example, a new teacher who was a former Marine Corps drill sergeant met his students on the first day of class with a baseball bat in his hands. As he strutted up and down in front of the class explaining his expectations, he repeatedly smacked his palm with the bat, implying that if students did not comply, he would hit them with it. They, of course, knew better and then set out to sabotage the class. In 3 weeks he had decided to give up teaching.

Several methods of negative consequences or punishment are used in assertive discipline:

1. One commonly used punishment advocated by Canter is time-out. Time-out is also known as isolation. In a classroom, the isolation area is often a corner in the classroom that is screened from the view of class members. Children may be sent to the time-out area for varying lengths of time. Isolation within the classroom works best with elementary schoolchildren. If assertive discipline is used on a schoolwide basis, a time-out room may be available to which teachers may send their disruptive students.

2.   Withdrawing a privilege is another commonly used punishment. For example, free time or recess may be taken away. Other preferred class activities may be taken away, such as physical education, art, field trips, or music. Children may be denied participation in such activities as interscholastic sports, debate, drama, cheerleading, contests, intramural athletics, student government, the school yearbook, or the student newspaper. Canter indicates that the more meaningful activities are, the more useful they are in forcing students to comply. Therefore, teachers should be sure that activities denied are particularly desirable ones.

3.   Detention, or staying after school, is also a recommended negative consequence in assertive discipline. Detention may take place under the teacher's direction, or students may spend their detention time in the principal's office. Sometimes there is a special room in the school set aside for detention. A detention room is a particularly effective punishment for children who have not completed their assignments during class time. Their detention time can be used to finish their work.

4.   Being sent to the principal's office is often used as a negative consequence. Larger schools commonly have vice principals who take primary responsibility for solving discipline problems. Principals and their assistants often can employ more drastic punishments than teachers can. They usually can administer detention, in-school suspension, suspension from school, transfer to another school, expulsion, and referral to other professionals.

5.   With assertive discipline, parents may be called on to help when their children are disruptive. Teachers can call students' homes or send notes when children act inappropriately. Conferences with parents can be held. Canter also recommends that teachers arrange with parents to provide punishments at home for infractions of school rules. For example, parents may lecture their children, take away their television privileges, require them to stay in their room, or keep them from various social activities. Just the fact that parents are involved is often a sufficient deterrent to misbehaving children.

6.   One highly effective means of curtailing the misbehavior of students is to send them to another class. Students ordinarily do not like being sent away. Embarrassment is not the intention of this tactic. Instead, it is meant to help children understand that their inappropriate behavior will not be tolerated. Misbehaving students are sent to another class for the purpose of doing the assigned work. Prior arrangements obviously have to be made with the other teacher. Before carrying out this punishment, teachers show the offending student the seat that will be assigned in the new classroom. One drawback to this approach is that students may find this action reinforcing not punishing.

7.   Some teachers who use assertive discipline make a tape recording of their disruptive students. The tape can then be played for the principal or parents. When parents have a hard time believing that their child could do the things of which teachers accuse them, a tape recording provides an exact record of what happened. It is essential that tape recordings be made with the full knowledge of target children. They should not be spied on. Instead, recordings should be made to provide an accurate record other adults can use to help misbehaving students. A tape recording gives a

more realistic and accurate picture of events as they take place. Often, these events are hard to describe adequately or to explain in believable terms.

In short, if teachers really care about students, they must be prepared to use any necessary and appropriate means to help them eliminate their inappropriate behavior. Students will sense their determination and quickly conclude that they have no choice but to comply with teachers' expectations. Following through on promised negative consequences cannot be overemphasized in the proper application of assertive discipline principles.

In making rules and applying negative consequences, distinctions need to be made between disruptive and nondisruptive off-task behavior. If a student is not paying attention, but is not bothering anyone, there is no need to impose negative consequences. His or her behavior just needs to be redirected. It is essential that teachers emphasize positive strategies for keeping students on task. To do this, teachers need to spend more time spotlighting students who are behaving properly and spend less time punishing misbehavior. Negative consequences should be kept to a minimum. The key to providing effective punishment isn't the severity of negative consequences, it's the consistency with which they are applied. Students don't need to be traumatized by punishment, but they do need to recognize that disruptive behavior will always result in negative consequences, every time for every student (Canter, 1996).

STEP 5: IMPLEMENT A SYSTEM OF POSITIVE CONSEQUENCES

What do teachers ordinarily do when their students act appropriately? Unfortunately, many teachers do nothing. The good behavior of students is frequently ignored while attention is given primarily to unacceptable behavior. Some teachers claim to spend so much time dealing with bad behavior that they have little time to devote to reinforcing good behavior. It is essential, however, for teachers to respond not only to children's bad behavior but also to their good behavior. Responding to good behavior as well as bad clearly establishes the types of behavior teachers will or will not accept. Children need to be provided with positive consequences so that they are more likely to repeat their good behavior. If only punishment is given as a consequence of students' behavior, the classroom will take on an oppressive feeling and tension will be created between teachers and their students. Praise and other kinds of rewards, on the other hand, will increase the positive regard students have for their teachers.

Canter proposes a less systematic reinforcement program than is recommended in the behavior modification approach to discipline. He does not include such tactics as token economies, in which students are told in advance of the specific positive behaviors and their accompanying rewards. Instead, in his system "catching children being good" is emphasized. He encourages teachers to respond to the good behavior of students (1) in a way with which they are comfortable, (2) with rewards children want and enjoy, (3) immediately after children behave appropriately, (4) as often as possible, and (5) after some advance planning.

Some teachers reward the whole class for good behavior. A jar is placed on the teacher's desk in front of the class, and marbles are dropped into it as long as students are attentive and do their assigned work. If they become disruptive, marbles are taken out. When the jar is full, a promised class party is held.

Canter suggests that the following positive consequences be used to reward acceptable behavior by students:

1. *Personal attention by the teacher.*   Personal attention can involve not only praise but also spending time with students. Students may be invited to work with teachers on special projects or just stay after school to help. Perhaps, on occasion, small groups of students may accompany their teacher to get treats at a local fast-food restaurant.

2. *Positive notes or telephone calls to parents.*   It is a refreshing experience for most parents, who hear reports from school only when their children are misbehaving, to receive good news. Teachers need to create methods to recognize all their students in positive ways. One teacher, who volunteers to teach all the difficult students in his school, makes a practice of calling the parents of his most difficult students without warning and giving them a variation of the following message: "This is Mr. Wong, Roberta's science teacher. Roberta has really been doing well in my class. In fact, she did something really wonderful today." The teacher then hangs up the phone. The call, of course, leaves the parents completely surprised. They no doubt have never received such a call. When the children arrive home, they are unable to explain the teacher's call because there has been no prior indication, either of misbehavior or of noteworthy accomplishments. By the time these students arrive in class the next day, they are completely baffled and much more subdued.

3. *Awards.*   Special awards for good behavior and academic performance can also have a positive influence on students. Plaques, trophies, certificates, and other awards may be given for excellence in whatever attributes you wish to encourage. These awards can be of your own design or copied from fellow teachers. Awards have a high degree of motivation for some students.

4. *Special privileges.*   Children can be rewarded for good behavior with attractive activities such as assisting the teacher, running errands, calling the roll, being the lab assistant, playing games, having an extra physical education period, being first in line, spending time in the reading corner, using the tape recorder, using the microscope, helping to correct papers, doing a special project, tutoring younger children, playing with the building blocks, spending a class period talking with friends, or using the word processor.

5. *Material rewards.*   Many tangible objects and edibles can be used as rewards: gift certificates, toys, marbles, books, dolls, models, coloring books, pencils, crayons, comic books, stickers, badges, ribbons, raisins, cookies, nuts, ice cream, and hamburgers.

6. *Home rewards.*   Teachers may collaborate with parents to provide a reward system at home. Students who complete their work may be given extra time to watch television or play video games. Other home rewards may include parties, movies, eating out, favorite home meals, ice cream treats, and even such things as radios, tape players, or use of the family car.

7. *Group rewards.*   Canter also advocates rewards for the whole class. As mentioned, one mechanism for rewarding the class is to drop marbles into a jar when the entire class works hard and remains on-task during the period. The benefit of using marbles is that they are easily noticed. Students can hear the marbles drop into the jar while they work, which encourages them to continue. Once the jar is filled, the class may have a party or some other special activity.

Canter emphasizes that positive rewards should not be used to replace limits and punishment. A balance is needed, he claims. Rewards should be used when possible, but there are times when it is necessary to punish students for misbehavior.

STEP 6: ESTABLISH STRONG PARENT SUPPORT

The success of assertive discipline depends on creating and maintaining strong parent support. Parents have a strategic role to perform in helping teachers maintain good classroom discipline. To promote better parent involvement, teachers should contact them before the school year, expressing in a general way the nature of classroom expectations. This can be in the form of a simple postcard. Then after school starts, a more detailed written explanation of rules and consequences along with the positive reinforcement program should be sent to parents. This more detailed explanation should be followed up by periodic telephone calls enlisting the support of parents. In these telephone conversations, the student's prior school experiences could be discussed along with parent suggestions. The critical importance of parent support could also be emphasized. Parents should not only be appraised of the discipline program but also learn of various student learning expectations. Homework requirements can be explained as well as parent responsibilities regarding this and other matters. Teachers should also explain their role.

Various follow-up conversations should be held with parents during the year. Student achievements can then be recognized. Calls could also be made when students are sick or when birthdays or achievement in various extracurricular activities deserve recognition. When parents are experiencing difficulty with their children, teachers should give expressions of empathy and provide appropriate information regarding how the school can provide assistance (Canter, 1997a).

Parents should also be invited to attend parent–teacher conferences. These conferences are essential to the success of the discipline program and student learning. Unfortunately, many parents do not attend regularly scheduled conferences. Lack of participation is due, in part, to the limited benefit parents see in these activities. To make conferences more productive and attractive, teachers need to help parents understand that their child's success depends on their being actively involved in these conferences. They should be given a special invitation that outlines what will transpire in the meeting. They should be told why their involvement is essential and why their input is valued. In the invitation, a brief questionnaire might be included in an effort to focus the parents' thoughts and prepare them for thoughtful interaction at the conference. The questionnaire might include reference to their perceptions regarding how their child is doing, concerns they have, and problems their child might be experiencing not only academically but also in terms of student friendships, attitudes about school, and problems the child has expressed.

Successful parent–teacher conferences include parents in a collaborative effort to improve their child's education. This collaboration can be promoted by teachers' presenting parents examples of their child's work that show various unique qualities. This might be done by sending the student's portfolio home in advance of the conference. Parent contributions and insights would then have the benefit of preparation and thought. Parents might also be appraised of how past problems have been resolved and any additional problems that have come up. When all this is communicated to parents before the conference, parents can come to the meeting with possible suggestions regarding how they think the school can help out as well as what they believe they can do to make improvements. In the conference itself, it is wise to start with a discussion of the parents' observations and concerns. The student's academic goals could then be reviewed and suggestions made regarding possible strategies for improvement. Finally, arrangements can be made for follow-up sessions. This shows parents that the teacher is truly interested in helping their child be successful (Canter, 1997c).

One way to improve parent–teacher communications is to create engaging activities during back-to-school nights. The success of these affairs depends on giving parents compelling reasons to attend. Proposed activities might include a video showing students during exciting learning experiences. In the invitation, parents might be promised a folder containing helpful ideas regarding their role in their child's learning and school success. A description of the student work that will be displayed might also be included. It might be especially enticing to have students demonstrating examples of exciting learning activities. Science students, for example, might be viewed conducting their experiments. Social science students might use some of the time interviewing parents to augment the research they are doing. Art students might be involved painting or drawing (Canter, 1997b).

Some Problems With Punishment or Negative Consequences

Punishment has a long tradition and is unquestionably the most used kind of discipline. Even corporal punishment is commonly applied in the schools, though more and more states are outlawing its use. In 1986, four states expressly prohibited corporal punishment (Englander, 1986). By the summer of 1996, twenty-three states forbade its employment while most other states had specific restrictions regarding its use (Hyman, 1996). Despite increased restrictions, about three fourths of the parents, school board members, school administrators, teachers, and principals approve of corporal punishment. This is true even though at present there are no published reports of any experimental study to support its application in normal classrooms.

Although physical punishment has not been carefully studied in normal classrooms, researchers have consistently found that children subjected to physical punishment tend to be more aggressive than their peers and likely to grow up and use violence on their own children. These effects are not confined to victims of what may be legally classified as abuse. Even "acceptable" levels of physical punishment may perpetuate aggression and unhappiness (Eron, Huesmann, Dubow, Romanoff, & Yarmel, 1987; Holms & Robins, 1988).

Punishment of all kinds generally provokes resistance and resentment, which children may take out on other people such as peers. Commonly, punished children feel worse about themselves and resent those who punish them (Kohn, 1993, p. 167). Perhaps more importantly, punishment is ineffectual in the long run in eliminating the kind of behavior it was designed to eradicate. Punishment leads to three possible outcomes, calculation of risks, blind conformity, and revolt (Kamii, 1991). Calculation of risks involves children spending their time trying to figure out how they can get away with something or avoid something. Children who blindly conform fail to learn self-government. Their wills are broken by punishment. These children are prone to accept what they are told unquestioningly, including slogans and propaganda, and are inclined to draw illogical conclusions (Kamii, 1984). Children who revolt openly oppose the teacher's influence. Teachers must decide if they really want to punish their students and thus pursue these adversarial relationships with them. They also must determine whether or not to believe students are naturally nasty, selfish, antisocial, and desist from behavior only because they fear possible punishment.

The effects of punishment have generally been studied in laboratory settings. In these situations, it has been found that punishment can be an effective means of controlling behavior if and only if certain specific conditions prevail. However, many, if not all of these conditions are impossible to obtain in a normal classroom.

Timing is one of the conditions that has to be met for punishment to be effective. In a study by Aronfreed (1968) with fourth- and fifth-grade boys, punishment was found to be effective if it was administered at the onset of the misbehavior. It was also discovered that after punishment, unless students were monitored continuously, they soon engaged in misbehavior again. As little as 12 seconds' delay was all that was needed to render the punishment relatively ineffective. Walters, Parke, and Cane (1965) confirmed the conclusions of Aronfreed but also discovered that, even though children are trained through punishment not to violate a rule, they will violate these rules if they observe others do it. This suggests that, for punishment to be effective, it not only must be dispensed early in the sequence of misbehavior, it must also be administered consistently to every individual who violates the rule.

The intensity of punishment and complexity of the task being performed in the class are other conditions that influence the effectiveness of punishment. Intensity refers to how strong a stimulus is, how loud a teacher might yell at misbehaving students, for example. Complexity is best illustrated by the appropriateness of student talk in the classroom. On some occasions students' talk is unacceptable, like when the teacher is addressing the entire class. At other times talking may not only be acceptable but encouraged. A recitation exercise is an example of this. In addition, talking is sometimes tolerated but not fostered, like when students are working in small groups. Knowing when to talk is a complex thing for students. They are rarely sure how to respond, because teachers have different expectations for different situations, which they commonly administer with a good deal of inconsistency. The research shows that when the discriminating task is simple, severe punishment has the greater effect.

However, when the discrimination between right and wrong behavior is more difficult, milder punishments are more potent (Aronfreed, 1968; Azrin & Holz, 1966).

Another factor that influences the effect of punishment is escalation. It has been found that if the intensity of punishment is increased gradually over successive administrations, it is unlikely to suppress the misbehavior. Maximum effect of punishment only occurs if it is sudden and substantial. Unfortunately, escalation is ordinarily practiced by most classroom teachers. They start out by administering a mild punishment and gradually increase intensity successively as students resist their influence. Ironically, the Supreme Court in its 1975 decision on punishment supported escalation by mandating that punishment must first be less abrasive and that it can then escalate into paddling (Azrin & Holz, 1966).

The frequency of punishment also determines its effectiveness. Every instance of misbehavior must be punished for it to be most effective. If punishment occurs periodically, the misbehavior will continue unabated until the individual anticipates that it is time for punishment to recur. To be really effective, teachers would have to station themselves next to any misbehaving student, poised to punish every time misbehavior occurred, right at the point the misbehavior is initiated.

Suppressing misbehavior with punishment is a very complicated affair, involving a number of factors. No single factor ensures that punishment will have the desired effect on misbehavior. Each condition requires that punishment be administered in a very prescriptive and precise way. In addition, the effects of the various conditions are additive. Therefore, to really work, punishment needs to be administered expertly, incorporating a number of conditions simultaneously. Even under these ideal conditions, which were research laboratory settings, one can expect only about half of the students to comply with what punishment is designed to dictate (Englander, 1986). It is unlikely that profitable learning would occur in classrooms where only half the students conformed to expectations enforced by punishment. Given the complexity of the normal classroom situation, there appears to be little hope of punishing effectively.

In appraising the effects of punishment, reducing the incidence of misbehavior is only part of the issue. Certain side effects must also be considered. Reference has already been made to many of these. To summarize, punishment can promote aggressiveness, revenge, withdrawal, poor teacher–student relationships, and it can inhibit learning. The inhibition on learning, in addition to disruptiveness and restlessness, can take place even when the individual only observes someone else being punished (Kounin & Gump, 1961).

One commonly used kind of punishment advocated by Canter is suspension or expulsion. These are punishments of the last resort and either are administered by school administrators or, in the case of expulsion, may require school board approval. Such little success has been achieved with these measures that adjustments have commonly been made, such as in-school suspension. Students who are suspended or expelled from school ordinarily get further behind in their schoolwork and make no improvement in behavior when they are allowed to return to class. With in-school suspension, students are required to complete their classroom assignments. This kind of suspension keeps students up to date on their schoolwork and may help by getting unruly students out of the classroom, but there is no evidence that it eliminates misbehavior. Some students are routinely sent to in-school suspension. Some of these students obviously find in-school suspension reinforcing.

Warning students of potential punishment by writing their names on the board may also be a way of reinforcing student misconduct. Some students take this as a challenge. Teachers who use the Canter model observe that some students routinely get their names on the board. Others not only do this but misbehave to the degree that they get a check or two by their names almost every day. Each of these students is apparently willing to accept a given level of punishment. They likely find the punishment program to be reinforcing up to a point and punishing beyond that. The result is for some teachers to issue warnings instead of punishing students. This is particularly true if the next level of punishment involves the principal or parents. In a sense, having difficulties that require the attention of the principal or parents is an admission of failure to some teachers. When students, as a consequence of misbehavior, are warned of possible punishment for future misconduct, they are reinforced for their unruliness. Because warnings are an inherent part of Canter's model, reinforcing misbehavior is always a potential problem.

In summarizing the research on punishment, Burden (1995) outlines the following problems:

1. Punishment is ineffective in changing student behavior and actually causes an increase in misbehavior when its use is expanded.
2. Punishment does not teach the appropriate behavior that can replace misbehavior.
3. Punishment commonly causes students to avoid contact with whomever has punished them and to engage in such avoidance behaviors as lying, cheating, skipping class, becoming sick, hiding, withdrawing, and doodling.
4. Punishment can inhibit socially desirable behaviors such as spontaneity, cooperativeness, assertiveness.
5. Punishment promotes aggressiveness in students. This aggressiveness is often directed toward others less powerful than themselves.
6. Students who are punished value learning less and are less successful in school.
7. When additional academic work or lowering grades are given as punishments, students form negative attitudes toward school.
8. Effects of punishment are usually specific to particular context and behavior. For example, punishing a student for being out of his or her seat on one day may not be a deterrent to this behavior on another day.

Preventing Discipline Problems

Assertive discipline is designed primarily as a reactive method of discipline with a less well-defined preventive component. It is a preventive method only insofar as students try to achieve rewards or avoid punishments. Teachers using this approach generally observe whether students' behavior is good or bad and then supply rewards or punishments as appropriate. There is no assumption that misbehavior will be prevented if children become more responsible and self-governed. Proper discipline is achieved when teachers are assertive and control students in their classrooms. Force must be employed to get children to behave properly.

The establishment of firm rules gives assertive discipline a somewhat preventive orientation. When children know the rules and the associated punishments, these punishments act as deterrents. If the punishments are visible enough and applied consistently, many students will try to avoid them. However, some children will go to great lengths to avoid control. They may, for example, do things for which they know they will be punished. Some even feel rewarded when they are punished because of the attention punishment brings. Canter believes that if a child finds a particular punishment rewarding, more severe punishments should be applied. However, with the increase in severity of punishment, negative feelings will also increase, and it may be hard for children in these circumstances to feel comfortable in class again. They may not misbehave, but they may decide to drop out mentally.

Schoolwide Discipline

Assertive discipline can be organized on a schoolwide basis. The first step is to create rules. These rules usually define unacceptable behavior on the school grounds, in the hallways, in the lunchroom, and even off the school grounds when children are traveling to and from school. Students may be permitted to play or congregate only in designated areas. Playground rules usually involve safety and courtesy. In the hallways, students ordinarily have to refrain from running, shoving, and throwing objects. Lunchroom rules usually govern queuing up, disposing of unused food, returning trays and utensils, and cleaning up, and they remind children to follow directions and not to throw food.

Negative consequences for violating schoolwide rules are similar to that implemented in individual classrooms. Children are given a slip for each rule violation. On the playground, for example, the following punishments might be applied: The first slip means the loss of playground privileges for 3 days. A student who receives a second pink slip loses playground privileges for a week and must help clean up the playground as well; the student's parents may also have to sign the slip. After a third slip is given, the student's parents are called in for a conference with the student and the principal. A fourth slip earns the student automatic expulsion.

Rule infractions in the lunchroom might be punished first with a warning. After being caught throwing food once, students might be given a slip that would have to be signed by parents and returned. The punishment for a second offense might be the loss of lunchroom privileges for a week, and a signature from the parents would again be required. A third slip might bring the loss of lunchroom privileges for 2 weeks and a conference between the student, parents, and the principal. If a student received a fourth slip, suspension from the lunchroom might be permanent.

The breaking of attendance rules, such as unexcused absences and tardy arrivals, can be handled in a similar manner. Students would ordinarily be detained after school for tardiness. Unexcused absences would receive more severe punishments.

Punishments would become increasingly severe if students continued to violate attendance rules, and parents and school officials might be involved in cases of habitual infraction.

More serious rule violations may incur harsher punishment. Canter and Canter (1981) suggest three criteria for determining the seriousness of an offense:

1. A student willfully inflicts physical harm on another student.
2. A student willfully destroys property.
3. A student blatantly refuses to follow instructions.

Strengths and Weaknesses of Assertive Discipline

STRENGTHS

1. It is simple to use.
2. The personal desires of the teacher can be enforced.
3. It involves parents and administrators in the discipline process.

WEAKNESSES

1. The practice of warning students by putting their names on the board may entice some students to misbehave who otherwise would not.
2. Students angered by warnings and sanctions may go further in their rebellion than they ordinarily would.
3. Students may be embarrassed by having their names on the board.
4. This approach fails to promote self-direction in students.
5. It fails to deal with the underlying causes of discipline problems, such as emotional illness, divorce, poverty, racism, and so forth.
6. It advocates suspensions for extreme misbehavior when far too many children are out on suspension already.
7. Although Canter recommends using positive reinforcement while emphasizing negative consequences, in actual practice, positive reinforcement may be excluded.
8. Canter recommends strictly enforced rules in the cafeteria. Children frequently go to fast-food restaurants for lunch without supervision and cause no problems. Perhaps schools could learn something from this fact.
9. Negative consequences or punishment stimulates rebellion and promotes the very behavior it is designed to eliminate.

▼ SUMMARY

Assertive discipline is a system in which negative consequences are consistently meted out for rule infractions. Rules are determined by the teacher or other school personnel and given to students to be obeyed. The severity of punishments is increased when students persist in misbehaving. When students continue to misbehave, teachers can enlist the help of parents and the principal. Conferences with the principal or parents are held in an effort to force unruly students to change their behavior. In addition to rules and punishments, teachers should use a program of rewards to encourage students to behave properly in school. The best discipline program is one in which both rewards and punishments are given in proper balance.

Some research on punishment shows that it promotes resistance and rebellion on the part of students. In addition, instead of eliminating undesirable behavior, it is likely to promote the very behavior it is designed to curtail. Punishment must be applied in very specific ways for it to be effective. Most teachers find meeting these application conditions nearly impossible to achieve.

CENTRAL IDEAS

1. Canter believes that teachers have the right to
   a. Establish classroom rules
   b. Insist that students follow rules
   c. Receive help from parents and school administrators in disciplining their students
2. Being assertive is the key to discipline. Teachers must create and enforce rules assertively to be successful in the classroom.
3. Assertive discipline involves
   a. Establishing rules
   b. Punishing students who violate rules
   c. Rewarding students for good behavior
4. What Canter calls *consequences* is the same as punishment in the view of other discipline theorists.
5. Punishment stimulates rebellion and usually promotes the very misbehavior it is designed to eliminate.

▼QUESTIONS AND ACTIVITIES

QUESTIONS TO CONSIDER

1. How is Canter's approach to discipline similar to and different from behavior modification? What do you believe the differences in the outcomes would be for each of these approaches?
2. What obstacles would you be likely to experience in implementing assertive discipline in the schools?
3. What do you believe are the strengths and weaknesses of assertive discipline?

CLASSROOM ACTIVITIES

1. Use role playing to simulate the following classroom situations: The teacher applies the principles of assertive discipline in handling a student who
   a. Refuses to be quiet in class and work on the assigned task
   b. Is habitually tardy
   c. Fights with other students
   d. Throws spit wads at other students
2. Break the class into two groups, and debate the relative merits of assertive discipline and behavior modification.

STUDENT APPLICATIONS

1. Think about the problems you may encounter in the school. Create a list of rules that you believe will be necessary to eliminate these problems. Prepare a list of punishments you would apply to deal with various infractions. Your list should allow for variations in punishment for increasingly serious violations.
2. Prepare a system of rewards you could use in your classroom. Include various categories such as edibles and special privileges.
3. Create a schoolwide discipline program for the type of school in which you plan to teach.

EXPLORE YOUR PHILOSOPHY

1. Defend or refute the assumption that children must be controlled and forced to comply with classroom rules and teacher expectations.
2. Defend or refute the assumption that punishment will promote positive classroom discipline and learning.
3. Defend or refute the practice of using parents and school administrators to regulate student's behavior in the classroom.
4. Defend or refute the practice of providing children warnings in advance of punishing them for misbehavior in the classroom.
5. Defend or refute the assertive style of teaching and classroom management.
6. Compare the principles contained in your educational philosophy with those of assertive discipline. Determine consistencies and inconsistencies. Make adjustments to your philosophy as you believe appropriate.

▼ REFERENCES

Aronfreed, J. M. (1968). In Arnold, W. J. (Ed.), *Nebraska symposium on motivation* (pp 271 320). Lincoln, NE: University of Nebraska.

Azrin, N., & Holz, W. (1966). In W. K. Honig (Ed.), *Operant behavior areas of research and application.* New York: Appleton-Century-Crofts.

Burden, P. R. (1995). *Classroom management and discipline.* White Plains, NY: Longman.

Canter, L. (1989). Assertive discipline: More than names on the board and marbles in a jar. *Phi Delta Kappan, 71,* 57–61.

Canter, L. (1996). First the rapport—then the rules. *Learning, 24*(5), 12–14.

Canter, L. (1997a). Act now! Limited time offer. *Learning, 26*(1), 14–15.

Canter, L. (1997b). Standing room only. *Learning, 26*(2), 39–41.

Canter, L. (1997c). Take pleasure in conferences. *Learning, 25*(5), 31–32.

Canter, L., & Canter, M. (1976). *Assertive discipline: A take-charge approach for today's educator.* Seal Beach, CA: Canter & Associates.

Canter, L., & Canter, M. (1981). *Assertive discipline follow-up guidebook.* Los Angeles: Canter & Associates.

Englander, M. E. (1986). *Strategies for classroom discipline.* New York: Praeger.

Eron, L. D., Huesmann, L. R., Dubow, E., Romanoff, R., & Yarmel, P. W. (1987). Aggression and its correlates over 22 years. In Crowell, D. H., Evans, I. M., & O'Donnell, C. R. (Eds.), *Childhood aggression and violence.* New York: Plenum.

Holms, S. J., & Robins, L. N. (1988). The role of parental disciplinary practices in the development of depression and alcoholism. *Psychiatry, 51,* 24–35.

Hyman, I. A. (1996, March). *The enemy within: Tales of punishment, politics, and prevention.* Paper presented at the annual meeting of the School Psychologists, Atlanta, Georgia.

Kamii, C. (1984). Obedience is not enough. *Young Children, 39*(4), 11–14.

Kamii, C. (1991). Toward autonomy: The importance of critical thinking and choice making. *School Psychology Review, 20,* 382–388.

Kohn, A. (1993). *Punished by rewards.* Boston: Houghton Mifflin.

Kounin, J. S., & Gump, P. V. (1961). The comparative influence of punitive and non-punitive teachers upon children's concepts of school misconduct. *Journal of Educational Psychology, 52,* 44–49.

Walters, R., Parke, R., & Cane, V. (1965). Timing of punishment and the observation of consequences to others as determinants of response inhibition. *Journal of Experimental Child Psychology, 2,* 10–30.

5

Logical Consequences: Rudolf Dreikurs

OBJECTIVES

This chapter is designed to help you

1. Distinguish between different motives.
2. Use Dreikurs's discipline model to
   a. Ascertain students' motives.
   b. Help students understand their motives.
   c. Help students exchange their mistaken goals for useful ones.
   d. Help students learn the consequences of their actions.
3. Understand how to deal with misbehavior designed to satisfy students' mistaken goals.
4. Apply Dreikurs's plan for preventing discipline problems.

ASSUMPTIONS

1. Inappropriate behavior is motivated by a need to gain attention, exercise power, exact revenge, or display inadequacy.
2. If the motive for attention is satisfied, inappropriate behavior associated with other motives will not be manifested.
3. Inappropriate behavior can be terminated by helping students find legitimate ways to satisfy their needs.
4. Children can learn to understand their own motives and consequently eliminate misbehavior by having teachers help them explore why they behave as they do.
5. Students behave more appropriately in the classroom when they suffer the logical consequences of their behavior.
6. Presenting students with a choice between two alternative behaviors offers a sufficient basis on which they can learn to be responsible.

Introduction

Rudolf Dreikurs was a native of Vienna, Austria. After he received his degree in medicine from the University of Vienna, he became an associate of Alfred Adler, the famous psychiatrist. Dreikurs emigrated to the United States in 1937 and became the director of the Alfred Adler Institute in Chicago. Although his primary interest was child and family counseling, he became interested in classroom discipline and with various colleagues wrote several books on the subject. He died in 1972 at the age of 75.

▼ Max is a second grader who for a couple of weeks was constantly out of his seat, leaning on his desk, and doing his work from a half-standing position. His teacher finally asked him whether he preferred to stand or sit while doing his work. Max said that he would prefer to stand. The teacher explained to him that he would no longer need a seat and that his chair could be used somewhere else in the school. Max's chair was immediately removed, and he had to stand up for the rest of the day. The following day, at the beginning of the period, Max was asked whether he preferred to stand or sit for the day. He said that he preferred to sit. His chair was replaced. Max no longer tried to do his schoolwork from a half-standing position.

▼ One day a group of junior high school students seemed particularly restless. Several students were talking rather belligerently and interrupted the teacher's lesson repeatedly. Finally, the exasperated teacher informed the students that she would be in

Max's frequent out-of-seat behavior was dealt with by removing his chair.

her office at the back of the classroom reading and that when they were ready to have her teach, they could come get her. The teacher was fearful as she started reading her book, but in a few minutes two serious-faced youngsters came in and said, "We're ready now—if you will come and teach us." After this incident, whenever the class became unruly and the teacher appeared annoyed, someone would say, "Be careful, or we'll lose our teacher again."

These two examples illustrate the application of the logical consequences model and how children may be expected to respond. A key tenet of logical consequences is that children should be given a choice rather than forced to behave as directed. Dreikurs believed that although some degree of force could be applied a generation or two ago, present social conditions necessitate the use of more democratic procedures. In the past, large groups of people—poor people, women, people of color, laborers—could not openly rebel against authoritarian domination. The same, of course, was true of children. Although they may occasionally have defied their parents or teachers, they could be satisfactorily controlled if sufficient force was applied. Most rebellion could be adequately suppressed. In this day and age, however, people are far less likely to submit to the control of others. They consider themselves to be of value and worthy of respect and thus refuse to permit others to deprive them of liberty and dignity.

In addition to changes in the social scene, more enlightened views of personality development have emerged, giving rise to new ways of interpreting human experience and dealing with human beings more productively. Believing that behavior is driven by an individual's purposes is one critical aspect of these new assumptions about human personality and behavior (Dreikurs, 1960). Even behavior that appears destructive is purposeful. Each behavior has the goal of self-determination. We do not simply react to forces that confront us from the outside world. Our behavior is the result of our own biased interpretations of the world. We act not according to the reality that surrounds us but rather according to our own subjective appraisal of it. For example, when a teacher selects one child to be a classroom leader, other children may interpret this selection as a personal rejection.

Unfortunately, when situations are open to personal interpretation, all of us routinely make unavoidable mistakes in perception. When we choose how to behave, we almost never have all the facts we need to make adequate choices. Our choices, therefore, are very subjective; they lack the validity more unbiased information would provide. Few humans make a habit of investigating the conditions present in particular situations and analyzing the assumptions they make about them. Nevertheless, we tend to act on these assumptions and conditions as if they were true. Of course, as we mature, we are more able to evaluate possible consequences in advance and choose our course of action in a more knowledgeable way.

Human beings all have a need to belong and be accepted. The combination of our human need for acceptance and our biased human perceptions sometimes helps to create distortions in our relationships with others. Children, for example, may not realize that acceptance by others depends on an individual's contributing to the welfare of the group; instead, they may strike out against the very people who could best satisfy their needs. When children's misguided perceptions lead them to abuse others, they commonly feel the acute rejection such actions engender. When they sense rejection, they begin to withdraw and experience even greater deprivation.

Dreikurs believes that the disposition to view the world as unaccepting is in part related to the order of one's birth (Dreikurs & Grey, 1968). The only child is the sole object of parental attention. With the arrival of another sibling, however, the older child is always dethroned. Older children then attempt to regain lost status. They may or may not feel successful in this attempt. Older children are prone to maladjustment.

Second children are always in a position of having older, more capable rivals to overtake. If they are successful, or if they find a different but constructive direction, they usually make satisfactory adjustments. If these children gain the recognition they want, they may develop more daring and flexible personalities. However, if they fail to achieve the status they desire, they may turn to destructiveness as a way to gain recognition. Often second children are very competitive.

When a third sibling arrives, second children may feel squeezed out. They often find that their older siblings have assumed a position of greater responsibility and their younger ones play the role of the baby. Second children may not have the rights of older children or the privileges of younger ones. They may then interpret life as unfair and feel that there is no place for them.

Youngest children, although they are often babied and spoiled, appear to have a somewhat easier time than the others. For one thing, they are never displaced. They remain the baby for the rest of their lives—even if they outdo their siblings—and consequently get a disproportionate amount of attention from parents. It is common for youngest children to get attention not only from parents but from older siblings as well. Older brothers and sisters serve as substitute parents and often must perform parenting duties assigned to them.

In large families, the effects of birth order also extend to groups of siblings. There may be a group of oldest children, a group of middle children, and a group of youngest children. Within these groups, there may be an oldest child, a middle child, and a youngest child. Knowing a student's place in the birth order helps teachers better understand the basis for development of the student's personality and lifestyle.

Motives for Behavior

Attaining recognition as a worthy, able individual is central to personality development. Dreikurs accepts the basic idea of Alfred Adler that all behavior—including misbehavior—is orderly and purposeful and directed toward achieving social recognition (Dreikurs, 1968). Unfortunately, our culture does not furnish sufficient means for children to achieve this recognition. In many children, the desire for attention goes unfulfilled. When children solicit recognition without success, they usually misbehave to gain it. All misbehavior is the result of a child's mistaken assumption about how to find a place and gain status. Parents and teachers need to be aware of what children do to be recognized and appreciated so that they can more fully accommodate them. They must also learn to avoid falling for the unconscious schemes children use to achieve their mistaken goals. Dreikurs has identified four such goals and the schemes used to achieve them:

1. Gaining attention
2. Exercising power
3. Exacting revenge
4. Displaying inadequacy

These motives have a hierarchical relationship to one another. Children first try to achieve recognition and status through strategies designed to gain them attention. If these strategies do not work, the children employ power. Power may be followed by revenge. Finally, children use inadequacy as an excuse when earlier strategies have proven unsuccessful.

GAINING ATTENTION

Attention is by far the most common goal for most young children. Children who seek excessive attention are often a nuisance in class. They distract their teachers by showing off, being disruptive, being lazy, asking special favors, needing extra help on assignments, asking irrelevant questions, throwing things around the room, crying, refusing to work unless the teacher is right there, or being overly eager to please. They seem to function appropriately only as long as they have their teachers' approval. Teachers often respond to these children by giving them too much attention—reminding them often, coaxing them, showing pity for them, or feeling annoyed at them.

Giving attention to attention-seeking children does not necessarily improve their behavior. When attention is given in response to children's misbehavior, the misbehavior increases. Although the search for attention is usually manifested in the form of misbehavior, even the cooperative behavior of very young children may stem from a desire for special attention. Often, these children try to do better than others, and they are very sensitive to criticism and failure. As with other misguided children, these youngsters must be helped to realize that they do not need constant testimonials to affirm their worth. They also need to learn that greater satisfaction comes from cooperating in groups than from provoking group members to get attention.

Four different attention-seeking behavior patterns have been identified: active-constructive, passive-constructive, active-destructive, and passive-destructive (Dreikurs, Grunwald, & Pepper, 1982) (see Table 5.1).

Active-Constructive Behavior.   Active-constructive children are very cooperative with adults and conform readily to their expectations. These children are highly success-oriented but usually have poor relationships with children their own age. They are very industrious and have an exaggerated conscientiousness. They tend to be perfectionists and are often spurred on by parents who are themselves overambitious and perfectionistic. Active-constructive children are very competitive and try at all costs to maintain their superiority over others; in doing so, they accept the role of the model child or the teacher's pet. Their goal is to receive praise and recognition, and they sometimes tattle on others who fall short of their high standards. The following example illustrates active-constructive behavior in an elementary school child:

TABLE 5.1
Attention-seeking behavior patterns.

	Constructive	Destructive
Active	*Behavior:* • Tattle on others • Overly cooperative • Conform readily • Highly success oriented • Perfectionist *Goal:* • To receive constant praise and maintain superiority	*Behavior:* • Want their own way • Impertinent • Defiant • Clown around or bully others • Perpetually pester others *Goal:* • Immediate and continuous attention
Passive	*Behavior:* • Charm others • Manipulative • Manipulate by helplessness • Vain, cute, flattering • Cling to others • Self-centered *Goal:* • To get others to serve them	*Behavior:* • Bashful, dependent, untidy • Self-indulgent, lazy • Lack of concentration • Claim tasks are too hard • Lack of positive action *Goal:* • Force others' concern • Get help from others

▼ Jane looked up from her drawing assignment just long enough to observe her classmates. It required only a glance to see that they were far behind and that their drawings were of much poorer quality than her own. Smugly, she busied herself again, humming as she worked. In a few minutes she raised her hand. "Look, Mr. Lowe," she said to her teacher, "I'm all done. Is there something else I can do?"

Mr. Lowe replied, "Jane, you always finish your work so quickly. You have done an excellent job, as usual. Class, look at Jane's picture. Don't you like the way she has blended her colors?"

Passive-Constructive Behavior.   Passive-constructive children try to achieve their goals by charming others. In this way they manipulate adults into serving them, often by putting on a façade of helplessness. These children are never involved in destructive, disruptive behavior. To be so occupied would only diminish their power. They give an appearance of being interested in others, but in reality they are very self-centered. They are the vain, cute, flattering children who are always clinging to those on whom they depend. The story of 10-year-old Robby illustrates this behavior:

▼ Robby entered the classroom wearing brand-new slacks and a sports jacket. He walked around the classroom so everyone could see his clothes. "My, Robby," Mr. Wallace remarked delightedly, "what a sharp-looking outfit!" Robby beamed and took his seat, looking pleased. "Look at Robby's new clothes," continued Mr. Wallace.

"Don't they go well together? Robby is always dressed so neatly. We could all use him as an example."

Active-Destructive Behavior.   Children who are impertinent, defiant, clownish, or bullying are classified as active-destructive. These children may be confused with those who seek primarily power or revenge. Power-oriented children want more than momentary attention; they want their own way all the time and keep pestering others until they get it. Active-destructive children, however, will stop provoking others when they receive the attention they desire. For example:

▼ "I won't do this dumb assignment," yelled Rose as she threw down her pencil in anger. Ms. Phippen looked at her momentarily and immediately turned her attention to the papers on her desk. "Ms. Phippen, you can take this assignment and choke on it for all I care." Ms. Phippen looked up again, smiled, and then returned to her work. Rose sat grumbling to herself for a while and started on the assignment.

Passive-Destructive Behavior.   Passive-destructive children are characterized as "lazy." Through their lack of positive action, these children force others to be overly concerned with them and to help them. They claim that what they are asked to do is too hard. Often, they claim not to understand what is expected. Their behavior patterns include bashfulness, dependency, untidiness, lack of concentration, and self-indulgence. The story of Dwayne provides an illustration:

▼ Dwayne sat looking out the window as his classmates busied themselves with their math assignment. Ms. Clegg watched him for a moment and then suggested that he start his work.
"I can't do these problems," whined Dwayne.
"You're going to have to start them sometime," replied Ms. Clegg.
"I just need a little help to get me started," implored Dwayne.
Ms. Clegg went to Dwayne's desk and began helping him with his problems. With each problem, Dwayne claimed to have difficulty understanding. By the end of the period, Ms. Clegg had helped Dwayne finish all his work.

EXERCISING POWER

When children fail to gain all the attention they seek, they often engage in a power struggle with parents and teachers. Teachers should avoid putting pressure on these children in an attempt to make them behave properly because such pressure usually leads to a power contest. As teachers apply pressure, they are likely only to increase the frustration of these children, which in turn provokes even more irrational, power-seeking behavior in the children. Teachers almost never win in these power contests. Children win because society expects adults to behave in a responsible, moral way. The same behavior is not expected of children. They can argue, cry, contradict, throw temper tantrums, lie, and be stubborn and disobedient. Adults are expected to be composed, trusting, loving, honest, and helpful. These expectations for adults are often exploited by power-seeking children for their own purposes, as the following example illustrates:

▼ Ching sat in the back of the room talking with friends as his fifth-grade teacher, Ms. Finch, tried to explain the meaning of the Bill of Rights to the rest of the class. She stopped a number of times in her lesson to remind Ching to be quiet, but after a minute or two he continued talking. Eventually, Ms. Finch became angry and demanded that Ching leave the room and stand out in the hall. He told her that he would not go. Ms. Finch then went to Ching's seat and demanded that he leave immediately. He looked back at her defiantly. She tried to pull him from his seat forcibly. He would not budge. Ms. Finch started screaming at Ching uncontrollably. Soon her voice cracked and her vision blurred with frustration. As she retreated from the room, visibly shaken, Ching sat with a look of contentment on his face.

Ms. Finch was handicapped by assuming that she had the responsibility to subdue defiant children. She felt an obligation to show misbehaving children who was boss and to make them follow orders. In addition, she became personally involved in the power struggle, and her fear of losing face and prestige as the teacher proved to be a stumbling block. She will continue to fail to resolve power conflicts as long as she fears humiliation. She must learn not to fight and not to give in. Instead, she must focus on the problem. She needs to realize that power-hungry children will always try to defeat those who try to control and suppress them. Unfortunately, their success in defeating adults who try to control them adds to their power. With the support of the whole class, they are able to wield considerable influence over teachers. This power can be reduced through discussions in which all class members are given an opportunity to comment about power-seeking behavior.

EXACTING REVENGE

When children's efforts at control are thwarted, they usually claim to have been dealt with unfairly. They believe that others have deliberately tried to hurt them, and they attempt to get even. Commonly, they take out their revenge on anyone around them. They are convinced that nobody likes them and create proof of this dislike by provoking others to retaliate. These children lash out by tripping, hitting, kicking, or scratching others or by destroying their property. They may knock books and supplies on the floor or scribble on classmates' papers. They may also seek revenge against the teacher by marking the teacher's desk, ripping pages from books, insulting the teacher publicly, or deliberately breaking equipment. Revenge-seeking children are very difficult to help. Teachers must realize that they hurt others because they feel hurt. Causing them more pain will only provoke more revenge-seeking behavior. Instead, teachers must offer understanding and assistance. They need to ensure that other children do not retaliate when revengeful children behave improperly. In the following example, Mr. Bright plays into the hands of a revenge-seeking student:

▼ Carter was the only student absent in Mr. Bright's seventh-grade music class that day. When Mr. Bright sat in the puddle of glue on his chair, he knew immediately who had put it there. He even caught a glimpse of Carter peering through an outside window in an effort to see what the teacher's reaction would be. Screaming at the top of his voice, Mr. Bright dashed to the window and threatened Carter with expulsion. He then stormed out of the room to report the incident to the principal.

DISPLAYING INADEQUACY

Children who fail to achieve a sense of self-worth through attention, power, or revenge often become so discouraged that they give up and seek to wrap themselves in a cloak of inadequacy. They are joined in this misguided quest by other children who at an early age conclude that they are not as capable as others and also give up. These children strive to be left alone and avoid the humiliation group participation inevitably brings. They attempt to retain what little self-esteem they have left by avoiding any kind of public display. They believe that others will leave them alone if they are believed to be inadequate. The purpose of this behavior in a student, like that of other behaviors, is to somehow affirm the student's significance. A display of inadequacy is a last-ditch effort to reach this ultimate goal of being accepted for what one is, even if one is inadequate.

▼ When the PE teacher is organizing softball teams, Wendy positions herself behind other students and moves toward the back of the group, hoping not to be seen and selected to play on one of the teams. When she is finally selected in last position, she says she is not feeling well enough to play today.

Teaching Styles

The reaction of teachers to students' misguided goal-seeking behavior can be instrumental in either reducing or increasing the incidence of misbehavior in the classroom. Avoiding these discipline problems depends to some degree on teachers' personalities. Different teachers tend to react to their students in different ways, and their reactions produce different results. Dreikurs identifies three types of teachers: autocratic, permissive, and democratic (Charles, 1992).

AUTOCRATIC

Autocratic teachers force their will on their students. They take firm control and refuse to tolerate any deviation from the rules. They force rather than motivate students to work, and they punish those who refuse to conform. Autocratic teachers use no humor or warmth in their classes. Instead, they enforce their power and authority over their students. Students are not very receptive to the tactics of autocratic teachers. They usually react with hostility to the demands, commands, and reprimands of these teachers.

PERMISSIVE

Permissive teachers are also ineffective when working with students. They fail to realize how critical rules are in the classroom. In addition, they do not follow through on consequences. The need for students to develop self-discipline is unimportant to them. Instead, they allow their students to behave as they wish. The usual result is general chaos and a poor learning atmosphere. These teachers encourage the misguided goal-seeking of their students rather than help them to adopt a more responsible lifestyle.

DEMOCRATIC

In a democratic classroom, teachers provide firm guidance but do not promote rebellion. Students are allowed to participate in making decisions about what is studied as well as in formulating rules. Democratic teachers help students understand that making decisions is firmly tied to responsibility. Students are allowed freedom, but they are expected to assume responsibility for what they do. These teachers do not feel compelled to habitually correct the behavior of their students. Allowing students some leeway, they believe, is the best way to help them eventually learn to be self-governing. Democratic teachers have a way of establishing order and limits without usurping their students' right to autonomy. They are firm and yet kind, and they involve students in cooperative learning experiences. Children in their classrooms are free to explore, discover, and choose their own way as they increasingly assume personal responsibility. Children in a democratic classroom develop a sense of belonging to and having a stake in the class.

Helping Students Correct Their Misbehavior

The following steps, suggested by Dinkmeyer and Dinkmeyer (1976), are useful for helping students correct their misbehavior. Some of the steps can be applied to preventing discipline problems. Keep in mind that for this approach to work successfully teachers must already have established a good relationship with the students they are trying to help. A relationship of trust is essential in using logical consequences.

1. Teachers attempt to ascertain students' motives.
2. Students are helped to understand their motives.
3. Students are helped to exchange their mistaken goals for useful ones.
4. Students are encouraged to become committed to their new goal orientation.
5. Students are taught to apply logical consequences.
6. Group discussions regarding class rules and problems are held.

UNDERSTANDING STUDENTS' MISTAKEN GOALS

Before teachers can help children alter their mistaken goals and improve their behavior, it is imperative that they understand children's behavior from a psychological point of view. That is, teachers need to understand the private logic of their misbehaving students (Dreikurs et al., 1982). Private logic consists of what a person really believes and intends. Included are a person's long-range and short-range goals and the reasons and rationalizations created to justify related behavior. Individuals begin in childhood to explain to themselves, with varying degrees of insight, the appropriateness of their behavior. Even maladaptive behavior can thus be judged acceptable if it can be rationalized.

Children have limited conscious understanding of their goals or motives. However, when the purpose of their behavior is explained to them, they recognize its connection to their goals. Younger children will either willingly admit that they misbehave for the reasons suggested or betray themselves by exhibiting an obvious recognition reflex: a smile, an embarrassed laugh, or a twinkle in the eye. Older children are too sophisticated to admit the motives behind their contrary behavior. They recognize the fact that society looks on such behavior as childish and therefore resist disclosing their motives. They put on deadpan expressions in an effort to hide their recognition, but they give themselves away with their body language. Their lips may twitch or their eyes may blink or bat more frequently; they may adjust their seating position, swing a leg, tap the desk with their fingers, or shuffle their feet.

To get children either to reveal their goals or to expose themselves through a recognition reflex, Dreikurs et al. (1982) recommend that you ask the following questions:

1. "Do you know why you _____?" (Even if a child does not know the reason for the misbehavior, this question is raised in preparation for the next step.)
2. "I would like to tell you what I think." (Ask one or more of the following questions from the group that is related to the mistaken goal.)

Gaining Attention:

"Could it be that you want me to notice you more?"
"Could it be that you want me to do something special for you?"
"Could it be that you want to be special to the group?"

Exercising Power:

"Could it be that you want to be the boss?"
"Could it be that you want to show me that I can't stop you?"
"Could it be that you insist on doing what you want to do?"

Exacting Revenge:

"Could it be that you want to punish me?"
"Could it be that you want to get even with me?"
"Could it be that you want to show me how much you hated what I did?"

Displaying Inadequacy:

"Could it be that you want to be left alone because you believe that you can't do anything?"
"Could it be that you want to be left alone because you can't be on top?"
"Could it be that you want to be left alone because you want me to stop asking you to do something?"

One way of reaching a child who is particularly resistant to your questions is to use the "hidden reason" technique. This technique is applied when a child says or does something out of the ordinary. You try to guess what is on the child's mind. If a child answers "no" to your initial question, ask a follow-up question. Continue asking follow-up questions until the answer is "maybe" or "perhaps." This response will lead you to a correct guess. The following example shows the use of this technique:

> ▼ Darryl has on several occasions refused to do as the teacher directed. Now, in yet another episode, Darryl has been told to start an assignment and has again refused to do it in class. But this time the teacher decides to look more closely into Darryl's behavior.

Teacher	Darryl, could it be that you want to make me feel guilty and sorry for something I did to you?
Darryl	Well, not exactly.
Teacher	Could it be that you want to show me how much smarter you are than I am?
Darryl	No.

Recognizing that Darryl appeared to be very popular with most of the other students in the class, the teacher decided to explore the possibility that Darryl's behavior reflected a desire to be the group leader.

Teacher	Darryl, do you have a lot of close friends in the class?
Darryl	Yes, I do.
Teacher	Do your friends try to be like you and do what you do?
Darryl	Yeah, sometimes.
Teacher	Could it be that you want me to give you control over what you and your friends do in class so that you can have control over them?
Darryl	Yeah, I guess that's right.

Teachers can use two additional methods to discern their students' motives (Charles, 1992). The first method requires teachers to analyze how they feel when a student responds.

- If they feel annoyed, the student is probably seeking attention.
- If they feel threatened, power-seeking behavior is being expressed.
- When teachers feel hurt, the student probably wants revenge.
- A feeling of being powerless is an indication that the student is displaying inadequacy.

A second way teachers have of determining a student's motives is to observe the reactions of the student.

If the student:	*The student's goal is to:*
Stops the behavior and then repeats it	Gain attention
Confronts or ignores authority	Exercise power
Becomes devious, violent, or hostile	Exact revenge
Refuses to participate or cooperate	Display inadequacy

Determining a child's motives can be difficult and complex. However, if teachers use the recommended techniques, they will get a better idea of the nature of these mistaken goals. These mistaken goals must be revealed to children before teachers can successfully help them pursue more worthwhile goals.

HELPING STUDENTS CHANGE THEIR MISTAKEN GOALS

Once teachers understand children's mistaken goals, they can take more valid and decisive action. Until they know these motives, they are more likely to do more harm than good. In fact, they may unwittingly reinforce bad behavior. Children's behavior can then become painful and intolerable. Dreikurs believes that it is essential to identify the mistaken goal correctly. Otherwise, the behaviors encouraged to satisfy an assumed motive will not be appropriate to the situation.

Dealing With Attention-Seeking Behavior.   Attention-seeking children seem unable to tolerate being ignored. They prefer the pain of humiliation or other forms of punishment to receiving no attention. If they fail to receive the attention they desire, they do things that cannot be ignored. When a small disturbance elicits no response, more provocative behavior can be expected. Teachers ordinarily pay attention to these behaviors by nagging or scolding the misbehaving students. However, they should avoid falling into the trap of reinforcing bad conduct. When students behave unacceptably, teachers must ignore them. If their misbehavior is consistently ignored, children will not learn to associate attention with inappropriate behavior. Sometimes teachers complain that ignoring bad behavior "does not work." They commonly reach this conclusion when in fact they are giving children attention through the use of various nonverbal cues. For example, students' bad behavior may be reinforced when their teachers stand and glare at them with hands on hips and say impatiently, "All right, class, we'll have to wait until everyone is ready to continue with the lesson." Ignoring misbehavior is also more effective when accompanied by reinforcement of good behavior. Teachers need to be on the lookout for occasions when their students are listening attentively or working on their lessons productively. When they do, attention should be drawn to the fact. Teachers may give them a pat on the back or tell them how much they appreciate their cooperation.

Dealing With Power-Seeking Behavior.   It is commonly believed that teachers must react decisively and with force if students try to usurp their authority. It is indeed very difficult for teachers to restrain themselves when children make a play for power. Teachers are usually unprepared to avoid power struggles with students who threaten their authority and prestige. Consequently, struggles for power are waged in most classrooms. Teachers fight back to avoid letting students get the best of them. After all, they believe, teachers must avoid losing face at all costs. Unfortunately, fighting with students—even though teachers may win the contest—breeds more hostility.

One way to avoid power struggles is to make it necessary for errant students to confront the whole class in the quest for power. Most students will realize the futility of this confrontation. For example, if a student constantly disrupts your teaching, stop the work of the entire class, and wait for the disruptive behavior to cease before continuing the lesson.

Teachers must also make sure that they do not give in to the demands of power-seeking children. To children who are trying to provoke them, teachers may say, "I am sure you prefer to be the leader, but the class has decided to rotate the leadership among all members during field projects" or "I can see that this situation is a difficult one for you. However, the class has agreed not to be disruptive during discussions and demonstrations." To children who refuse to do their work and say that the teacher cannot make them, the teacher may respond, "You're right. I can't make you. You will have to decide whether or not you want to participate with the rest of the class on your project."

Teachers need to remember that they must not fight with students. They can often avoid power struggles simply by refusing to play the role of authoritarian. Students cannot meet their mistaken goal of power if there is no one with whom to fight. Children rebel in direct proportion to the autocratic level of their teachers' behavior.

David refused to give in to his teacher's controlling demands.

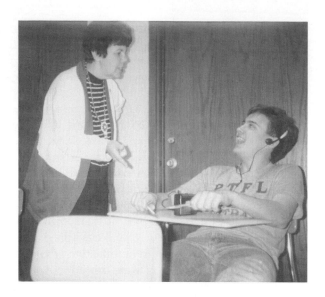

Autocratic teachers complain about the unruliness of their students, and the misbehaving students protest the controlling rigidity of their teachers. Each party sees the other as being in the wrong; both are unable to see their own part in the difficulty. If a child initiates a confrontation with an autocratic teacher and the teacher takes the bait by responding negatively, the student will usually become more resistant and disruptive. This reaction is illustrated in the following example:

> During a chemistry lesson, David was listening to his portable stereo and beating on his desk in time to the music. Ms. Edwards told him to stop, but he just looked back at his teacher and continued drumming on the desk. Ms. Edwards then scolded David and threatened to take away his stereo if he did not stop. David just smiled back at her and continued to keep time with the music. Infuriated, Ms. Edwards demanded that David wipe the silly grin off his face. David's smile broadened, and he started to move his whole body in rhythm with the music as he continued banging on his desk. Ms. Edwards stormed over to David's desk and in a rage snatched the earphones from his head, knocking the stereo to the floor. For an instant, shock registered on David's face, but it quickly faded. In its place came an enormous grin as he started again to thump his hands against the wooden surface of the desk. Ms. Edwards's face was red with anger as she demanded that David come with her to the principal's office. David just continued drumming. Ms. Edwards grabbed David's arm and tried to pull him from his seat, but David grabbed the side of the desk and held on. The smile on his face was accompanied by a defiant laugh.

This example shows a teacher becoming increasingly demanding and controlling and a student becoming more resistant and defiant. The grin displayed by the student was a sure way to infuriate the teacher. It was the student's way of publicly belittling the teacher. The student was able to remain calm and under control, but the teacher was out of control. If the whole class witnessed this episode, they would likely side with the student, not with the teacher. Certainly, the student's peers would provide reinforcement for the daring confrontation with the teacher. The teacher should have avoided a confrontation with the student about his behavior. If the inappropriate behavior continued, even though the teacher ignored it, the student might be asked to provide a leadership role in the class, like being the chairperson for a group activity, helping the teacher take roll, operating a video camera, or similar activities.

Classmates also sided with the student in the following episode. The example is given as an illustration of a student making a play for power, although another student exhibiting the same behavior could simply be pulling a prank.

▼ As the students in Mr. Larsen's biology class slowly filed in, their attention was drawn to Gordon, who was standing near the display table in the front of the room on which Mr. Larsen had placed his prized stuffed fox. From his pocket Gordon took a cigarette. He put it to his lips, lit it, and placed it in the fox's mouth. Hurrying along, he took his place near the front of the room and pretended to read his book. Smoke from the cigarette curled up toward the ceiling as Mr. Larsen strode into the room. His attention was immediately drawn to the ludicrous sight of the smoking fox. Complete surprise registered on his face, and then rage as he demanded that the culprit who put the cigarette in the fox's mouth come forward and stand in front of him. Nobody moved. The entire class was immobilized with fright. Then an audible snickering was heard from the front of the class. Mr. Larsen demanded to know who thought a smoking fox was so funny. Gordon raised his hand. Mr. Larsen went straight to where Gordon sat, grabbed him by the arm, and spirited him out the classroom door. A few minutes later a red-faced Mr. Larsen appeared at the door and marched to the front of the room. He ordered the students to take out their texts and begin reading silently. There was to be absolute quiet. It was so quiet for nearly 5 minutes that you could have heard a pin drop. Then Ruth, unable to contain herself any longer, giggled softly to herself. Miggs followed suit. Then Lois started in. Mr. Larsen looked up from his desk and glared at the class. Another snicker was heard from the back of the class. Mr. Larsen demanded to know who had snickered and promised to make an example of that student. No one responded. Then more laughing erupted. Mr. Larsen stood and moved toward the back of the room in an effort to detect the source of the noise. He had not gone two paces before Gordon appeared at the classroom door with a grin on his face. He defiantly walked to his seat, laughing loudly. The rest of the class joined his laughter and then began clapping. Mr. Larsen continued to move toward the back of the room and proceeded on out the door.

Both Mr. Larsen and Ms. Edwards were successfully drawn into a power contest with students. In each case, coercive control was increased in an effort to maintain order. However, both teachers failed. Instead, the students became more defiant. In the case of Mr. Larsen, the whole class turned against him. Had Mr. Larsen come into the room and burst into laughter when he first saw the smoking fox, Gordon's play for power would have been undermined, the class would have had a good laugh, and Mr. Larsen's reputation and status would have been preserved.

Sometimes students' desire for power can be redirected. They may be satisfied with taking a leadership role in the class instead of confronting their teachers. A child who seeks power by disrupting the class may, for example, be asked to be in charge of maintaining order during class activities. The student could be asked to report on which techniques helped in keeping order or to make recommendations for improving the atmosphere of the class.

Doing the unexpected is another way to deal with power-seeking students. When children misbehave, teachers usually have an immediate emotional reaction. Reactions ordinarily are predictable because most people tend to react in the same way in a given situation. Children commonly have ready-made responses to these standard reactions. Therefore, teachers can nip an impending power struggle in the bud by doing the exact opposite of what they feel like doing. Children are put off balance because the teacher's behavior is new and unanticipated.

Dealing With Revenge-Seeking Behavior. The desire for revenge is often closely tied to the desire for power. It may sometimes be hard to differentiate between the two. Revenge is usually the motive in children who are convinced that they are right and can do whatever they please. They often try to hurt others and feel that those who try to stop them are their enemies. They feel the need to hurt others because they have been hurt themselves. Ordinarily, their need for attention and acceptance has gone unfulfilled because others view them with contempt and refuse to associate closely with them, sometimes because they are different in some way or because they exhibit bizarre behavior in their attempts to gain the attention they so desperately desire. It is difficult to reason with these children. Convinced that they are hopelessly disliked by everyone, they distrust any effort to persuade them otherwise.

Children who pursue their desire for attention or power are sometimes unaware of the purpose behind their behavior. Those who feel hurt and disliked, however, are very much aware of their goals. They seem oblivious, though, to their own suspiciousness. They are also unaware of the hostility they provoke and the fact that their own behavior dictates how they are treated. They rarely accept the responsibility for the destructive relationships they have with teachers and classmates. It is always others who are wrong. These children are firmly convinced that they are right in what they believe and justified in retaliating against those who, they believe, are their enemies.

Helping revenge-seeking children is a very delicate matter. Teachers can enlist the help of other class members, but they should do so with care. Children often will side with teachers by shunning revengeful children. Unfortunately, teachers may be prone to accept such alliances because of their own sense of failure in dealing with these children. Instead, teachers need to encourage the class to be more positive. They could, for example, persuade more popular peers to take a special interest in outcast children. Such a program will take considerable effort, and teachers will have to give their helpers the support they need to stay with this task. Revenge-seeking children are likely, in the beginning, to be antagonistic in the face of friendliness and kindness. They will obviously retain a sense of distrust for a time. Even after trust seems to be developing, they may put everyone to the test by doing something outrageous. When they do, children whose help has been solicited should be encouraged to avoid rejecting their revengeful peers but at the same time not to accept their behavior. The following example illustrates this point:

▼ Tui disdainfully watched the other students successfully working on their experiments in the biology lab while at the same time feeling unsure of himself and the results he was obtaining on his own experiment. He was particularly incensed by the way certain students sought and obtained special help from Mr. Bingham. It wasn't fair that when they asked for help Mr. Bingham ignored the rest of the class and gave the teacher's pets all the help they wanted. A clever idea suddenly clicked in Tui's mind. He turned in his seat and looked toward the back of the room. A sinister grin spread across his face as he quietly slipped from his seat and made his way stealthily to a cage on the back counter. Throwing a quick glance in Mr. Bingham's direction, he noiselessly opened the cage and took out the huge bullfrog that was kept inside. He promptly put the enormous amphibian behind his back and walked unobtrusively toward a group of A students who were working together at a lab table. While they were looking down at their experiments, he set the frog on the table and quickly returned to his own seat and pretended to be immersed in his own experiment. The frog suddenly croaked and jumped right into the middle of the area where the group was working. To Tui, the pandemonium that ensued was beautiful to behold. All five let out a yell and jumped back from the table, knocking over stools and lab equipment and strewing papers everywhere. Three of them made such a mess that it took them nearly 10 minutes to clean up after Mr. Bingham had captured the frog and returned it to the cage. The rest of the class was laughing uproariously, some doubled over with tears running down their cheeks. Mr. Bingham was seething, and his face was bright red. As the students began to notice their teacher's rage, the room grew quiet. No one dared breathe. Mr. Bingham searched the room with penetrating eyes, looking for the guilty party. His gaze settled on Tui. He noted the satisfied look on Tui's face. "You,"

Tui sought revenge by releasing a frog in his biology classroom.

Mr. Bingham said with feigned control as he pointed at the door, "go to the principal's office immediately. I'll be following you."

This situation was obviously handled badly if Mr. Bingham sincerely wanted to help Tui overcome his vengefulness. Had Mr. Bingham quickly captured the frog, reassured the flustered students, and helped them to laugh at the situation, he would have not only taken the wind out of Tui's sails but also added to his credibility in the classroom. The momentary fright and embarrassment caused by the incident could not be ignored, of course, but revengeful behavior on the part of the teacher would not solve the problem either.

Dealing With Displays of Inadequacy.   If children have been sufficiently rebuffed in their efforts to gain attention, they may become so discouraged that they behave like blobs. When they do not achieve their goals of attention or power or revenge, they may just give up. These children wish to be left alone. They believe that their case is hopeless and want their teachers to believe it too. Many teachers do give up on these children.

Students who display inadequacy do so for one of the following reasons:

1. *They are overly ambitious.*   This is probably the most frequent cause of giving up. These children despair of not doing as well as they want to do. If they cannot be first, make the best grades, be the leader, be the star athlete, or the like, they refuse to put forth any effort. Children with debilitating overambition will not participate in an activity unless it provides them an opportunity to prove their superiority. These children must be helped to see how they defeat themselves. They must learn to continue trying even though others may outperform them.

2. *They are overcompetitive.*   Some children are convinced that they have no chance to do as well as others. They believe that they are not good enough to be successful, and comparisons with others usually serve only to confirm their belief. Unfortunately, parents and teachers sometimes try to motivate these children by making such comparisons: "When I had your sister in my English class, she was my best student." "Why don't you do as well on your tests as your brother?" These comparisons should be avoided for all children, but especially for those who are overcompetitive.

3. *They are oversensitive to pressure.*   Students who are oversensitive to pressure feel that they cannot do as well as others expect. They therefore refuse to live up to others' expectations. Two of the misfortunes of our present educational system are the emphasis on avoiding mistakes and the practice of trying to motivate children through criticism and competition. Teachers need to tell children that they are all right as they are and to remove pressure by being less critical. Children need to learn and grow in a less competitive environment. They must be given sufficient time to achieve at their own speed.

Teachers must learn never to give up on students who believe themselves to be inadequate. They must provide these students an abundance of support and encouragement. Encouragement is especially needed when students make mistakes. These students need to feel successful and accepted for what they are. Because of the competitive environment found in most schools, students who are more successful are likely to reject their less productive peers. One of the most important duties teachers can perform is to help other students accept those who feel inadequate.

Preventing Discipline Problems

It is obviously better to prevent discipline problems than to correct them after they occur. Unfortunately, many children have long-standing problems that need correction. These tenacious problems are often extremely difficult to solve. Misbehavior that has become a habit is very resistant to change. Children may be convinced that their way of behaving is the only one that can adequately satisfy their needs. Dreikurs suggests several procedures that can be used not only to deal with these problems but to prevent them as well.

ENCOURAGEMENT VERSUS PRAISE

Encouragement is a useful technique for preventing discipline problems because it corresponds so well to children's goals. Children seek approval, and encouragement provides a legitimate means of receiving it. Encouragement focuses on effort rather than achievement; it thus gives positive feedback to children who are trying hard but may be somewhat unsuccessful. Encouragement stimulates them to continue trying. When encouragement is properly given, students gain status and satisfaction more from learning than from relative achievements. Test scores, for instance, have less value than learning itself. Children who have been encouraged accept themselves as they are, even when they are less than perfect. Encouragement can also solidify their place in the group. They can feel that they are contributing members of the group and that the group accepts their efforts as valid. In this process, students become aware of their strengths without undue focus on their weaknesses. When children exhibit more realistic confidence in their abilities, they are less likely to cause discipline problems.

Praise needs to be differentiated from encouragement. Praise focuses on the level of accomplishment or achievement; encouragement highlights the value of learning. Praise is given for high achievement and is ordinarily reserved for those who are more successful according to some measure of performance. Praise fosters the idea that only test performance is worthy. Students who receive praise for their efforts do not work for self-satisfaction. Instead, they are governed by extrinsic rewards. Encouragement, on the other hand, stimulates cooperation rather than competition, effort and enjoyment rather than quality of performance, independence rather than dependence, and helpfulness rather than selfishness. The following examples show the difference between praise and encouragement:

Your artwork is excellent.	You seem to really enjoy art.
You got the highest mark on your exam.	I can tell that you worked hard to prepare for your exam.

You always work quietly without disturbing others. Thank you.	It seems important to you to do your own work.
You're doing a wonderful job with these new dance movements.	You have obviously been spending a lot of time perfecting these new dance movements.

Teachers need to appreciate children who have diverse abilities, not just those who perform well on tests. Limiting what is acceptable or valued always restricts the number of students who feel encouraged to work for success in school. Teachers also must be careful not to add restrictions ("but's" or "however's") when they offer compliments to their students. Avoid such compliments as "Your drawing is very elaborate, but you must remember to incorporate proper perspective."

LOGICAL CONSEQUENCES

Regardless of how encouraging teachers are, they are still likely to encounter misbehavior in students. While encouraging their students, teachers should identify logical consequences in advance and prepare to apply them as behavioral problems develop. Logical consequences need to be distinguished from natural consequences as well as from punishment. Natural consequences are those that occur without a teacher's intervention. For example, if children throw snowballs or rocks at one another, someone may get hit in the head and injured. Students who do not study for tests often get poor test scores. These consequences are not arranged; they happen naturally. Teachers do not need to threaten children with natural consequences. Children can discover them on their own.

Logical consequences are contrived and then applied as necessary to influence students' behavior (Dreikurs & Grey, 1968). They do not happen naturally, but they do have a reasonable connection to some action. For example, a student who breaks something may be expected to replace it. Logical consequences generally express the reality of the social order and are the results that can be expected whenever an individual fails to abide by the rules of living that all humans must learn in order to function effectively. These consequences are logically related to the misbehavior the teacher hopes to correct and are devoid of any moral judgments. In addition, they are concerned only with what is happening at the present time and not the future. Logical consequences are given to students in a pleasant, helpful manner, not angrily and coercively (Dreikurs & Grey, 1970).

Sometimes the use of logical consequences is confused with punishment. Punishment, however, does not have a logical connection to a particular behavior. Instead, it is arbitrarily administered and usually designed to be painful enough so that misbehaving students have no choice but to change their behavior. If students, for example, talk during lectures and discussions, the teacher may punish them by subtracting points from their grades. In reality, grades have little to do with talking during instruction. A logical consequence may be to have students leave class until they indicate that they will no longer talk during instruction. Students may be punished by being kicked out of class for a week for talking disruptively. This action is punitive because the length of time students are excluded is arbitrary. For such an action to be a logical consequence, students would have to be kept out of class just until they were able to make a plan to improve their behavior.

Punishment promotes revenge and causes students to feel that they have a right to retaliate (Dreikurs & Cassel, 1972). Students do not associate punishment with their own behavior but rather with the person providing it. Because children's main objective is to feel acceptable and accepted, they will not meekly endure punishment. They will feel humiliated and try to punish the teacher for how they feel. They believe that it is their right to do so. Employing logical consequences helps them understand that it is their unacceptable behavior that brings unpleasant results, not the arbitrariness of teachers.

To be effective, consequences have to be applied consistently. If a teacher applies them a few times and then discontinues their use, students will soon take advantage of the teacher's inconsistency. They will gamble that the teacher will be in a good mood or that they will have good luck. Applying consequences consistently in school helps students become acquainted with the reality of the society in which they live.

Logical consequences must be explained, understood, and agreed on by students. Students more readily accept consequences they have helped determine. Teachers should avoid applying consequences that have not been agreed to by students. When consequences are administered at the time of misbehavior without prior discussion, they have an effect similar to that of punishment. Consequences promote good behavior. Punishment fails to teach correct behavior and often encourages more inappropriate behavior.

Dreikurs et al. (1982) suggest the following examples of logical consequences:

1. If a student pushes someone on the stairway, the teacher may let the student decide whether to avoid pushing in the future or go back to the class and wait until everyone else has cleared the stairway before going down.
2. If a student hands in an incomplete or dirty paper, the teacher may read the paper only if the student submits a complete, clean copy.
3. If students write on the walls, they can either clean them or pay the janitor to clean them.
4. Students who mark their desks can be required to sand and refinish the desks or pay for having them refinished.
5. Students who fight during recess may be barred from recess until they provide the teacher with a plan outlining how they propose to avoid fighting.
6. If students disturb others, they may be isolated from the group until they agree to disturb the class no longer.
7. If students are late for class, they may be directed either to come on time or to wait at the door until they receive a signal that their late arrival will no longer disturb the class.

Sometimes the discrimination between logical consequences and punishment is inappropriately made. Even Dreikurs is accused of failing to make the necessary distinction when he recommends that a child who is late for dinner might be sent to bed without food as a "logical consequence" (Gordon, 1989). Gordon suggests that a more logical consequence would be for the child to eat the dinner cold, or have to heat it up in the microwave oven. If no leftovers are available, the child may have to fix a sandwich. To send a child to bed without dinner is an attempt to control punitively, he says.

Another questionable aspect of applying logical consequences is the recommended practice of providing children a choice between two competing (and perhaps equally aversive) consequences rather than letting them consider the entire range of possible consequences associated with their misbehavior. In addition, imposing the consequence selected may be judged by the student to be punitive. Allowing an examination of a full range of consequences, on the other hand, may be a better deterrent to future misbehavior. One example of this is the boy referred to earlier in the chapter who was constantly out of his seat and who was informed by his teacher that he could either keep his chair and sit in it to do his work or he would have his seat permanently removed. Another example supplied by Dreikurs is to tell students who lean back in their chairs that they can either keep all four legs of their chairs on the floor or have the front two legs continuously blocked up. Neither of these examples provides consequences that are particularly logical and free from punitive control. This illustrates, perhaps, the difficulty experienced in determining logical consequences and conveying to students that these consequences are not simply arbitrary punishment. The way teachers' actions are interpreted by their students is far more important than what teachers intend. For example, a teacher may ask a student to leave the classroom as a "logical consequence" for talking out during a lecture. This may be the same punitive thing that has happened to this student routinely in other classroom situations. How will he or she interpret this action? That probably depends on how consequences are determined and the role students play in this process. If students together determine, in advance, that the appropriate consequences for disturbing class by talking is to have to leave until they come to the teacher with a plan of how to avoid such behavior in the future, they will more likely interpret removal from class as logical instead of punitive.

DISCUSSIONS IN THE CLASSROOM

Classroom discussions are helpful in preventing discipline problems. Group influence can have a positive impact on the behavior of almost all children. Group discussions, which are imperative in a democratic setting, have several purposes. First, they provide an excellent atmosphere in which students can better learn interpersonal skills and effective communication. Second, they can be used to create common goals and procedures so that class members know their roles and how to perform them; children learn to accept responsibility and understand the consequences they may expect. Third, students can learn more about themselves and others as they take part in discussions. This knowledge provides them with a basis for cooperating with one another and working successfully together.

Teachers must provide expert leadership in group discussions. They should make sure that students are free to express themselves in the group without feeling intimidated. More dominant students should not be allowed to monopolize. Everyone's rights must be respected (Dinkmeyer & Dreikurs, 1963). Teachers should promote active, voluntary participation. Teachers must avoid taking too dominant a role, although they do need to ensure that these discussions are productive, implementing a minimal amount of manipulation if necessary.

Group discussions can serve the class as a forum for determining class values and expectations as well as a means of enforcing them. If some students fail to follow group directives, the unacceptable behavior they exhibit can be brought up for group discussion. Bringing up the names of offending students should be avoided. Only the types of misbehavior need be discussed. The teacher must provide the necessary leadership to ensure that a group discussion does not degenerate into a free-for-all.

Group discussions should promote an inner freedom for both students and teachers. All must feel free to choose and take responsibility for their choices. The mutual respect that is thus generated will encourage the free exchange of ideas and a greater tolerance for one another. Proper classroom order can be expected as a result. Dreikurs believes that children should gradually develop more self-management skills. This development must take place in an atmosphere of social reality. Children must learn the rules we live by in society, become accustomed to them, and adopt them as their own. These same rules should be applied in the classroom. All students must accept responsibility for themselves and their behavior and learn to respect themselves and others. They should realize their strategic role in helping others in the group and develop a sense of group responsibility.

PREVENTIVE DISCIPLINE SUGGESTIONS

Dreikurs offers some specific suggestions for preventing discipline problems. Some of these suggestions are based on developing a positive relationship with students (Dinkmeyer & Dinkmeyer, 1976). First, teachers must avoid reinforcing or provoking misbehavior. Students have motives they attempt to satisfy through misbehavior. Teachers should, therefore, avoid behaving inappropriately in response to students' provocations. For example, if a student's motive is attention, he or she may do something to annoy the teacher. If the motive is power, the student may try to provoke anger. Desire to retaliate may be stimulated when a student seeks to satisfy his or her revenge motive. Teachers should not respond to student provocations designed to satisfy these motives.

The second thing teachers can do to prevent discipline problems is to establish a relationship of mutual respect between them and their students. This involves not only being kind to students but also displaying an appropriate level of firmness. Teachers should not make threats or fight with students. If a conflict looms, it is best to withdraw, refusing to fight, while at the same time not giving in to student pressure.

Third, teachers should look for assets in each of their students. Looking for positive attributes in students ensures more positive relationships. Looking for student assets encourages them to more fully display the positive behavior exemplified by these assets. Assets like cooperativeness, persistence, and loyalty can be encouraged when teachers expect their students to have them.

Fourth, teachers need to be flexible in their attitudes toward students. Misbehaving students are commonly discouraged and sense they are not accepted by others. Their misguided efforts to satisfy their motives may have promoted an attitude of unacceptance by their peers and teachers. They sense this and commonly misbehave even more. Teachers must be flexible enough to act as if their students have desirable attributes if they hope to encourage them to develop such characteristics.

Dreikurs also suggests that students be involved in determining rules for the classroom (Dreikurs et al., 1982). A broad range of rules should be addressed. For example, there may be rules regarding borrowing personal belongings, using classroom equipment, playing with other children on the playground, table manners in the cafeteria, calling other children names and swearing, bicycles, getting help from classmates on schoolwork, cleaning up work areas, talking during class discussions and lectures, and entering and exiting the classroom.

Students should also be allowed to work at their own pace, display spontaneity and enthusiasm, explore personal interests, and learn to accept responsibility for themselves. These natural impulses of students need to be expressed and should be sanctioned within an acceptable format in the classroom.

A final way to better prevent discipline problems is to have discipline-oriented class discussions. In these discussions, the five following topics should receive the focus of attention:

1. The good things that have happened since the last discussion are addressed. This aspect of the discussion may well deal with problems that have been overcome and learning that has been enhanced by class decisions that have been made earlier.
2. The class should examine ways to avoid specific problems and improve the class during the next week or so. Here, problems that have plagued the class should be brought up without making reference to particular students. Specific ways to overcome these problems should be brought up and agreed upon.
3. Personal problems should be reviewed. Students should be allowed and even encouraged to bring up problems that affect them personally. When these problems are discussed, children can attain a greater sense of community with their classmates and achieve an increased commitment to help one another.
4. Examine responsibilities of class members for how the class operates. Students should feel a sense of responsibility for what happens in class. This way they can assume responsibility for being a contributing member of the class. Students who feel no sense of class responsibility commonly obstruct classroom activities in an effort to satisfy their own needs.
5. Formulate future plans that provide a sense of class direction. Students will be more enthusiastic about pursuing goals that they have helped develop. These plans can include items such as proposed curricula, projects, future discussion, guest speakers, and equipment purchases.

Schoolwide Discipline

Although Dreikurs does not provide specific instructions for the implementation of logical consequences on a schoolwide basis, its basic principles could be applied in a whole-school setting, but with a few possible drawbacks. Particularly recalcitrant students could be referred to administrators or other designated professionals who would diagnose students' motives and help them change mistaken goals for more productive ones in the same way teachers do in their classrooms. These more difficult cases may be handled by administrators in their offices or in a central clearing house created in the school and staffed by professionals trained in logical consequences techniques. These cases may be those that teachers find difficulty working with and still carrying on their instructional program. Unfortunately, moving unmanageable students out of the classroom may just shift the focus of problems and not solve them. For example, revenge or power motives may originate in a particular classroom with a particular teacher and may best be solved in that context. Because this discipline approach deals with motives whose development may be situation specific, schoolwide applications could be less potent and less appropriate than those applied by individual teachers. Teachers may be in a better position to provide students appropriate options to their mistaken goals, which fit their particular classroom. Because situations in various classrooms may differ, it would be difficult for personnel unfamiliar with these conditions to guide students in determining appropriate alternative behaviors. Also, because trust relationships are critical to the operation of this model, individual teachers may be better equipped to work with these students than personnel in a centralized referral facility.

Strengths and Weaknesses of the Logical Consequences Model

STRENGTHS

1. It promotes a degree of autonomy for students.
2. It incorporates a preventive approach to discipline.
3. It helps students understand why they behave as they do.
4. It helps students learn correct behavior.
5. It promotes mutual respect between teachers and students.
6. It relies on logical consequences instead of arbitrary punishment and systematic reinforcement.
7. It helps teachers focus on causes for behavior before they take action.

WEAKNESSES

1. Teachers have trouble determining the actual motives of their students.
2. Students may not admit their real motives, either because they believe that their motives are unacceptable or because they do not know what they are.
3. Teachers may find it difficult to respond to students in a noncontrolling way.
4. Teachers may have a problem dealing with the complexity of engaging in a dialogue with their students.

▼ SUMMARY

Democratic principles are central to Dreikurs's approach to discipline. Teachers who are democratic will be more successful in helping children become more responsibly self-governed. These principles can also be used more effectively to deal with students who have mistaken goals. Teachers' effectiveness can be improved when they realize that the behavior of all students is an outgrowth of a desire to be accepted on a social level. Misbehavior results when children pursue the mistaken goals of gaining attention, exercising power, exacting revenge, and displaying inadequacy. Children's disposition to seek these mistaken goals is often related to their family experiences as well as to their treatment in school.

A summary of Dreikurs's recommendations for good discipline can be found in his list of *don't*s and *do*s (Dreikurs et al., 1982):

A List of **Don'ts**

1. Do not be preoccupied with your own prestige and authority.
2. Refrain from nagging and scolding, which may reinforce misbehaving children's quest for attention.
3. Do not ask children to promise anything. They will use a promise to get out of an uncomfortable situation with no intention of fulfilling it.
4. Avoid giving rewards for good behavior. Doing so will only condition children to expect rewards.
5. Refrain from finding fault with children.
6. Do not hold your students and yourself to different standards.
7. Do not use threats.
8. Do not be vindictive.

A List of **Dos**

1. Always try first to understand the purpose of children's misbehavior.
2. Give clear-cut directions for actions expected of children.
3. Focus on children's present, not their past, behavior.
4. When children misbehave in class, give them a choice either to remain where they are without disturbing others or to leave the room.
5. Build on the positive and avoid the negative.
6. Build trust between yourself and children.
7. Discuss children's behavior problems only when neither you nor they are emotionally charged.
8. Use logical consequences instead of punishment.
9. Treat children with consistency.
10. Use cooperative planning to establish goals and solutions to problems.
11. Let children assume increasingly greater responsibility for their own behavior and learning as they are able to do so.
12. Use the whole class to create and enforce rules.
13. Be kind but firm with children.
14. Show that you accept children but not their misbehavior.
15. Help children become more responsibly independent.

16. Make sure that students understand the limits.

CENTRAL IDEAS

1. According to Dreikurs, students misbehave because their needs are not met.
2. The needs to gain attention, exercise power, exact revenge, and display inadequacy form a hierarchy: If one need (attention, for example) is unmet, the next need in the hierarchy (power) becomes predominant.
3. To avoid having to deal with a variety of misbehavior, teachers should make sure that their students' need for attention and acceptance is met.
4. Discipline problems can be prevented through the use of class discussions and the application of logical consequences.

▼ QUESTIONS AND ACTIVITIES

QUESTIONS TO CONSIDER

1. What evidence is there that the purpose of misbehavior is to achieve social acceptance?
2. What motives besides the ones Dreikurs accepts do you think explain misbehavior?
3. How does your own experience corroborate or contradict the conclusions Dreikurs reaches regarding the influence of birth order on behavior?
4. To what extent have social conditions changed sufficiently to require more democratic methods of working with children?

CLASSROOM ACTIVITIES

1. Compare Canter's assertive discipline (Chapter 4) and Dreikurs's logical consequences.
2. Divide the class into groups of four or five members. One member of the group is given a list of behaviors and associated motives. This person describes each behavior to the other group members. They try to determine the motive behind the behavior by asking questions of the group member holding the list. For example:

   Behavior (Motive)

   A student digs into the desk with a knife.   *(Revenge)*
   A student fights with other students.   *(Attention)*
   A student is late for class.   *(Power)*
   A student cuts into the lunch line.   *(Attention)*
   A student uses foul language in class.   *(Power)*
   A student talks boisterously.   *(Attention)*

3. Have students change the following praise statements into encouragement statements:
   a. Look at the stitching on this dress you have sewn. You did an excellent job.
   b. Class, you should see Robert's research paper. It was the best one in the class.
   c. Your trumpet playing is absolutely remarkable, Bill.

d. Mark, you're the best basketball player we have this year.

STUDENT APPLICATIONS

1. With two classmates, use role playing to discover how a teacher can apply logical consequences to help a misbehaving student in the following situations. One person plays the role of the teacher; another plays the role of the student. The person playing the student should be told only what the misbehavior was. That person then decides on one of the mistaken motives without revealing it to the person playing the teacher. The third person is to observe and help the two other participants analyze the situation.
   a. Bill makes paper airplanes and flies them around the classroom.
   b. Shon trips other students as they walk up the aisle.
   c. Steve rips pages out of textbooks.
   d. Lynette spends time talking instead of working quietly at her desk.
2. With a group of classmates, use role playing to simulate a class discussion in which learning goals as well as classroom rules are determined.

EXPLORE YOUR PHILOSOPHY

1. Defend or refute the assumption that humans are motivated by their need to gain attention, exercise power, exact revenge, or display inadequacy.
2. Defend or refute the assumption that the preceding human needs are related to one another in a hierarchy so that satisfying attention needs will preclude the manifestation of the other needs.
3. Defend or refute the assumption that appropriate behavior changes will take place only when children understand the motives for their behavior and embrace acceptable alternatives to satisfy their needs.
4. Defend or refute the assumption that the best way to determine behavioral manifestations of children's needs is to explore the reasons why they behave as they do.
5. Defend or refute the practice of providing children with consequences in the form of two alternative behaviors from which to choose, instead of allowing them to examine the full range of possible consequences.
6. Compare the principles contained in your educational philosophy with those of logical consequences. Determine consistencies and inconsistencies. Make adjustments to your philosophy as you believe appropriate.

▼ REFERENCES

Charles, C. M. (1992). *Building classroom discipline: From models to practice* (4th ed.). New York: Longman.

Dinkmeyer, D., & Dinkmeyer, D., Jr. (1976). Logical consequences: A key to the reduction of disciplinary problems. *Phi Delta Kappan, 57,* 664–666.

Dinkmeyer, D., & Dreikurs, R. (1963). *Encouraging children to learn.* New York: Hawthorne Books.

Dreikurs, R. (1960). *Fundamentals of Adlerian psychology.* Chicago: Alfred Adler Institute.

Dreikurs, R. (1968). *Psychology in the classroom: A manual for teachers* (2nd ed.). New York: Harper & Row.

Dreikurs, R., & Cassel, P. (1972). *Discipline without tears.* New York: Hawthorne Books.

Dreikurs, R., & Grey, L. (1968). *A new approach to discipline: Logical consequences.* New York: Hawthorne Books.

Dreikurs, R., & Grey, L. (1970). *A parent's guide to child discipline.* New York: Hawthorne Dutton.

Dreikurs, R., Grunwald, B. B., & Pepper, F. C. (1982). *Maintaining sanity in the classroom. Classroom management techniques* (2nd ed.). New York: Harper & Row.

Gordon, T. (1989). *Discipline that works: Promoting self-discipline in children.* New York: Penguin Books.

6

Transactional Analysis: Eric Berne and Thomas Harris

OBJECTIVES

This chapter is designed to help you
1. Understand how human ego-states develop and how they influence behavior.
2. Consider the evidence that our entire life's experience is recorded in the brain in the form of sounds, sights, other sensations, and feelings.
3. Determine which ego-state students are in when they make various statements.
4. Know the four life positions and how each is achieved.
5. Analyze verbal transactions and determine whether the transactions are compatible.
6. Learn how to remain in the Adult ego-state in transactions with students.
7. Understand the games students play that create problems in the classroom and how to react to them.

ASSUMPTIONS

1. Behavior is an outgrowth of information stored in the subconscious mind that has been learned by interacting with others.
2. Most of our experiences in life are recorded unaltered in our subconscious minds.
3. Behavior designed to control others is nearly automatic and comes from the Parent ego-state.
4. Exuberance and self-centeredness come from the Child ego-state.
5. Children can learn to be more responsible by learning how to let their Adult ego-state monitor both their Child and Parent and alter the automatic behaviors that would ordinarily occur.

Introduction

Eric Berne, a psychiatrist from California, is credited with originating transactional analysis, a method of dealing with behavioral disorders. In creating this new approach to psychiatry, Berne relied heavily on the research of Dr. Wilder Penfield. Penfield found that stimulating various parts of the brain with a mild electrical impulse evoked images of past experiences in the minds of patients. He concluded that all our life experiences are faithfully recorded in the subconscious mind and later influence how we behave.

Thomas Harris, as Director of Education at DeWitt State Hospital in Auburn, California, spent 10 years studying with Berne. *I'm OK—You're OK,* Harris's book about the principles of transactional analysis, spent more than a year on *The New York Times* best-seller list. The popularity of this book contributed to a widespread interest in transactional analysis, interest that led to its eventual use in the schools to manage students' behavior.

▼ Mr. Brown was a few minutes late returning to his classroom after being summoned to the office. When he got back, three students were dancing on the top of their desks while others were running around the room playing tag. Mr. Brown yelled at the students to go immediately to their desks and sit down. He then ordered the three students who were dancing on top of their desks to go to the principal's office immediately and indicated he would follow them shortly. He then lectured the rest of the class about their bad behavior and threatened to send them to the principal's office too if they were not sitting quietly reading when he returned. He then left the classroom.

▼ When Ms. Winger discovered that two students from different classes had turned in the same research paper, she asked them to meet with her after school. She told them that she was aware they had both turned in the same research paper and then waited for them to respond.

After 2 or 3 minutes of painful waiting, one of the students said, "This situation can't be helped. You make these assignments too hard. How can we be expected to do all you expect of us?"

Ms. Winger responded, "What is it you need to do about this situation? You need to figure out what needs to be done to rectify this problem and how similar difficulties can be prevented in the future. What do you suggest?"

What are the differences in these two episodes? Mr. Brown is angry and controlling, while Ms. Winger is under control and allows the students to think through the problem and how to solve it. Where do behavior patterns like these come from? According to Berne and Harris, they are based on behaviors that have been observed and/or enacted during previous experiences and faithfully recorded by the brain for future use. As children go through life, they accumulate experiences with other children as well as adults. Much of what they learn comes from interactions with parents and siblings. These interactions and the feelings associated with them are filed away in the brain for later use in similar situations.

Behavior and the Brain

This conception of the brain as an information storage system is supported by the work of neurosurgeon Wilder Penfield. During the course of brain surgery used to treat patients with focal epilepsy, Penfield conducted experiments in which he touched the temporal cortex of a patient's brain with a weak electric current transmitted through a galvanic probe (Penfield, 1952). The experiments were conducted under local anesthesia, and consequently the patients were fully conscious. Penfield found that by touching the brain with an electrode, he could produce what were clearly recollections of the patient's past. He concluded that all experiences of which we are consciously aware are "recorded" in detail in the brain and that they can be "played back" later with the clarity of the original recording. In Penfield's experiments, patients not only recalled various events but also experienced again the emotions and feelings that were associated with them. Penfield also concluded that each time he touched the brain with the electrode, a single recollection was evoked. Memories were not mixed, and generalizations were not created. Instead, a single memory was elicited. The following example, reported in Penfield's work and related by Harris (1967), illustrates the results of some of these experiments:

When the probe was placed in a specific location of the right temporal lobe of a patient, the individual reported that there was a piano playing somewhere. A second touch of the probe brought the response, "Someone's speaking to another." A name was mentioned. When the probe was touched to the brain a third time, the patient said, "Yes, *Oh Marie, Oh Marie!*—Someone is singing it." When the same area was stimulated a fourth time, the patient heard the same song and explained that it was the theme song of a certain radio program.

When a different place on the brain of a second patient was stimulated, the individual stated, "Something brings back a memory. I can see the Seven-Up Bottling Company . . . Harrison Bakery." When this patient was told that he was being stimulated but in fact was not, he reported no evoked memories.

In a third case, the superior surface of the right temporal lobe was stimulated within the fissure of Sylvius. The patient reported to be hearing a specific popular song being played as though by an orchestra. Repeated stimulation brought the same report. While the electrode was kept in place, the patient hummed along with the orchestra she was hearing.

Sometimes a single stimulation produced just an image. One patient, for example, saw a man walking a dog along a road near his home in the country. At other times the person reported just hearing a voice. On one occasion a patient whose brain was stimulated heard a voice she could not understand. When the probe was placed at approximately the same place again, she heard a voice distinctly calling, "Jimmie, Jimmie." Jimmie was the nickname of the young man she had recently married.

Penfield also concluded that the response of patients to the probe was involuntary. In one instance, a patient had a familiar experience appear in his consciousness on which he did not necessarily want to focus his attention. A song he had heard on a previous occasion went through his mind. He found himself becoming part of that occasion, which unfolded just as it had originally. He was experiencing a second time what he had experienced before. He had the sense of being both the actor and the audience, both subjectively experiencing the feelings he had experienced before and objectively watching himself re-experiencing them.

One of the most significant discoveries of Penfield was that feelings associated with past events are also faithfully stored in the brain, recorded in great detail. Apparently, the events in our lives are inextricably connected with feelings. One cannot be elicited without the other. When an image or experience was evoked by the probe, the individual experienced anew the original feelings associated with the image or experience. Thus, a memory evoked by the probe is not like a photograph or videotape. Instead, it is an exact reproduction of what the individual felt and understood as well as saw and heard.

To evoke an exact reproduction of previous experiences does not necessarily require one's brain to be probed. These experiences can also be stimulated by signals from the environment. For example, a 40-year-old woman was walking down the street one morning and, as she passed a music store, heard some music that created in her an overwhelming melancholy. She felt herself gripped by a feeling of sadness she could not understand. The intensity of it was almost unbearable. There was nothing in her conscious mind that could explain how she felt. Several days later she reported that she had continued to hum the tune over and over till suddenly, in a flash of recollection, she saw her mother sitting at the piano and heard her playing this song. The mother had died when the woman was just 5 years old, and the song had somehow been associated with her death. The woman now had the experience of reliving the same feelings she had at that time.

Good feelings can also be evoked. Most of us have had smells or sounds arouse pleasurable feelings that can be traced back to enjoyable childhood experiences. The smells associated with joyful trips to the old swimming hole during the heat of summer can bring back the same feelings one had as a youth during those special times. In people of a certain age, the smell of bread baking can often elicit feelings of love and contentment associated with coming home from school and eating their mother's fresh-baked bread.

The work of Penfield is cited as evidence that all our experiences are permanently recorded in our brains, to be called forth as needed by stimuli in the environment. The responses stimulated by these recorded messages are not intentional. Instead, they appear automatically and are ordinarily carried through faithfully unless the person makes a conscious effort to modify them.

The Three Ego-States

An ego-state is "a consistent pattern of feeling and experience directly related to a corresponding consistent pattern of behavior" (Berne, 1966). An individual's ego-states are developed from life experiences and retained both consciously and unconsciously in the brain. Many behaviors appear as if from nowhere, without any conscious thought. Even so, they are well articulated and purposeful and appear to have been carefully formulated. Displaying these behavior patterns is somewhat like automatically turning on a tape machine: Information recorded long ago is simply played back. But words and feelings too are expressed as they were once learned, and they require little or no conscious effort to produce. According to the principles of transactional analysis, all people have three ego-states that form the basis of their behavior: the Parent, the Child, and the Adult.

THE PARENT

The Parent ego-state is a huge collection of recordings of unquestioned or imposed external events experienced by the person during the first 5 years of life. This recorded information includes the pronouncements made by real parents or parent substitutes. Everything these individuals are observed to do is also recorded in the Parent ego-state of the child.

Because these experiences are recorded during the early years of life, they are unedited. Young children have no way of knowing how to modify what they experience. Therefore, if parents are malicious or hostile toward their children or toward one another, their conduct is recorded as it occurred without the benefit of interpretation. Young children will also record the terror they feel as they observe the very people on whom they depend for sustenance and love battle with one another or abuse them. There is no way for children to deal with extenuating circumstances. For example, abusive parents may have personal problems unrelated to their children; if the children understood these problems as an adult might, they could better interpret their parents' behavior. But young children have no such capacity.

The Parent ego-state is the repository of all the admonitions, rules, and laws issued by parents and other adults during the course of children's early life. In addition to spoken words, such things as tone of voice, facial expressions, and physical contact are also recorded. Included in this set of experiences are the many thousands of *nos* and *don'ts* with which children are ordinarily bombarded as they attempt to express their native curiosity and understand their world. No amount of new experiences can erase these recordings. They will always be part of the person's history. For example, positive, nurturing experiences in adulthood will not change the reality of abuses in childhood. However, once the individual has new experiences, either can be selected as reminders to guide transactions with others (Woollams & Brown, 1979).

The Parent ego-state also contains the smiles, hugs, pride, and delight of parents, grandparents, teachers, and other important adults—and the contexts in which the approval was given. These positive experiences are important components of children's growing-up years. Their sense of well-being depends on receiving them in abundance.

As children grow, they make a mental record of the complicated, well-intentioned platitudes and precepts to which they are subjected—pronouncements of which they have only a vague understanding:

Remember to wear your coat when it's cold.
Don't go out at night alone.
Associate only with people of your own kind.
Never tell lies.
Pay your bills.

Clean up your plate.

Eat your dessert last.

Do unto others as you would have them do unto you.

Do unto others before they do unto you.

The idle mind is the devil's workshop.

You will be judged by the company you keep.

You have to dress the part.

You can never trust a cop.

Haste makes waste.

These admonitions can be judged by adults as good or bad when interpreted with a reasonable ethical standard. Children, however, record them as truth. After all, they come from their source of security, the people on whom they depend for survival. Once these bits of advice are recorded, they are available for immediate replay, and they exert a powerful influence all through a person's life. They determine whether our behavior will be permissive or coercive. We tend to internalize them rigidly and depend on them as patterns for dealing with other people in most situations. The internal Parent ego-state serves the same purpose as our physical parents served in protecting us as young children. It continues to issue warnings and admonitions to protect us from harm.

Sometimes messages received from parents are inconsistent. One parent or parent substitute may contradict another. When faced with such contradiction, children suppress the Parent so that it has less influence on their behavior. There may also be data stored in the Parent that are no longer valid but are heeded anyway. For example, a child was once told by her mother never to put her hat on a table or her coat on a bed. She followed this admonition throughout her life and insisted that her own children follow the same practice. Finally, when her mother was very old, she asked why she was told never to put a hat on a table or a coat on a bed. Because, her mother replied, some of the neighborhood children years ago were infested with lice (Harris, 1967).

THE CHILD

While the Parent is being recorded, the Child ego-state is being recorded simultaneously. This recording consists of the responses children make to what they see and hear. Because children have little or no understanding of the meaning of language during their early years, most of their reactions are feelings. During this time, children are faced with numerous uncompromising demands with which they must comply, regardless of how they feel or what they want to do. To receive parents' approval, children must satisfy expectations. This conflict between the desires of children and the demands of parents creates a good deal of frustration for children. On the basis of these feelings, children often conclude that they are "not OK." Even children of "good" parents carry a burden of not being "OK." So it is not hard to imagine how much heavier an emotional load abused children have to bear.

Like the Parent, the Child ego-state also strongly influences people's reactions as they engage in transactions (give-and-take verbal exchanges) with others. Many situations similar to those experienced in childhood have the power to arouse the same feelings. The original frustration, rejection, or abandonment can surface again as individuals relive earlier experiences. They may respond by becoming withdrawn. They may throw tantrums. They may lose control emotionally, letting anger dominate reason. This is called natural anger. Anger may also be expressed in an adapted form. In this case anger is interrupted by thinking or fear. It is ordinarily expressed in a socially appropriate way and is generally effective in setting boundaries and maintaining contact with others (Garcia, 1995).

Fortunately, there is a more positive side to the Child ego-state. The Child also contains such positive traits as creativity and curiosity. The Child is filled with the happy first discoveries of life: the first taste of homemade ice cream, the first puppy, the way a cereal bowl bounces across the floor when thrown from a high chair, the feel of a kitten's fur against your face, the warm water in your first bath. The delightful feelings these experiences create are also recorded. These "OK" feelings may also be relived in day-to-day transactions. Unfortunately, in many of us the "not OK" feelings predominate. For this reason, Harris (1967) concludes that most of us have a "not OK" Child inside us.

The Child functions in two basic ways: the Natural Child and the Adapted Child. The Natural Child expresses herself or himself spontaneously without concern for the reactions of the parents of the world. The Adapted Child, on the other hand, behaves as if a parent were watching or listening, and consequently is much more restrained. The Adapted Child may either be compliant, industrious, or rebellious, or may act in any other way that has a payoff with parent figures (Woollams & Brown, 1979).

THE ADULT

Until the age of about 10 months, children are bound by their own ineptness. They respond mainly to external demands and stimulations. After this time, however, they are able to move around and more successfully manipulate their surroundings. Eventually, they learn that they are able to do things that arise from their own awareness and original thought. When this realization occurs, the Adult ego-state starts to emerge. The Adult grows as children find out for themselves the difference between the "taught concepts" of the Parent and the "felt concepts" of the Child. The outgrowth of this process is the development of "thought concepts."

The Adult during these early years is fragile and subject to injury and distortion, which may occur when too many commands come from the Parent or too many fears emanate from the Child. Without such interference, children would be able to tell the difference between life as it was taught and demonstrated to them, life as they felt it or wished it or fantasized it, and life as they figured it out for themselves. If it is not excessively distorted, the Adult can examine rules from the Parent to determine their trustworthiness and current applicability and then accept or reject them. The Adult can also examine the Child to ascertain whether feelings stored there are acceptable in present circumstances or are just responses to obsolete dictates of the Parent. This examination does not automatically erase the data stored in either the Parent or the Child ego-state. Instead, it provides a way to restrict their influence. For example, a young child may initially experience fear of snakes or anger at not being allowed to play with them. A later awareness that most snakes are not dangerous or that parental caution may have been warranted will not erase that fear or anger. However, in the Adult ego-state, the child can choose just to turn it off.

The day-to-day task of the Adult is to monitor both Parent and Child and ensure that the behavior each may promote is valid and useful under present conditions. It tests the rules and information of the Parent to determine whether they can be wisely used. It also determines when the feelings of the Child can be appropriately expressed. People have two major ways of organizing and dealing with the information from their thinking. One of these is intuitive and creative, and the other is rational. A fully functioning person uses both intuitive and logical thinking in ways that combine and enhance the benefits of both types (Woollams & Brown, 1979).

▼ Betty Jane had left Ms. Tobler's cooking class every day that week without cleaning up her work station. She pretended to be cleaning, and then when the bell rang, she dashed out the door before Ms. Tobler could stop her. Ms. Tobler decided that she would make a point of standing by the door on Monday to intercept Betty Jane. When Monday's class ended, Betty Jane saw Ms. Tobler by the door and quickly cleaned up her area and left with the rest of the class. Ms. Tobler, who had been watching her, decided to let her go. On Tuesday, Ms. Tobler again stood by the door, and again Betty Jane cleaned up her area. Ms. Tobler decided that Betty Jane had changed her ways. However, on Wednesday, while Ms. Tobler busied herself answering the questions of other class members, Betty Jane again left a mess and slipped out of the room unobserved. Ms. Tobler made up her mind to somehow confront Betty Jane and so on the following day pretended not to be paying attention as the students began to leave at the end of the period. She watched Betty Jane out of the corner of her eye and could see that Betty Jane was also scrutinizing her. Ms. Tobler deliberately turned her back

Ms. Tobler insists Betty Jane clean up her work station before leaving class.

for a few moments and then walked toward the door. Betty Jane was on her way through the door when Ms. Tobler stopped her and brought her back to her work station. The area was covered with cookie crumbs and drips of batter from the day's baking lesson. Ms. Tobler asked, "Betty Jane, what do you need to do now to make sure that your work station is as it should be when you leave class?"

In dealing with Betty Jane, Ms. Tobler acted correctly in terms of transactional analysis theory. She responded primarily from the Adult ego-state, approaching the situation rationally and helping Betty Jane to think through the problem herself.

Had Ms. Tobler responded from her Parent ego-state, she might have scolded Betty Jane: "I'm sick and tired of your sneaking out of class without cleaning up your work station, Betty Jane. When are you going to learn to keep your area neat and tidy like the other students?" or "Look at the mess you have left here. You are the messiest student I have ever had in class."

Had Ms. Tobler responded from her Child ego-state, she would probably have complained petulantly: "Betty Jane, how come you always leave this mess for me to clean up?" or "Betty Jane, you make me so mad. I'm not going to let you do any more cooking for the rest of the week!"

It is easy to see that responses expressed from the Parent or Child ego-states are not helpful. Students will usually fail to improve their behavior when approached in this way. Yet it is a very common way for teachers to interact with their students. Greater success can be achieved when teachers understand the nature of the transactions they make with students and how their own behavior patterns can determine the way their students respond. If teachers learn to respond from the Adult ego-state, fewer discipline problems will occur.

The Four Life Positions

If the Adult is not unduly subdued by abuse, it will help to make appropriate modifications in both the Parent and the Child. For example, the Adult will help the Child learn to express feelings safely that may otherwise be communicated in socially unacceptable ways. When these adjustments are successfully made, children are able to make fruitful transitions from the control-bound existence they have experienced as children to autonomous self-regulated living as adults. This transition is critical to becoming a fully functioning person. Failure to make this transition creates problems that are resistant to correction. The individual then may become locked into a behavior pattern that prohibits good personal and social adjustment. Discipline problems may be the result.

Harris (1967) identifies four possible outgrowths of this transition process, which he calls life positions (see Table 6.1):

- I'm Not OK—You're OK
- I'm Not OK—You're Not OK
- I'm OK—You're Not OK
- I'm OK—You're OK

TABLE 6.1
Life positions.

	Life Experience	Results	Formation of Life Position
I'm not OK—You're OK	No stroking	Life adjustment hindered	Unconscious through feelings
I'm not OK—You're not OK	Limited stroking 1st year; none thereafter. Excessive punishment	Extreme withdrawal	Unconscious through feelings
I'm OK—You're not OK	Brutal battering	Self-stroking, blames others, lacks conscience	Unconscious through feelings
I'm OK—You're OK	Consistent stroking	Fully functioning personality	Conscious through thought and faith

Source: Harris, 1967.

I'M NOT OK—YOU'RE OK

I'm Not OK—You're OK is the universal life position of early childhood. Because children are much smaller than adults as well as much more inept, they naturally perceive that they are Not OK. If they are helped through stroking (the process of positive approval) to feel good about themselves and gradually appreciate the genuine contributions they are able to make, they will eventually feel OK about themselves. If they are unsuccessful, Not OK feelings will persist and hinder their life adjustment. Children's perception of themselves is not based on their own assessment. They depend on others to provide this information. Children lack the mental acuity and experience to form an accurate picture of themselves. Sensing this lack, they constantly question adults about their performance in various situations in an effort to assess their own worth. Because of their inherent insecurity, they require a lot of stroking and recognition. Without assurance from adults, children usually conclude that they are unacceptable and unable.

The emphasis on social recognition as the source of positive personal development is a major difference between transactional analysis and the work of Sigmund Freud. Freud (1915) believed that sex is the basis of human struggles in life. Adler and others believed that feelings of inferiority are more critical adjustment factors (Harris, 1967). Although both Freud's psychoanalytic theory and transactional analysis focus on the subconscious life of human beings, there is another important difference between the theories. Freud believed that experiences stored in the subconscious mind have unalterable effects on human behavior. It thus becomes necessary to bring these subconscious experiences to consciousness, where they can be understood. Once understood, they no longer have debilitating influences. Adler, Berne, Harris, and others who promote transactional analysis believe that behavior is driven by unconscious experiences.

However, through conscious thought, these behaviors can be altered before they are expressed. Unlike Freud, Adler and his associates believe that behavior can be controlled and directed.

I'M NOT OK—YOU'RE NOT OK

Sometimes children who have experienced only a limited amount of stroking during the first year of their lives later receive none. Life, which in the first year had some comforts, now has nothing to offer them. If this lack of approval continues throughout the second year, children conclude not only that I'm Not OK but also that You're Not OK. The Adult ego-state stops developing, and the child, seeing no hope, gives up. Such individuals commonly end up in mental institutions in a state of extreme withdrawal, hoping to achieve the kind of stroking they received as infants.

Once this life position has been established, all experiences in life are selectively interpreted to support it. These people are very hard to help because when they conclude that their parents are Not OK, they apply the same conclusion to all other people and reject stroking even though it may be genuinely given.

I'M OK—YOU'RE NOT OK

If children are brutalized long enough by parents whom they initially felt to be OK, they will move to the life position of I'm OK—You're Not OK. This position is decided in the second or third year of life and is resistant to change. These children are able to achieve an OK feeling through self-stroking. They are apparently able to realize that their parents will not provide stroking for them. In addition, they realize that despite their own inabilities as young children, they are better than their abusive parents. They survive in the face of extreme rejection and physical pain. This experience promotes hatred and a determination to strike back. This hostility is what sustains them. Because their treatment has been so bad, they lack the capacity for introspection; they cannot see their own role in what happens to them. They become persons devoid of moral conscience, who believe that whatever wrong they do is the fault of others. They are, therefore, extremely unwilling to change, because those who try to help them are seen to be the same as their parents. Essentially, there are no OK people in their lives. These children are likely to develop criminal psychopathologies.

I'M OK—YOU'RE OK

The fourth life position, I'm OK—You're OK, is dramatically different from the other three positions. Children who reach this life position are able to deal realistically with life and achieve a greater sense of fulfillment. The first three positions are based on feelings. The fourth position is founded on thought, faith, and the ability to act without the certainty of outcomes. These children are fortunate to have had repeated exposure to situations in which they could prove, to themselves, their own worth and the worth of others. The I'm OK—You're OK life position means that no one is inferior and everyone is entitled to the opportunity to be treated as an equal and to have his or her basic needs met, including the need for strokes. A stroke is a unit of attention that provides stimulation to an individual. Humans fail to develop properly without stroking. Strokes should be both external and internal. External strokes, or strokes from another person, are necessary to become an OK person. Internal strokes can also be a positive source of stimulation. This form of stroking consists of old memories, new fantasies or ideas, movement, and other forms of self-stimulation. We all have a collection of strokes stored in our memories, both our favorite positive ones as well as negative ones (Woollams & Brown, 1979).

Infants are potentially OK at birth because they have within them all the resources necessary to experience OKness in themselves or others. All that is needed is that they be treated as OK in response to their various expressions. Children need to be considered OK by others just for being human, regardless of how they act or what assets they bring with them. Love needs to be unconditional (Parry, 1979).

Analyzing Transactions

It is a fundamental premise of transactional analysis that all individuals need to feel adequate. Both the acceptable and unacceptable behaviors of children are designed to ascertain how others feel about them. From the reactions to their behavior, they decide how to think about themselves. Teachers, therefore, need to have an affirming attitude even toward students who display excessive misbehavior. They should apply stroking techniques: They must give attention and affection. They must learn to appeal to children's Adult ego-state by approaching them with their own Adult. And they must affirm the positive aspects of children's Parent and Child. Stroking promotes rational thought, which supports the Adult, affirms the positive aspects of restraint coming from the Parent, and facilitates the creativity that is characteristic of the Child.

RECOGNIZING EGO-STATES

Using transactional analysis effectively in the classroom to eliminate learning disruptions depends on how well teachers understand the principles of transactional analysis as well as how perceptive they are in determining their own internal state. It also depends on how skilled they are in discovering the internal states of their students and how adeptly they interact with them. How can you tell which internal state a student is operating from? Part of the answer is revealed in the verbal information that is transmitted—that is, what the student says. The rest comes from nonverbal cues. Nonverbal cues include facial expressions, gestures, and voice inflections. Evidence that the Parent is in control may be hands on hips, arms folded across the chest, tongue-clucking, sighing, pointing the index finger, head-wagging, a furrowed brow, pursed lips, a tapping foot, or a look of disgust. Confirmation that the Child is in charge may be tears, temper tantrums, complaining, pouting, the quivering lip, shrugging shoulders, giggling, squirming, laughter, or downcast eyes. The Adult ego-state is manifested as smiles of approval and looks that ask for more information.

Both verbal information and nonverbal cues should be considered in making an assessment of which ego-state is active. Taken together, they shed light on one another. Often, verbal information has more than one possible meaning. For example, the question "Where are my shoes?" coming from the Adult is just a request for information. There would be no innuendo in the voice. However, these same words spoken by the Parent could suggest that the person to whom the question is directed has stolen the shoes.

The verbal expressions of the Parent usually demand, command, and reprimand. They are designed to control and direct. They also contain criticisms and labels. The following examples show a Parent talking:

1. Pick up those books now!
2. Go back to your seat. You don't have my permission to sharpen your pencil!
3. I can't see why you continue to act like that.
4. You never remember to turn in your homework.
5. You are just like your brother/sister when it comes to cleaning up your messes in the lab.
6. How can anyone be so lazy?
7. You are just being ridiculous.
8. When are you going to stop blowing your nose in class?
9. You ought to be ashamed of yourself, the way you carry on.
10. You're always getting into trouble.

The verbal clues expressed by the Child usually take the form of uncontrolled emotion. They may be expressions of great exhilaration or declarations of uninhibited disgust; they may lack either concern or resistance. The Child may make such statements as:

1. I ain't gonna pick up my tools.
2. Why can't I go to lunch? Everyone else is.
3. Who cares about your old rules?
4. I want my ice cream now!
5. When I grow up, I'm going to be a millionaire.
6. I want the biggest one.
7. Give me that piece of cake. Yours is bigger than mine.
8. My dad can whip your dad.
9. My bike is better than yours.
10. I guess so.

One can tell that the Adult is in control by listening for the following kinds of questions and statements:

1. How much time will it take you to finish the job?
2. How does the job you did today compare with the one you did last week?
3. I think I understand what you mean.
4. When will you present your plan to your chemistry teacher?
5. I think that what you have in mind will be possible.
6. What do you think the consequences will be for failing to do your homework?
7. When do you plan to start on your experiment?

8. On what do you plan to base your decision?
9. In my opinion, you would be better off looking at more of the possible consequences before you make up your mind.
10. I have no idea what will happen if you don't show up for class.

AVOIDING INCOMPATIBLE TRANSACTIONS

When teachers are armed with clues to understanding ego-states, they can more effectively analyze transactions and help students improve their behavior. They can also more insightfully monitor their own transactions and alter how they respond to their students. Some transactions are incompatible—that is, they take place between individuals in different ego-states. These are the transactions about which teachers must be most concerned because they produce the most trouble. A student may, for instance, say to the teacher, "How am I going to finish this assignment by tomorrow?" The teacher could respond, "How much have you got left to do?" or "How can I help you finish your assignment on time?" These are Adult-to-Adult responses. The teacher could say, however, "Why don't you try working for a change?" In this case, the teacher's Parent would be making the response. Incompatible transactions (sometimes called ulterior transactions or crossed transactions) create conflict and impede students' work; they also erode student–teacher relationships.

Sometimes crossed transactions occur when one person receives the words of another and reads negative intent into them. For example, a student may ask, "When is this assignment due?" The teacher might respond sarcastically, "Why? Do you plan to turn it in late?" Another student could ask, "Should we bring our textbooks to class tomorrow even though we are having a test?" The teacher might reply, "Why? Do you plan to use it to cheat on the test?"

Let's analyze a lengthier transaction. Suppose that a student is visiting quietly with other students nearby. Assume that the class has been given time to work on a written assignment. Other members of the class are busy writing.

Teacher	Garn, you couldn't be done with your assignment already. Don't you have something more to do?
Garn	Yeah, too bad, but I do.
Teacher	Well, you had better get started on it. You have to turn it in at the end of the class. Why are you still sitting there when you have time to work? A lot of the work you have turned in lately isn't very good. Maybe if you'd spend time on it, you could make it look more decent.
Garn	Well, it's about as good as this class. How can we be expected to do an assignment like this when everything is so vague in here?
Teacher	You have been told repeatedly that you can't learn the content of this course unless you listen and take notes. You spend all your time talking with other students. It's no wonder you don't know what to do.
Garn	Yeah, well, this course is a waste of time. When are we ever going to use this stuff? I get bored to death in here.

Teacher	If you ever plan to go to college, you'd better sit up and listen. They won't put up with this kind of behavior in college.
Garn	Who says I'm going to college, anyway?

This episode illustrates how crossed transactions promote conflict. The teacher is acting out of her Parent, whereas the student is responding from his Child. When the teacher tries to get Garn to work, she assumes that he is lazy rather than just in need of help. She believes that she has to order him to work rather than ascertain why he is not working. Even when he claims that he cannot do the assignment because he is confused, she blames him for his predicament instead of providing the help he needs. Although what she claims might be true, confronting Garn in this manner will not help solve the problem. It would have been better to make an Adult response: "Garn, I see you haven't started your writing assignment yet. Is there some part of it you don't understand? I'd be happy to help you if you'd like." With this approach, the teacher avoids reading anything into the situation. Rather, she determines whether valid problems exist that need to be corrected. Instead of being helpful, however, the teacher scolds and judges Garn. He in turn displays an "I don't care" attitude. In reality, he has little choice. He cannot appear to be interested in the class when the teacher is so critical of his performance. It is inconceivable for Garn to try as hard as he can and yet fail to receive approval. It is safer for him to confront the teacher. In this way he can prove to himself that she is the cause of his poor performance. He probably believes that he could be successful if it were not for the teacher. The teacher fosters this belief when she interacts with him out of her Parent ego-state.

Now let's look at this same situation as it would be played out if the teacher handled it from the Adult ego-state:

Teacher	Garn, I see you haven't started your writing assignment yet. Is there some part of it you don't understand?
Garn	I don't understand any part of it. This class is so confusing. Why can't things be explained so I can understand them?
Teacher	Let's look at page 254 in your textbook. See that diagram of the Krebs cycle? Now look at the accompanying page. There you have an explanation of the chemical reactions that take place.
Garn	Oh, now I see. I never noticed this before.
Teacher	Have you been reading the textbook much during the year, Garn?
Garn	No, not much. I don't seem to get anything from it.
Teacher	When do you usually try to read your textbook?
Garn	I do it during class mostly.
Teacher	Are there things that happen in class that disturb your reading?
Garn	Well, some of the other kids talk to me while I'm trying to read.
Teacher	Where would you like to sit so this won't happen any more?
Garn	I guess I could take a seat up by your desk.

In this example, the teacher stays in the Adult ego-state. She does not try to correct Garn directly. Instead, by asking questions that both give Garn information and allow him to see his alternatives so that he can make responsible choices, she tries to get him to think through his problems and change his behavior himself. When the teacher stays in the Adult, students are encouraged to respond in their Adult. In this example, the student initially makes Child statements. When the teacher avoids making Parent responses, which the student's statements tend to encourage, the student is eventually drawn into using his Adult as well.

Even though it is advisable for teachers to act in the Adult and encourage children to do the same, there are times when Parent-to-Parent or Child-to-Child interactions are appropriate. These transactions do not create conflict and may be productive. For example, a student who has just won first prize in a contest may exclaim, "Wow, look what I did!" This is a Child statement. The teacher may respond from the Child and say, "Look at you! You took first place!" These Child-oriented interactions provide students with a healthy outlet for this part of their personality.

The Parent can also be constructive. Suppose that a student suddenly proclaims, "I'm not going to be able to finish this project here at school. I guess I will have to take it home and finish it over the weekend." The teacher could reply, "Yes, that's right. You'll need quite a lot more time to do this project right." Both of these statements have a Parent orientation, but they do not contradict one another. No conflict is produced. And the result is positive for the student as well as the teacher.

Transactional Analysis in the Schools

To some teachers it isn't apparent how transactional analysis can be effectively used for disciplinary purposes in the schools. This is in part due to the fact that it does not encourage teachers to actively correct student misbehavior like many discipline approaches do. Other discipline strategies commonly focus on actions teachers should take when students misbehave. With transactional analysis, teachers focus less on misbehavior and more on teaching students how to regulate themselves. Teachers are also encouraged to apply transactional analysis principles as they interact with their students. The role of the teacher is to stay in the Adult ego-state and teach students to apply transactional analysis principles as they interact with each other. Teachers also need to learn how to deal with the games students play as they try to cover up their Not OK feelings.

STAYING IN THE ADULT EGO-STATE

Because the Adult develops later than either the Parent or the Child, it seems to be in the process of catching up throughout life. In addition, Parent and Child occupy the "primary circuits" in the brain and tend to respond automatically (Harris, 1967); a conscious effort must be made to enter the Adult ego-state. It is therefore helpful when trying to stay in the Adult to become sensitive to Parent and Child signals. Child signals usually are accompanied by aroused feelings, feelings ordinarily associated with being Not OK. Just being aware that the Not OK Child is asserting itself is helpful. When you can attribute anger to your Child and know that your Adult can alter the course of this anger, you are better able to modify childish expressions. It is possible to detach yourself mentally from the Child and analyze it, quickly dousing the fire that might otherwise flare up and burn uncontrollably.

Parent signals can be monitored in a similar way. It is helpful to decide in advance how the Adult plans to deal with the tendencies of the Parent that automatically appear. For example, the Adult may interrogate the Parent, asking it a series of hard questions. The biting, irrational orientation of the Parent can be subdued if it is forced to respond to questions such as

- Where did this idea come from?
- Is it true?
- What evidence is there?
- What can happen if this response is made?
- Does this response really apply to this situation?
- Is this action appropriate in this situation?

Managing the Parent in this way short-circuits its automatic expression. The strength of both Parent and Child lies in their unconscious manifestation. They require no thought. They have been recorded in the past and stored in the subconscious mind, ready to be expressed when appropriate environmental stimuli appear. But if these automatic behaviors are scrutinized, consciously and rationally, their expression can be modified or eliminated.

TEACHING TRANSACTIONAL ANALYSIS TO CHILDREN

Obviously, if teachers intend to use the principles of transactional analysis, they must understand them and know how to apply them successfully in their own lives. In the classroom, teachers must not only use transactional analysis principles while interacting with students but also teach their students to use transactional analysis in regulating their verbal transactions with others. Children also need to understand transactional analysis and know how to apply it with their teachers as well as fellow students. Concepts that could be taught to students include

1. The three ego-states (Child, Parent, and Adult)
2. What it means to be trapped in the Parent or the Child
3. The four life positions
4. The basic need of human beings to feel capable and accepted
5. How to treat others so that they feel accepted and capable (stroking)
6. How to analyze transactions
7. How to increase the power of the Adult and more reasonably regulate the influence of Parent and Child in transactions with others

One of the goals of teaching transactional analysis in the schools is to help students achieve an OK life position. This is best accomplished once teachers have acquired a true sense of their own autonomy and are inclined to also provide students greater personal autonomy in the classroom. Being autonomous involves children not only achieving personal control and self-direction over many classroom activities but also accepting their own humanity and becoming comfortable with themselves. Autonomous people accept others wholeheartedly and delight in associations with them. Teachers can promote this attribute by demonstrating warmth and genuine caring for students and by having meaningful and stimulating interchanges with them. Students must be helped to feel important and accepted and enabled to express their thoughts and feelings freely.

Teachers should promote trusting relationships with their students. Students need to feel secure in the classroom and free from the requirement to defend themselves for who they are and what they do. They must also be unfettered by excessive dependency on their teachers. Their independence should include the capacity to give themselves credit for their abilities and achievements without requiring others to validate what they do. Students must be free to satisfy their essential needs reciprocally with others and in the process develop close ties with them. They should learn to live in the here and now, gaining a sense of satisfaction with life in the present without having to make reference to the past or future to achieve a sense of fulfillment. In personal transactions, students must learn to use the appropriate ego-state. To live more successfully within the classroom, they need to reduce the impact of their coercive Parent ego-state, free their Child for more open communication, and strengthen their Adult to improve the quality of interpersonal transactions (Downing, 1987).

Games Students Play

If teachers are to improve their transactions with students and help students cultivate better relationships, they should be aware that students play certain behavioral games. Games involve an ongoing series of complementary, ulterior transactions that progress toward a well-defined, predictable outcome (Berne, 1964). Students play these games for a reason—ordinarily to cover up Not OK feelings or to excuse themselves for not improving their behavior. Games are learned systems that are substitute ways of getting strokes and require the individual to discount himself or herself and/or another person (Woollams & Brown, 1979). But the people who play these games are essentially innocent in the sense that they are not fully aware of what they are doing. The subconscious behavior patterns of the Child and the Parent form the basis for most of the games, and the feeling of being Not OK provides the motivation.

Games are usually played for the benefit of the person who initiates them and at the expense of someone else. At other times, both parties benefit from the game and need one another to successfully play. Game players want to stimulate others to play so that they can receive their payoff: a solution to their problems, some stroking, or an excuse for themselves.

To keep students from playing these games, a teacher must first analyze the games and discover what the students' motives are. What are students hoping to gain from the game? Are they in need of stroking? From whom do they want stroking? It is also useful to determine the ego-state from which the students are operating and the ego-states of the teachers to whom they are appealing.

Once the game is understood, the teacher must refuse to play it. In making this refusal, the teacher suppresses the automatic reactions of Child and Parent and responds from the Adult ego-state exclusively. Games are played by the Child and Parent components of our personalities. When Adult responses are made, students will more readily see these games for what they are and avoid using them in the future.

Children should not be left without support when their games have been analyzed and exposed. The need behind their game playing is still unfulfilled. Students require stroking at this point. In fact, children require a lot of affirmation. They need to feel accepted and acceptable. When these needs are more fully realized, students will be far less active game players.

Finally, students need to be socially successful without playing games. They need alternative ways of responding that do not involve manipulating others. They need to learn to solve their own problems without creating games to excuse their own perceived ineptness. Students need encouragement from their teachers while they are learning to make these new responses. A good deal more stroking will be necessary.

The following list, drawn up by Ernst (1972), describes some of the games students and teachers play in school:

Uproar.   The primary goal of Uproar is to stimulate the teacher's Parent. Students try to provoke negative reactions by creating various distractions: talking out, turning around in their seats, rattling papers, dropping books on the floor, coming in late, drumming on the desk, clicking their pens, snapping their fingers, kicking their neighbors, or trying to sidetrack the lecture. When students succeed in getting the teacher to rebuke them, they claim that they are being picked on unfairly. This perceived persecution justifies continued provocations.

Clown.   Students who play the game of Clown entertain the whole class and are admired by their peers for their daring. It is difficult even for the teacher not to like them; their antics may appear playful and even enjoyable. However, when their games get out of hand, teachers who feel that they are losing control of the class may rebuke them. Most of the time clowns perform for the benefit of their peers, often making teachers the butt of their jokes and trying to avoid being discovered by them.

Stupid.   Students who play Stupid also need an audience. They try to appear dumb, affecting mannerisms that make them appear dim-witted. They become quite skilled in this portrayal, pretending not to know how to do assignments correctly and asking questions no one else would ask. They may also try to appear clumsy or inept. Their object is to get their peers to call them stupid—that is, to give them attention, even if the attention is insulting.

Chip on the Shoulder.   In Chip on the Shoulder, students who are asked to perform in some way fear that they may appear stupid to their peers, so they choose to be belligerent rather than run this risk. Their behavior is often interpreted as hostile. If they can create discord, they can easily avoid the possible failure they associate with a teacher's demands. They produce a smoke screen to cover their Not OK feelings.

Make Me.   Children who refuse to complete assignments may be playing the game of Make Me. These students refuse to budge unless extreme force is used. They try to provoke a clash of wills, daring the teacher: "Just try and make me do it." They may flatly state that they will not cooperate or just sit with a look of defiance on their faces.

Schlemiel.   Students playing Schlemiel, the physical equivalent of Stupid, give the appearance of being klutzes. They deliberately bump into others, knock things over, or drop things. They often make a mess of others' belongings and then lamely apologize, "It was an accident" or "I was only trying to help." They are always quite willing to help clean up the mess they make, but they usually succeed only in making matters worse.

Let's Find Out.   What can you do in school to create a little excitement? Discovering the answer to this question is the purpose of Let's Find Out ("Let's find out what would happen if . . . "). Students who play this game are always thinking up little pranks they can pull to stir things up. Usually, the participants try to pull their pranks without getting caught. They may, for example, throw a firecracker into the principal's office after planning how to escape undetected. They may also steal or vandalize school property.

Cops and Robbers.   Cops and Robbers requires more confrontation than Let's Find Out. Students who play this game try to see how far they can go without suffering any consequences. They may, for example, violate the school's no-smoking rule or dress code in front of their teachers, daring them to enforce these rules. They play "robbers" and try to entice their teachers to play "cops." Most teachers willingly play the "cop" game of Now I've Got You when students so blatantly flout authority.

I Want Out.   Some students complain that they cannot stand school and want to get out as soon as they can. They often are heard exclaiming how much they hate school. In reality, they would prefer to remain in school. But they match their actions to their words, and their games often get them expelled. As they leave the school, they usually explain to others how happy they are to be leaving and how much more exciting and desirable a life they can now live. After they are expelled, however, they are often found back in school wandering the hallways and attending some classes. Commonly, when these students are on the brink of suspension, they beg school authorities to give them just one more chance. If they fail in this quest, they may spend some of their suspension at school rather than at home or on the streets.

Sweetheart.   Sweetheart is a game played by "sugar-coating" a hurt intended for someone else. This game ordinarily starts with innocent-sounding comments. These remarks, however, are cutting and are intended as insults. Such comments come from the Child ego-state:

"I'm only telling you this because I'm your friend."
"It is really nice that they make some things in larger sizes now, don't you think?"
"I really admire the way you don't mind being around those people."
"I don't care what the others say about you, I like you."

Why Don't You . . . ?—Yes, But. . . .   This game is played to excuse oneself and evade responsibility. It consists of creating an extensive list of excuses in an effort to explain away any suggestion that problems could have been solved by taking some appropriate action. For example,

Teacher	Where is your homework assignment, Peggy? It was due yesterday.
Peggy	I didn't have time to do it. I had to work the last two nights.
Teacher	The assignment was given 2 weeks ago. You have had plenty of time to do it.
Peggy	When I don't work I have to tend my little brother. While I'm with him I can't do any homework.
Teacher	Why don't you tell your parents that you need more time to do your schoolwork?
Peggy	They would just tell me to finish my assignments at school before I come home.
Teacher	Why don't you do that?
Peggy	You can't study at school; there's too much noise.

Late Paper Game

▼   Jay failed to turn in his paper for his English class. Ms. Catanni reminded him that it had been due the week before. Jay said, "Gee, Ms. Catanni, I'm really sorry I didn't get my paper to you. I'll bring it tomorrow." Jay did not come to school for 3 days. When he finally did come to his English class, Ms. Catanni reminded him that he needed to turn it in as soon as possible. Jay responded, "I hope I can finish it by Friday. My uncle died last week, and the whole family has really been broken up about it." Ms. Catanni said, "Take your time, Jay. I know these things sometimes take a long time to get over." Jay has succeeded in getting the paper deadline put off indefinitely. His teacher believes that he has a legitimate excuse, but he is just playing games. Sometimes students even get their peers or siblings to falsely verify their excuses.

Buddy.   Teachers also initiate games. Buddy is one such game, sometimes started when teachers have an overwhelming need to be liked by their students. Teachers who play this game try to be pals with their students. They talk to selected students about their private lives and encourage these students to do the same. Commonly, they try to befriend the most popular students, giving them special privileges not available to others, accepting late assignments from them, and including them in choice activities. Other students usually view such teachers as wimps and their student friends as brownnosers.

Dealing With Students' Games

What should teachers do when students play games with them? First, they should determine the purpose of the game. Usually, these games are played to bolster students when they are feeling Not OK. Often, people who are Not OK want to avoid appearing inept and approach others with chips on their shoulders. Sometimes, because they are insecure about what they can do, they deliberately try to appear dumb in the hope that others will not expect much of them. Sometimes, they create a smoke screen to draw attention away from their performance, which they feel is woefully inadequate. The underlying problem, having Not OK feelings, is fairly common.

Second, teachers should avoid playing the game. To do so, they must remain in the Adult themselves. It does no good to scold, as the Parent would. This reaction is precisely what many games are designed to provoke. Students are more able to forgive their own feelings of ineptness while they are being abused by the teacher's Parent. Teachers, therefore, must resist the temptation to play the game from their Parent ego-state. Instead, they must formulate questions that will help students accept themselves as they are and understand that games are unnecessary.

Third, teachers should provide stroking. Statements of affection, touching, and smiling help students feel accepted. Stroking communicates that they are genuinely liked and are therefore worthy. Without stroking, the question of students' personal worth is left unanswered. This is the reason why children try to involve their teachers in games: They need verification of their self-worth (Berne, 1964).

Preventing Discipline Problems

No explicit distinction is made in the literature between procedures for preventing and procedures for correcting discipline problems using transactional analysis. However, if teachers help their students apply transactional analysis principles, they will foster prevention. Prevention, then, is a matter of teaching transactional analysis to students and encouraging its application. This type of instruction and encouragement amounts to a passive prevention program rather than a vigorously active one.

Schoolwide Discipline

Transactional analysis focuses on data transmitted between students and their teachers. Theorists do not describe a schoolwide program. However, administrators could conceivably be trained in transactional analysis so that in their own relationships with students they could support the work of teachers. Students referred to the principal for disciplinary action, for example, would be given the same kind of treatment as individual teachers would provide.

Strengths and Weaknesses of Transactional Analysis

STRENGTHS

1. It is derived from a well-documented examination of how information is stored in the subconscious mind.
2. It promotes self-analysis and self-correction.

3. It has applications beyond the classroom in students' personal lives.
4. It helps children avoid destructive roles often played in interpersonal relationships.
5. It helps children understand their own messages and those of others.
6. It provides a framework for communication and understanding.

WEAKNESSES

1. Overcoming the automatic behaviors coming from the Parent and Child ego-states may be difficult.
2. It cannot be applied as readily to discipline problems other than those involving verbal exchanges.
3. It may encourage students to "psychoanalyze" one another.
4. Students may not have the language, cognitive skills, or reasoning necessary to employ this technique.
5. Making necessary distinctions between Parent, Child, and Adult may be difficult.

▼ SUMMARY

Relationships between students and teachers depend on transactions—that is, everyday verbal exchanges with one another. These transactions, in turn, depend on the ego-state from which each person is operating and the compatibility of the transactions. There are three ego-states: (1) the Child, which is the emotionally reactive or exuberant inclinations of individuals; (2) the Parent, which is the component of a person's behavior that controls and directs; and (3) the Adult, which is the rational aspect of human personality. Incompatible, or crossed, transactions occur when the ego-states of interacting human beings conflict with one another.

Conflict is often produced when children play behavioral games with their teachers. Such games are designed to help compensate for their feelings of being Not OK. Children assume that they are Not OK when they fail to gain a sense of acceptance, which occurs when they do not receive the stroking they need. When children are abused, their Not OK feelings may become solidly established. If the abuse is extreme, they may instead come to believe that they are OK and that everyone else is Not OK. These individuals have extreme social difficulties and often end up in correctional institutions.

Teachers need to practice staying in the Adult ego-state when they interact with their students. They need to avoid playing behavioral games with their students and must remember to supply the necessary stroking. Finally, students also can benefit from understanding transactional analysis and learning how to respond to others from their Adult.

CENTRAL IDEAS

1. In human beings there are three collections of behaviors or ego-states, which have different functions:
   a. The Parent controls and directs.
   b. The Child is compulsive and expressive.

  c. The Adult applies conscious judgment and thought to behavior.
2. All of our experience is recorded in our brains in a subconscious state. This repository of experience is composed of feelings as well as basic sensory impressions. These stored, subconscious experiences are the genesis of much of our everyday behavior. Our behavior is therefore sometimes manifested without careful thought or a conscious decision on our part.
3. If children receive proper stroking, they will move from the life position of I'm Not OK—You're OK to that of I'm OK—You're OK. Children who fail to receive this assurance remain as they are. When children are abused, they may shift to the position of I'm Not OK—You're Not OK. If abuse is severe, they may move to the I'm OK—You're Not OK life position and end up with an antisocial or even criminal orientation to life.
4. Teachers need to remain in the Adult ego-state and teach their students to do the same.
5. Students play games such as Uproar, Clown, Stupid, Make Me, Schlemiel, and I Want Out to satisfy their needs. Because these games can adversely affect classroom discipline, teachers must stop them by
  a. Determining the purpose of the games
  b. Refusing to play the games
  c. Providing stroking for students

▼ QUESTIONS AND ACTIVITIES

QUESTIONS TO CONSIDER

1. What are the major differences between the ideas of Freud and those of Harris and Berne?
2. To what extent does the work of brain surgeons support the basic ideas behind transactional analysis?
3. How successful are teachers likely to be in teaching their students about transactional analysis?

CLASSROOM ACTIVITIES

1. Use role playing to study the use of transactional analysis in various school situations.
2. Have one member of the class play a student with a behavior problem.
3. Discuss the actions taken along with possible alternatives.

STUDENT APPLICATIONS

1. With one or two classmates, use role playing to act out discipline situations in which students have made the following initial statements. Apply the principles of transactional analysis. Include follow-up interactions.

a. To a teacher: "I hate this work. I can't understand how we can be expected to learn this junk."
b. To another student: "You're just going to have to turn it in to the teacher the way it is and suffer the consequences. I'm not going to help you finish it."
c. To a teacher: "You always have your pets."
d. To a teacher: "I'm not going to do those problems. You can't make me."
e. To another student: "Give me that book. You're too stupid to read it."

EXPLORE YOUR PHILOSOPHY

1. Defend or refute the assumption that behavior is an outgrowth of our experiences as stored in the subconscious mind and that many times behavior is enacted without conscious thought.
2. Defend or refute the assumption that efforts made by humans to control one another are automatic and stem from our previous experiences, which are recorded in the subconscious mind.
3. Defend or refute the assumption that children can be taught to act responsibly by helping them to monitor and to regulate automatic behaviors coming from the subconscious mind.
4. Compare the principles contained in your educational philosophy with those of transactional analysis. Determine consistencies and inconsistencies. Make adjustments to your philosophy as you believe appropriate.

▼ REFERENCES

Berne, E. (1964). *Games people play.* New York: Ballantine Books.
Berne, E. (1966). *Principles of group treatment.* New York: Oxford University Press.
Downing, L. N. (1987). *The OK school house.* Provo, UT: The Association for Human Relations.
Ernst, K. (1972). *Games students play.* Millbrae, CA: Celestial Arts.
Freud, S. (1915). *Instincts and their vicissitudes.* London: Hogarth Press.
Garcia, F. N. (1995). The many faces of anger. *Transactional Analysis Journal, 25*(2), 119–122.
Harris, T. A. (1967). *I'm OK—you're OK.* New York: Avon Books.
Parry, T. A. (1979). To be or not to be ok: The development of the child ego state. *Transactional Analysis Journal, 9*(2), 124–130.
Penfield, W. (1952). Memory mechanisms. *A.M.A. Archives of Neurology and Psychiatry, 67,* 178–198.
Woollams, S., & Brown, M. (1979). *TA: The total handbook of transactional analysis.* Upper Saddle River, NJ: Prentice Hall.

CHAPTER

Teacher Effectiveness Training: Thomas Gordon

OBJECTIVES

This chapter is designed to help you

1. Understand the detrimental effects of punishment and rewards
2. Know the coping behaviors children ordinarily display in response to coercion
3. Understand how to determine ownership regarding problems in the classroom
4. Avoid communicating unacceptance of students
5. Identify student needs, and modify the environment to reduce the incidence of misbehavior
6. Effectively engage in active listening to student problems
7. Decode complicated student communications
8. Send appropriately constructed I-messages for teacher problems
9. Engage in effective problem solving
10. Effectively deal with problems that involve value conflicts

ASSUMPTIONS

1. Human beings are self-regulating and can thus learn to manage their own behavior.
2. Students commonly rebel when their teachers actively regulate their behavior.
3. Rewards and praise may undermine intrinsic motivation.
4. Students can solve their own problems when teachers actively listen to them.
5. Students will alter their misbehavior when teachers deliver appropriately constructed I-messages.

Introduction

In the early 1940s Thomas Gordon, as a graduate student studying with Carl Rogers (1942), began the study of what took place behind the closed doors of counselors' offices regarding what helped or hindered patients in solving their emotional problems. These efforts ushered in a new field of scientific inquiry—the study of the process and outcomes of counseling.

Thomas Gordon is a licensed clinical psychologist who received his doctorate from the University of Chicago and later served on the faculty there. He once served as the president of the California State Psychological Association and is a Fellow of the American Psychological Association.

Dr. Gordon not only has worked extensively helping teachers more effectively teach and avoid discipline problems, he has also created written materials and sponsored training to help parents.

His book *P.E.T.: Parent Effectiveness Training* (1976) has been used extensively as a textbook in college classrooms. It has also served as the basis for training more than a million parents in the P.E.T. program. Several thousand instructors are authorized in the program, from every state and 25 foreign countries. The program has been in operation for the past 32 years.

Teacher effectiveness training (TET) has involved over 100,000 participants including school administrators, counselors, school psychologists, and teachers. More than 50 universities give college credit for TET. The U.S. Office of Education has officially sponsored TET workshops in a number of communities.

▼   Saundra, Elaine, Manuel, and Dan have made a habit, during the past 2 weeks, of talking loudly at the start of class, making it difficult for Mrs. Santiago to begin class. Usually, she stands watching them and waiting for them to quiet down. Today, none of them bothered to look at her. She wondered if they were deliberately ignoring her. Finally, she decided to call out to them, "Elaine, Saundra, Dan, Manuel, I cannot get class started when your group is talking so loudly, and I need to get class started because everyone else is waiting."

Dan replied, "Well, we are just trying to get our project finished up for this class. We only have 1 more week before we have to make our presentation."

"I see. You are hurrying to finish your project, and you feel you must spend this time at the beginning of class to meet the deadline," responded Mrs. Santiago.

"That's right," said Saundra. "If we don't get assignments made now, we won't be able to start our individual study assignments in time to finish by Friday."

"It sounds like you have mapped out your time and feel pressure to get assignments made today," said Mrs. Santiago. "I also feel that when I am unable to start class at a reasonable time, other class members just sit around wasting their time and then get distracted and disinterested. Do you have any ideas how we could solve the problem so we'd both feel OK?"

"Could our group use the seminar room at the end of class each day to do our planning?" asked Manuel. "That way we wouldn't disturb the class, and we could get

Students who act out in class are often reacting to the teacher's controlling behavior.

our coordination done here at school. Elaine has to catch the bus right after school, and we don't have time during the day, even during lunch, to do our planning."

"I can see how you might have a problem getting together during the school day," responded Mrs. Santiago. "No other group has asked to use the seminar room, so I can't see any problem with what you propose. Do you think you will be needing the seminar room every day? What if another group asks to use it?"

"As far as we know, we'd like to use it every day," Dan indicated. "Maybe if others want to use it, two groups could meet there. It would be crowded, but I think it would work all right."

A Case for Teacher Effectiveness Training

The case of Dan, Elaine, Manuel, and Saundra illustrates how problems can be solved by students in the classroom using TET. Gordon believes that this more democratic way of solving classroom problems helps satisfy both teachers and students. Neither party loses. It is a win–win solution.

Gordon feels that significant changes are needed in the way we work with children in all areas of society. We have long-standing traditions in how children are treated, which have even been supported by Supreme Court decisions. For example, in *Ingruham v. Wright* (1977), two teenagers had been beaten by their school principal with wooden paddles. The injuries were so extensive that, had it been their parents who had administered the beating, the hospital would have been compelled by law to file reports charging the parents with child abuse. Nevertheless, the Supreme Court ruled that the same protection offered adults, including prisoners, in terms of bodily harm, should not be guaranteed children. In a decision split five to four, the majority held that schoolchildren have no need for protection afforded citizens by the Eighth

Amendment, which forbids the use of cruel and unusual punishment. Justice Lewis Powell gave his opinion that enforcement of due process procedures in our schools, and consequently offering children the same rights as adults, would result in an impairment of the teacher's ability to maintain discipline in the classroom. He added that paddling of recalcitrant children has long been accepted as an appropriate method of promoting good behavior and instilling a sense of responsibility and decorum in the mischievous heads of schoolchildren (Gordon, 1989, p. xx).

Gordon points out that similar views are held in religious communities, whose members quote the Bible as justification for imposing a "spare the rod and spoil the child" approach to discipline. The religious antecedents for corporal punishment are represented in the belief that children are born in sin and are therefore inherently evil. This belief has had a powerful influence on child rearing in Western culture and is responsible for the practice of "beating the devil out" of children or the belief that "children's will must be broken."

By 1996, twenty-three states had outlawed corporal punishment in schools (Hyman, 1996). In other states, laws dictate an assortment of conditions under which corporal punishment may be administered. In some, the punishment must be reasonable. In others, it must be carried out without malice and not cause permanent injury. In some cases, the school district must authorize corporal punishment. In others, teachers and/or principals can beat children. In some instances, individuals other than teachers and principals are authorized to carry out corporal punishment (Hyman, 1990, pp. 262–268).

In a study in Pennsylvania, Reardon and Reynolds (1975) found that the following percentages of various personnel favored corporal punishment:

School board presidents   81%
Principals   78%
Administrators   68%
Teachers   74%
Parents   71%
Students   25%

Apparently, there is considerable support for the idea that good old-fashioned discipline can improve children's behavior. Many think that the answer to misbehavior as well as crime and violence is harsher and harsher punishment. It is becoming increasingly clear, however, that punishments of all kinds increase the incidence of misbehavior rather than reduce it. Punishment may be the least effective way to achieve good discipline at home or at school. One study showed that nearly 100% of corporally punished children had assaulted a brother or sister during the year of the study, while only 20% of children whose parents did not use physical force had done so. In addition, they found that 4 children in 100 are at risk of serious injury each year from parents using at least one of the following dangerous forms of punishment: kicks, bites, punches, burns, beatings, and threats with, or use of, guns or knives (Straus, Gelles, & Steinmetz, 1980).

If you were to ask parents to name the worst thing that their children could do, they would be likely to say, getting in trouble with the law. This is the very fear that lures many parents into the trap of providing punishment as the primary way to force their children to submit to authority. Their hope is that punitive discipline will promote the development of moral virtues required of law-abiding citizens. However, punitive discipline causes the delinquent or criminal behavior it is designed to prevent. Studies show a positive correlation between severe punishment and juvenile delinquency, violent crimes, murder, and vandalism (Gordon, 1989, p. 4).

Ironically, most parents and teachers believe that children will eventually become self-regulating automatically, as a direct result of adults applying external control. Considerable evidence now exists that refutes this conclusion. Children who have been coerced usually show very little self-control once they are outside the influence of adult controllers. Self-disciplined youngsters, however, have ordinarily been provided considerable personal freedom. In addition, contrary to conventional wisdom, punishment will not prevent children's aggressive behavior. Instead, harsh, punitive, power-based punishment actually causes aggression in children (Gordon, 1989, p. 4).

One of the interesting coping behaviors observed in children who are coerced is that of giving into authority, submitting, and obeying. Unfortunately, there is evidence that many hideous crimes have been committed in the name of obedience. The Nazi atrocities during World War II are just one example. This principle is further illustrated in the research of Milgram (Gordon, 1989, pp. 95–98), where subjects were told by the researcher to administer electric shocks to individuals (victims) who were strapped into a chair. The subjects didn't know that the victims were actually actors. The experimenter ordered the subjects to increase the strength of the shock each time the victim gave a wrong answer. Even though the victims screamed out as though they were in pain, some subjects continued to administer what they thought were shocks of increased voltage. Nearly two thirds of the subjects obediently carried out the directions of the experimenter. Although many of them experienced a lot of personal stress in the situation, and made frequent protests to the experimenter, they continued providing shocks up through the strongest voltage on the indicator. Later, some subjects acknowledged they knew they were doing wrong but admitted they could not bring themselves to disobey authority.

Parents and teachers alike use power-based control extensively to regulate children's behavior. This tactic seems to "keep a lid on things" until children enter adolescence. Gordon believes that the single most important cause of the severe stress and strain in families during the adolescent years is from parents continuing to use their power-based authority when in reality they no longer have any power. Inevitably, when children reach adolescence, they can do as they wish. Parents can no longer exercise the control they once had. Once parents lose power, they are often accused of being permissive. Because they no longer have power, they cease trying to impose their will on their children. In reality, they are not permissive, but rather impotent wielders of power.

In schools, teachers also run out of power. At about junior high school age, youngsters resist or ignore power-based discipline because teachers are not authorized to exercise the kind of punishment that would actually deter deviancy. They are left with only nonaversive, ineffective punishments such as making kids stay after school, referring them to the principal's office, or suspending them.

When power-based discipline is enforced, children engage in various coping mechanisms in a quest to achieve some degree of autonomy, or at least to make life miserable for those trying to coerce them. In the following list are the coping behaviors Gordon has noticed:

1. Resisting, defying, being negative
2. Rebelling, disobeying, being insubordinate, sassing
3. Retaliating, striking back, counterattacking, vandalizing
4. Hitting, being belligerent, combative
5. Breaking rules and laws
6. Throwing temper tantrums, getting angry
7. Lying, deceiving, hiding the truth
8. Blaming others, tattling, telling on others
9. Bossing or bullying others
10. Banding together, forming alliances, organizing against adults
11. Apple-polishing, buttering up, soft-soaping, bootlicking, currying favor with adults
12. Withdrawing, fantasizing, daydreaming
13. Competing, needing to win, hating to lose, needing to look good, making others look bad
14. Giving up, feeling defeated, loafing, goofing off
15. Leaving, escaping, staying away from home, running away, quitting school, cutting classes
16. Not talking, ignoring, using the silent treatment, writing the adult off, keeping one's distance
17. Crying, weeping, feeling depressed or hopeless
18. Becoming fearful, shy, timid, afraid to speak up, hesitant to try anything new
19. Needing reassurance, seeking constant approval, feeling insecure
20. Getting sick, developing psychosomatic ailments
21. Overeating, excessive dieting
22. Being submissive, conforming, complying, being dutiful, docile, being a goody-goody, teachers' pet
23. Drinking heavily, using drugs
24. Cheating in school, plagiarizing (Gordon, 1989, p. 83)

Sometimes controllers provide rewards instead of punishment. This assumes that controllers know what is best for children. Unfortunately, controllers sometimes choose consequences beneficial primarily to themselves rather than the children they are trying to control. There is little question that controllers can achieve power over children. This is particularly true when children feel deprived of the rewards the controller is able to dispense. Teachers can exercise control over students as long as students are kept in a continuous state of dependency or fear—dependency on the teacher for the rewards that can be offered, fearful of the punishments that can be inflicted. This works best if children can be kept locked in the relationship, unable to get for themselves what the teacher can offer as a reward or unable to escape the punishment the teacher can impose. On the surface, this state of affairs appears somewhat extreme, but in reality, it is the very relationship established in most school situations.

One interesting application of rewards in school is grading. Most teachers believe grades are rewarding and thus can motivate children to work harder and achieve more. However, because high grades are reserved for only the highest academic achievement, few children can obtain them. Consequently, to low-achieving students, grades have little reward value. Even for high-achieving children, grades may have deleterious effects. Instead of learning because of interest and desire, they may learn only when they are appropriately rewarded. We thereby run the risk of learning activities that would have provided children considerable pleasure intrinsically becoming chores that must be suffered through to achieve designated rewards. The intrinsic motivation that is ordinarily associated with these worthwhile learning activities is undermined by rewards. In addition, children who work for grades may compromise personal integrity by cheating, copying, and plagiarizing.

Another commonly used reward is praise. So common and accepted is this control tactic, its liberal use is rarely if ever questioned. Little children even appear to seek praise. However, the intention of adults who use praise is not solely the benevolent one of making children feel good and motivating them to engage in worthwhile learning. Rather, it comes from the teacher's desire to control, and it promotes the changes they desire in their students. More importantly, praise often conveys nonacceptance by implying that a certain behavior is required to be accepted.

Essentials of Teacher Effectiveness Training

Teacher effectiveness training maintains that rewards and punishments are ineffective ways of achieving a positive influence on children. Gordon indicates that having an influence on children is entirely different from controlling them. Influencing requires teachers to forgo using power methods that promote resistance, rebellion, and blaming and instead to use those that foster self-regulation. Very little controversy is encountered about whether self-regulation is desirable for children. In reality, nearly everyone places considerable value on children becoming self-regulated, self-controlled, and self-disciplined. There is considerable controversy, however, about the most appropriate way to foster these desired traits. Most parents and teachers believe these traits are a natural outgrowth of children being rewarded, regulated, coerced, and even severely punished. From this perspective, children are seen by adults as naturally misbehaving. Misbehavior, however, is exclusively parent and teacher language and constitutes any behavior that creates an undesirable consequence for adults. The "badness" of the behavior is defined by adults. Children see the situation differently. In their minds, they are doing what they believe will best satisfy their needs. In other words, the adult, not the child, experiences the badness. When teachers understand this distinction, changes in attitudes are possible. Teachers can then understand that everyone's behavior is basically need-satisfying, not good or bad. Hopefully, this will make teachers more accepting of children. This doesn't mean that teachers necessarily become more accepting of what children do. It means that they begin seeing children as need-satisfying beings like themselves, not motivated by ulterior motives.

PROBLEM OWNERSHIP

In helping children solve the difficulties they encounter in the classroom, it is essential to first identify who owns the problem. Teachers commonly try to force changes in students regarding problems owned by students and consequently block the flow of communication needed to help students solve their problems. The following are typical teacher behaviors that block effective communication between them and their students. The first five types of responses communicate unacceptance and try to solve the students' problems for them:

1. Ordering, commanding, directing. Example: "Stop what you are doing now, and start on your homework."
2. Warning, threatening. Example: "You better start turning in your homework everyday, or you won't get a good grade in this class."
3. Moralizing, preaching, giving "shoulds" and "oughts." Example: "It is important that you learn how to behave in class. How can you ever expect to become a good citizen otherwise?"
4. Advising, offering solutions or suggestions. Example: "What you need to do is organize your time. Then you could get your work done and your assignments turned in on time."
5. Teaching, lecturing, giving logical arguments. Example: "Now just look at the roll book. You can see that you have 12 missed assignments of the 25 given during the term. Certainly, you can see you won't be successful that way."

The next three types of responses communicate judgment, evaluation, or put-downs. Teachers typically believe that it is helpful to point out students' faults and inadequacies.

6. Judging, criticizing, disagreeing, blaming. Example: "You're always putting off starting on your homework. I hope that's not a permanent impediment you have."
7. Name-calling, stereotyping, labeling. Example: "You're acting like first graders instead of like sixth graders when you line up to go out for recess."
8. Interpreting, analyzing, diagnosing. Example: "You're just trying to purposely create problems in the class. I can see why you get your friends to torment Alan."

The next two response categories are designed to make the student feel better, to make the problem go away, or to encourage students to deny there is any real problem:

9. Praising, agreeing, giving positive evaluations. Example: "You're always so conscientious. I'm sure you will complete all your assignments and get them in by the deadline."
10. Reassuring, sympathizing, consoling, supporting. Example: "You're not alone in feeling the way you do about failing this test. Everyone feels that way about their failures. I've had a few myself. The thing is, you can make up for this by doing well on your tests for the rest of the term."

The next roadblock is probably the most frequently used one. It is composed of questions that ordinarily produce student defensiveness. Teachers use these questions when they feel the need for more facts in a situation because they intend to solve the student's problem by coming up with the best solutions themselves:

11. Questioning, probing, interrogating, cross-examining. Examples: "Do you have other activities that interfere with your ability to complete your assignments?" "How much time do you usually allot to completing your assignments?" "When should you have told me regarding the trouble you are experiencing working these problems?"

Category 12 consists of communication-blocking messages, which teachers send to change the subject, to divert students efforts, or to avoid having to deal with students and their problems.

12. Withdrawing, distracting, being sarcastic, humoring, diverting. Examples: "Lets deal with this problem later. I can see you're not ready to do anything about it." "Let's get on with your homework." "I can see that you didn't get enough sleep last night" (Gordon, 1974, pp. 48–49).

The roadblocks in the preceding list are commonly used by teachers. Some may be judged to be inappropriate, despite their frequent use. For example, many teachers can see the inappropriateness of blaming and labeling. Some of the roadblocks, however, have more subtle problems. Suppose a student tells you that she is unhappy because she told another student a joke about her chemistry teacher, which the teacher overheard. You might be tempted to say, "You either have to be more discrete in your telling of jokes or avoid doing it altogether. Perhaps things would be better if you went to your chemistry teacher and apologized." This response has a number of hidden messages. Among them are the following:

"You don't have much tact."
"You have bad judgment."
"You can't figure out what to do to rectify the situation on your own."
"You are your own worst enemy."

Help of this kind is ineffective for students who are experiencing problems. When students are preoccupied or have distressful problems, this kind of "help" is either unwelcome or resisted and interferes with the problem-solving processes. The 12 roadblocks generally communicate unacceptance to students. This is because these roadblocks inform students that they must change, because they are somehow unacceptable as they are. It may even communicate that it is unacceptable to even have a problem and that something must be wrong with the problem owner. Teachers must be able to communicate genuine acceptance of their students. Developing effective helping relationships with students depends on it.

The roadblocks derail communication primarily by enforcing control or by taking responsibility for problems students should assume themselves. When teachers notice students having problems, or when students request assistance to solve problems best solved themselves, teachers would be more helpful if they responded by asking questions like the following:

1. When would be an appropriate time to address this problem?
2. What is the first step you need to take to solve this problem?
3. What are some alternative solutions to this problem?

Notice that these questions do not have suggested solutions embodied in them. They are also devoid of criticism, demands, preaching, logical arguments, praise, and the like.

Sometimes it is the teacher who owns problems in the classroom. Clues that a particular problem is owned by the teacher are feelings of annoyance, frustration, resentment, anger, distraction, and irritation. These feelings often promote tension, discomfort, upset stomach, headache, and jumpiness.

Some common situations that the teacher owns include the following:

In chemistry lab, students squirting acid at one another from micropipettes
Students taking the teachers personal things from his or her desk
Students disturbing lectures by talking loudly to one another
Students stealing chemicals from the chemical storage area in an effort to create their own bomb

When these kinds of problems occur, nearly all teachers send confrontational, roadblocking messages to students. These messages cause students to resist change, to feel incapable and unacceptable, to feel guilty or ashamed, to feel less self-esteem, to feel they must defend themselves, to feel anger, or to withdraw. With confrontational messages, teachers hand out solutions to problems and expect students to accept them. They are messages laden with negative judgments, designed to put students in their place. These messages are either simply discounted by students or internalized by them as proof of their own inadequacy. Confrontational messages do little to help solve problems.

Sometimes teachers send indirect messages to students in an effort to solve problems that the teacher owns. Indirect messages may come across as kidding and teasing or as just sarcasm. They seldom work and are often misunderstood. For example, teachers may say,

"Your best attribute is blocking the door."
"Now that you have had your chance to teach us, maybe you can turn it over to me."
"When did you become everyone's daddy?"
"You girls seem more interested in hair styles today than biology."

IDENTIFYING STUDENT NEEDS

In addition to avoiding roadblocks and properly identifying problem ownership, teachers need alternative ways to solve classroom problems. One important alternative is to accept students' behavior as an attempt to satisfy needs instead of categorizing it as misbehavior. To do this, teachers should listen carefully and accurately to student messages. Keep in mind that children's behavior always has a reason behind it. With practice, teachers will be able to remove whatever it is that is causing the unacceptable behavior or supply whatever it is children need and can't provide for themselves.

Children do not always give clear signals regarding how they want their needs fulfilled or what is keeping them from satisfying their needs adequately. Teachers, therefore, need to make clarifying inquiries. For example, a child may give messages like the following:

"I am so angry!"
"Why do we have all this homework to do on the weekend?"
"When are we going to have an opportunity to say what we would like to learn?"

If a student says he is angry, it may not be evident why the anger has been created. Perhaps the student has failed to achieve the control he wishes because another class member has just won the election for class president. The teacher may correctly conclude the reason for the student's anger in this case; however, what if the anger is because he has just been cut from the basketball team for failing to keep training rules? This provocation will be far less evident and more difficult to ascertain.

Teachers can obtain information about a student's behavior by making direct inquiries. For example teachers may ask,

"Why are you so angry?"
"What is it you want?"
"Why are you screaming at Amy?"
"Why aren't you getting ready to go to your next class?"

MAKING A TRADE

Another effective nonpower method for altering unacceptable behaviors, particularly for younger children, is to get them to trade an unacceptable behavior for one that is acceptable to you. A student may, for example, be clowning around and perhaps even endangering himself or classmates. You might invite him to help you get the video ready you are about to show the class. Another example would be to hand a shovel to a child to help build a snowman as a trade for throwing snowballs at classmates. What could be offered as a trade for a child who is talking too loudly during class discussion? She might be asked to come to the board and make a drawing to help you explain the concept being taught or to respond to a question about the lesson. If what you offer as an alternative is compelling, you can expect students to focus on the new productive task and forget the disruptive one.

MODIFYING THE ENVIRONMENT

Many times teachers would be more effective if they modified the classroom environment rather than trying to alter unacceptable behavior. Sometimes the learning environment is too "rich" in stimuli, and other times it is too impoverished. Children who are bored or have too little inclination to learn what their teachers propose tend to fidget and annoy one another or to generally disrupt the class. Other times, children are bombarded by so many stimuli they seem to be "bouncing off the walls." Any teacher who has tried to conduct class Friday afternoon just before the school's basketball team is to play in the state championship game has experienced this kind of problem. Children may be stimulated by pep rallies, unresolved decisions about how to get to the game, excitement of being in the tournament, anticipation of being with friends, expectations about getting out of school, and a host of other things.

When students are overstimulated, it may be wise for teachers to provide learning experiences that allow them to be more active. Role plays, debates, interviews, discussions, and labs are examples of these kinds of activities. Sometimes an activity that directly relates to the event students are excited about can help keep things under control as well as promote better learning. Unfortunately, some teachers fear that more active learning experiences will further stimulate students who are already overactive and that pandemonium will break out. This may occur if the activity is poorly managed or if it has little value to the learners. However, well-managed, interesting activities should have the desired effect.

An impoverished school environment needs to be modified so children become excited to learn. Many times the problem occurs because children are not allowed to help decide what they learn. There also may be too many adult rules, regulations, and procedures that children don't feel inclined to follow. Children become listless and easily distracted when they are compelled to do things in school for which they have no interest. The solution to this problem is simply to provide students more opportunities to learn what they wish and to allow them to have a say in classroom rules and regulations.

Other times children become bored because there is too little stimulus variation. Teachers may drone on and on lecturing, or they may provide only a single type of activity for an entire class period. Student learning should be shifted from among a number of different activities to satisfy children's need for stimulus variation. In a study of classrooms across America, Goodlad (1984, p. 265) found that teachers ordinarily limit classroom learning activity to only two options, lecture and quiet seat work. This was less true of elementary classrooms, but in all cases, there was an alarming poverty of methods used by teachers. Sensitive teachers not only provide a large number of different learning activities for children, they also extend the learning environment into the outside world—such as field trips, library use, playground, gymnasium.

ACTIVE LISTENING

One of the most difficult ideas for teachers to understand is that they can help their students to solve their problems by just listening. Counselors have learned that a good deal of progress can be made just listening to their patients, even when the individual is severely troubled. This approach to solving problems provides a release of distressful feelings and emotions as well as allowing the person who owns the problem to solve it. In addition, listening provides the teacher with a format for showing a willingness to help and communicates an acceptance of the students despite their troubles. Listening works just as well in teacher–student relationships as it does between counselors and their patients.

Sometimes passive listening is called for. In this case, the teacher remains silent and allows the student to do all the talking. It is wise to remember that students cannot talk to you about what is bothering them if you are doing the talking. Most teachers, when confronted with student problems, feel compelled to talk. In the process, they tend to assume too much responsibility for solving problems, and they curtail communication. Sometimes the actual problems students suffer remain hidden when teachers launch into a series of recommendations about how to solve student problems before the students have had an opportunity to adequately express them.

Verbal and nonverbal cues sometimes help the communication process. These cues are acknowledging responses. When you nod, lean forward, smile, frown, or use other body movements, you let students know that you really hear them. Verbal cues like "Uh-huh," and "Oh," and "I see" let students know that you are attentive and interested in listening to them and that you accept them.

Door openers can also promote better communication and help students open up and explore more completely what is bothering them. Some examples of door openers include

"Would you like to tell me more about that?"
"That is an interesting idea, would you like to go on?"
"It sounds like you feel what you are saying is important."
"I'm really interested in what you are telling me."

Notice that these questions and statements contain no evaluative content.

The use of silence and acknowledgment in a student–teacher interaction may look like the following:

Student	No one ever does their part in these cooperative learning activities. I think I will quit and not do anything either.
Teacher	(Silence, nods.)
Student	Other group members agree to do some of the work, but the next time we meet, they haven't done anything. They just leave it up to the rest of us. And we don't get to learn what they are supposed to teach us.
Teacher	Uh-huh.
Student	We're just going to have to find some way to get them to do their part. Maybe if those of us who do all the work got together, we could come up with a plan to get the others to do what they have agreed to do.
Teacher	(Nods.)
Student	No. I've got a better idea. We should just all meet together and talk about how we feel about this project. They need to understand how we feel. It won't do any good to lecture them, but they need to understand that we depend on them to teach us the things they are researching.
Teacher	I see.
Student	I think I'll call a meeting during class tomorrow and get this problem resolved.
Teacher	OK.

Silence, acknowledgment responses, and door openers have their limitations. Teachers also need to engage in active listening to help students solve their problems. Active listening promotes even deeper probing of problem situations. It helps students explore underlying causes and feelings and communicates that you not only are tuned in to their problems but also are accepting of them and their messages. Active listening helps assure students that their teachers not only have heard them but have also understood.

Teachers must understand that when students attempt to communicate, they are not ordinarily portraying their feelings accurately. Not only is it difficult for them to accurately communicate how they feel, they may also encode their messages to avoid incrimination. Most humans feel vulnerable to potential incriminating interpretations of what they say. They therefore make guarded statements about their true feelings, until they develop a sense of trust in the person with whom they are communicating. This is why active listening is more likely to bring out true feelings. It communicates acceptance and nonjudgment and promotes trust. When students gain confidence in you, more progress can be made in helping them solve their problems.

Following are some examples of how students encode messages to protect themselves. They perhaps indicate why teachers may have difficulty correctly interpreting them:

The student is feeling:	*His coded message:*
Concern about failing an exam.	"Why do we have to memorize the Krebs cycle? I don't see what good it will be."
Fear of not being selected by classmates on one of the teams.	"I didn't remember to bring my gym shorts today. I'm not going to be able to dress today."
Overwhelmed by getting behind in completing homework assignments.	"This homework is just too hard. When I get home I just can't figure it out."
Feeling rejected by peers.	"I just can't stand cliques. They are all around school, and I think they should be broken up."
Disappointment in not getting first place in the science fair.	"I hate science. I'd never want to be a scientist."

Students' messages not only are encoded to avoid incriminating judgments, they are uniquely encoded by each person. This not only makes it difficult for teachers to understand but also makes it foolish for them to respond to the coded message at face value. The following dialogue between a junior high school boy and his principal provides an example of how teachers may appropriately decode messages from their students:

Student	(Hesitantly) I . . . I thought I would tell you about the problem I am having with my science teacher, Mr. Jones.
Principal	You appear not to be to sure you want to talk to me about your problem with Mr. Jones.
Student	Well, I don't like to talk about others behind their back, and if he found out, I don't know what he would do with my grade. I'm afraid he would really be mad at me.
Principal	I see. You're worried that if Mr. Jones found out you came to see me about the problem between you it may have an adverse affect on your grade.
Student	Yeah.
Principal	I don't plan to tell anyone about our conversation unless you say it's OK.
Student	That's a relief. Do you know what happened? Mr. Jones got so angry with me when I got some acid on Amy Brower's dress that he won't let me in the lab any more. If I don't get into the lab, I won't be able to

finish my assignments. Anyway, Amy squirted some acid on my pants, and now there's a big hole in them. Wait until my mom sees that. She says she is sick and tired of buying me new clothes. She'll just tell me I should be more like my brother Jake. He's so good in school and always does what Mom asks.

Principal   You are concerned about your grade mostly because of what your mother will say and because she is always comparing you with your brother.

Student   Yeah. She is always on my case about how I should be more like Jake. She never lets up. I don't think I can ever be like him. He gets straight As and does all the other things that please Mom.

Principal   You find it impossible to please your mother, and you think you are not able to do much in school when you are always compared with your brother.

Student   Yeah, I guess so. I never do very well. I never feel like trying, especially when I have to do as well as Jake.

Principal   I hear you saying that you could do better in school, but having to measure up to your brother puts you off doing much at all.

Student   You've got that right. I know I could do good in school. I think I could do a good job in science, particularly. But now Mr. Jones won't let me in the lab. That's the part of science I like the most. I know I didn't obey the safety rules in the lab, but other kids were doing the same thing. I was just the one that was caught.

Principal   You'd really work hard in science and your other classes if you were given another chance in your science class.

Student   I guess that's what I mean.

Notice how the student moves from a vague encoded message to one that more clearly indicates how he proposes to solve the problem. Notice also that the principal checks out the accuracy of his decoding by eliciting verification from the student. The principal focused on how the student felt about the various situations brought up, not on the situation itself, thus allowing the student to assume responsibility. To be effective active listeners, teachers and school administrators must avoid coming across as insincere, patronizing, or manipulative. They must also avoid appearing mechanical, unnatural, and wooden to their students. To be effective, teachers must achieve the following:

1. Have a deep sense of trust in students' abilities ultimately to solve their own problems. Students may ramble and sound inconclusive, but teachers need to have faith in the process and to realize that finding solutions to problems may take weeks or even months.
2. Be able to genuinely accept the feelings expressed by students. This must be done despite what is felt about how students should think or feel about their problems. Students can escape from troublesome feelings when they believe their feelings can be openly expressed, examined, and explored.
3. Understand that feelings are often quite transitory; that through active listening, students will move from momentary feeling to momentary feeling, and in the process, feelings can be defused, dissipated, and released.

4. Want to help students with their problems and take the necessary time to be effective.
5. Be able to show empathy for students and yet maintain a separate identity. Teachers must not get caught up in the feelings expressed by students to the point that the separateness is lost. They need to understand students' feelings but not own them.
6. Understand that students initially seldom can share their real problems. How deeply students can share their problems depends on how skillfully the teacher listens.
7. Respect the privacy and confidential nature of whatever students reveal about themselves and their problems. Students must have confidence in the absolute confidentiality of what they share (Gordon, 1974, pp. 75–76).

Active listening can help students deal with and defuse strong feelings that may be detrimental, can help students own their own emotions, can facilitate problem solving, can help students assume responsibility for analyzing and solving problems, and can promote closer, more meaningful relationships between teachers and students.

Many teachers incorrectly identify student problems as their own. They then confront students with one of the roadblocks in an attempt to force them to change their feelings about what they have done or problems they are trying to solve. They may even take a more active role and solve problems for their students. When this occurs, students soon learn to distrust their own feelings, to develop a dependence on "safe" ways to feel, and to allow others to tell them how to feel and behave. If teachers actively listen, students will learn to assume ownership of their feelings and problems and undertake solutions to conflicts and problems while gaining greater independence and self-responsibility. The greatest disservice teachers can perform is trying to protect their students from personal problems and denying them the opportunity to deal with the consequences of their actions.

SENDING CONFRONTING I-MESSAGES

It is undeniably difficult and frustrating for teachers to manage classrooms and promote a good learning environment when many of their students attempt to meet their needs through annoying, boisterous, stubborn, loud, aggressive, forgetful, selfish, inconsiderate, absentminded, or destructive behaviors. In the classroom these may be problems owned by the teacher. Teacher-owned problems cannot be handled through active listening. Instead, confronting I-messages are necessary. As mentioned, clues to teacher-owned problems include annoyance, frustration, resentment, anger, distraction, and irritation. Some common situations of teacher-owned problems include the following:

1. Students rip pages out of their textbooks.
2. Students dig into their desks.
3. Students throw spit wads and paper airplanes in class.
4. Students leave their candy wrappers on the floor.

When students own problems, teachers take a role of being active listeners, are primarily interested in the students' needs, and are more passive in problem solving. When teachers own problems, they send messages to their students, are primarily satisfying their own needs, and take an active part in problem solving. In modifying unacceptable student behavior to get their own needs met, teachers work with three variables—the student, the environment, and themselves. To modify student behavior, for example, a teacher may tell a student to be quiet and not interrupt her while she is helping someone else. She may modify the environment by providing the student with an answer book so he doesn't have to come to her for answers. She may modify herself by giving a student more of her time when she recognizes this may be a need he has.

In training teachers to use TET, Gordon (1974, pp. 126–141) found that when students do disturbing things, 90% to 95% of the teachers commonly confront them with messages that have the following effects or outcomes:

1. Cause students to resist changing their behavior.
2. Encourage students to believe the teacher thinks they are stupid or incapable.
3. Make students feel that the teacher has little consideration for their feelings and needs.
4. Make students feel guilty, ashamed, or embarrassed.
5. Promote poor student self-esteem.
6. Cause students to defend themselves.
7. Provoke student anger.
8. Cause students to withdraw or to give up.

These outcomes are achieved when teachers warn, order, preach, give logical arguments, advise, judge, criticize, stereotype, interpret, analyze, praise, probe, interrogate, and reassure. These directions are commonly sent as you-messages:

You sit down and shut up! (Ordering)
You had better put that down or else! (Warning)
You know what will happen if you keep that up! (Preaching)
You can get organized if you put your mind to it. (Logic)
You're not using your time effectively. (Criticizing)
You didn't really try. (Analyzing)
Why did you do that part first? (Probing)

When teachers send you-messages, they convey to students that they are to blame for whatever prompted the message to be sent, even though it is an encoded message about teacher frustration. It is in fact a teacher-owned problem. Teachers need to determine problem ownership and then send I-messages that address problems and their ownership as it exists. Gordon indicates that properly constructed I-messages are composed of three parts. The first of these is to clearly communicate what is creating a problem for the teacher. It is a nonblaming, nonjudgmental description of what the teacher finds unacceptable. For example:

"When I see spit wads being flipped around the room . . . "
"When I see marks made on the desks . . . "
"When I get interrupted during discussions . . . "
"When students cheat on their tests . . . "

Notice that these statements refer to specific student behaviors and yet do not blame, evaluate, provide solutions, or present moral judgments. Observe the difference when the message includes evaluative content:

"When I learn you can't be trusted to keep your eyes on your own paper . . . "
"When you are mean and inconsiderate of other class members . . . "
"When you are sloppy and make messes everywhere . . . "

Notice that I-messages begin with *when*. This conveys to students that it is just at particular times their specific behaviors are a problem. There is something they can do to solve these problems. It is a matter of changing a behavior rather than adopting some label or negative attribute.

The second component of an appropriate I-message is a statement of the tangible or concrete effect the specific behavior has on the teacher. For example:

"When you use the same scoop to get different chemicals (nonjudgmental description),
    they can become contaminated . . . " (tangible effect).
"When you play in the aquarium (nonjudgmental description), I am afraid some of the
    fish will die . . . " (tangible effect).
"When you look at someone else's paper during the test (nonjudgmental description),
    I'm not certain your work is your own . . . " (tangible effect).

This I-message component needs to appear to be real in the eyes of students. It cannot appear unreasonable or unlikely. Most students dislike being thought of as "bad guys." They want their teachers to like them. In addition, they often don't know how their behavior is affecting others. They tend to be preoccupied with satisfying their own needs. When the effects of their behavior are brought to their attention, their reaction is commonly to confess they didn't realize the negative impact they were having.

The third and final part of the I-message is a statement of the feelings generated within teachers by their students. For example:

"When you talk during class discussions (description of behavior), many of your class-
    mates find it hard to hear (tangible effect), and I'm afraid they will be unprepared
    for the exam (feeling)."
"When you throw chemicals around in the lab (description of behavior), someone could
    be seriously hurt (tangible effect), and I'm afraid I'll be held liable (feeling)."
"When you push other students while playing on the slide (description of behavior),
    someone might fall (tangible effect), and I'm afraid that they may experience a seri-
    ous injury (feeling)" (Gordon, 1974, pp. 142–145).

These statements communicate precisely what the troublesome behavior is, what effect can logically be expected, and how you as a teacher feel about it. They can be counted on to encourage students to change their behavior without negative consequences. In addition to influencing students to change, I-messages let them know that their teachers are human: that they have feelings, needs, wants, and limits. I-messages communicate a level of equality between students and teachers that helps students assume more control over their own behavior and develop a greater sense of responsibility to others.

SHIFTING GEARS TO REDUCE RESISTANCE

Despite using well-constructed I-messages, teachers can expect to occasionally experience resistance, defensiveness, guilt, denial, discomfort, or expressions of hurt feelings from their students. It is understandable that these responses may sometimes be provoked, given the fact that I-messages confront students with the prospect of having to change their unacceptable behavior. Students often express surprise about how teachers feel regarding their behavior. Apparently, the kind of feedback they ordinarily get is quite unlike that provided in I-messages.

It does little good to keep providing assertive messages to students when they offer resistance. I-messages communicate how teachers feel and what they want. However, sometimes students couldn't care less regarding what their teachers want or feel. They have their own needs and interests in mind and considerable commitment to achieving them. When you experience resistance to your I-messages, it is wise to quickly shift from sending them to a listening posture. This communicates a willingness to be sensitive and patient regarding your own needs. Shifting gears in this way often causes an immediate reduction in students' resistance. When their feelings are acknowledged despite what teachers may wish, students are much more willing to modify their behavior appropriately. Children find it easier to change if they feel their teachers understand how hard it might be for them to do so. The following dialogue illustrates how to shift gears when a student is having problems getting his assignments in on time:

Teacher	Raul, your turning in work late is causing me problems. I have to hurry my assessment, and I'm afraid I won't be able to provide you with valid and useful feedback.
Student	Yeah, well I've had a lot to do the past few weeks, and I just can't manage to get it all done.
Teacher	(Shifting gears to listening) I see. You have problems of your own that are interfering with getting your work done.
Student	That's right. I've had three term papers assigned in other classes, and they are all due within the next 2 days. My grades will really be affected if I don't get those papers in on time.
Teacher	There is no way you can get your work done in this class, because you have important term papers in other classes that must be completed.
Student	Yeah. I know you need me to get my work in on time, and I think I can start Wednesday. Right now I have to finish my work in other classes. I don't think I will have this problem again.
Teacher	It sounds like you will be able to solve this problem shortly. I appreciate finding out what you are experiencing and what you are doing about it.

In this incident, the teacher expressed her concern in an initial I-message, but then experiencing resistance, shifted to a listening posture. This enabled Raul to understand the teacher's problem and to indicate how he could help solve it.

PROBLEM SOLVING

Occasionally, neither using I-messages nor shifting gears is sufficient to cause students to modify their behavior right away. When this happens, it may be time to initiate mutual problem solving. This involves the following six steps:

1. Define the problem.
2. Generate possible solutions.

3. Evaluate each solution.
4. Make a decision.
5. Determine how to implement the decision.
6. Assess the success of the decision (Gordon, 1974, p. 228).

Problems cannot be solved until they are properly defined. Many times, problems are hidden in the encoded messages transmitted by students and, therefore, are not immediately apparent. Sometimes, teachers fail to properly articulate how they feel, or they make statements about solutions before the problem has been identified and expressed. You wouldn't, for example, tell your students that you want it quiet in the class. This is a solution. Instead, you might say, "I can't hear the group I'm working with at the moment." In defining problems, it is appropriate for teachers to provide I-messages so their students know exactly how they feel. These messages should fit the problem and be an accurate expression of the teacher's feelings. Teachers should also engage in active listening so their students can give an accurate expression of their needs. They may at first have trouble separating their needs from solutions they want. Remember, in defining problems, conflict of needs should be expressed, not competing solutions.

Once the problem has been accurately defined, both teacher and students can offer possible solutions. It is often best to get students to suggest some ideas before teachers offer their own. It is also wise not to evaluate proposed solutions at this point. The invitation to offer possible solutions should indicate that all suggestions are accepted without having to justify them. Each proposed solution should be written down for future reference.

When an acceptable number of suggestions has been made, the evaluation process can begin. Start by asking students to state what they believe the best solution to be. Solutions that produce negative ratings from anyone for any reason should be crossed off the list. Teachers should not hesitate to state their own opinions and preferences. I-messages can be used to do this. For example, "I couldn't accept that idea because . . ." Students should be encouraged to tell the group why solutions they support have merit. Teachers should do the same. They should also encourage the participation of all class members. Students will feel a greater sense of ownership if they give their input in the discussion.

In making a decision, it is wise to avoid voting except for taking straw polls to find out the general feeling of the class as the discussion proceeds. What is wanted is consensus. Once movement toward an agreed-on solution appears eminent, test the proposed solution by asking students to tell how they believe the solution will work. Do not adopt a solution until everyone agrees to at least try it. This will communicate that the proposed solution is not necessarily final. It is something to be tested.

Problem-solving efforts often end in frustration because decisions are never implemented. When this happens, it is generally because the group has failed to determine who is to do what and when they are to do it. Teachers should ask their students what they need to do to implement the solution. They also need to define the standards for setting their plan in motion. Undefined standards or shoddy implementation are unacceptable. Standards should be defined and monitored by the group. Problems encountered in this process can be used as topics for future discussions. The agreed-on solution and the means for implementation must be written down and used as a reference. The timing for implementing solutions should be included.

Because problem solving is an ongoing process, solutions should be carefully monitored and evaluated. Students can be invited periodically to assess the effects of their decisions. Teachers should be on the lookout for student commitments that were enthusiastically entered into but that later turn out to be unrealistic or difficult to carry out. Checking with students about their decisions should, therefore, be routine. When this is done, poor problem solving won't be allowed to continue and perpetuate additional difficulties. When unexpected difficulties appear, students should feel free to discard unwise solutions and seek new ones.

WHEN VALUES COLLIDE

Sometimes student–teacher conflicts cannot be successfully resolved in classroom problem-solving sessions. These conflicts usually involve cherished beliefs, values, personal preferences, personal tastes, lifestyles, ideas, and convictions (Gordon, 1974, pp. 283–284). They may involve things like gang membership, religion, drug use, profanity, manners, moral behavior, justice, honesty, sexual behavior, or beards and moustaches. Commonly, people refuse to bargain about these issues and put their cherished beliefs at risk. Teachers need to recognize these value conflicts for what they are and differentiate them from the conflict-of-need situations, which are properly solved in classroom problem-solving sessions.

In value conflicts, students are rarely willing to engage in problem solving. They do not buy your I-messages. They don't see that there is a problem. Students will likely resist problem solving, believing the problem is either in your imagination or none of your business.

How then can teachers deal with value conflicts? The first step is to gain acceptance by students as a consultant regarding value matters. This may be achieved only when students believe you are not evaluating them or trying to force them to change. You should indicate a willingness to discuss various issues and share your ideas without promoting your own point of view. In addition, you need to be prepared and appear knowledgeable. Students will discount your ideas if they are not based on a solid understanding of value issues from a broad perspective. They will correctly interpret your bias if you present ideas in a one-sided way.

Teachers should not pester their students about value questions. Share your ideas only once. Otherwise, greater resistance and defensiveness will be provoked. Students can be expected to be somewhat defensive about their beliefs. They have commonly had to defend themselves against various attacks. They may become programmed to resist new information because of a history of confrontations. They are likely to fight your ideas and defend their own vigorously. When resistance is encountered, it is wise to shift gears and engage in active listening. An effective consultant must correctly interpret students' resistance and defensiveness and communicate acceptance of how they feel. You may say, for example,

"You think that idea is not too sound."
"What I have said doesn't fit your experience."
"You find what I have said hard to believe."
"You appear to have reservations about what I have said."
"What I'm suggesting doesn't make sense to you."

Students need to be left with the responsibility of problem ownership when it comes to their values. If problems are encountered because of what they believe or feel, they must address these problems. Your role as a teacher-consultant is to provide information about new ways of thinking or behaving. Teachers should not feel obligated to have their students accept their views to be successful. Students have the ultimate responsibility to learn and to change their views in connection with what they learn (Gordon, 1974, pp. 293–298).

One thing teachers can do is to model what they value. One problem commonly encountered in doing this is the double standard prevalent in most schools. Usually, different rules apply to students and teachers. For example, teachers may have a different menu in the cafeteria or be able to go to the front of the line, while such privileges are denied students. Teachers may be provided separate and unequal toilet facilities or have comfortable lounges where they can relax and enjoy themselves. Students may have no such accommodations. Teachers and school administrators may promote the virtue of student self-determination with their words while at the same time restricting them in a multitude of ways. Nothing so infuriates students as adult hypocrisy—when one set of values is publicly pronounced and another practiced, particularly when the end result is a caste system with students at the lowest level (Gordon, 1974, pp. 298–299). Modeling cannot be expected to automatically alter student values. However, teachers who honestly model their values, devoid of hypocrisy, will earn the respect and admiration of their students. Even if the values teachers model are generally rejected, students may accept the lack of hypocrisy as a model for themselves.

Promoting student value changes involves maintaining good student–teacher relationships. Sometimes this involves teachers making modifications in their beliefs that more closely correspond to student values. This may not be as hard as it first appears. Some teachers have, for example, become more flexible, fun-loving, and intimate and less rigid and demanding. This changed role may be a complete contradiction to what has been assumed to be appropriate teacher behavior. It is unnecessary to change beliefs about values like honesty and integrity; society as a whole accepts such values, and students sense their appropriateness. But some changes may be necessary when it comes to how students dress, the music they listen to, or sexual behavior. It may be in the best interests of students to change their views of these matters, but these changes will occur only when students decide to do it. Teachers can provide only additional information and opportunities to explore the implications of what they value. It is appropriate for teachers to also spend time examining their own values. They may wish to make changes that may make their values more compatible with student attitudes and beliefs (Gordon, 1974, pp. 301–302).

Preventive Discipline

Teacher effectiveness training has few suggestions regarding the prevention of discipline problems. Some reference is made, however, to holding student-centered discussions to deal with such distractions as upcoming holidays, unusual weather, fights on the playground, pep rallies, and sporting events. It is recommended that teachers set aside their instructional plans temporarily and conduct open-ended discussions in which students are free to discuss anything they want. Conceivably, some classroom problems may be addressed in these meetings, although they are not specifically designed to do so.

THE PREVENTIVE I-MESSAGE

When teachers desire to receive future support and cooperation from their students, they may wish to send preventive I-messages. Whereas confrontational I-messages attempt to get students to modify unacceptable behavior that has already occurred, preventive I-messages are designed to modify future student behavior in some anticipated set of circumstances. These messages let students know ahead of time what teachers might need or want. When preventive I-messages are provided, students can sense more involvement in what teachers plan to do. These messages help avoid the possibility of surprises later and alert students to possible changes teachers may wish to make. The following are examples of preventive I-messages:

"I'd like to discuss what you plan to have ready on your report for Friday so I can anticipate what I need to prepare for that day."

"I'd appreciate having you begin thinking about what rules may be needed during our field trip to the art museum next week so that any problems that you anticipate can be prevented."

"We need to figure out what can be done when any members of your group are home sick while you are preparing for your presentations. Otherwise, only part of the work will get done, and you will be unable to coordinate your final presentations."

In communicating preventive I-messages, it is critical not to sound aggressive, demanding, or authoritarian. When these messages are properly transmitted to students, teachers can anticipate a number of important benefits:

1. Teachers maintain awareness of and control over their needs and feelings.
2. Students learn what their teachers' needs are and how they feel about them.
3. Teachers model openness, directness, and honesty and thereby foster similar behavior in their students.
4. Future conflicts and tensions from unknown or uncommunicated needs can be avoided, thus reducing the unpleasant surprises that can occur when problems are not anticipated.
5. Teachers are encouraged to assume full responsibility for future plans and needs.

6. Through openness, honesty, and mutual need satisfaction, better student–teacher relationships can be fostered (Gordon, 1989, pp. 119–121).

MODIFYING THE CLASSROOM ENVIRONMENT

Teachers can also prevent unacceptable student behaviors by modifying the classroom environment. This involves making changes in the physical and psychological characteristics of the classroom. Instead of discussing how to avoid specific discipline problems, the focus is on altering the physical environment of the classroom so that students spend their time learning more effectively, thus avoiding distracting influences.

The typical classroom commonly is a 960-square-foot room with a wooden or asphalt-tile floor, hard wall surfaces, large glass windows, chalkboards, and bulletin boards. Lighting and ventilation are frequently inadequate, and seating is so uncomfortable that few adults would put up with it. In many classrooms, temperature control is either inadequate or impossible. School rooms need more comfortable seating, better temperature control, better acoustical control, and more access to flexible furniture arrangements. In addition, classrooms need to be more beautifully and colorfully decorated. Children need places where they can go to concentrate, to work in groups, to build things, to experiment, or to listen to the teacher. Children of all ages need classrooms that are pleasant and where a variety of activities can be engaged in simultaneously. Classrooms might well have learning centers, libraries, art centers, audiovisual centers, and seminar rooms. Sometimes students also need locations where they can go to let off steam or cope with personal problems that prohibit productive work in the classroom. Teachers need places where they can confer with students privately as well as areas for instructional planning. Arrangements like these are unavailable in most classrooms but can be created through teacher ingenuity along with a bit of wood and some nails (Gordon, 1974, pp. 173–175).

Strengths and Weaknesses of Teacher Effectiveness Training

STRENGTHS

1. It promotes autonomy and self-regulation for students.
2. It promotes good student–teacher relationships.
3. It allows students to deal with personal problems and feelings.
4. It helps teachers communicate their needs to students so that students can appreciate how their behavior affects others.
5. It helps students understand that teachers have needs and feelings just like they do.

WEAKNESSES

1. Teachers may find some difficulty changing their role from directing and controlling students to actively listening.

2. Teachers may have difficulty accepting value differences between themselves and their students.
3. Transmitting I-messages instead of you-messages will be understandably difficult for teachers to master.
4. A more comprehensive preventive discipline approach may be needed to help teachers avoid having to deal with the number of possible problems likely to surface.

▼ SUMMARY

Attempting to control student behavior through rewards and punishment is unlikely to succeed. Punishment promotes aggression and violence. Most violent criminals have been recipients of abusive punishment. To be successful, teachers need to avoid controlling and directing their students' behavior. Far less criticism and regulation are needed in the classroom. Instead, teachers need to foster self-regulation along with positive student–teacher relationships. Good relationships provide an atmosphere in which students can learn productively about themselves and various instructional topics. Good relationships can be developed as teachers speak the language of acceptance to their students and avoid roadblocks like ordering, threatening, preaching, criticizing, and labeling. They also need to avoid communications that keep students from directing their own affairs. Praising and reassuring are two kinds of roadblocks that encourage students to avoid solving their problems. Praise and other types of rewards are commonly accepted and encouraged. However, there is good reason not to praise students. Ordinarily, the purpose of praise is designed to make an adult, not a child, feel good. Teachers praise in an effort to obtain student compliance. Instead, students need an opportunity to think through problems and feelings and choose courses of action without undue interference.

Teachers need to learn how to determine whether they or their students own particular problems. Otherwise, the problems are impossible to solve. Teachers can help students solve problems through active listening. This involves clarifying student messages without judging them. Students need to believe that their teachers not only understand them but accept them.

Teachers can effectively inform their students of how they feel about their behavior through well-constructed I-messages. I-messages must first inform students regarding the specific behavior that is creating a problem for the teacher. Next, the concrete effects of the problems must be communicated. Finally, students must be informed about the feelings these effects create.

When I-messages are unsuccessful in solving classroom problems, teachers may wish to engage students in classroom problem solving. In this process, problems are carefully identified and solutions determined and evaluated. Some problems are value laden and consequently difficult to solve. In this case, teachers are wise to offer their knowledge about a particular value topic but to refrain from forcing students to change their values. Such tactics will only undermine teachers' overall effectiveness.

CENTRAL IDEAS

1. Corporal punishment is generally accepted by educators and parents as an appropriate means of disciplining children, even though its use promotes violent behavior in recipients.
2. Children respond to power-based discipline by resisting, rebelling, retaliating, lying, blaming, bossing, bullying, apple-polishing, withdrawing, becoming emotional, getting sick, taking drugs, and other destructive behaviors.
3. Rewards undermine intrinsic motivation, encouraging children to be productive only when rewards are forthcoming.
4. The ownership of problems must be determined before these problems can be solved.
5. Students can more effectively solve their problems when they believe they are accepted as they are.
6. Teachers communicate unacceptance of their students by ordering, warning, moralizing, preaching, judging, labeling, praising, reassuring, interrogating, and being sarcastic.
7. Active listening involves properly decoding student messages, having a deep sense of trust for students to solve their own problems, and genuinely accepting the feelings expressed by students.
8. I-messages tell students exactly what their inappropriate behavior is, its tangible effect, and how their teachers feel about their behavior.
9. When resistance is experienced in response to I-messages, it may be appropriate to shift gears to active listening.
10. Problem solving involves helping students define the problem, generating possible solutions, evaluating each solution, making a decision, determining how to implement the decision, and evaluating the success of the decision.
11. When classroom problems are the result of value conflicts between teachers and their students, it is best not to force value changes. In this case, teachers can provide information about the value question but should not pester their students.

▼ QUESTIONS AND ACTIVITIES

QUESTIONS TO CONSIDER

1. What are the similarities and differences between TET and transactional analysis (Chapter 6)?
2. How does TET compare to logical consequences (Chapter 5)?
3. Why is corporal punishment so popular among educators and parents?
4. How can rewards and praise fail to encourage productive behavior?

CLASSROOM ACTIVITIES

1. Have students research the nondirective counseling methods of Carl Rogers (1942) and then report their findings to the class.

2. Have the instructor demonstrate active listening in class by role playing with students in class.
3. Have the instructor demonstrate the delivery of I-messages by role playing with students in class.

STUDENT APPLICATIONS

1. With classmates, use role playing to study how a teacher could use active listening in the following situations:
   a. A student comes into class in tears.
   b. Two students come to class still involved in a fight that started on the playground regarding who had first claim on a particular swing.
   c. A student sits and daydreams most of the time she is in class.
   d. A student is put down by another student who says the skirt she made in her sewing class looks stupid.
2. With classmates, use role playing to study how a teacher could send properly constructed I-messages for the following situations:
   a. A student is constantly interrupting the teacher during discussions and lectures in class.
   b. A student is caught cheating on a test.
   c. A student rips pages out of her book.
   d. A student digs holes in his desk.
   e. A student trips other students as they walk up the aisle.
   f. A student leaves candy wrappers on the floor under her desk.

EXPLORE YOUR PHILOSOPHY

1. Defend or refute the assumption that children inherently rebel when others try to regulate their behavior.
2. Defend or refute the assumption that rewards and praise undermine intrinsic motivation.
3. Defend or refute the assumption that students can solve their personal problems if teachers actively listen to them.
4. Defend or refute the assumption that students can solve problems that involve their teachers if teachers provide them with I-messages.
5. Compare the principles contained in your educational philosophy with those of TET. Determine consistencies and inconsistencies. Make adjustments in your philosophy as you believe appropriate.

▼ REFERENCES

Goodlad, J. I. (1984). *A place called school.* New York: McGraw-Hill.
Gordon, T. (1974). *T.E.T.: Teacher effectiveness training.* New York: Peter H. Wyden.
Gordon, T. (1976). *P.E.T.: Parent effectiveness training.* New York: Wyden Books.
Gordon, T. (1989). *Discipline that works: Promoting self discipline in children.* New York: Penguin.

Hyman, I. A. (1990). *Reading, writing and the hickory stick.* Lexington, MA: Lexington Books, D. C. Heath.

Hyman, I. A. (1996). *The enemy within: Tales of punishment politics and prevention.* Paper presented at the annual meeting of School Psychologists, Atlanta, Georgia.

Reardon, F., & Reynolds, R. (1975). *Corporal punishment in Pennsylvania.* Harrisburg, PA: Department of Education, Division of Research Bureau of Information Systems.

Rogers, C. R. (1942). *Counseling and psychotherapy.* Boston: Houghton Mifflin Company.

Straus, M., Gelles, R., & Steinmetz, S. (1980). *Behind closed doors: Violence in the American family.* New York: Anchor Press/Doubleday.

8

Reality Therapy/Choice Theory: William Glasser

OBJECTIVES

This chapter is designed to help you
1. Follow the steps of reality therapy to correct students' unacceptable behavior.
2. Understand the difference between reality therapy and choice theory.
3. Recognize human needs and know how to help students satisfy their own needs without depriving others of the opportunity to satisfy theirs.
4. Understand the difference between boss-management and lead-management.
5. Implement a preventive discipline program that incorporates Glasser's concept of a quality school.

ASSUMPTIONS

1. Human beings are basically self-regulating and can thus learn to manage their own behavior.
2. Children learn to be responsible by examining a full range of consequences for their behavior and making value judgments about their behavior and its consequences.
3. Avoiding an exploration of motives will help children accept responsibility for their behavior and not make excuses.
4. Human behavior consists of an effort on the part of each individual to satisfy needs for love, power, freedom, and fun.
5. Each person has a unique way of satisfying needs.
6. Children cannot be forced to change what they believe about how to best satisfy their needs.

Introduction

William Glasser is a prominent psychiatrist who gained national attention with the publication of *Reality Therapy: A New Approach to Psychiatry* (1965). His rejection of classical psychotherapy in favor of a more behavioral approach has been acclaimed by many as an enlightened move away from the beleaguered field of Freudian psychology. Instead of looking for the antecedents of inappropriate behavior in the subconscious mind, Glasser helped his patients find solutions to their behavioral problems in the present.

Through his work with juvenile offenders, Glasser became interested in helping teachers deal with school discipline problems. He now conducts workshops across the country for teachers and others in the helping professions.

▼   Ricardo was still upset. He had been sitting in the time-out room for 2 days, chafing because Ms. Danielson had told him that she would allow him back in class only if he made a plan that would guarantee no more disruptions. He had been routinely talking out in class and throwing spit wads. Ricardo was a high school junior, popular among his peers, and respected as one of their leaders. He had won his leadership status, in part, by boldly confronting teachers when they tried to correct his bad behavior. Right now he wanted desperately to be back in class with his friends, but he did not want to comply with Ms. Danielson's demands. He felt that he would lose face with his friends as well as forfeit some of the power he had acquired. In the past, because he demonstrated high achievement as a student and because his father served on the school board, teachers had usually backed down eventually. This time, however, Ms. Danielson was really holding out. He decided that it was just a matter of time until she caved in and let him come back to class.

Ricardo must come up with a plan before being allowed back in class.

As Ricardo sat pondering, Mr. Boden, the time-out supervisor, sat down next to him and asked to see his plan. Ricardo had only a blank sheet of paper to show. Mr. Boden asked, "Do you plan to go back to class?"

Ricardo replied, "Of course I do. I don't know why I have to sit here, though. This isn't doing anyone any good."

"If you really do want to go back to class, you'd better start on your plan," advised Mr. Boden.

Ricardo sat and considered the situation. What could he do, he wondered, that would help him save face with his friends and still satisfy Ms. Danielson?

Mr. Boden broke the silence. "What is the only way you will be able to get back to class?" he asked.

"I guess I'll have to write a plan," admitted Ricardo.

"When do you plan to start?" prompted Mr. Boden.

"I guess I should start now," volunteered Ricardo.

"I'll check back with you in 15 minutes to see how you are coming along," said Mr. Boden.

Reality Therapy

The case of Ricardo illustrates what happens to students whose unacceptable behavior is excessive. In this case, although Ricardo had been involved in creating classroom rules, he had chosen to violate them repeatedly. He therefore had to prepare a plan outside class that would solve the problem. Before his removal from class, Ms. Danielson may have taken Ricardo aside on one or more occasions and gone through the steps in Glasser's reality therapy to get him to change his unacceptable behavior. In Ricardo's case, these efforts failed, so he was assigned to the time-out room until he prepared a plan for readmittance to class.

Over the years, Glasser's views on dealing with discipline problems in the school have evolved. Glasser's initial background and training were in Freudian psychoanalysis. He eventually rejected these ideas in favor of an approach oriented more toward responsibility, an approach that made different assumptions about human needs and motives. Whereas psychotherapists assume that basic needs are psychosexual in nature, Glasser believes that human needs are defined more in terms of successful social relationships. Psychotherapists might attempt to uncover the source of poor psychological adjustment among various repressed, subconscious experiences; Glasser instead tries to help people live successfully in the conscious world. He does not accept the psychoanalytical axiom that the source of present behavioral and psychological difficulties consists of unconscious mental conflicts. To him, traumatic events experienced earlier in life do not unconsciously direct behavior. Rather, he believes that social and psychological problems are an outgrowth of bad decisions made about social relationships. His approach is to help people identify behaviors that are inconsistent with accepted social norms, accept them as irresponsible, and replace them with more socially desirable ones. He believes that good psychological health depends on loving and being loved and feeling worthwhile to ourselves and others. According to Glasser, being responsible is essential in successful relationships with others. Individuals must learn that their own needs can be satisfied only in a reciprocal way. The gratification of personal needs depends on how successfully each person can satisfy the needs of associates (Glasser, 1965).

CORRECTING UNACCEPTABLE BEHAVIORS

Children who fail to satisfy their needs create problems in school. They tend to be lonely, angry, frustrated, and openly rebellious. The teacher's role is to help them learn a way to behave that better satisfies their needs. Teachers must help students take responsibility for acknowledging their own behavior and for changing it as necessary. Teachers can do a number of things to help unruly students act more responsibly. Interviews with students in which the following steps are followed can be useful. Note that for interviews to be successful, teachers must already have established good relationships with their students. A relationship of trust is essential in reality therapy (Glasser, 1969):

1. Help students identify their inappropriate behavior. Do not accept excuses. Do not invite excuses by asking students why they behave as they do.
2. Have students identify various consequences if their inappropriate behavior continues.
3. Have students make value judgments about their behavior and its consequences.
4. Help students create plans to eliminate inappropriate behavior.
5. Help students stick to their plans or suffer the consequences if they fail to do so.

These steps are discussed in detail next and illustrated with student–teacher dialogues. Explanations of teacher responses are also given to show the rationale behind these reactions and how they are consistent with reality therapy principles.

Identifying Inappropriate Behavior.   People find it difficult to admit doing something wrong. Commonly, they deny bad behavior by shifting blame or claiming that they could not help what they did. However, to improve behavior, students must first admit their misbehavior. The teacher helps by getting students to identify the behavior considered inappropriate. No attempt is made to judge the behavior as good or bad.

Commonly, teachers invite students to excuse their misbehavior by asking them "why" they behaved inappropriately. For example, a student coming late to class is ordinarily asked why he or she is late. When students are caught cheating on examinations, they are usually asked why. When homework is habitually turned in late, teachers are also inclined to ask why. Students are full of excuses and ready to offer them even without being invited. Glasser believes teachers should avoid inviting excuses by asking why. If students try to excuse their bad behavior, teachers should ignore the excuse and direct the student to address the problem.

Consider the case of Gordon, an elementary school student whose teacher is trying to help him identify his role in fighting with other students:

Teacher	Gordon, what was it you did to Owen out on the playground during the morning recess?
Gordon	I didn't do anything.

Teacher	What did you do to Owen just as he was starting to use the swing?
Gordon	I hit him, but he hit me first. He never shares the swing with any of the rest of us.
Teacher	So what did you do to him?
Gordon	I hit him.
Teacher	Who else have you been fighting with this past week?
Gordon	Nobody.
Teacher	Who were you shoving yesterday by the drinking fountain?
Gordon	Sarah.
Teacher	And who did you throw sand at on the playground during the afternoon recess?
Gordon	Ruth.

Gordon tries to excuse his behavior by explaining that Owen started the fight. He also justifies himself by telling his teacher that Owen never shares. To claim that another person started a conflict or problem is the usual way in which youngsters shift the blame for misbehavior. Misbehaving children can then claim that the bad behavior of others justifies their own. When students attempt to excuse their behavior in this way, teachers need considerable skill to avoid ridiculing them or giving support to their excuses. One way teachers can avoid these pitfalls is to bypass the students' remarks by asking them to state their own role in the difficulty. In this way, conflict about "who started it" can be avoided. Trying to resolve a "who started it" conflict usually interferes with helping students take responsibility for their inappropriate behavior.

Making students describe their behavior is better than having their teachers do it. It is unlikely that students will "own" their behavior if teachers identify it for them. Questions, therefore, must be asked that direct students to state what they have done to cause problems. They will, of course, resist admitting fault. They will even lie to avoid accepting blame. If students do tell a lie about their role in a problem situation, just ignore it. Ignoring lies is unnatural for most adults, who feel that not challenging the lies of children will somehow corrupt them or encourage them to lie even more. However, children often would rather have parents and teachers focus on lying than admit the inappropriate behavior in question. When interrogated about lying, children often create a diversion by accusing parents and teachers of not trusting them. Discussions about trust usually weaken teacher–student relationships and fail to help children act more responsibly. Fortunately, once children get used to being more responsible for their own behavior by having to admit it, they are less likely to lie.

Notice in the dialogue that Gordon is given clues about the specific way in which he is expected to respond to the teacher. For example, Gordon is asked what he did to Owen at morning recess just as Owen was about to use the swing. These clues are designed to make it difficult for Gordon to claim that he does not know what the teacher is talking about. Children often say that they do not know what is meant by teachers' questions. Clues help avoid this problem. They also define the domain in which students are expected to respond. Without these clues, students can direct attention to many different areas and get the conversation off track. Notice also that Gordon is required to identify several instances of fighting. This pattern helps establish that there is a serious problem that needs solving. There is no reason to have a meeting if the student has misbehaved only once. It is only when misbehavior persists that it must be corrected.

Identifying Consequences. The next step in reality therapy is to help students identify whatever adverse consequences are associated with their inappropriate behavior. Gordon identifies such consequences for fighting:

Teacher	You have indicated that you have been involved in fighting with several class members. What can be the result of this?
Gordon	I can get into trouble.
Teacher	What kind of trouble?
Gordon	Maybe I'll get sent to the principal's office.
Teacher	Yes, perhaps. What action do you think the principal might take in a case such as yours?
Gordon	I don't know.
Teacher	What might happen to your privilege of being in school?
Gordon	I guess the principal might kick me out.
Teacher	Yes, I suppose you might not be allowed to remain in school. In your fight with Jon, you were back by the aquaria and the science equipment. What could have happened to those items during a fight?
Gordon	They could have been broken.
Teacher	If you broke them, who would have to pay for them?
Gordon	I would, I guess.
Teacher	Yes, I agree. When you fight with others, what could happen to you or the other person physically?
Gordon	I guess somebody could get hurt.

In this dialogue, several points need to be emphasized. Notice how the teacher responds when Gordon says that he could be kicked out of school for fighting. Gordon's suggestion indicates his belief that school administrators act arbitrarily. He tries to claim no responsibility. The teacher clarifies the situation—by fighting, Gordon could forfeit his participation in school—to help him understand that being excluded is a consequence of decisions he makes, not some arbitrary punishment imposed by the principal.

Notice also that Gordon is helped to understand the consequences he will undoubtedly experience if he breaks school equipment. Note that Gordon is specified in the teacher's question as the cause of the breakage. The teacher might have asked instead, "What is likely to happen if school equipment gets broken during a fight?" Had this been the question, Gordon might have said that the school would have to replace it, implying that he had no responsibility himself. The way questions are formed, therefore, is important in helping students accept responsibility for their behavior.

In addition, notice that the teacher's questions contain clues about what responses are expected. These clues help students learn what their teachers wish to discuss with them. They limit the kinds of responses that may be made and allow teachers to deal more directly with problems without getting sidetracked. For example, the question

"What might happen to your privilege of being in school?" confines the topic to staying in school. Focus is kept on the problem and away from other topics that might come up if questions were more general. The teacher could have asked, "What do principals do when students fight?" There are a number of ways to respond to this question. Gordon might say that the principal would call his parents, give him a spanking, or put him in detention. These punishments may have little to do with what might actually happen.

Finally, notice that Gordon is allowed to formulate the consequences himself. Observe also that in contrast with the logical consequences model (Chapter 5), he considers a number of consequences rather than having the teacher simply give him two alternatives from which to choose. In the logical consequences model, students must choose between two consequences and then have their choice imposed on them. In reality therapy, a range of possible consequences is explored so students can visualize the potential hazards of their misbehavior. They are encouraged to change their behavior so it is consistent with consequences they find acceptable.

Making Value Judgments.   After the consequences have been identified, students are asked to decide (1) whether or not they want the consequences to occur and (2) whether or not they judge their behavior to be inappropriate. The teacher in our example asks Gordon questions that help him make such value judgments:

Teacher	Gordon, you have said that you could possibly get yourself expelled from school by fighting. In addition, you have indicated that school property could be broken, in which case you would have to pay for it. And what is most important, you have said that someone could get hurt, perhaps even seriously. Do you want that to happen?
Gordon	No.
Teacher	What do you think about fighting, then?
Gordon	I guess I need to stop.

In this step, it is wise to have students make a statement about all the consequences collectively. Eliciting such a statement increases the likelihood that students will answer in a responsible manner. If consequences are presented one at a time, students may deny that some of them are significant problems. Another useful tactic is to embellish the students' responses with helpful additions. In the example, the teacher raises the stakes: "And what is most important, you have said that someone could get hurt, perhaps even seriously." The teacher has added the idea that getting hurt is a more serious problem than the other consequences. It is wise not to discuss this statement with students, however. Such discussions are usually counterproductive. The same is true of discussions involving the seriousness of injuries received during a fight. Actually, death sometimes is the result of mindless scuffling and brawling. Severe injury is always a possibility. However, children are more likely to think of outcomes in terms of their intentions than what could actually happen. They may not truly believe that debilitating or life-threatening injuries could occur if they did not plan to inflict them. They will claim that you are just overreacting. In addition, such discussions may degenerate into disputes about who is at fault or how the seriousness of an injury is defined.

Creating a Plan. When students no longer accept their behavior as appropriate and wish to avoid the consequences associated with it, a plan can be devised to overcome the problem. Students must make value judgments about their behavior because, in the process of making a plan, they may resist changing behavior with which they have found some satisfaction in the past. If they put up resistance, you just have to ask them what they have already said about changing their behavior. Then help them formulate a specific strategy for eliminating the behavior. Gordon shows some initial hesitation in developing his plan:

Teacher	Now that you have identified the consequences of fighting, you are ready to devise a plan for eliminating it. What do you think you could do to avoid fighting in the future?
Gordon	(After a long pause) I don't know. I can't think of what I could do. Maybe you could try to keep Dee and some of the others from picking on me.
Teacher	What did you already say you felt about fighting?
Gordon	I said I thought I should stop.
Teacher	I have noticed that some of your fights take place in the hall just outside the classroom. What could you do immediately as you come to class to get involved more productively and be less likely to fight?
Gordon	I could come into class, take my seat, and start to work.
Teacher	What specifically could you do, say tomorrow, when you come to class?
Gordon	I have a book I'd like to bring.
Teacher	Do you think that would work?
Gordon	Yes.
Teacher	Why don't you try it for a week, and then let me know how you think you are doing.

Gordon is initially resistant and perhaps unable to think of how to avoid fighting. This way of thinking is new for most students, so their inability to make plans for avoiding difficulties is understandable. At first, teachers will probably have to provide clues that suggest possible plans. It is also necessary to have students be specific. When Gordon proposed what he thought was a good plan—he would come into class, take his seat, and start to work—it was still necessary for him to specifically identify what he would read. To follow through, the teacher should make sure that Gordon does in fact bring his book to class the next day.

Sometimes students are much less cooperative than Gordon appears to be. In such cases, a positive relationship still must be maintained. Teachers commonly react to students' rash behavior. When students are obnoxious, teachers are tempted to treat them harshly to show them that they cannot get away with such behavior. Such reactions must be avoided. Maintaining a positive relationship with students is critical. To illustrate, assume that when Gordon is asked to identify his fighting behavior, he responds in the following way:

Teacher	What did you do to Owen out on the swing at morning recess?
Gordon	I didn't do anything! I'm always getting blamed! Why can't you leave me alone? Nobody ever blames Owen! He's the one who started it!

Teacher	But what did you do to him?
Gordon	(Silence.)
Teacher	You probably need to think about what I asked. I need to work on a project at my desk. When you feel you would like to talk about the episode on the playground today, let me know. (The teacher leaves Gordon to think about the problem and to cool down.)

In this situation, little will be accomplished by maintaining contact with Gordon and trying to force him to respond. He will only become more hostile. It also does little good to sit and expect him to respond. It is better to move away and indicate a willingness to talk when he is ready. Students must realize that their problems cannot be resolved until they are willing to talk and that the teacher can wait as long as necessary. Sometimes the teacher must wait quite a while. However, the necessary time should be provided. If teachers try to force students to respond, they may become hostile and more inclined to shift the blame. Also, students know that if they wait long enough, they can usually avoid accepting responsibility for misbehavior. Teachers must be willing to wait longer than their students.

TIME-OUT

Sometimes students make a commitment not to misbehave and are unruly anyway. These students should be cycled again through the steps of reality therapy. They may also be required to suffer the consequences they have already identified. If students refuse to cooperate with reasonable classroom expectations, or if they violate rules they have previously agreed to accept, they may be candidates for isolation from the class. When students are a threat to the instructional program, it is appropriate to exclude them. These isolation (time-out) procedures are not intended to be punitive. Students are not assigned some arbitrary period of time-out as punishment. They are expected to stay in isolation only as long as it takes to produce a workable plan for returning to the classroom. If there is a schoolwide program for reality therapy, there will be a designated time-out room, monitored by a staff member. If teachers use reality therapy on their own, they can create a time-out area within the classroom by partitioning off a corner of the room. Assignment to the time-out area may be necessary when students habitually refuse to abide by class rules.

During time-out, students are directed to create a written plan that they believe will solve their discipline problems. The purpose of requiring a written plan is to help students achieve a greater sense of commitment. The plan becomes a statement of intentions, a contract between students and their teachers. If problems persist, students can be referred to other professionals as necessary.

Choice Theory

In 1984, Glasser wrote *Control Theory*, later called choice theory (Glasser, 1997b), which on the surface may appear to be a radical departure from his initial work in reality therapy. Although there are some significant additions to his earlier ideas, choice theory is compatible with reality therapy. Actually, it is better to view choice theory as an extension of reality therapy, with choice theory being primarily a preventive approach to discipline and reality therapy being a corrective one. Glasser's intention is for teachers to use reality therapy as the vehicle for teaching students the principles of choice theory (N. Glasser, 1989). The major difference between reality therapy and choice theory has to do with the central role of need gratification.

BASIC HUMAN NEEDS

The focus of reality therapy is on helping students become more responsible in a behavioral sense. When students behave more responsibly, their needs for social acceptance can be satisfied and their status among their peers enhanced. As a result, their sense of personal worth increases.

Choice theory has an expanded list of human needs, which are more central to its basic application. Glasser suggests that children be taught about these needs as well as ways of more legitimately satisfying them (Glasser, 1998). The list of needs associated with control theory includes

- Love
- Control
- Freedom
- Fun

Love. The need for love is similar to the need for social acceptance in reality therapy. As human beings, we need to love and be loved. We need to belong. We need to be accepted by others as significant and important. We need to believe that we are accepted by others for what we are and that this acceptance is unconditional. Children usually try to satisfy their need for love and acceptance through behavior designed to get attention. Children are constantly trying to get the attention of parents and others as a sign of love and acceptance. If others give approval, the children are satisfied. Unfortunately, children often want more attention than teachers and parents can provide. When their efforts fail, children commonly resort to more drastic measures. These measures are the source of much misbehavior. Although it is difficult in a class of 30 or more students to see that each one gets sufficient love and attention, the need remains and must somehow be met.

Children who are lonely and ignored often behave outrageously in their quest to belong and be accepted. Even suicide may be considered when this need is not met. For these children, death is more desirable than living with the pain of loneliness. Sometimes love given on a conditional basis creates similar reactions. Love is conditional when acceptance depends on a child's conforming to expectations. Teachers as well as parents often communicate to a child that their love is conditional ("I'm happy when you make good grades"). Children need to be told, over and over, that they are loved—not because of what they do, not in spite of what they do, but just for who they are.

Control.   All of us need sufficient power to regulate our lives as we desire. Unfortunately, teachers usually deny children the opportunity to satisfy this need. Children are considered too immature to make responsible choices. Therefore, when children assert themselves, teachers ordinarily increase their own control. This increase in control only encourages greater rebellion. It is ironic that rebellion is promoted by excessive control and that control is the usual means by which teachers and school administrators attempt to quell rebelliousness. When teachers stimulate rebellion in this way and then punish children who act out, they usually reinforce bad behavior in the process. It would be far better to provide students a way to satisfy their need for control in legitimate ways.

Students not only need to have reasonable power and control over their lives but also need to use power properly to satisfy other needs, such as love. For example, if children exercise power in abusive ways, they will not obtain the love and acceptance they desire. They must achieve an appropriate balance in satisfying these potentially contradictory needs. Children and adults often mistakenly think that they can force others to love them, which of course they cannot. In fact, love can occur only when needs for control are moderated. Children must understand how this relationship between love and power works to avoid having their need for love thwarted.

The need to control cannot simply be renounced. It is a legitimate need. However, the way in which control is exercised must usually be modified. People ordinarily use control to manipulate the environment or another person so as to satisfy their needs in a desired way. This use of control is appropriate so long as others can satisfy their needs as well. When we manage our needs and curb their gratification, we are able to create predictability in our lives. We can regulate important happenings and outcomes, defend ourselves against the arbitrariness of others, and avoid involvement in unpleasant situations. In a world where power is often abused, self-regulation is desirable and satisfying.

Children's efforts to obtain control are often awkward and lacking in consideration for others. So teachers may react negatively to students' efforts to manage themselves. They assume that students are irresponsible and immature. However, children's irresponsible behavior is often just a reaction to control by teachers. For example, a teacher may suggest that students be courteous and take turns with other children using the swings on the playground. Children may react angrily to such a suggestion, however, because they want to decide for themselves when to swing. They feel that the teacher's controlling behavior threatens their ability to maintain personal power, which is essential to them. Even if they are aware that their exercise of power often irritates or alienates others, some children are unable to modify their need for control sufficiently to avoid causing these reactions. Confronted with disapproval from others, such children may overreact and become even more controlling when teachers suggest that they take turns.

Young people often find it difficult to see that their power needs can be met by understanding subject matter. This is because educators emphasize grades instead of the power inherent in a good education. Because tests are emphasized as the way students demonstrate understanding instead of encouraging students to communicate their knowledge in more pervasive and powerful ways, students don't get to feel the strength that is achieved when their knowledge is shared and communicated through personal writings. It is rare that creative thinking, the most empowering of all human behaviors, is encouraged in school (Glasser, 1986b)

Freedom.   Children not only need to be in control of their own lives but also need to be free from control by others. However, satisfying this need can also create conflict. Teachers usually interpret children's efforts to obtain freedom as affronts to their authority. In addition, they may doubt the ability of children to use freedom responsibly. Thus, opportunities for free expression are withheld pending evidence of maturity. Freedom, however, is a necessary component of learning to be responsible. It therefore cannot be used as a reward for becoming responsible. Wise teachers provide an increasing level of freedom as students show an inclination and ability to use it wisely. One way of providing freedom is to teach children decision-making skills. Even young children can learn to make valid decisions about various issues that concern them. For example, students can help make decisions about class rules and topics to be studied.

It is important to realize that providing freedom is no guarantee that it will be used responsibly. Unrestrained freedom can cause chaos. However, if too much control is exercised, rebellion occurs. Teachers therefore need to provide freedom gradually as children become more able to govern themselves. They must offer children several choices and at the same time teach them about the consequences of those choices. Choosing between various possibilities may be new to some children. They may not realize the nature of the consequences they can expect from specific choices. Some consequences can best be learned by experience; some can be learned only by experience. Children must learn that freedom exists only when consequences are carefully taken into account—that ignoring consequences will likely deprive them of the freedom they desire. For example, students who fail to take the consequences of drug abuse into account may find themselves deprived of the opportunity to complete an education, restricted by ill health or injury, or perhaps incarcerated.

Fun.   Children are driven by the need for fun, far more than parents and teachers are usually willing to accommodate. Even adults have a greater need for fun than they usually admit. Glasser believes that fun is as basic as any other need (Glasser, 1984). People of all ages desire it. In addition, he believes that a relationship exists between learning and our genetic need for fun. Learning, he says, is a lifelong pursuit, and fun is inherently a part of it. It is ironic that the academic part of schooling, however, is usually devoid of fun. Most students do not take pleasure in what they are currently learning. How can we expect them to do well in school if they do not enjoy much of what they do? In fact, students are told, often by teachers, that learning is not supposed to be fun. Rather, it is hard work. This admonition implies that work is not fun either. If tasks are not fun, they become a forced drudgery. When we have fun, we are able to work for long hours and look forward to doing it.

Children's need for fun is evident in their common query to one another, "Was it fun?" Fun is obviously important to them; it is a gauge against which to measure many different experiences and activities. Adults often ask the same question. They seek fun just as children do. One has only to look at the multibillion-dollar industries that supply us with an ever-increasing number of opportunities for "fun." But adults, forgetting that fun is a human need, often misapply the term fun exclusively to forms of entertainment. Many experiences can provide pleasure or enjoyment. But if they do not also provide a real sense of satisfaction, then, according to Glasser's usage, they are not fun.

BALANCING NEEDS

Balancing needs is an important part of choice theory. As the following story illustrates, needs must be balanced, because overemphasis of one need may make satisfying other needs more difficult.

▼ One day three 11-year-olds were trying to decide how they would spend their day. Each suggestion proposed by one was swiftly rejected by the others. It was obvious that what mattered most was not to participate in a particular activity but to have one's suggestions accepted. One of the three suggested that they go to the union building at the university. The second favored playing video games at the arcade in the mall. The third had just picked up a new game and wanted the others to come over and play it.

"I want to go to the Wilkinson Center," said Chris. "I'm getting tired of sitting around playing games all the time. I want to do something more creative."

"Well, I think we should go to the mall," responded Alma. "We went to the Wilkinson Center last week. Besides, you can't do anything creative there."

"I've been wanting to play my new game," interrupted Bailey. "I got it especially so we could play it today. If we don't do it, then I shouldn't have got it in the first place."

This conversation went on for several minutes, with each child trying to take the lead and persuade the others to follow. Finally, Chris and Alma decided that they would go to the Wilkinson Center and stop by the mall on the way back. Bailey was unbending, complaining to the others that they never did what anybody else wanted, and stomped angrily home to find someone else to play with.

A week later the same three children were having a similar discussion. This time Bailey wanted to go to the Wilkinson Center, Chris wanted to hang out at the mall, and Alma wanted to stay home and have the other two come over to play. They argued awhile, and then Alma and Bailey went off to the Wilkinson Center while Chris was left behind fuming.

This story of conflict between friends is a common scenario. Each child is hoping to maintain friendship and not give up control. Sometimes friendship wins out, and sometimes control does. Control is hard to forfeit, even when temporary loss of friendship is the result. Glasser advocates teaching children to balance their needs by having them forgo some control in favor of developing friendships. Each child needs to feel accepted and loved. These needs can be met if friendships are cultivated. It is therefore unwise to be so controlling that potential friends are alienated.

The needs for freedom and control must also be balanced. Conflicts between freedom and control can be a problem when children want freedom but are unwilling to grant the same privilege to their peers. They want to be the ones who always get to tell the others what to do and yet never accept suggestions from them. This self-centeredness usually thwarts the playmates' need for fun and causes them to reject one another. Balancing personal needs with the needs of desired associates is, therefore, one of two interactive dimensions of need balancing. A second is the balance that must be achieved between our own competing needs.

UNFULFILLED NEEDS AND MISBEHAVIOR

Unfulfilled needs promote misbehavior in many forms. Teachers can avoid these problems by discerning children's needs and by helping them satisfy their needs legitimately. Needs should be recognized and satisfied before patterns of inappropriate behavior develop.

For example, children's sense of well-being may depend on getting attention from teachers; they may perpetually seek approval as a sign that others accept them. In a class of 30 or more students, teachers cannot satisfy everyone's needs on demand. So some students resort to misbehavior, which is a sure way of getting the teacher's attention. It would be better for the teacher to anticipate students' needs for attention and satisfy them in advance rather than wait and react negatively when students misbehave. For instance, teachers could call attention to students by having them share their hobbies with the rest of the class or by giving them responsibilities in class that provide status.

It is not uncommon to claim that certain children require too much attention because they are used to getting it, even when in fact they come from an attention-deprived background. It is normal for children to want attention from adults. The problem is not so much a desire for too much attention as a result of receiving too little. Children may misbehave to make up for this deficiency.

Another common cause of misbehavior is the failure to satisfy students' legitimate needs for freedom and control. Teachers commonly believe that they must exercise control over their students. Students, on the other hand, desire more freedom. Children do in fact need more freedom than what is offered in most school situations. When teachers are too controlling, students may become rebellious. When students rebel, teachers may become more coercive. Rebellion by students is accepted as evidence that they are not responsible enough to use freedom wisely. Even when children simply get out of hand in an overexuberant effort to have fun, teachers often react negatively and conclude that the children are unable to govern themselves wisely. But when teachers apply more control to quell students' misbehavior, they can usually anticipate even more misbehavior.

THE PICTURES IN OUR HEADS

Glasser believes that each of us has a unique way of determining how our basic needs can best be satisfied, which he describes as a set of pictures we have in our heads. These pictures are stored in our minds as long as they continue to satisfy us. When we no longer consider them worthwhile, we remove them and replace them with more satisfying pictures (Glasser, 1984). Sometimes the pictures we have do not correspond to the real world, and irrational behavior is often the result. Teachers and students, for example, are likely to have vastly different pictures of how each wants to be satisfied by the other. Children may have a picture of teachers who let them out early for recess, who always explain complex concepts in an understandable way, who pay special attention to them, who lecture in an entertaining way, who give easy tests, who never give homework or pop quizzes, or who provide treats and lots of parties. Teachers may visualize students who sit quietly in their seats, who promptly turn in all work, who study hard, who pay attention, who become deeply involved in class discussions, or who write excellent papers. Obviously, these pictures are somewhat incompatible. And, unfortunately, both the teacher and the student find it difficult to adopt the other's pictures. To complicate matters for teachers, different students have different pictures of what is most satisfying to them. Consequently, meeting all students' needs is difficult if not almost impossible. Teachers must realize, however, that what students do is the most satisfying choice they have at the time (Glasser, 1997a). It is, therefore, difficult to change how children behave. Teachers and students must both learn that the only behavior they can change is their own (Glasser, 1997b).

Glasser emphasizes that we do not picture ourselves doing badly. We all have a view of being successful and happy. We may at times choose to do self-destructive things, but we do not intend to destroy ourselves. Our pictures make sense to us; otherwise, we would not have them (Glasser, 1984). Students may, for example, take drugs despite repeated warnings about the hazards of doing so. Teachers who issue the warnings undoubtedly believe that these students are determined to destroy themselves, and they cannot understand why they would choose to do so. The students, on the other hand, may picture drugs as the only way to escape the misery they confront in life.

CONFLICTS IN SATISFYING NEEDS FOR CONTROL

According to Glasser, we always have control over what we do, even when we behave destructively. We react to the environment but are not directly controlled by it. For example, if we are hurrying to take someone to the hospital and are confronted by a powerful external stimulus such as a red light, we will not simply respond to the light and stop. Instead, we will make a decision based on other factors as well. Most of us in this case would check the traffic and go on through the light. Therefore, even those who appear to be controlled are not being controlled in a strict sense. They will continue to follow others' directions only as long as they find it satisfying to do so.

Part of this satisfaction, says Glasser, must include a sense of personal control. To illustrate, Glasser points out that even animals seek to maintain control. Piglets who are trained to respond to a stimulus of food by climbing up a ladder and going down a slide will not continue to perform indefinitely. They can be depended on to repeat these actions for only a few weeks (Glasser, 1984). Humans undoubtedly are even less susceptible to the control of others. We like to control but despise being controlled, which causes problems in our relationships with others. Although we are in a continual struggle for control to ensure that our needs are satisfied, we cannot in the process deprive our friends of the opportunity to satisfy their needs. Otherwise, our need for love and acceptance may be put in jeopardy.

If control can be successfully negotiated with our close associates, we can anticipate relative harmony. But the need to control is potent. When others interfere with our need to maintain control at a level we desire, we react in various ways. Small children usually cry or throw tantrums. Later, when these methods prove ineffective, children may resort to a manifestation of depression or even threats of suicide to gain control. These drastic steps usually have the desired effect, at least for a while, but they also create a level of misery beyond what the children anticipated and from which they find it extremely difficult to remove themselves. Once depression is established, its associated feelings become automatic, and the individuals who experience it may be convinced that they have nothing to do with its occurrence.

All our needs require satisfaction and play a very significant role in how we behave. Teachers must realize that students cannot deny their needs. Instead, they are dedicated to fulfilling them. Unfortunately, none of the needs Glasser describes is sufficiently satisfied in school, at least for many students. Because their needs are not adequately met, these students drop out in one way or another. Many of them create discipline problems. Glasser contends that a radical restructuring of the schools is necessary before students' needs can be met and that discipline problems will continue until conditions change. Glasser believes that students do what is most satisfying under the circumstances. We can safely assume that if students are more satisfied doing something other than their schoolwork, they will spend whatever time they can doing it. Sometimes they doodle or daydream or just look out the window. More often, they try to enhance their relationships with their peers and carry on various social interactions during times when their teachers expect them to study.

The Quality School

The *Quality School* is Glasser's (1992b) latest effort to improve the schools. He has taken a leadership role in implementing his quality school ideas in selected demonstration schools. One prominent example is in Johnson City, New York, where all the schools in the district use choice theory. In addition to teachers becoming proficient in using choice theory, students are being taught the same principles. Glasser reports that the behavior of these students is markedly improved. In this work, he emphasizes that schools must provide students a better way to satisfy their needs, which involves a complete change in the nature of school management. He believes that schools make the mistake of forcing students to acquire knowledge or memorize facts that have no value for them in the real world (Glasser, 1998). Glasser has taken his school management model from the work of W. Edwards Deming, whose ideas about management have had such a profound effect on the economic growth of Japan since the end of World War II. In presenting his plan for the schools, Glasser criticizes current school managers for accepting low-quality work. He claims that no one, students included, will expend the effort necessary to learn unless they believe that "there is quality in what they are asked to do" (Glasser, 1992a). Glasser contends that a manager cannot make people do quality work. In fact, no one can make anyone do anything. However, if students are allowed to do quality work, they will perform without coercion.

Glasser explains that the main complaint of students is not that school is too hard. They say that they could do the work if they wanted to. Instead, they claim that schoolwork is boring and fails to satisfy their basic needs. He points out that many proposals for school reform are too coercive, such as the recommendations contained in *A Nation at Risk* (National Commission on Excellence in Education, 1983): a longer school day and year, stiffer graduation requirements, and more homework. These recommendations fail to address the problem that doing more of what is currently offered would achieve nothing except to put more pressure on children to accomplish what they have already rejected as unsatisfying (Glasser, 1992a). These efforts will not solve the problems. They are the problem (Glasser, 1998).

BOSS-MANAGEMENT VERSUS LEAD-MANAGEMENT

Glasser believes that what school officials say are student discipline problems are in reality school management problems. School administrators fall into the trap of thinking that discipline problems, not unsatisfying education, cause low achievement levels. The real problem is that students struggle to resist the low-quality, standardized, fragmented curriculum that is being forced on them through coercive administrative practices. When students who fail to become involved register their disinterest, some educators apply more coercion, which only serves to alienate them further. Glasser (1992a) calls this approach boss-management and describes some of its characteristics:

1. The administrator or teacher (boss) establishes the task and standards for students. Students must simply adjust to the job as the boss defines it.
2. The boss usually tells, rather than shows, students how to do the work and rarely asks how it can be done better.
3. The boss is the exclusive evaluator. Students are considered unable or biased. Bosses tend to settle for just enough quality work to get by.
4. When students resist, the boss uses coercion, usually in the form of punishment, to obtain compliance. In the process, teachers and administrators create an adversarial relationship between themselves and students.

Glasser recommends a change from boss-management to lead-management:

1. The lead-manager encourages students to discuss the quality of the work they want to perform and the time constraints they wish to put on themselves.
2. The lead-manager constantly tries to fit the learning task to the skills of students.
3. The lead-manager provides students with models of how they should perform and allows them to evaluate their own work, acting on the assumption that students know not only what high-quality work is but also when they are producing it.
4. The lead-manager is a facilitator, establishing a nonadversarial classroom atmosphere without coercion.

A productive work atmosphere develops because the leader authentically does everything possible to provide students not only the best tools with which to learn but also the autonomy to govern themselves in the process. This autonomy helps students to satisfy the ever-present need to be in control as much as they possibly can.

THE QUALITY SCHOOL PROGRAM

Quality is defined by Glasser as any experience students have that is consistently satisfying to one or more of their basic needs (Glasser, 1993). In a quality school, education is defined as the process through which we discover that learning adds quality to our lives. Teaching is the process of imparting knowledge to students who want to acquire this knowledge because they believe it will add quality to their lives. Teachers must provide educational experiences that students judge will add quality now and in the future (Glasser, 1992b). No one will work hard at school without believing that there is value or quality in what is asked. They also need to have a clear idea of what a good education is (W. Glasser, 1989). Quality almost always includes caring for others, is always useful, always involves hard work, and for both teachers and students, it provides a high degree of satisfaction. Because it is so satisfying, we all carry in our heads a clear idea of what quality is for ourselves (Glasser, 1992a).

Glasser (1992a) has made a number of suggestions intended to help educators understand the specific attributes of quality schools:

1. School experiences should satisfy the basic needs of love and acceptance, control, freedom, and fun. The traditional practice of rewards and punishments must therefore be abandoned. Punishment often promotes misbehavior. Rewards satisfy needs, but students may still resent the power of teachers to give or withhold them. The competition established in a reward system automatically produces losers and winners instead of a high level of learning for all students. Teachers should not attempt to give rewards as an inducement for students to do what they find no satisfaction in doing. Giving students rewards only conditions them to the rewards and fails to promote excellence.

2. Learning teams should be organized as a basic instructional strategy. Students will satisfy more of their needs in a cooperative learning environment than in a traditional competitive one.

3. Teachers should allow for considerable variation in how students satisfy their needs. Each of us has a personal picture of how best to satisfy our needs. We are generally unable to adopt the view of someone else. Students need to include high-quality school experiences as a significant part of the picture they have of themselves and their world.

4. If teachers want to become a positive part of students' pictures of how to best satisfy their needs (the quality world of students), they must encourage students to express themselves and then listen carefully to what they say.

5. Teachers are ultimately in charge of what goes on in the classroom. However, they must avoid making their power an issue as they manage a class.

6. Teachers should make it clear to students that the higher the quality of their work, the more they will be in charge of it. Because high-quality work leads to greater independence and success in life generally, the message is conveyed that students are more in charge of their lives when they increase the quality of the work they do in school.

7. There is little lecturing in a quality classroom. Students are involved in discussions and in work done in groups or independently.

8. Students should be helped to understand the importance of delayed gratification. It often pays to endure some immediate short-term pain to increase the chance of obtaining some later, long-term pleasure.

9. If students are asked whether it takes hard work to get a good education, they will answer "Yes." If they are asked whether they are smart enough to get a good education, almost all will answer "Yes." However, if they are asked whether they are working hard in school, most will answer "No." Students will work harder to obtain a quality education when they are taught what it consists of and how it can be obtained.

10. If teachers treat their students coercively, students will waste time, size up their teachers, and try to outwit them.

11. When students are coerced, they usually refuse to accept ownership of the work they are asked to do. They will not accept the responsibility of evaluating their own work and improving it. Students need to set their own standards for quality, not just do well according to the teacher's standards.

12. In a quality school, there are no bad grades. All permanent low grades are eliminated. A low grade would be considered temporary, a problem to be solved by students and teachers working together. Hopefully, students would conclude that it is worthwhile to expend more effort to achieve a higher level of quality. High grades would be retained in a quality school because, if they are fairly earned, their coercive power is not destructive.

13. The lowest grade would be a *B*. The level of quality expected for the grade of *B* would be about as it is now. Students could also earn As and A+s.

14. Quality schools would not concern themselves with outside measures of productivity such as state-mandated achievement tests. Students would be involved in advanced placement programs.

15. Mandatory homework, which is ordinarily intended to increase students' productivity, in practice severely reduces it. The emphasis on compulsory homework should be drastically reduced and the importance of class work stressed.

16. Classroom rules should be few and simple. If there are too many rules and teachers assume the role of enforcing them, an adversarial relationship develops between teachers and their students. Students should be involved in the formulation of rules. Teachers will probably need to help students understand that if they are courteous with one another, they are unlikely to need many rules.

17. Teachers should avoid accepting the role of the punishing authoritarian. Consequences for breaking rules should be discussed with students, and students should accept the consequences when they break rules. Those who break rules should be asked to suggest ways to prevent rules from being broken in the future.

18. Teachers should show an interest in students' personal lives and reveal selected information about their own lives that will help students appreciate them as human beings.

19. Teachers should ask students for help and advice when a need actually exists and the students can give valid assistance. Such requests help to break down barriers between teacher and student and create a friendlier atmosphere in the classroom.

20. Teachers should avoid calling students' homes when the students experience difficulties in school. When students' families are notified of problems at school, students correctly perceive the school to be the cause of problems at home. In addition, some students will misbehave in school with the intention of getting an ambivalent parent involved, even when negative attention from that parent is expected.

21. In disciplining children who have broken the rules, teachers may find the following sequence of questions helpful: (a) "What were you doing when the problem started?" (b) "Was it against the rules?" (c) "Can we work it out so that it does not happen again?" (d) "If this situation comes up in the future, what could you do and what could I do so that we do not have this problem again?"

22. Schooling should promote continuing education. Learning should be useful and enjoyable at the present as well as later. Students should see the implications of their learning for the world of work.

23. In a quality school, emphasis should be on speaking, writing, calculating, and problem solving, both for students as individuals and as members of groups.

24. There should be no memorized facts. There should be no objective tests, and all tests should be open book. The curriculum should not be designed to pass tests like the SAT and ACT. Tests should consist of written or oral opinions, written or oral evaluations, and problem solving.

25. A corps of good students should be trained to serve as tutors for any student who needs one-on-one tutoring. Student tutors can use this experience to raise their grades in the subject.

26. All teachers and students should be taught choice theory. All teachers should be taught how to council using reality therapy.

27. Student self-evaluation should be emphasized, with subsequent learning being based on that evaluation. Students should be invited to improve their work based on their evaluation.

28. Disruptive students should not be treated with threats and anger. Students who rebel are usually reacting to a frustrating system. It is the teacher's job to make school less frustrating for students.

29. Very difficult students may be sent to a time-out room for counseling and to do their work. If disruptions continue, they may be sent home for a period of 3 days. If they choose not to follow the school rules, they can be asked to drop out of school and try it again the following year.

30. Community service should be emphasized in the quality school. This service should never be pure physical labor. It should always have an intellectual component—something the students have learned in school that they can make use of in community service (Glasser, 1992b).

31. It would be appropriate for students to become involved in the economic operations of the school. Part of their education should involve working in the school and regulating the expenditure of funds. This way children learn important lessons regarding financial responsibility (Glasser, 1998).

32. Students will listen to their teachers and take them seriously as long as they perceive their teachers as need fulfilling, teaching enthusiastically, and seeking to share pictures (or goals) in common with their students (Parish, 1992).

33. Students should be asked to keep a portfolio containing examples of their quality work. Each piece of work should include a self-evaluation.

34. The staff of a quality school should be expanded by enlisting the help of volunteers so that each classroom has at least three full-time assistants (Glasser, 1998).

Correction Strategies

Although much of Glasser's choice theory appears to have a prevention orientation, applying the principles he suggests can also help to correct discipline problems. When students' rebelliousness is extreme, teachers and administrators may have to work with them on a one-to-one basis using reality therapy. The following steps are helpful in this process:

1. Establish a quality school program with a lead-management orientation. The coercion–punishment model should be replaced.
2. Provide the target students with school experiences that are meaningful to them and that satisfy their basic needs of love and acceptance, control, freedom, and fun. Help them believe that they can achieve a high level of quality.
3. Help students identify their inappropriate behavior and its consequences.
4. Encourage students to make a value judgment about their inappropriate behavior and its unacceptable consequences.
5. Have students make a plan that has a real possibility of helping them be more autonomously productive in school.
6. Periodically meet with students and give them the opportunity to evaluate their school experience and make changes as necessary.

It is unlikely that students' disruptive behavior patterns will change in an immediate and dramatic way, particularly if the students have been significantly abused by the current boss-management system. The help of teachers and administrators is vital if such students are to gain confidence in the school and its programs.

Preventing Discipline Problems

Preventing discipline problems, in Glasser's view, depends to a large extent on establishing principles and procedures associated with a quality school and supplanting the coercive boss-management system with lead-management. Glasser's methods of discipline always include a significant prevention component. In *Schools Without Failure,* he recommends three types of classroom meetings designed to prevent discipline problems: social-problem-solving meetings, open-ended meetings, and educational diagnosis meetings (Glasser, 1969).

The purpose of social-problem-solving meetings is to encourage students to solve discipline problems as a class. Class expectations are established in these sessions, and the types of behavior the class finds unacceptable are discussed. Consequences for violating class expectations are determined in these sessions, and necessary, periodic changes are negotiated. Open-ended meetings serve as meaningful supplements to the regular curriculum. Glasser believes that one reason children misbehave in school is that they find the curriculum irrelevant. Discussions in open-ended meetings permit them to raise whatever questions they have that pertain directly to their classroom situation. Educational diagnosis meetings, on the other hand, are intended to enable students to evaluate their educational experiences. In these meetings, students can determine how effectively they learn and ascertain what gaps exist in their educational experiences.

The following steps will be useful in class discussions to prevent discipline problems:

Goals of instruction
Classroom rules
Classroom operations

Commitment

Consequences

Each of these five steps is discussed in detail next. They are designed to help students accept ownership for their program of studies along with the necessary commitment to learn. Student ownership and commitment provide the basis on which responsible decisions about classroom rules can be made along with consequences for breaking rules that students have helped determine. It also provides students with an opportunity to give input regarding classroom operations and teaching.

1. *Determine as a class what the goals of instruction will be.* This involves an effort by the teacher to provide students with sufficient information that they can make valid curriculum decisions. There are many options regarding legitimate topics for study to include in the curriculum. This, of course, varies from subject to subject, but even in subjects like mathematics, some decision making by students is possible. In making these choices, students must understand that what they decide will have an impact on their future plans and desires. For example, if they wish to attend college, they need to include topics that best prepare them for university work. Some topics may have greater application to more students or be more critical in practical living situations than others. Choices need to be made taking this information into account.

The purpose of giving students an opportunity to make decisions about the curriculum is to aid in promoting student ownership. This way, students can achieve the level of commitment necessary to be more self-regulating and responsible regarding this and other classroom matters. Classroom rules make more sense to students when they are cast within the context of self-determined classroom purposes and activities.

2. *Formulate classroom rules that are instrumental in achieving the specified class goals.* Connections need to be made between what students propose to study and the rules necessary to best promote these activities. Teachers should ask class members to formulate rules that they believe will help them achieve their goals while avoiding impediments to their learning. Making these connections helps students see the purpose in formulating rules and promotes adherence to them. Here again, ownership is important. Students are better served by rules they create themselves within the context of selecting their own learning activities.

3. *Allow students to make suggestions regarding class operations that they believe will promote a more enjoyable and productive learning environment.* For example, unannounced quizzes and weekend homework assignments may be an irritation to students. They may also be unnecessary from the teacher's point of view. Such suggestions can improve the climate of the classroom. It must be kept in mind that students may be interested in making life in the classroom easier rather than more productive. The difference between these two perceptions needs to be addressed in this phase of preventive discipline. An issue doesn't need to be made of this during the discussion, however. Rather, the teacher needs to preface the discussion by such statements as, "We have made some important decisions about what we will study during this course and the rules that will promote a better atmosphere for accomplishing your goals. You may also have some suggestions to make regarding the kinds of classroom activities that you

think would further enhance your learning. What arrangements can be made in class that will help you learn better and enjoy yourselves?" Statements like this direct discussion toward more responsible suggestions and decisions.

4. *Achieve commitment by all students for goals, rules, and procedures decided on.* The entire class needs to be committed to the decisions that are made. Everyone needs to have an opportunity to state this commitment or to suggest what changes need to be made to make the plan more acceptable. In the event students are unable to commit themselves, they may be invited to consider transferring to another class or to take a day or so to reconsider their opposition. If they do decide they want to transfer, it is wise to allow them the option to return if they find their circumstances less acceptable in the new class. The condition of their return, however, is to accept and abide by the plan the class members have decided on.

5. *Decide on the consequences that should apply in the event any student behaves contrary to the proposed rules.*   Students will likely need help identifying consequences that are nonpunitive and make logical sense. They will likely be well acquainted with the usual punishments commonly administered in schools for rule infraction and suggest these be used. They should be shown that many of these punishments are arbitrary and inappropriate to use as a consequence. Students must accept ownership for consequences and consider them not as punishments, but as appropriate, temporary outcomes for violating commitments.

One educational strategy Glasser advocates to promote more meaningful learning and reduce discipline problems is cooperative learning, also known as the learning team model. He believes that this kind of learning provides students a better way to satisfy their basic needs. Glasser recommends that students work on long-term projects with other students to go deeper into a subject and become more involved in the experience of learning. For this purpose, he suggests that teachers organize teams of from two to five students who have reached different levels of achievement. He lists several benefits to be gained from cooperative team learning (Glasser, 1986a):

1. Working in teams provides students a sense of belonging, which helps motivate them to work harder and achieve more.
2. The more advanced students find it fulfilling to help less able team members because they want the power and friendship that go with a high-performing team.
3. Less able students also have their needs fulfilled. In the group, they are able to accomplish something, whereas they did very little before. Their contribution to the team is appreciated more than their previous individual efforts were.
4. By working in teams, students gain a greater sense of independence from the teacher and discover themselves able to make valuable contributions to the class.
5. Learning teams serve as a structure within which students can obtain a deeper understanding of school subjects. Unless students understand the subjects they study more deeply, they will be unable to make the vital connection between knowledge and power that must underlie any attempt to improve today's schools.
6. Teams provide a framework within which students can better evaluate themselves. More than just grades may be considered as evidence that students are learning.

Schoolwide Discipline

In a quality school, there would be no boss-management by principals, counselors, or teachers. Traditionally, the school principal exercises veto power over students' decisions. To provide lead-management, principals need to give students greater autonomy, particularly as they demonstrate greater maturity. When children sense that opportunities for self-government are the result of responsible decisions and behavior, they will increasingly demonstrate trustworthy conduct. Principals need to anticipate that students will become more responsible when given more freedom instead of assuming that they will dream up devious, antisocial activities.

Within the classroom, each individual class would have the responsibility for determining rules. Outside the classroom, the student council would serve as a genuine governing body, and students would take an authentic role in determining school rules and procedures. The student council would have the duty to make sure that students behave appropriately in such places as the lunchroom, halls, and school grounds.

Student councils should be organized in the elementary and junior high schools as well as in high schools. If such councils were consistently implemented, students would be more adept at self-government by the time they reached high school age. In the elementary school, participation in student council might be restricted to the older children, but children in the earlier grades could be taught how to take an active role later in school government.

Not only do students need opportunities to create their own rules, but they must also learn how to police themselves. There is always the possibility that students will want to deal punitively with those who break the rules. In a quality school, however, punishment in the traditional sense is unacceptable. Children should learn to apply appropriate consequences for breaking rules rather than seek retribution.

No standardized achievement tests would be administered. These tests are designed to separate students into categories based on a normal distribution curve. All students would be expected to achieve at a high level. There would be no need to give tests designed only to make comparisons among them or between them and group norms.

Quality Communities and Quality Schools

In an effort to create quality schools, Glasser has organized the William Glasser Institute. Through the work of the institute, he has promoted not only quality schools but also quality communities. Quality communities make the founding of quality schools much easier. The work has involved teaching parents choice theory and encouraging the practice of choice theory in various community agencies and organizations. In a quality community, domestic violence would decrease. When it occurred, there would be something tangible that could be done about it. A child who was abused or was not getting along in the community would become a community problem. Various agencies as well as the school and the home could be enlisted to help. All individuals involved would be able to present a united front in the application of choice theory principles (Glasser, 1998).

In a quality school, students take a major role. They are taught choice theory principles and given the autonomy to apply them in their school experiences. One school that has applied choice theory is Apollo High School, an alternative high school of 400 students in the Simi Valley Unified School District in southern California. Students at Apollo High School are appointed to leadership positions and then given leadership training based on choice theory. Selected students are thus not involved in a popularity contest to achieve leadership status. It is more a matter of having demonstrated responsible behavior in the past. Each month the entire student body is divided into five teams. Each team is headed by trained student leaders and staff. Each team is given the responsibility to identify and decide on important issues and resolve concerns. Teams make decisions regarding budget. In the past they have made the decision to allocate part of available discretionary funds for instructional supplies and field trips. To deal with graffiti problems, they decided to have students design and paint murals on the walls. The result was the lowest graffiti problem in the district. They also tackled the problem of substance abuse. They organized teams to present a program on drug education for students in neighboring elementary schools. These high school students used their own experience to teach those younger students. They also created a program to deal with behavior problems. As a result, behavior problems were greatly reduced.

Perhaps one of the most influential parts of the Apollo High School program was the Community Service Program. As part of this, students initiated a tutoring program for elementary children, as well as for the deaf and orthopedically challenged. They also helped to build a kindergarten playhouse and initiated a senior citizen outreach program.

The emphasis on quality and choice theory at Apollo High School achieved amazing results. Test scores were significantly improved. All but one student passed the district proficiency test. Teen pregnancies were reduced to a level well below the national average. There was a marked increase in graduates who attended college and assumed responsible positions in the adult world. School attendance greatly improved, while suspensions were drastically reduced. Vandalism was decreased to zero (Uroff & Green, 1991).

Strengths and Weaknesses of Reality Therapy/Choice Theory

STRENGTHS

1. Reality therapy and choice theory promote a high degree of autonomy and responsibility for students.
2. They help students see a wide range of possible consequences for their behavior.
3. They allow students to determine solutions to their own discipline problems.
4. They help students understand their needs and how to satisfy these needs legitimately.
5. They help teachers avoid promoting rebellion.

6. They delineate clearly what a teacher needs to do for every misbehaving student.
7. Problem behaviors can be handled in classroom meetings involving the entire class, which helps all students understand the various discipline problems and what to do about them.

WEAKNESSES

1. It is difficult for teachers to help students satisfy their need for control without feeling threatened themselves.
2. It is difficult to react properly when communicating with students about their inappropriate behavior.
3. It is difficult to avoid giving responses that encourage students to make excuses for their bad behavior.
4. It is difficult to help students experience the true sense of autonomy implied by control theory if outside influences dictate what is taught in school and how children should be disciplined.
5. Classroom meetings may consume more time than is desirable.
6. It may be difficult to help students who do not want to be in school to make plans to improve their behavior.
7. Students may not have the necessary skills to make plans that will help improve their behavior.

▼ SUMMARY

Glasser's ideas about discipline have evolved over the years. In his initial work, he recommended that students be allowed to suggest ways to make school more meaningful and to formulate appropriate rules for classroom use. Students who misbehaved were to be corrected through the use of reality therapy, which involves four basic steps: (1) Help students recognize and describe their behavior, (2) ask them to identify the consequences of their actions, (3) have them make value judgments about both the consequences of the behavior and the unwanted behavior itself, and (4) help them formulate plans that they believe will help eliminate their problems. If these efforts fail, students can be given time-out until they come up with a more workable plan.

In his work on reality therapy, Glasser identifies successful social relationships as essential components of a happy, ordered life. In choice theory, Glasser stresses the importance of a student's need for love and acceptance, and he expands his list of basic human needs to include control, freedom, and fun. Reality therapy focuses on correcting students when they misbehave; choice theory places a greater emphasis on helping children achieve their needs responsibly. Glasser claims that when children's needs are met, they find little cause to create trouble. The task of the teacher is to help them satisfy their needs legitimately and to help them learn to balance their needs. Balance is essential because full realization of various needs sometimes creates conflicts. Conflicts can also occur when the fulfillment of needs depends on others who are also trying to satisfy their own needs.

Glasser has recently begun advocating a change in the pattern of leadership used in schools, from boss-management to lead-management. He believes that such a change will create a more conducive atmosphere in which students can better satisfy their needs, and he urges the use of lead-management in the development of quality schools.

CENTRAL IDEAS

1. In reality therapy, teachers help students
   a. Identify their inappropriate behavior.
   b. Identify the consequences of that behavior.
   c. Make judgments about their misbehavior and its consequences.
   d. Create and stick to a plan to eliminate problem behavior.
2. When Glasser created reality therapy, he identified successful social relationships as basic needs for humans. With the development of choice theory, the needs of love, control, freedom, and fun were added.
3. Applying choice theory involves helping students satisfy their needs in a legitimate way and abandon antisocial means of satisfaction.
4. A balance must be achieved between competing needs within an individual and between a person's own needs and the needs of others.
5. Low achievement levels may be more the result of an unsatisfying education than the result of discipline problems.
6. A quality school satisfies children's needs, aids cooperative learning, allows for variation, provides for autonomy, has expectations for high-quality work, avoids coercion, promotes students' ownership of their work, increases students' productivity, involves students in classroom decisions, and is relevant to students' personal lives

▼ QUESTIONS AND ACTIVITIES

QUESTIONS TO CONSIDER

1. What are the fundamental ways in which reality therapy and choice theory differ from one another? To what degree are these differences compatible or incompatible with one another?
2. What changes would have to be made in most schools to implement Glasser's ideas and principles?
3. What evidence is there that Glasser's ideas about human needs are correct?
4. How can students be helped to balance need gratification?
5. To what extent will students create valid classroom rules if they are allowed to participate in this process?
6. How do unfulfilled needs stimulate misbehavior?
7. What evidence is there that humans have personal ways of satisfying their needs?
8. What kind of valid input can students give in determining the goals of a particular class?

9. How might Glasser's ideas about choice theory in the community be implemented? What obstacles are likely to be encountered?

CLASSROOM ACTIVITIES

1. Create an outline of a comprehensive discipline program that is consistent with Glasser's ideas. Include provisions for
   a. The curriculum
   b. Class organization
   c. Activities that will satisfy students' needs for love and acceptance, control, freedom, and fun
   d. Formulating classroom rules
   e. Schoolwide discipline
   f. Grading procedures
   g. Adopting the characteristics of a quality school
2. Break into two groups, and debate the relative merits of Glasser's approach to discipline and another approach.
3. Visit a school where reality therapy/choice theory is used. Talk with teachers and administrators about this discipline approach.
4. Have teachers and administrators visit your classroom who use reality therapy/choice theory in their school. Have them discuss the strengths and weaknesses of their program.
5. In a demonstration, role play the part of a misbehaving student while having the class collectively act as the teacher using reality therapy to make a plan to change behavior.

STUDENT APPLICATIONS

1. With two classmates, use role playing to study how a teacher would use reality therapy to help a misbehaving student in the following situations. One person plays the role of the teacher. Another person plays the role of a student who has made a habit of disrupting the class. The third person observes and helps the other two participants analyze the situation.
   a. Jane is habitually tardy for class.
   b. Marjika never turns her homework in on time. Some assignments are never turned in.
   c. Randy has a long history of throwing spit wads in class.
   d. Ruth chatters incessantly during quiet study time as well as during lectures and discussions.
   e. Glen has carved his artwork into his desk.
   f. When Claron takes the hall pass to go to the restroom, she is usually gone for more than half an hour.
   g. Norm frequently uses profanity in class.
2. Use role playing with several classmates to examine the process of establishing classroom rules and procedures. Define class learning objectives and requirements as well as expectations about students' behavior.

EXPLORE YOUR PHILOSOPHY

1. Defend or refute the assumptions that human beings are self-regulating and that their behavior is purposefully directed.
2. Defend or refute the assumption that children can learn responsible behavior through examining a full range of behavioral consequences and making value judgments about their behavior and its consequences.
3. Defend or refute the assumption that children can best learn to behave responsibly without exploring the motives for their behavior.
4. Defend or refute the assumption that human behavior is motivated by the need for love, power, freedom, and fun.
5. Defend or refute the assumptions that every person has a unique view of how best to satisfy his or her own needs and that this perception of need satisfaction is very resistant to change.
6. Compare the principles contained in your educational philosophy with those of reality therapy/choice theory. Determine consistencies and inconsistencies. Make adjustments in your philosophy as you believe appropriate.

▼ **REFERENCES**

Glasser, N. (1989). *Control therapy in the practice of reality therapy: Case studies.* New York: Harper & Row.

Glasser, W. (1965). *Reality therapy: A new approach to psychiatry.* New York: Harper & Row.

Glasser, W. (1969). *Schools without failure.* New York: Harper & Row.

Glasser, W. (1984). *Control theory: A new explanation of how we control our lives.* New York: Harper & Row.

Glasser, W. (1986a). *Control theory in the classroom.* New York: Harper & Row.

Glasser, W. (1986b). Discipline is not the problem: Control theory in the classroom. *Theory Into Practice, 24,* 241–246.

Glasser, W. (1989). Quality is the key to the disciplines. *The Education Digest, 55*(1), 24–27.

Glasser, W. (1992a). *The quality school.* New York: Harper & Row.

Glasser, W. (1992b). Quality, trust and redefining education. *The Educational Forum, 57*(1), 37–40.

Glasser, W. (1993). *The quality school teacher.* New York: HarperCollins.

Glasser, W. (1997a). Choice theory and student success. *Education Digest, 63*(3), 16–27.

Glasser, W. (1997b). A new look at school failure and school success. *Phi Delta Kappan, 78*(8), 597–602.

Glasser, W. (1998). *Choice theory: A new psychology of personal freedom.* New York: HarperCollins.

National Commission on Excellence in Education. (1983). *A nation at risk.* Washington, DC: U.S. Department of Education.

Parish, T. S. (1992). Using "quality school" procedures to enhance student enthusiasm and student performance. *Journal of Instructional Psychology, 19*(4), 266–268.

Uroff, S., & Green, B. (1991, November). A low-risk approach to high risk students. *NASSP Bulletin, 75,* 50–58.

Judicious Discipline: Forrest Gathercoal

OBJECTIVES

This chapter is designed to help you

1. Understand how the First, Fourth, and Fourteenth Amendments to the U.S. Constitution provide for personal freedom.
2. Understand how personal rights and compelling state interests are related and how they apply to operations in a democratically run classroom.
3. Learn to teach students how their right to due process and right to equal protection under the law apply to the classroom.
4. Learn how to teach students the way compelling state interests regarding property loss or damage, legitimate educational purposes, health and safety, and serious disruption of educational processes apply to behavior in the classroom.
5. Understand both inductive and deductive methods for creating rules and consequences for a democratic classroom.

ASSUMPTIONS

1. School is an appropriate place to prepare students for living in a democratic society.
2. Students can learn to responsibly use their personal freedoms as guaranteed by the Constitution.
3. Students can learn to regulate their personal behavior so it does not violate compelling school interests.
4. Students can help create valid rules for the classroom.
5. Consequences provide a better way to improve the classroom behavior of children than punishment.

Introduction

Forrest Gathercoal holds two degrees from the University of Oregon, a bachelor's in music and a J.D. from the School of Law. Currently, he serves as a professor in the Department of Educational Foundations at Oregon State University, where he has taught law for educators for more than 20 years. He has also offered courses in educational psychology and has conducted workshops for educators regarding discipline and school law. Additionally, he serves as a consultant to many school districts across the country and as a presenter at numerous educational conferences. Before his involvement at the university, he was a classroom teacher, coach, and high school vice-principal. While at Oregon State University, he has been Director of the Placement Office and Assistant Dean of the School of Education.

Gathercoal has created a discipline model that acknowledges individual differences between students but at the same time recognizes the need for an educational environment free from disruptive forces. Simply stated, the focus of the classroom in terms of discipline is that students may do what they want so long as it doesn't interfere with the rights of others. When teachers apply this approach, they administer discipline in an evenhanded manner, respecting the constitutional rights of their students. At the same time, this model allows teachers and students to relate to one another in a democratic way and teaches students about their responsibilities to other members of the class.

Judicious Discipline is based on the democratic principles established in the Constitution and the Bill of Rights. This creates an educational and ethical perspective for the development of school rules that map directly onto citizenship responsibilities, which students need to apply to the world outside the school. It is, in reality, authentic training for students to live successfully in a democratic society. This approach provides students with an opportunity to understand their rights and responsibilities as citizens and to experience the individual liberties attendant to this role. Through their school experiences, students are expected to become empowered to govern themselves within a social context and to learn to think for themselves and make decisions that are an adequate blend of personal rights and social responsibilities. To accomplish this, the school and the classroom serve as models of the same system of laws under which students will live when their compulsory schooling is completed.

▼ Roxanne has always been a very popular girl in school. Through the encouragement of her teachers, she has been involved in student government and has been elected to various class and student body offices over the years. Currently, during her senior year, she is serving as student body president. At home, her parents are going through a painful separation and possible divorce. During this time, Roxanne has had various parts of her body pierced, to which she has attached rings and other ornaments. In addition, she has been staying out late on school nights with friends who are not approved by her parents. Her parents also object to her clothing styles, which recently have become far less modest than in previous years. But, though they object to the changes they see taking place in Roxanne, they are too preoccupied with their own trouble to do more than criticize her actions and threaten her with various punishments.

On Friday morning, Roxanne's mother experienced an especially trying argument with her husband, and she exploded at the breakfast table when she saw the gaudy makeup her daughter was wearing. When Roxanne yelled back at her mother, she got her face slapped and then stalked out of the house with no breakfast. It was just 2 weeks before graduation. On her way to school, Roxanne decided she needed to do something to stir things up at school.

When she arrived, she talked several other student body officers into helping stage a food fight in the cafeteria at lunch time. Spaghetti was being served, and on Roxanne's signal, the student body officers began throwing it all over the lunch room. Soon all but a few students were launching handfuls of spaghetti at one another. Mrs. Gunderson, the lunch supervisor, arrived 5 minutes late to perform her duties and found the whole lunch room in a state of pandemonium. As she rushed through the door, screaming at the top of her voice to get the food throwing stopped, she unfortunately slipped on a pile of spaghetti and broke her arm as she fell to the floor. The whole episode looked so comical that the entire student body broke out laughing while Mrs. Gunderson writhed in pain. Mr. Rosetti, the principal, soon arrived on the scene and quelled the laughing. He helped Mrs. Gunderson to her feet and led her to the main office to initiate the medical attention she needed.

When Mr. Rosetti returned to the lunch room, he learned quickly who had instigated the episode. Soon Roxanne was standing in front of his desk with a defiant look on her face. Mr. Rosetti told her, with an expression of disgust, that she was the most pathetic student body president he had ever seen. First he criticized her for the revealing clothes she wore and then for the assortment of jewelry she had used to decorate her nose, ears, navel, and eyebrows. He said he planned to suspend her from school and would recommend to the board that she be expelled. Her graduation

Roxanne is reprimanded by the principal for her role in staging a food fight in the cafeteria.

was threatened as well. He further said that she was being punished so severely because as the student body president she had a responsibility to serve as an example to other students. Finally, he said that Roxanne must clean up the cafeteria and that she would have no right to eat there again.

Roxanne's face first bore a look of disbelief and then rage. She picked up Mr. Rosetti's pen set from this desk and heaved it through the window. With tears starting to form in her eyes, she turned on her heel and ran out of the office and through the front doors of the school. She continued running until she reached the city park, where she sat down on a bench and cried for more than an hour. Afterward she went home and locked herself in her room, refusing to come out. She continued quietly sobbing as she listened to her parents engage in their usual round of arguments.

Does a suspension seem to be the right action to take in this situation? The school did have a rule against food fights in the cafeteria. This rule had been approved by the board of education and widely publicized to all students. A copy of it appeared prominently along with other school rules in the student handbook. A suspension of at least 3 days was the designated punishment. The rule allowed for no exceptions. The school administration felt that the rules should apply fairly and evenly to all students.

Was Mr. Rosetti justified in his actions? Was the example he made of Roxanne appropriate, given the important student body office she held? Were the other students in the school well served by this action? Would the actions taken best serve Roxanne? What rights do students have in school when they break rules? Does insisting on the same punishment for all serve the students and the school best? Who should pay for Mrs. Gunderson's medical expenses? Who has the responsibility for cleaning up the cafeteria? Is there anyone besides Roxanne who should be held responsible for the food-fighting incident? Answers to these questions are not that "cut and dried." They depend on various assumptions and principles that might be applied in a variety of situations. The Judicious discipline model provides answers to these questions that depart dramatically from those applied by Mr. Rosetti and from those commonly implemented by school administrators and teachers.

The Legal Perspective

When students graduate from school, they enter into a system of constitutional government that is designed not only to provide for the needs, interests, and welfare of the majority, but to bestow specific rights and freedoms on individuals. In America most of us are aware that the majority rules. This understanding is used from childhood in settling various disputes like playground arguments or in seeking consensus on the rules of a game being played. Far less is understood regarding individual rights. To be well-adjusted, responsible citizens, children must learn that in a constitutional democracy individual rights are as important as the needs and interests of the majority.

Constitutional liberties come from the first 10 amendments known as the *Bill of Rights*. The First Amendment, which guarantees freedom in terms of religion, speech, press, and assembly, is the cornerstone for protecting individual rights. The Fifth Amendment protects citizens from unlawful searches, while the Fourteenth Amendment provides for "due process of law" and "equal protection." These amendments have important implications for protecting the rights of individuals. These rights are not self-explanatory. Their meaning within the political, legal, and educational realms is generally translated by the Supreme Court of the United States.

The Constitution guarantees the protection of citizens regarding three important values: freedom, justice, and equality. Students need to understand these values within the context of a free society. They must realize that they can't do whatever they please, that they have a responsibility to others in the community. This means that *freedom* must be limited. Much of the controversy in our democratic society revolves around how, when, and where to limit individual freedom so that there is an appropriate balance between one's personal rights and the needs and interests of the community. The difficulty lies in creating a precise formula to determine when freedom has exceeded rightful bounds. Thus, *justice* is involved with due process and with the issue of fairness. We are all aware of criminals who have been set free by the legal system or of innocent persons who have been sent to prison. Though the system is not perfect, it strives to guarantee the rights of individuals while appropriately representing important community expectations. The third value, *equality,* concerns the distribution of burdens and benefits. Problems of equality are especially difficult when members of a community have less opportunity than others due to race, gender, or other characteristics. The courts have tried to promote equality, but we often discover that additional problems are created by their decisions.

STUDENT RIGHTS

Some students are fond of claiming that "they should have their rights" when they feel excessively controlled or when they wish to do something that others seem to disapprove of. Their actions may defy the controlling influence of teachers and parents, and at times they are offensive to others or violate others' rights. Sometimes, however, students' rights have been violated. Such violations are commonly due to the assumption by teachers and other school officials that they act *in loco parentis* (in the place of parents) in disciplining schoolchildren. In the past this rule of law could be appropriately applied in schools. This application, however, was changed in 1969 with the ruling of the U.S. Supreme Court in the case of *Tinker v. Des Moines Independent School District* (1969). In this case a high school student was suspended from school by the principal for wearing a black armband to protest the U.S. involvement in the Vietnam war. The court ruled that the protection of the First Amendment applies to schoolchildren, just as it does to citizens generally. Under the *in loco parentis* justification, most schools acted unilaterally, making rules that fit the values of the school, the teachers, and the administrators, with no regard to the wishes or values of the students. With the *Tinker* case, schoolchildren were guaranteed important rights set forth in the First, Fourth, and Fourteenth Amendments (Wolfgang, 1995).

THE FIRST AMENDMENT

Congress shall make no law respecting an establishment of religion or prohibiting the free exercise thereof; or abridging the freedom of speech or of the press;

or of the people peaceably to assemble, and to petition the government for a redress of grievances.

In the school, such questions as the following may be raised regarding First Amendment rights:

1. What right do students have to publish and distribute material on school property?
2. Can students refuse to read assigned material that is contrary to their religious practices and beliefs?
3. Can children wear clothing that violates school rules but is an expression of religious beliefs?
4. Can children wear clothing that is an expression of political beliefs or an expression of their opposition to government activities?
5. Can students be released from school to attend religious classes and not be punished or lose the opportunity to learn the regular educational content of the school?

THE FOURTH AMENDMENT

The right of the people to be secure in their persons, houses, papers, and effects, against unreasonable searches and seizures, shall not be violated, and no warrants shall issue, but upon probable cause, supported by oath or affirmation, and particularly describing the place to be searched, and the persons or things to be seized.

Principally, this amendment raises such questions as the following:

1. Can a teacher or other school official search students' property, including lockers, pockets, purses, and vehicles in the parking lot?
2. Can teachers or other school officials seize student property?

THE FOURTEENTH AMENDMENT

All persons born or naturalized in the United States, and subject to the jurisdiction thereof, are citizens of the United States and of the State wherein they reside. No State shall make or enforce any law which shall abridge the privileges or immunities of citizens of the United States; nor shall any State deprive any person of life, liberty, or property, without due process of law; nor deny to any person within its jurisdiction the equal protection of the laws.

From this amendment have come two clauses, the *due process* clause and the *equal protection* clause, which have had significant impact on public schools. They raise such questions as the following:

1. Can a teacher discipline students by removing them from the classroom and moving them into the hall or isolation room? Can school administrators suspend or expel students, thereby depriving them of the property right to be educated, without due process? Can a student insist on having legal counsel present during a hearing?
2. Can a student's grades, which may be considered a property right, be lowered or withheld because he or she is truant or late for class?

Due process refers to a legal effort to balance individual rights with the need to protect the interests and welfare of society. If the state cannot demonstrate a compelling interest in its favor, then individual rights prevail and should receive the protection of the state. Public school students won their right to due process in the case of *Goss v. Lopez* (1975). In this case several high school students, including the plaintiff, Dwight Lopez, were suspended for acts of violence. Certain students' acts were clearly documented, but those of Lopez and a few others were not. None of the students were provided a hearing regarding their suspensions, nor were they told the nature of the charges against them. The court ruled that their right to due process had been violated (Hoover & Kindsvatter, 1997). In the case of Roxanne, the principal suspended her and initiated actions to have her expelled from school and to have her graduation postponed. In addition, he stated that the severity of the punishment being applied was due primarily to her position as student body president, which necessitated making an example of her actions, and to the inappropriate costumes she wore to school. Did the circumstances warrant depriving Roxanne of an education? Would other punishments be more appropriate? Were the principal's actions legal? Did Roxanne have a right be represented by an attorney during the hearing with the principal?

With regard to due process, the state can deprive someone of established rights if a compelling state interest can be shown with regard to one of the following:

1. Property loss or damage
2. Legitimate educational purpose
3. Health and safety
4. Serious disruption of an educational process (Gathercoal, 1990)

Loss or destruction of property is involved in such actions as putting graffiti on restroom walls, breaking windows, destroying textbooks, tearing up term reports of other students, digging holes in desktops, and walking on the gym floor with cleated shoes.

Failing to satisfy a legitimate educational purpose occurs when students do things like not bringing textbook, pencil, and notebook paper to class as directed; not bringing appropriate clothing to a physical education class; not completing assignments according to the designated schedule; or failing to do their own work on examinations and papers.

Health and safety concerns include such actions as failing to wear appropriate protective clothing and equipment during a chemistry lab, running in the hallways, releasing hydrogen sulfide in the school venting system, failing to obtain appropriate vaccinations before attending school, throwing various items in the classrooms and hallways, and engaging in food fights in the cafeteria.

Disruption of the educational process may occur when students roughhouse with their peers during quiet study time, use rough and loud talk that interferes with the learning of peers, engage in gang activity on school premises, dress in ways that disrupt class, release animals from their cages in the biology classroom, and carry on political protests in class while the teacher is trying to teach a lesson.

The school must show that the student's behavior violates one of these state rights before the behavior can be prohibited. It must be shown that the welfare of the school and its purposes are being thwarted. However, the school, even in these instances, cannot act arbitrarily. The following procedural criteria must be met:

1. There must be *adequate notice*. There must be an oral or written notice of the charges and a description of the rule that was violated. Rules must be publicized in advance so that all students have had a reasonable opportunity to be informed about them.

2. There must be a *fair and impartial hearing*. This implies that the personal preferences of teachers and school administrators do not predominate and that the circumstances in which the hearing takes place do not take advantage of a student's gullibility or lack of maturity. There must be a meaningful opportunity to be heard, state a position, and present witnesses.

3. There must be *evidence* to support the claims made against the student. There should be a written summary of the evidence, including the names of witnesses.

4. The student must have an opportunity to mount an adequate *defense*. The student must have appropriate time to prepare and opportunity to present his or her side of the conflict. The student is entitled to be represented by others, if desired.

5. Students must have the right to *appeal* any decision rendered by school officials. This appeal may be made at increasingly higher levels in the school district's administrative structure and may advance from the school district to higher state or federal administrative agencies and finally to an appropriate court. If necessary, appeals may even be made to the U.S. Supreme Court.

The preceding elements of due process are *procedural*, designed to allow students maximum opportunities to show whether or not a rule of law has been violated. There are also *substantive* aspects of due process, which refer to the nature of the law itself, the basic fairness in the substance of the decision rendered. To satisfy this due process imperative, school rules must meet the following criteria:

1. *Have some rational need for adoption.* The rules must fit the purposes of the school and not be confused with the personal preferences of teachers and school officials. For example, in the case of Roxanne, some of the jewelry she had attached to her body might be a hindrance to learning or health considerations, while the rest of it might not. The principal's values regarding her appearance and her responsibility to set an appropriate example might not be relevant to compelling state interests.

2. *Be as effective in meeting the need as any alternative that reasonable people would have developed.* In effect the rules implemented must represent the most appropriate way to ensure that the purposes of the school are most fully met. Some school rules and the consequences of breaking them may fit the values of school officials but be excessive from a broader perspective. For example, having Roxanne and her cohorts clean up the cafeteria and pay the medical bills of the lunchroom supervisor might be reasonable. Canceling Roxanne's graduation or even suspending her for a period of time might be excessive.

3. *Be supported by relevant and substantial evidence and findings of fact.* This requirement implies that rules be clearly connected to established knowledge of ways of promoting student behavior that is most likely to achieve school purposes. For example, rules and procedures that denigrate a student's self-concept should not be employed.

The Fourteenth Amendment is also designed to protect individuals from discrimination of all kinds, including discriminating actions related to one's sex, race, national origin, disabilities, marital status, age, and religion. Students with disabilities have additional rights to educational opportunities and considerations that are not necessarily available to students who are not disabled. Some children with disabilities engage in behavior that is sufficiently disruptive that it would result in suspension for normally functioning peers. Federal and state laws require that students with disabilities be held to different standards and that procedures be used that take their disabilities into account. Not to deal differentially with students with disabilities constitutes a breach of their constitutional rights. Specifics regarding treatment of students with disabilities are dictated by state and federal law and do change periodically. Educators need to stay abreast of changes in these laws (Gathercoal, 1992).

DEMOCRATIC LAW AND THE SCHOOLS

One of the more significant contradictions in public education is the autocratic system of managing student behavior, which is assumed to provide a model for responsible citizenship in a democratic society. There is little doubt that applying discipline procedures that enable students to think as and act like responsible citizens will be much more effective for this purpose than requiring blind obedience. Schools furnish an excellent environment in which to teach democratic principles and values. Groups of students can act as communities under the expert tutelage of caring teachers. They can learn to appreciate their individual rights and to articulate these individual rights with social rights and responsibilities. Such articulation involves helping students to appreciate a full range of personal desires within a social context and helping them understand that personal desires often have social implications that can either enhance or distract from the realization of their fondest wishes.

When school rules and expectations are based on democratic principles, a framework is established that weighs student's rights against the compelling interests of the state. The burden of proof remains with teachers and school administrators to demonstrate that a student's behavior violates one of the state's four compelling interests. Rules, as well as explicit definitions of inappropriate student behavior, should provide a clear protection of the state's interests or should be abandoned or revised. These expectations promote better citizenship and are educationally sound. Students who are allowed to discipline themselves democratically and to guide their own classroom activity become much more interested and involved in the learning process (Goodlad, 1990).

Many educators take it for granted that the most effective procedure for managing student behavioral problems is a system of rewards and punishment. With such a system, once rules and consequences are established, the teacher's only responsibility is to consistently apply them. In addition, many educators believe that the rules and consequences should not be bent. All students are to be treated exactly alike. To do otherwise, it is believed, would be unfair.

Such educators also conclude that punishing students is consistent with what they will experience in the "real world" and that such treatment teaches them to be responsible for their own actions. However, punishment only has an appearance of justice. It is usually antithetical to our educational mission and professional objectives. Punishment ordinarily creates an adversarial relationship between teachers and their students. This relationship often generates retaliation, mental drop out, or some form of deviousness. Instead of teaching students to learn more effectively, it teaches them to avoid learning and to fight against the system.

If judicious discipline is to work, educators must understand human growth and development, learning theory, and classroom management as they teach their students to become democratically involved in the classroom. Rather than punish, educators need to know how to motivate and encourage. Otherwise they will not be able to help their students learn and behave appropriately (Gathercoal, 1990).

RULES AND CONSEQUENCES

Beginning teachers often lack understanding of the legal aspects of teaching. They want to know how various laws pertain to their teaching, as well as how to protect themselves from litigation. A broad range of legal decisions have been issued by various courts. There are also federal and state regulations, as well as school district and school directives of which teachers need to be aware. Some rules derive directly from these sources and consequently must be followed. Teachers should examine state department administrative rules and codes, school board policies, collective bargaining agreements, school building rules and regulations, and student handbooks.

Rules should first be created in broad general terms, inclusive enough to account for all possible student behaviors. The four compelling state interests provide a good outline to follow, particularly because they are all-inclusive. From these general considerations, the specific classroom rules can be generated. It is wise to include along with the general rules a list of specific examples of student behavior. The rules should be written at a level and in a style students can understand. It is also important that students not only accept rules but also feel positive about them. Students should understand that rules are intended to help them negotiate possible perils in school and to enhance their learning. Students should agree that the rules reasonably apply to them and that the rules are useful. Wise teachers will help student understand the value of and the necessity for the rules they create. The following is a list of rules that might be created in this way:

1. *Act in a safe and healthy way.*   Use playground equipment appropriately, follow the laboratory safety rules, walk in the building and other designated areas, avoid tripping or hitting other students, go straight home after school, and follow the bus regulations.
2. *Treat all property with respect.*   Protect textbooks and library books from damage, ensure that school furniture and equipment are not abused, ask permission to use someone else's property, and use only the proper shoes on the gym floors.
3. *Respect the rights and needs of others.*   When you are to work independently, do your own work; when you work in groups, do your part to make learning successful. Be courteous to classmates and teachers, use appropriate language, and don't crowd in front of others.
4. *Take responsibility for learning.*   Complete all assignments on time, come prepared for examinations, carefully listen to teachers and compare your own thinking with what

Discussion is a critical part of creating rules in a judicious classroom.

you are taught, keep track of your learning materials and bring them to class as directed, and do the very best you can in all your learning activities (Gathercoal, 1990).

Punishment is generally used to prevent misbehavior or to keep inappropriate behavior from being repeated. However, punishment designed to be aversive is often found by students to be reinforcing; thus it promotes more misbehavior (Madsen, Becker, Thomas, Koser, & Plager, 1968). Commonly, punishment is arbitrary and unrelated to the particular rule that has been broken. This is likely the reason students tend to rebel against rules and punishment. In contrast, consequences are designed to be *commensurate* with the rule. When they are commensurate, students are more likely to accept them as appropriate and to learn more acceptable behaviors and better attitudes. Commensurate consequences flow logically from a student's misbehavior (Dreikurs, Grunwald, & Pepper, 1982).

Consequences should also be *compatible*, representing a broad view of the problem and including attention to students' needs including personal self-worth and academic achievement. For example, a student might be required to scrub graffiti from the restroom walls but have to do it after school to prevent time missed from class and ridicule from peers. This arrangement may also prevent possible school disruptions from taunting and resultant fighting.

Consequences should relate not only to problems in the school, but also to those from other environments like the home. For example, in the case of the punishments given for the food fight spearheaded by Roxanne, no consideration was given to the problems she was experiencing at home. Extreme dress and body piercing could have been addressed by school authorities earlier as behavior inconsistent with Roxanne's usual style. The tell-tale signs were clearly manifest but ignored by school officials and parents alike. Perhaps the whole episode could have been prevented. From this perspective, the principal, Mr. Rosetti, had a responsibility to monitor student behavior and detect possible problems and solve them before they got out of control. With Roxanne's high visibility due to the office she held, he was certainly in a position both to recognize the symptoms and to solicit the necessary help. He placed the whole responsibility on Roxanne, when he and other school officials and teachers could have provided some intervention and were, therefore, accountable to some degree for what happened.

Assuming school officials had been unable to diagnose changes in Roxanne's behavior before the food fight, it would have been prudent for the principal to attempt to ascertain what conditions might have led to the situation rather than just administering punishment. Certainly in this case mitigating circumstances demanded attention and should have affected how the case was treated. In addition, the principal should have considered the fact that Roxanne had enlisted the help of other student body officers and that nearly all the other students present in the cafeteria had joined in. This participation sent a message that the administration and teachers certainly needed to address rather than blaming and punishing just one student.

The compatible nature of judicious consequences is a holistic approach that implies a balance between various ramifications and possible courses of action. Issues central to the educational and self-esteem needs of students, as well as the mission and ethical practices of professional educators, need to be identified and properly addressed. Questions like the following need consideration:

1. What needs to be learned regarding the situation?
2. How would a true professional educator manage the problem?
3. What additional information is needed about the student or the student's family?
4. What strategies are most likely to keep the student in school?
5. How will the student perceive the consequence? Will it be seen as a logical result of the behavior?
6. How will the student's behavior and the consequences applied affect the school community?
7. What actions will be needed to ensure that mutual respect is kept intact and that strong student–educator relationships are maintained? (Gathercoal, 1990)

In applying judicious consequences, educators need to examine all the relevant issues of a student's education. All sides of a question must be considered before responding to a problem. Sometimes intervention of any kind should be avoided, and natural forces should be allowed to bring about a resolution.

The way in which consequences are applied depends on individual differences among students. Flexibility is essential if students' educational and self-esteem needs are to be appropriately considered. This requires that consequences not be identified and published before behavioral problems occur, although examples could be given. Otherwise, actions cannot be made to depend on circumstances. In addition, students often play games when they know consequences in advance. For example, knowing that a third infraction in class results in being sent to the principal's office may invite disruptive students to draw the line at two disruptions each day.

Some educators express concern regarding individualizing consequences. They fear that they will be judged unfairly. Fairness is less of an issue for consequences than for punishment. When consequences are applied, it is easy to recognize them as a suitable reaction to the misbehavior. When the reaction is perceived as suitable, students show little interest in making comparisons between their situation and that of other students. Consequences convey an attitude of helpfulness and educational appropriateness.

With judicious discipline, the following consequences might be appropriate: make an apology, clean up messes made, return stolen property, make restitution, do community service, receive counseling, have a private conference, have a conference with parents, for plagiarism prepare a paper on a new topic, for cheating take a different form of a test, complete an alternative assignment, study with a tutor, lose privileges regarding extracurricular activities, be placed in time-out, be suspended or expelled from school.

Judicious Application of Rules and Consequences

Although the usual actions taken when students break school rules are aversive and designed to thwart further infractions, judicious discipline encourages application of legal standards and sound educational principles. The following are examples of ways judicious discipline may be applied to various discipline problems:

Discipline Issue: Unexcused absence or tardiness.

Usual Actions: Lowering grades in the case of absence or tardiness.
Judicious Procedure: Grades should not be lowered because of lateness or absences. Special classes could be held in the evenings or on weekends. Tutoring could be made available. Students should be given credit if they can demonstrate that they have learned course content by other means. Alternative methods of demonstrating mastery of the course content might be offered.

Discipline Issue: Suspension or expulsion.

Usual Actions: Students are suspended or expelled for a specified time without due process. Ordinarily, they are told of the action being taken by the school and the reason for it.
Judicious Procedure: The student has a right to due process if he or she is being deprived of the right to an education. Appropriate notice should be given, with a summary of the evidence against the student and a list of witnesses. The student should be given an opportunity to tell his or her side of the story and to be represented by counsel.

Discipline Issue: Withholding privileges.

Usual Actions: Withholding privileges like participation in the graduation ceremony, athletics, debate, or other school activities as punishment for rule breaking.
Judicious Procedure: The right to graduate cannot be withheld if the student has completed all requirements, but the right to attend the graduation ceremony could be denied if the gravity of the offense dictates this kind of consequence. A consequence must be demonstrated to be appropriate for the age and mental, emotional, or physical condition of the student.

Discipline Issue: Punishing a whole class for the misbehavior of a single student.

Usual Actions: Keeping the whole class seated after the bell rings, or giving an unannounced test when rules are violated, and similar actions.

Judicious Procedure: This should not be permitted. Students cannot be punished for the misbehavior of their peers.

Discipline Issue: Disciplining a student through public attention or ridicule.

Usual Actions: Having a student sit outside the classroom or putting his or her name on the chalkboard. These strategies are often used when a student disturbs the class by talking to friends.

Judicious Procedure: Because these tactics engender ridicule by peers and have detrimental psychological effects, they should not be used.

Discipline Issue: Keeping students after school.

Usual Actions: This may be done for a variety of reasons such as disrupting class, not completing assignments, or coming to class late.

Judicious Procedure: Keeping students after school is unacceptable, due to possible safety problems with a child returning home at a time or in a way that is unusual.

Discipline Issue: Restricting students' classroom participation.

Usual Actions: Having the student not participate with the class due to not bringing pencils and other school supplies. Students may not have materials necessary for full class participation for a variety of reasons. They may have been unable to get into their locker, someone may have stolen the supplies, or they may have left them home.

Judicious Procedure: Students should not be kept from participating. Community equipment and materials should be available to borrow. The whole class may be asked to contribute to this stock of materials.

Discipline Issue: Destroying school property.

Usual Actions: When students destroy school property, they often receive such punishments as denial of privileges or suspension. These punishments have little to do with the actual offense.

Judicious Procedure: The consequences applied should be proportionate to the severity of the damage and the student's feeling of remorse. Parents are liable for the cost of the damage, but children could be required to compensate the school through work or community service. The school may use small claims court to recover costs.

Discipline Issue: Destroying or stealing another student's property.

Usual Actions: Students occasionally act carelessly with another student's property or take it without permission. They are often punished by suspension or expulsion. No actions may be taken to recover the stolen property.

Judicious Procedure: Make sure parents and students are informed of the risk involved in bringing items from home. Means may be sought to secure valuable items. Parents of a student suffering a property loss may take a classmate and his or her parents to small claims court to recover losses.

Discipline Issue: Inappropriate dress and appearance.

Usual Actions: Due to changes in what is acceptable clothing for school, students sometimes wear what is judged as inappropriate. Children are often punished for wearing clothing that conflicts with the school dress code.

Judicious Procedure: A dress code must be clearly stated, and its relationship to the educational environment should be explained. The personal preferences of teachers and school administrators should not be included if items do not create learning distractions for students. Parents should be informed when their children are dressed in ways that are patently vulgar or clearly inappropriate. A certain amount of self-expression should be protected. Cases should be handled on an individual basis with involvement of parents.

Discipline Issue: Insubordination, open defiance, profanity, indecent gestures, and bigoted statements.

Usual Actions: Students may engage in these kinds of behaviors when they feel their rights are threatened or when they wish to threaten the teacher or avoid punishment. Usually, students suffer expulsion from class. Ordinarily, the reasons for the student's actions are not examined.

Judicious Procedure: These behaviors can interfere with learning by undermining the teacher's credibility or by promoting negative reactions and confrontations. The teacher has the right to terminate these student behaviors. However, it is wise to ascertain the student's motives before taking any action. Too often, teachers take these behaviors personally, but such reactions should be avoided. It is better to correct the problems that may have precipitated the behavior. Teacher reactions can often make matters worse.

Discipline Issue: Searching lockers, cars, and personal items.

Usual Actions: Teachers may inappropriately search student property on occasions when they think they might find things that are not allowed. The searches are commonly unannounced. When disallowed items are found, they are often confiscated.

Judicious Procedure: Though no search warrant is necessary, teachers and school administrators should have a reasonable cause to search students' lockers, cars, and personal effects. The student should be present during the search, and there should be witnesses. When random searches are planned, prior notice should be given where possible, unless school authorities are looking for misplaced school property or spoiled food that may cause health risks. Bomb threats make random searches legal for safety reasons.

Discipline Issue: Conducting body searches or "strip searches."

Usual Actions: Sometimes students will attempt to hide forbidden materials on their person, believing they are legally immune from being searched. When educators suspect forbidden items have been hidden on a student's person, they may conduct a strip search.

Judicious Procedure: Conducting strip searches can be risky if the student fails to cooperate. Teachers could easily be badgered by students into using excessive force. There must, of course, be reasonable cause to believe that the person is hiding sensitive items. It may be appropriate for parents or police to perform the search if the situation is serious.

Discipline Issue: Seizure of student's property being used to disrupt learning.

Usual Actions: Teachers sometimes seize toys, fad items, and similar materials brought from home that the student uses for entertainment but that distract either the student's own learning or that of his or her peers. Items that distract the teacher are also sometimes brought. Often, teachers confiscate these items and in some cases permanently deprive a child of his or her property.

Judicious Procedure: The teacher may confiscate items that disrupt the class, but these items should be returned to the student as quickly as possible, probably after school. It is wise for the teacher to give a receipt for the item, indicating that the student is the owner.

Discipline Issue: Placing limitations on what students may publish.

Usual Actions: Students often believe they have rights to publish whatever they please, especially when they think their individual rights have been abridged or when various controversies arise regarding school practices or general social problems. Sometimes educators censor any student writing that they consider inappropriate.

Judicious Procedure: Because students cannot be legally sued for libel, they enjoy only some substantive rights regarding what they publish. What students can publish needs to be clearly communicated to them. This should be done in a manual of written guidelines, created by an advisory board composed of a student editor, advisor, student-body representative, teacher, administrator, school board member, and possibly a local newspaper editor.

Discipline Issue: Student refusing to participate in class activities for religious reasons. Some activities like frog dissections may be objected to on religious grounds.

Usual Actions: Teachers may lower a student's grade for refusal to participate in any learning activity that is part of the class curriculum.

Judicious Procedure: Students should be excused from activities to which they object for religious reasons without suffering any grade reduction. They should be given alternative work that is relevant to or a desirable substitute for the activity from which they are excused.

Discipline Issue: Wearing religious attire, performing religious music, and decorating the school with religious artifacts.

Usual Actions: Sometimes a student's religious attire may be criticized by peers. If this creates disruptions, school officials may ask students to wear regular clothing. Christmas and other religious holidays may be observed in the school. Religious symbols may be used to decorate the school.

Judicious Procedure: Students may wear religious attire if they wish; however, teachers cannot wear religious dress if it appears to advocate a particular belief. Teachers should protect students who wear religious attire from the ridicule of their peers, as these students have a right to be protected against discrimination. Religious music may be used in a secular manner. Musical or artistic renditions that are objectionable to a minority should not be advocated by the school. Students should have bulletin board space allocated on which to express their religious preferences. They should be allowed free expression of their ideas but not be allowed wide distribution of them through the school.

Judicious Discipline in the Classroom

Good discipline depends on educators' valuing their students as persons and respecting their students' capability for making wise judgments about rules and consequences. They must believe that their students' opinions are worthy. Only when students are significantly involved in making rules will they achieve the level of ownership required to make democratic principles operative in the classroom. In applying judicious discipline to classrooms, teachers must help students learn the implications of constitutional rights and principles, not only for life generally, but for life in the classroom. It is best if students sense the general applicability of discipline in the school to what they can expect in life beyond the classroom. This can be accomplished in two ways, through inductive teaching and through deductive teaching. These two approaches are illustrated here as they might occur at the high school level. Less sophisticated language would be necessary for younger students.

INDUCTIVE APPROACH

The purpose of this approach is to use classroom discussions to help students discover their personal rights and explore ways that these rights might be kept in balance with society's needs. Students need to understand that the loss of personal rights may occur when there is a compelling state interest. In the school the compelling state interest consists of the needs of the total school community regarding property rights, legitimate educational purposes, health and safety, and serious disruption of the educational process.

The following is an example of how this approach might apply:

Teacher   Take out a piece of paper and pencil. Write down all the personal rights you think you have as citizens of our country.

When students have completed their lists, the teacher writes all their contributions on the chalkboard.

Teacher   Now make a list of all the rights you think you have in school.

The teacher writes all of these contributions on the chalkboard.

Teacher   It may surprise you to know that your rights as citizens of our country and your rights in school are nearly the same. Today we will be discussing your rights as citizens of the school and looking at ways these rights may be forfeited. Knowing what our rights are and how to retain them is a critical part of becoming a responsible citizen in a school society.

Now let's examine the rights listed on the chalkboard and try to group them into categories. In preparation for this we need to talk about the United States Constitution and the amendments, which guarantee our rights and privileges. The First, Fourth, and Fourteenth Amendments are the ones that apply to us in school. The First Amendment provides us freedom of speech, press, and peaceful assembly, along with the right to petition the government for redress of grievances. This doesn't mean that we can say or publish anything we want regardless of who it might injure, but it does mean that our rights cannot be arbitrarily restricted. If we feel our rights have been unfairly limited, we have the right to have our case heard through an orderly judicial procedure.

The Fourth Amendment protects us from unreasonable searches and seizures. For example, your lockers should not be searched unless it is probable that they contain something illegal. If the school administration is concerned about weapons and drugs in the school, and they have reason to suspect these items may be in student lockers, they have the right and social responsibility to conduct a search. This is because they have the responsibility to protect the health and welfare of the students. Your personal property cannot be seized unless it is clearly being used to disrupt learning in the school.

The Fourteenth Amendment provides for due process along with equal protection. Due process mandates conditions that must be met if citizens are to be deprived of their rights. Rights can be taken away only when there is a compelling state interest. The due process rules help to balance personal rights with social needs. Compelling state interests include four categories of social needs: the right to avoid property loss or damage, the right to ensure legitimate educational experiences for all students, the right to ensure the health and safety for all, and the right to protect the learning environment from serious disruptions. Personal rights cannot be considered more important than these compelling interests. *Equal protection* involves all the laws and rules prohibiting discrimination. All students regardless of sex, race, national origin, disabilities, marital status, age, and religion are assured an equal educational opportunity. Now, let's have you identify which of the rights listed on the board come from each of the three amendments I have told you about.

The class helps the teacher categorize the list of rights in terms of the three amendments.

Teacher   Rights vary depending on where you are and what role you have. For example, you have more rights in this classroom than I do. You could wear a political button for a particular candidate at school, but I could not. Also, I could not teach you the doctrine of a particular religious sect, but I could teach those doctrines to members of a religious congregation in my church, even if some members of this class were in that congregation. What restrictions are there on my personal rights as a teacher and on your rights as students who are members of the school community?

A class discussion is held about the various rights listed and ways they may have to be modified so as not to violate the rights of the whole educational community.

Teacher   Now I want you to get into your four-person groups and discuss the question of when society can take away our rights. See if you can discover any patterns. When society takes away our rights, it is done because of a compelling state interest. I can't throw a rock through a store window, because I am destroying someone else's property. I can't run a red light, because doing so would endanger the lives of other citizens. I can't yell "fire!" in a crowded theater, because it would endanger the health and welfare of those present. In your groups, discuss how this applies to the rights we listed on the chalkboard.

Students use whatever time is necessary to discuss situations in which the personal rights they have listed would be overruled because of a compelling state interest. A whole-class discussion could be used to share group findings.

Teacher   Now that you have considered how to balance personal rights with compelling state interests, let's think together how we might use this information to develop rules or procedures for our class. What rules do you think appropriately match each of the compelling state interests?

The class should work through each of the four compelling state interests in relation to classroom rules. Ideas can be recorded on the chalkboard. The teacher may wish to provide clues to help students identify certain rules that they have not included.

Teacher   Now that we have discussed your citizenship rights and compelling state interests, you are ready to discuss judicious consequences. Consequences are different from punishment. While punishment may be arbitrary and unrelated to specific inappropriate behavior, consequences are designed to be a logical result of breaking rules. You have listed the rules. The next step is to create a list of consequences you believe are fair and make sense. Keep in mind that we are not interested in causing pain; consequences should be appropriate and reasonable as well as educational. Keep in mind too that we don't want to make an exhaustive list of rules. The rules should cover the different compelling interests, but the number should be kept to a minimum.

The class would then devise judicious consequences, which the teacher would record on the board. The teacher may want to point out appropriate consequences students fail to include.

DEDUCTIVE APPROACH

Some teachers teach five or six classes a day and wish to ensure consistency in the rules established for all their classes. Consequently, they may prefer to use a deductive approach in establishing classroom rules. The following scenario illustrates how this might be done:

Teacher   Historically there have been changes in the way school rules are determined. Before the 1969 U.S. Supreme Court decision regarding student rights, school officials and teachers used to base rules on what is called *in loco parentis*. This Latin term gave legal permission for school officials to act in behalf of parents in disciplining children in school. It was as if they were the parents when it came to disciplining. From this perspective students were limited to the same rights at school that they had at home. With the 1969 Supreme Court decision, students received nearly the same rights at school as any other citizen, though they still had restricted rights at home. Therefore, as we formulate rules for this class, we will make sure they are consistent with your civil rights.

The teacher then discusses with the class the concept of *in loco parentis* and points out the changes that have been made and the effects of these changes in students' civil rights. The teacher helps students understand that their rights in school are the same as the rights of any citizen but that these rights are modified in the home.

Teacher   As your teacher, I want to ensure that you understand your rights and responsibilities and that you learn how to balance your personal rights with the needs and interests of the school community. You need to know how a compelling community interest can override individual rights and that this is the reason for creating rules and determining consequences for breaking them.

   My responsibility is to ensure that your personal interests are not violated, except by compelling interests of the class. I also want to be sure that consequences for breaking rules are fair in terms of what you have done and how you are going about correcting your behavior, and that these consequences do not interfere with your educational needs and opportunities.

   You need to be aware of how and when you can forfeit your personal rights and what can happen when you do. You also need to understand that I will be your advocate in dealing with problems. I will help ensure your civil rights are safeguarded, and I will help you learn how to achieve an appropriate balance between these rights and matching social expectations. What do you understand about how your personal rights might interfere with the rights and needs of the class?

This question should be discussed until the teacher is satisfied that students understand this important concept.

Teacher   I'd next like to explain some of your rights, as set forth in the First, Fourth, and Fourteenth Amendments to the Constitution. These amendments guarantee your rights of speech, press, and peaceable assembly and the right for redress of grievances. In addition, you have the right for protection against unreasonable searches and seizures. Searches and seizures can only be made with probable cause. This means that any official who is searching you or your property must have reason to suspect you are holding or carrying something illegal like drugs or weapons.

You are also guaranteed *due process* and *equal protection* of the laws. The purpose of due process is to ensure that you have adequate notice any time your civil rights are in question because of your behavior. It also guarantees your right to a fair and impartial hearing and your right to appeal any decision reached. Due process is required any time you are accused of violating the compelling interests of the educational community. This includes being responsible for the loss or damage of either public or private property in the school, failing to undertake the legitimate purposes for which you have come to school, endangering the health and safety of anyone in school, or disrupting the learning process in class.

Equal protection of the laws is designed to protect citizens from discrimination in all forms, including discrimination based on sex, race, national origin, disabilities, marital status, age, and religion. You should receive the same opportunity for an education as anyone else, regardless of personal attributes and conditions. We should have no prejudice in our classroom, and no one should be deprived of any educational opportunity offered in school. You all have a right to an education as long as you abide by the rules set forth to protect the compelling interests of the whole class.

What are some ways in which discrimination might take place in the classroom? How can you be sure that you have received due process when you are being accused of violating a classroom rule?

The preceding questions should be discussed to ensure that students understand what due process means in practical terms as well as to make students aware of discriminatory actions that might come from the school and the teachers as well as from fellow students.

Teacher   We next need to talk about some specific behaviors that are protected under the law. First, what is protected under our right to free speech and expression? Dress and appearance codes are among the most controversial and perplexing problems on which schools have to make decisions.

Difficulties occur because styles change, and things that were conspicuous enough to be disruptive at one time might not be disruptive today. You will need to be aware of what the current rules say about things like short skirts, long skirts, shorts, short shorts, hats, coats and jackets in class, knickers, jumpsuits, coveralls, frayed trousers or jeans, shirttails outside pants, tie-died clothing, tank tops, bare midriffs, low necklines, jewelry, clothing with slogans and pictures, hair styles and colors, jewelry attached to unusual parts of the body, and unusual facial makeup. The school may also mandate that students wear socks, shoes, shirts, and bras.

This list of items is not exhaustive, because what is judged to be disruptive may change with style changes.

The school will try to maintain standards of dress designed to satisfy the four compelling school interests. For example, you may be required to wear robes at graduation or white shirts and ties on game days because they serve a legitimate educational purpose. Health and safety are compelling school interests that require you to wear shoes to school or protective gear when participating in sports or in science laboratories. Lewd or indecent dress or expression may violate the compelling school interest of promoting good mental health of students. Finally, gang dress and activities are unacceptable because they are likely to cause serious disruptions of the learning in school. You might be curious about the current dress code. For a few minutes, let's address questions you have about any item in the code.

The teacher should discuss the dress code and clarify any component that students do not understand. Students should understand that modifications are possible as time goes by, but that there are better ways of making changes than violating the code. An item on the code will not be modified as long as wearing it could interfere with a compelling school interest.

Teacher   One thing you should realize is that insubordination or open defiance of teacher's authority violates the law and often results in suspension or expulsion from school. Teachers won't always react in the same way to this kind of student behavior. Some will be more patient than others. You need to be aware, however, that the law considers behavior like swearing at a teacher or refusing to leave the room when told to do so as inappropriate, and doing these things can result in serious disciplinary action. The law will not tolerate a student acting in this way. It is a violation of the state's interests for students to use profane language, display indecent gestures, or make bigoted statements. This behavior would be judged as disrupting the operation of the school. In this class, if you feel upset, let me know privately about the problem so that disruptions can be avoided. Students' free speech rights do not take precedence over the need to maintain order in the classroom. Let's discuss what distinctions need to be made between statements that disrupt the classroom and those that might be controversial but not inappropriate.

A discussion should be held to help students make distinctions between appropriate and inappropriate classroom language.

Teacher   Sometimes students get confused about proper religious expressions. Some think it is illegal for teachers to mention anything religious or to support values that may be advocated by various religions. A distinction needs to be made between some of these values and specific religious doctrines. For example, some churches oppose premarital sex. Because this is a biology class, students sometimes raise questions about this topic.

Keep in mind that this is a social and psychological question, even though various religions take a stand on it.

Then there is the topic of evolution. You will find that the state-approved textbook assumes that evolution occurred and that an understanding of current plant and animal life depends on knowing their evolutionary history. Many religions oppose teaching evolution. Our state approves of teaching it, however, as evidenced by approving biology textbooks that include a study of evolution. In our class we will teach about evolution, referring to it not as a fact but as a scientific theory, because that's what it is. That way we won't show antagonism toward religion. Avoiding antagonism toward religion is an important school responsibility.

In school we cannot support a particular religious sect, but we also cannot oppose religion. The U.S. Supreme Court has ruled that schools should include the comparative study of religions to show the role of religion in the advancement of civilization. They have ruled that it is appropriate to study the *Bible* both for its literary as well as historic qualities. In fact, deliberately excluding the study of religion in the schools is in violation of the law. In addition, it is your privilege as students to study whatever you want regarding religion and to make statements about your beliefs. However, we will not have discussions in class about your religious beliefs. You are also free to create art subjects, wood shop projects, musical expressions, and other projects that have a religious theme. But as your teacher, I can't do this at school. That would be interpreted as advocating religion, and it is not allowed. You're probably also aware that we cannot have prayer in the school. What questions do you have about religion and the schools you would like to discuss?

Questions the students raise about religion and the schools should be discussed.

Teacher   Another right you may have wondered about is freedom of the press. What exactly can you write or publish at school? First, freedom of the press prohibits *prior restraint*. This means that our government has no legal authority to restrict in advance what anyone may or may not publish. However, if what is published injures another person, the injured party may sue for libel. Publishing material that urges violent overthrow of our government or something which is obscene may result in criminal prosecution.

The Supreme Court has ruled that some modifications are appropriate for school-sponsored publications due to the age and impressionability of the students and the fact that students cannot be held legally liable for what they publish. Consequently, some prior restraint may be reasonably imposed on student publications. Schools are responsible to exercise editorial control over the style and content of student speech and writing in school-sponsored expressive activities, as long as their actions are reasonably related to legitimate educational concerns. The Court has suggested that experience in school writing should help students learn whatever the lesson is designed to teach, that material that is inappropriate for students' level of maturity should not be included, and that the views of the individual writer or speaker should not be attributed to the school.

You shouldn't experience difficulties if you follow the publication guidelines put out by the Publication Advisory Board. They are quite specific and cover most issues relating to publication. Keep in mind that there are many issues that you are free to write about. You just need to be wary of materials that are obscene, profane, libelous, or demeaning—in short, materials that might disrupt the education process.

Occasionally, you may wish to distribute or post off-campus publications on school grounds. This is permissible as long as these materials meet the standards included in the publication guidelines. What questions would you like to discuss about your freedom of speech rights?

The teacher should conduct a discussion regarding the questions raised about freedom of speech rights.

Teacher The Bill of Rights also provides rights regarding unlawful search and seizure. However, search and seizure may take place as long as appropriate standards are met. If school officials have reasonable cause to suspect students are concealing such items as textbooks, school equipment, drugs, weapons, or the personal property of other students, a legal search can be made. It is not necessary for them to obtain a warrant before making such a search. Students' pockets and automobiles may also be searched. None of these searches should be made, however, just to see what might turn up. This is not reasonable. Schools can also undertake random searches. This might take place near the close of the school year in an effort to recover lost or misplaced school property, as well as to remove items that are a health hazard. You will be advised in advance if the administration plans to make random searches. You will be asked to be present for any search made. If there is a bomb threat, lockers might be opened without warning. In this case, there is a clear and present danger, which must be dealt with quickly.

I hope you will not bring items to class that are potentially disruptive. If you do, they will be taken from you until after school. I will give you a receipt, which you must return to recover your property. If illegal drugs, firearms, or contraband are found in the school, they will be turned over to law enforcement authorities. As you can see, rules for conducting searches and seizures in school are different from those in society generally. What questions do you have about specific rights in this area?

A discussion about search and seizure should follow, clarifying exactly how school situations are different from those of society generally.

Teacher Now let me talk to you about my attitudes toward education, so you can understand why I organize learning the way I do. First, I prefer that you assume as much responsibility as you can by helping to set classroom goals. I also believe that you all have different needs and learning styles that require different teaching approaches. I think you will learn more and enjoy school better if you are successful in pursuing many of your own goals in ways that make sense to you. If problems come up, particularly when your personal rights are not being respected or when compelling school needs are violated, I will try to ensure that your due process and equal protection rights are secure. It is important that we maintain good relationships with one another, even when problems occur. To do this you must help me understand how to help you learn in the best way possible and let me know when your needs and expectations are not being met. It is better to prevent problems in the first place, but when they occur it is best to solve them before they have a chance to escalate.

Now that we have discussed the various rights you have, along with compelling school interests, you are ready to examine classroom rules that are associated with these rights and compelling interests. The rules in this handout apply (Gathercoal, 1990).

The teacher distributes the following information in writing:

1. *Act in a safe and healthy way.*   Use school furniture appropriately, walk in hallways and classrooms, follow laboratory rules, always clean up after yourself, follow bus riding rules, keep your hands to yourself, and your feet under your desk.
2. *Treat all property with respect.*   Take proper care of textbooks, library books, school furniture, school bathrooms, computers, and the personal property of others. Borrow others' property only with permission, and return it in a timely way undamaged.
3. *Respect the rights and needs of others.*   Do your own work as directed, cooperate with others as assigned, be courteous to others, use appropriate language, and take pride in the work you do.
4. *Take responsibility for learning.*   Always do your best work, come to school prepared, turn all assignments in on time, listen carefully to all instruction, participate in discussions, bring textbooks as well as notes and paper to class, keep your work organized, and take the initiative in learning.

The teacher should explain that modifications may be necessary in this list of rules. The class should examine them together and make suggestions.

Teacher   I hope that the list of rules is in a form that is acceptable to the class. As I look at the rules, I believe they will help protect your personal rights, and at the same time ensure that the compelling interests of the school community are not put at risk.

The next question is, what should we do as a class if there are rule violations? You are probably well aware of the nature of punishment commonly given to those who break the law. You may also have witnessed punishment given for breaking rules in school. In our class we will follow a different approach. Consequences will be given for violating rules. For example, if you fail to follow safe procedures in the lab, you will not be allowed in the lab until you have prepared a statement on how you intend to follow the rules in the future. If you turn in a paper exactly like that of someone else, you will have to prepare another paper on a different topic. If you do not do your own work on a test, you will be given an alternative test, perhaps an oral one. If you do not complete your homework assignments, a conference will be arranged with your parents to formulate a plan for helping you consistently complete your homework. If you destroy another student's property or school property, you will be required to pay to replace it. If you disturb the class by excessive talking during learning activities, you will be asked to leave class until you create a written, workable plan for solving the problem. These are some examples of the kinds of consequences that will be used. Notice that they are designed to help you take responsibility for improving your behavior. Are there any comments or questions about how consequences are different from punishment or how they will be used in class?

A discussion is held on students' questions about consequences.

Once rules and consequences have been created and applied to the classroom, teachers may find it necessary to periodically review them. Students who have not previously been in a class that uses judicious discipline will require a period of adjustment. Most students are used to discipline based on punishment where they have little or no input regarding the rules that are imposed. Students are also likely to have distorted views of what their rights are and how compelling school interests apply in the schools. Changes toward applying democratic principles to the school will require patience and continued instruction while students become accustomed to a greater degree of self-government.

Preventing Discipline Problems

Though it is designed primarily for dealing with rule infractions, judicious discipline has a powerful preventive component as well. Prevention is promoted mostly through teaching students about their rights and helping them recognize the need to regulate their behavior in terms of compelling school interests. Because students are involved in determining rules and expectations along with consequences, they are more prepared to take a responsible role in self-government. When students understand the implications of their behavior, they are better able to anticipate consequences and constrain themselves, thus avoiding the need for corrective measures.

Schoolwide Discipline

Though Gathercoal doesn't specifically show how this model can be applied on a schoolwide basis, this application can easily be made. In fact, creating schoolwide applications provides an opportunity to more fully implement various aspects of the U.S. legal system in student governance. A student legislative body would be elected and empowered to enact rules that would have schoolwide applications. These might include rules governing activities on the playground, in the cafeteria, on school buses, at school activities and assemblies, in gymnasiums, on athletic fields, and in hallways. It might deal with such things as after-hours use of the building and expected behavior at activities away from the school, as well as general vandalism.

A court system could be created with three levels of student courts for the school: a court of original jurisdiction, an appellate court, and a supreme court. The court of original jurisdiction would provide the initial rulings for cases involving the violation of schoolwide rules. The appellate court would hear appeals brought to them from various classrooms as well as provide an appellate level court for appealing schoolwide rule violations. The supreme court would constitute the final level of appeal at the student level. Student attorneys would be appointed to represent student clients.

In some instances the student court system would be bypassed in favor of submitting grievances to administrative councils or to the school board. Students and their parents would have the right to confine their appeals to authorized school officials. In these cases representation by competent professional counsel would be likely. Serious cases might end up being tried in the regular court system outside the school.

Strengths and Weaknesses of the Judicious Discipline Model

STRENGTHS

1. It provides students a more valid sense of how violation of their rights may be addressed after they leave school.
2. It helps children understand how the legal system works in a democratic society.
3. It helps students learn to balance their rights against compelling school interests.
4. It helps students get a truer picture of their rights and responsibilities in a democratic society.
5. It provides a format for students to become actively involved in school and community affairs, including learning the operation of the legal system.

WEAKNESSES

1. It takes considerable time for students to become involved in the schoolwide aspects of judicious discipline.
2. The application of personal rights and compelling school interests may be confusing to students when they exit the school at graduation.

▼ SUMMARY

Judicious discipline is based on democratic principles embodied in the Constitution and the Bill of Rights. Of particular importance for the schools are the First, Fourth, and Fourteenth Amendments. These amendments provide for the free exercise of religion, speech, and press, as well as the right to assemble and the right to petition the government for redress of grievances. They also protect citizens from unlawful search and seizure. Finally, individuals are provided due process as well as equal protection under the law. Applied to the schools, this means that a student who appears in violation of established rules must be given adequate notice, be provided a fair and impartial hearing, be provided statements of evidence of the rule broken, have an opportunity to mount an adequate defense, and have the right of appeal as due process rights. Students are to be protected from all types of discrimination. A student can be deprived of established rights only if it can be shown that he or she is in violation of a compelling school interest.

School rules should be created to protect the health and safety of all students. Such rules should show students how to respect the rights and needs of others as well as take responsibility for their own learning. Rules should also be produced that protect personal and school property. When rules are violated, consequences should be provided that are directly related to the rule infraction and that tend to teach students the right way to behave in school.

Judicious discipline can be applied on a schoolwide basis. To do this, various levels of courts are established to review rule violations and to render judgments. Serious matters should be referred to the proper authorities. School administrators or the school board should take care of problems of this kind. Law enforcement personnel should be summoned in matters involving weapons, drugs, and contraband.

CENTRAL IDEAS

1. Judicious discipline is based on democratic principles embodied in the Bill of Rights, as applied to school discipline.
2. The First, Fourth, and Fourteenth Amendments provide for basic student rights, including the rights of speech, press, peaceable assembly, and protection against unlawful searches and seizures, along with the right to due process and to freedom from discrimination.
3. The schools no longer can operate *in loco parentis* with respect to student misbehavior. Students have a full range of rights, modified only as necessary in accordance with their age and maturity.
4. Schools have a compelling interest in matters regarding property loss and damage, student health and safety, protection of the learning environment, and support for legitimate educational purposes in school.
5. Students have the right to receive adequate notice regarding charges that they have violated school rules, the right to be given a fair and impartial hearing, the right to receive and examine evidence put forth to convict them, the opportunity to mount an adequate defense, and the right to appeal any judgment made against them.
6. Classroom rules should be those necessary to protect the school's compelling interests regarding property loss and damage, student health and safety, the learning environment, and unacceptable disruptions.
7. When classroom rules are breached, consequences should be supplied that are directly related to the particular infraction and that help students learn a better way to behave.

8. Schoolwide discipline involves establishing a legislative body to define schoolwide rules, along with a court system to hear grievances, render judgments, and deal with appeals.

▼ QUESTIONS AND ACTIVITIES

QUESTIONS TO CONSIDER

1. How does judicious discipline compare to the logical consequences and reality therapy/choice theory models of discipline?
2. What problems might be encountered in using judicious discipline on a schoolwide basis?
3. How can teachers help students recognize the differences in their rights as students in school and as citizens in the society at large?

CLASSROOM ACTIVITIES

1. Have students debate whether or not it was appropriate for the Supreme Court to eliminate the perspective of *in loco parentis* for teachers and school administrators.
2. Discuss the difference between the kind of problems that might be kept within the student legal system of the school and those that might find their way into the state and federal courts.
3. Discuss the extent to which a properly operating student legal system might reduce the instances where students and their parents might seek redress in the state and federal courts.
4. Role play with the class the establishment of a set of rules for judicious discipline using both the inductive and deductive methods.

STUDENT APPLICATIONS

1. In a role play situation with a group of your peers, using the inductive approach, create a set of rules and consequences for a class you may be preparing to teach.
2. Using the deductive model, role play the creation of classroom rules and consequences.
3. With a group of your peers, create a description of a student who is unusually disruptive in school. Talk about a likely scenario that could be expected as the student's misbehavior is acted on and the student appeals the decision all the way to the school supreme court.

EXPLORE YOUR PHILOSOPHY

1. Defend the assumption that students are capable of regulating their own behavior in concert with rules relating to compelling school interests.

2. Defend or refute the assumption that applying consequences is a more effective way to discipline than providing punishment.
3. Defend or refute the assumption that students are capable of creating valid sets of classroom rules.
4. Compare assumptions in the judicious discipline model and those outlined in the logical consequences model.

▼REFERENCES

Dreikurs, R., Grunwald, B. B., & Pepper, F. C. (1982). *Maintaining sanity in the classroom: Classroom management techniques* (2nd ed.). New York: Harper & Row.

Gathercoal, F. (1990). *Judicious discipline* (2nd ed.). Davis, CA: Caddo Cap Press.

Gathercoal, F. (1992). *Judicious parenting.* San Francisco: Caddo Gap Press.

Goodlad, J. I. (1990). *Teachers for our nation's schools.* San Francisco: Jossey-Bass Publishers.

Goss v. Lopez, 419 U.S. 565 (1975).

Hoover, R. L., & Kindsvatter, R. (1997). *Democratic discipline: Foundation and practice.* Upper Saddle River, NJ: Merrill/Prentice Hall.

Madsen, C. H., Becker, W. C., Thomas, D. R., Koser, L., & Plager, E. (1968). An analysis of the reinforcing function of "sit down" commands. In R. K. Parker (Ed.), *Readings in educational psychology* (pp. 265–278). Boston: Allyn & Bacon.

Tinker v. Des Moines Independent School District, 393 U.S. 503 (1969).

Wolfgang, C. H. (1995). *Solving discipline problems: Methods and models for today's teachers* (3rd ed.). Boston: Allyn & Bacon.

The Jones Model:
Fredric H. Jones

OBJECTIVES

This chapter is designed to help you
1. Learn to make seating arrangements in the classroom that give teachers greater control.
2. Implement the praise–prompt–leave sequence of instruction.
3. Effectively use nonverbal language to set limits on students' behavior.
4. Describe how students react to limit setting by their teachers.
5. Create a program of preferred activity time that can be applied in a specific type of classroom.

ASSUMPTIONS

1. Children need to be controlled to behave properly.
2. Teachers can achieve control through nonverbal cues and movements calculated to bring them closer and closer to students physically.
3. It is appropriate to pressure students to behave by reducing the time they are allowed to spend in preferred activities.
4. Reinforcing good behaviors will increase their frequency.
5. The involvement of parents and school administrators in classroom discipline helps the teacher gain control of students' behavior.
6. Stopping instruction to deal with discipline problems helps eliminate these problems.

Introduction

Fredric Jones is a psychologist who conducted research on classroom practices while working at the UCLA Medical Center and at the School of Medicine and Dentistry at the

University of Rochester. From this work he created his discipline model, which is now promoted in the classroom management training program he directs. Teachers who are trained in this California-based program go on to train their colleagues. Jones emphasizes the need for teachers to employ just enough of their physical presence in the classroom to ensure that students remain on-task and avoid disrupting their neighbors.

▼ LaVern glanced expectantly at Dale, wishing that he could work up enough courage to say something. He knew, however, that Mr. Bell was still looking straight at him. It was almost as if Mr. Bell could read his mind. Even when Mr. Bell was dealing with a commotion in some other part of the classroom, he would still look back at LaVern. His eyes seemed to be everywhere at once. No students escaped his attention if they were even the least bit disruptive in class. The look on his face always showed little emotion. It was hard to tell what he was thinking. Sometimes he would come right to your desk and stand there looking at you. LaVern always went right back to work rather than challenge Mr. Bell. The way Mr. Bell carried himself seemed to communicate his authority and let everyone know who was in charge.

This episode illustrates a few of the tactics Jones recommends for improving classroom discipline. He believes that classroom management procedures must be positive. They must affirm students while setting limits and promoting cooperation. Coercion must be avoided. Jones also believes that discipline procedures must be practical, simple, and easily mastered. They must ultimately reduce the teacher's workload. Teachers should use discipline techniques that take the least amount of planning and effort and involve the least amount of time and paperwork. Jones believes that it is erroneous to assume that discipline refers primarily to handling major crises. Instead, it involves the management of many small problems and potential problems. Teachers make 500 management decisions each day, which makes their work second only to that of air traffic controllers in complexity and stress (Jones, 1987a). Learning how to manage these many situations effectively is necessary if teachers are to avoid burnout before they reach age 35. To help teachers cope with management problems, Jones recommends that they

1. Properly structure their classroom.
2. Learn how to maintain control in the classroom by using appropriate instructional strategies and by setting limits.
3. Build patterns of cooperation.
4. Develop appropriate backup systems.

Classroom Structures

Many discipline problems teachers experience are the result of mismanaging various routines and procedures in the classroom. Rules may be misunderstood. Seating arrangements may hinder easy access to students, making it difficult to monitor their behavior. Interactions between teachers and their students may promote misbehavior. Successful teachers know how to manage their classroom and avoid these problems.

RULES, ROUTINES, AND STANDARDS

Jones believes that the following common misconceptions about rules create problems for teachers:

1. *Misconception:* Students already know how to behave when they reach your class.
   Reality: They usually have a vague idea about rules, but in reality they wait to find out "your rules" first. Until rules are clarified, students go as far as they can to determine limits.

2. *Misconception*: Teachers should avoid spending too much time going over the rules because doing so takes too much time away from the instructional program.
   Reality: Teachers should take whatever time is necessary to help their students understand class rules. It is reported that teachers who have the fewest discipline problems may spend most of the first 2 weeks of the school year teaching rules, routines, standards, and expectations (Evertson & Anderson, 1979).

3. *Misconception*: Rules are general guidelines.
   Reality: General rules have their place, but they must always be backed up by specific requirements. Teachers must spell out exactly what they expect and how students can comply with these expectations.

4. *Misconception*: Announcing the rules of the class will ensure that they are understood.
   Reality: Rules have to be taught. They have been taught only when they are properly understood. Informing students of rules and procedures will usually not give students a sufficiently clear understanding of what teachers desire. Students should be involved in a dialogue with their teachers regarding the rules.

5. *Misconception*: If you do a good job teaching your rules at the beginning of the school year, you will not have to refer to them again.
   Reality: If teachers are to avoid discipline problems, they must reteach the rules periodically throughout the school year. Not only do students have a tendency to forget the rules, but they also need to have them reinforced occasionally. Otherwise, they will behave as if the rules were never given.

6. *Misconception*: Discipline is essentially a matter of strictly enforcing the rules.
   Reality: Rules should not be enforced through dictatorial means. Students' cooperation must be enlisted to ensure compliance with rules. Good disciplinarians are relaxed and emotionally warm, not harsh like drill sergeants.

7. *Misconception*: Students inherently dislike and resent classroom rules.
   Reality: On the contrary, students appreciate teachers who systematically organize their classrooms. When rules are lacking, the resulting chaos makes learning difficult. Most students recognize the benefits of an orderly classroom and prefer teachers who exercise control through the proper use of rules.

Rules, routines, and standards are critical aspects of any classroom. Imagine a classroom in which there is no rule prohibiting talking out of order during quiet study time or during discussions and lectures. Or imagine what a chemistry lab would be like if students were not required to adhere to safety standards. In a chemistry lab, rules such as the following are absolutely essential:

1. Use proper safety precautions when inserting glass tubing into a stopper.
2. In the lab, always wear safety goggles to protect your eyes.
3. In the lab, always wear an apron to protect your clothes.
4. Avoid letting strong bases and acids make contact with your skin.
5. Do not dispose of chemicals by pouring them down the drain. Place them in the appropriate disposal receptacles.
6. Use all chemicals only in the prescribed way.

Students should be thoroughly familiar with the procedures to follow in case of fire, chemical spills, and chemical contamination of clothing, skin, or eyes. Rules are also necessary regarding lab cleanup as well as equipment and chemical storage. Sometimes special rules are necessary in labs where expensive equipment is used.

Jones believes that teachers should teach rules, routines, and standards as they would teach any other subject. This teaching differs from the usual practice of making a few pronouncements about rules during the initial class period or lecturing students after rules have been violated. Students should understand and be able to follow the rules. There should be no misunderstanding about how rules are to be interpreted. To enlist the support of students for the rules, teachers should conduct discussions in which students can express their views about (1) what characterizes a good classroom, (2) what their role should be, (3) what obligations and responsibilities both teachers and students have, and (4) what kinds of behavior can ruin a class.

SEATING ARRANGEMENTS

In addition to establishing rules, teachers need to arrange classroom furniture in ways that maximize their mobility and allow greater physical proximity to students. This proximity provides moment-by-moment access to each student. Teachers need to put the least distance and the fewest physical barriers between themselves and their students. Any arrangement that provides quick and easy access to all students is likely to be successful. The teacher's desk should not be in the front of the room. In this location it restricts the teacher's movement and reduces proximity to students. Students' desks should be located near the board. There should be just enough space to allow mobility for the teacher (Figure 10.1).

Some teachers believe that students should have the freedom to select their own seats in the classroom. Jones prefers to have assigned seats. Good students tend to locate themselves near the front, where they can participate more fully and thus get better grades. Chronic disrupters, on the other hand, are inclined to seat themselves near the back of the classroom as far away from the teacher's scrutiny as possible. This naturally occurring seating arrangement is a potential powder keg as far as discipline is

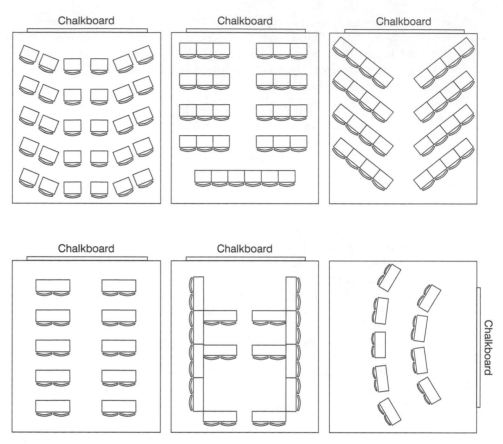

FIGURE 10.1
Accessible seating arrangements.

concerned. Wise teachers will seat potential disrupters close to them and place more conscientious students near the back of the room.

What kind of a seating arrangement can be made at the beginning of the year before you are sufficiently acquainted with students to know where to seat them? They should be seated either alphabetically or randomly and told that changes will be made in seating within a few weeks. If you forewarn students, you will encounter less resistance when actual changes are made. It is also wise to tell students that you intend to change seating periodically to help maintain a good learning environment.

STUDENT–TEACHER RELATIONSHIPS

Building positive relationships is a particularly critical task of teachers in their initial contact with students. Students are more susceptible to the influence of teachers they like and respect. If students respect the teacher, they are also more likely to enjoy the subject being taught and be more successful learning it. Positive student–teacher relationships are built on trust. Trust is promoted in an atmosphere of freedom. Children need to gradually receive more responsibility for making their own decisions in school. As they mature in an atmosphere of freedom, they will learn to make appropriate choices without coercion. Many teachers ordinarily perceive children as lazy—requiring force to get them involved in worthwhile activities—and naturally prone to misbehavior. Thus, many teachers feel that students need to be threatened and punished before they will behave well. However, with proper training most students can learn to be more self-governing and responsible.

To build proper relationships with students, teachers need to get as much information about their students as possible. On the first day of class, it is wise to have students provide basic information such as their name, address, home phone number, hobbies, and interests. This information can be recorded on an index card. Ice-breaking activities can be used to help teachers become better acquainted with their students. Students can be assigned to interview one another and then report on what they find. Teachers can help structure these interviews by giving students a list of topics to be covered. Teachers also can interview their students. Even in secondary schools, interviews could be completed in 2 or 3 weeks if teachers interviewed three students each day. Another excellent way for teachers to become acquainted with students is to take their photographs and post them on the bulletin board.

To develop relationships, teachers not only must learn about students but also must allow students to become better acquainted with them. Teachers need to talk about themselves. Opening up to students helps them see their teachers as human beings with desires and goals similar to their own. Teachers can tell students about their interests and hobbies; some students may have similar hobbies and thus share a common bond. Teachers can share their teaching aspirations with their students, explaining why they chose the teaching profession and what gratifications they find in teaching. Teachers may discuss attitudes, feelings, and such matters of mutual concern as respecting others and taking personal responsibility for learning. Teachers also need to show their students that they are active, interested learners, not merely dispensers of information; students can easily detect the hypocrisy of teachers who do not enjoy learning.

Classroom Control

Rules define what the limits are, but they do not establish them. Establishing limits can be done only in the give-and-take of the classroom. Students by nature will test the limits. They need to find out how the rules will actually be applied. They know what the teacher said about the rules, but they need to see whether what was said was truly meant. For example, the teacher may say that whispered talking is allowed during quiet study time, but what level of noise will actually be permitted? Students have learned that different teachers have different levels of tolerance for noise. They want to know how far they can go. Teachers who "mean business" can give students the clearest picture of what they can and cannot do in the classroom. These teachers are more successful than their less direct counterparts.

Jones's initial attempts to define how teachers show that they mean business were not successful, mostly because he concentrated exclusively on verbal cues. Body language is also a subtle yet powerful way for teachers to communicate their intentions. When appropriate body language is integrated with spoken messages, a teacher's resolve is adequately conveyed.

Power, or control, is almost always an issue in the classroom. Students will assume all the power they can. It is very desirable to control one's own life in school to make it as pleasant as possible and to avoid difficult learning situations. The question is, who is going to control whom? Jones, of course, believes that teachers must maintain control. Successful teachers know how to exercise interpersonal power in a way that is typically described as diplomatic, confident, and self-assured. In other words, they mean business. Interpersonal power is best exercised calmly. Conveying calmness establishes the ability of teachers to exercise control over themselves. Children commonly attempt to gain control of their teachers by getting them upset. Children almost always acquire control when teachers lose their tempers.

Jones believes that maintaining control in the classroom depends on two interrelated components: the teacher's instructional strategies and limit setting.

INSTRUCTIONAL STRATEGIES

Teachers often lose control of their classes when they spend too much time with each student. While they are working with one student, others goof off. Teachers can escape this predicament by avoiding universal helping interactions and instead using the praise–prompt–leave sequence of instruction.

Avoiding Universal Helping Interactions.   In his research, Jones found that teachers commonly experienced discipline problems when they finished a lecture or discussion and began helping students individually at their seats. Students usually began immediately to ask their teachers for help. Teachers usually responded with a "universal helping interaction." They tried to

1. Find out where a student was having difficulty.
2. Re-explain the portion of the lesson the student did not understand.
3. Supply the student with additional explanations and examples.

Jones contends that this process ordinarily takes at least 5 minutes for each student. If the practice period lasts 30 minutes, no more than six students can receive help. While the teacher is helping these students, the rest of the class, particularly those who are unsuccessfully seeking help from the teacher, will talk and goof around. This result, according to Jones, helps explain why talking to neighbors in ways that are disruptive constitutes 80% of the discipline problems in a typical classroom. Not only does discipline break down, but the students who do receive help are unable to use the teacher's long, drawn-out explanations to successfully complete their work. The universal helping interaction is too slow and inefficient. Teachers tie themselves up for too long a period with too few students and leave too many students unattended and unrewarded for too much of the work period (Jones, 1987a).

Teachers should be aware of how most universal helping interactions between students and teachers are initiated and avoid getting caught up in them. The following are actions that might be avoided:

1. Asking students where they are having difficulty is the most common and straightforward means of initiating a helping interaction. Teachers often ask, "Where are you having difficulty?" or "What is it you don't understand?"

2. Teachers are often aware of the difficulties students experience and identify these difficulties as they offer to help. For example, they may say, "I see you are having trouble carrying the correct digit. Let me show you how it is done."

3. Focusing on the students' strengths before calling attention to the problems is a common tactic among teachers who are aware of the necessity of giving students support during feedback. They believe that giving good news first will diminish the negative effects of the bad news that follows. A teacher might say, "You did the first few problems correctly, but when you got to the ones requiring long division, you did them all wrong."

4. Some teachers express their exasperation with students in the way they use body language, such as shaking the head from side to side, as if to say, "I have never seen anything like this. How could you have worked these problems this way?"

5. Sometimes, before they help students, teachers give voice to comments that are simply derogatory (for example, "How can you be so stupid?"). Jones calls these comments "zaps and zingers." Considerable harm can be done to students to whom these comments are directed.

Using the Praise–Prompt–Leave Sequence.   In place of universal helping interactions, Jones recommends the three-step sequence of praise, prompt, and leave (Jones, 1987b).

The first step is to praise.   In giving praise, the teacher reviews what the student has done right, which not only provides a positive experience for the student but also defines the starting point for new instruction. For teachers to become good at giving praise, they need to avoid the common habit of looking for errors in students' work. This tendency causes teachers to communicate dissatisfaction as well as frustration and exasperation. Teachers should build on adequately completed work, not defects. They need to develop an aptitude for seeing the positive and make it a reflex action. Once the strength of a student's work is identified, appropriate words can be used to describe it. This language must be a specific description of exactly what is well done. Avoid statements such as "Nice job" and "You're off to a good start." Instead, say "You have organized this paragraph well. There are transitions between all the sentences."

The second step is to prompt.   To prompt is to tell students exactly what to do next. Prompting should be clear and simple. Ordinarily, mastery of concepts involves many steps. Students, however, can perform these steps only one at a time. Teachers therefore should provide a prompt that requires a one-step performance. Asking students to perform many steps tends to produce cognitive overload. Teachers tend to bog students down with excessive, complex verbiage. They talk too much and explain more than students can keep straight at one time. Instead, teachers should prompt students about the next action to take and then encourage them to act on the prompt. Prompts can either direct a student to do something or not to do something. An initiating request asks a student either to begin something or to do it more. A terminating request asks a student to stop something or to do it less. The following are examples of terminating (T) and initiating (I) requests:

T: You will be unable to subtract fractions until you have first found a common denominator.
I: First you need to find the common denominator and then subtract.
T: You shouldn't hand your math test in without showing all the calculations.
I: Recopy all these equations showing all your calculations, and then turn them in.
T: You need to avoid using darker colors for highlighting.
I: If you want to highlight an object, use light colors on the side of the object that shows the source of light.

The third and final step is to leave.   Once a clear and simple prompt is given, teachers should leave and turn their attention immediately to other students. They must not take time to observe how students act on prompts. Leaving will cause many teachers discomfort, given their inclination to stay at students' desks long enough to see how they respond to instructions. Even so, teachers must avoid the temptation to stay longer. Not only does leaving convey confidence in students' ability to act on the instruction given, but it also gives teachers more time to circulate in the class. With this system, teachers can see more students and see the same student more than once in one class period. At the same time, the teacher gains greater control by being able to move around the entire classroom more quickly.

LIMIT SETTING

Along with particular instructional strategies, Jones believes that teachers must employ very specific, limit-setting discipline techniques (Jones, 1987a). These techniques primarily involve the use of body language designed to convince students that their teachers are in control even when provoked. Body language communicates a teacher's interpersonal power to students. The teacher's objective in using limit-setting techniques is to resolve the power issue and have students return to their work. Limit setting always entails the same series of steps. How many steps are taken depends on how quickly disruptive students return to work.

Step 1: Having Eyes in the Back of Your Head.   The first step in limit setting is to be aware of and simultaneously monitor the behavior of all students in the classroom. Sometimes this skill is called "withitness" or "having eyes in the back of your head." Teachers who have withitness have an uncanny ability to track even those activities students try to hide, thus increasing their effectiveness in stopping students' misbehavior. Students need to be convinced that their teachers know what is really going on (Kounin, 1970). Otherwise, disruptive behavior persists. Some students apparently are drawn to see how far they can go in creating problems for the teacher. If the teacher knows what is going on (is "withit"), there is no need to continually test the limits.

Withitness is also demonstrated when teachers show proper targeting and timing. Mistakes in targeting are of two types:

1. The teacher corrects (desists) the wrong child or an onlooker for misbehavior.
2. The teacher desists a less serious display of misbehavior while overlooking a more serious one occurring at the same time.

Sometimes teachers fail to track an entire sequence of their students' behavior and thus fail to properly identify the student who initiates a problem. Instead, they catch a student who is reacting to another's provocation. When teachers confront students who are just reacting to classmates, they encourage more such provocations. When real perpetrators can consistently avoid detection, other class members are less fearful that they may be observed if they too step out of line. In addition, the class is likely to make a joke of the teacher's ineptness at catching on to what is happening.

Ignoring a more serious classroom infraction and attending to a less serious one also limits the effectiveness of a desist. For example, a teacher may order a student to put a library book away and go to work on the genetics exercise while failing to deal with two students in the back of the room who are trying to catch goldfish from the aquarium. Likewise, if a teacher desists a child who is observed whispering to a neighbor while two other children fight in the back of the room, the teacher obviously is attending to the wrong target. Students react to mistargeting with increased misbehavior. They sense that their teacher is not really aware and are more willing to misbehave without fear of being caught. Teachers' credibility depends on selecting the most serious discipline problem on which to focus attention.

Timing is a critical aspect of withitness. Correct timing is determined by whether or not misbehavior is allowed to become more serious before the teacher takes action. The timing for a desist is correct if the misbehavior is not more serious at the time of the desist than at the time it started. The interval between the onset of the misbehavior and the desist is not the critical element in determining whether timing is correct or not; rather, it is seriousness of the misbehavior.

It is a timing mistake to wait until misbehavior spreads before doing anything about it. For example, if a couple of students left their seats and went to the back of the room and were then joined by three or four others before the teacher intervened, the desist may be too late. Once the misbehavior spreads, it is much more difficult to deal with. When the two students started toward the back of the room, the teacher should have immediately requested that they take their seats.

Successful desists also depend on overlapping. Overlapping is the management of more than one activity simultaneously. When teachers fail to attend to one discipline situation in order to deal with another, the one not receiving attention may become more difficult to defuse subsequently. Class members being temporarily ignored usually become distracted and have difficulty refocusing themselves once the teacher returns to deal with them.

Overlapping does not consist exclusively of verbal directions. A short remark or a simple look can convincingly communicate to students that the teacher is aware of what is happening. For example a teacher while helping one student at his or her desk may observe another student about to throw a classmate's shoe out the window. This is happening at the same time a third student is about to throw his pencil across the room. The teacher could motion to the student at his desk with one hand to wait. At the same time he could point at the student who was about to throw the pencil and verbally stop the third student from throwing the shoe out the window while at the same time walking toward him or her. The ability to handle all three situations simultaneously strengthens the perception of the class that the teacher can deal with any and all problems and that students can not "get away with anything" in the class.

Remarks and looks are more effective when they are given with clarity and firmness (Kounin & Gump, 1974). Clarity refers to the amount of information the teacher gives to the misbehaving student. Rather than saying to the student who is about to throw the shoe out the window, "you need to take your seat," the teacher should say, "Carlos, please give Jake his shoe now and take your seat." The attribute of firmness has to do with the tone of voice and/or facial expression. Firmness can be increased by (1) making the desist more emphatically, (2) looking directly at the student being desisted, (3) walking toward the student, and (4) touching or otherwise guiding the student toward the proper behavior (Kounin, 1970).

Withitness and overlapping have been studied to determine both their individual and their combined effectiveness. These studies indicate that although withitness plays a somewhat more important role in classroom management, withitness and overlapping are significantly related. The most effective desist will show that the teacher knows what is going on in the classroom; it will be properly timed and targeted and have firmness and clarity. It also will not interfere with the other tasks the teacher is performing.

Obviously, the seating arrangement in the room helps teachers exhibit withitness. They can also increase their effectiveness by placing themselves where they are able to see the entire class. When teachers cannot see the class, they must monitor it by listening. Most of us have learned to focus our attention on one thing at a time and block out other sensory information. As a teacher, however, you have to make a conscious effort not to filter out extraneous noises. Teachers must learn to attend to everything that occurs in the classroom.

Step 2: Terminating Instruction. Suppose that while you are helping one student you glance across the room and notice two other students talking to one another; you catch one of them looking at you. Some teachers believe that disruptions should not be attended to during instruction, because this attention only reinforces bad behavior. Jones argues that discipline should always take precedence over other class activities and must be dealt with immediately. He believes that if you ignore the discipline problem, even temporarily, and return to giving instruction, you reinforce the discipline problem. He recommends that when you encounter a discipline problem while you are giving instruction, you should stop in mid-sentence, make a hand gesture to the student being helped to indicate that you are temporarily stopping instruction, and then proceed to deal with the problem. In addition to making a hand gesture, you may quickly ask to be excused: "Excuse me for a moment. I'll be right back."

Step 3: Turning, Looking, and Saying the Student's Name. As soon as instruction has been terminated, you should turn from the student being helped and focus attention on disruptive students. Turn around completely, and face the misbehaving students squarely. Turning to face students conveys the message that you are dealing with them exclusively. They have your full attention. Failure to face students squarely signals them that you are less than 100% committed to disciplining them.

Next, look them in the eye. Your gaze must be unwavering. Do not allow your eyes to dart around or otherwise break contact. Darting eyes tell students that you are uncomfortable and anxious. It is also important not to show disgust or irritation. You do not want to convey anger. Instead, you want students to see you in complete control of yourself. A steady look that is free of emotion will communicate the desired message. Along with eye contact, you should maintain an appropriate facial expression. Facial expressions can send either the intended message or one that is contradictory and confusing. For example, if teachers smile in a particularly stressful discipline situation, they may communicate submission rather than limit setting. A fiery look accompanied by a slight smile may be interpreted by students as "I don't want you to talk. I'd like you to go back to work, but I'm not going to insist on it." It is better to remain expressionless as you continue to maintain perfect eye contact with the student causing the most trouble. Even if students smile at you, be sure to sustain your expressionless look. You want to convey the message that you find nothing amusing about bad behavior and that you are simply waiting while the student decides what to do next. There are other cues you can give with your body. Some of these cues should be avoided. For example, hands on hips or folded arms usually indicate impatience or upset. Instead, let your arms hang comfortably at your side or, if your prefer, place your hands in your pockets.

Then say the names of disruptive students—only once and in a flat, matter-of-fact fashion. If your voice is bland, it will convey your calm and self-control. Learning how to remain calm and relaxed in response to provocations is the most crucial aspect of limit setting, and yet it is the most difficult to master. Commonly, it is forgotten when students do irritating things.

The limit-setting process explained so far may be all you need in many instances. After having said the students' names, you should wait while you take two relaxing breaths. Continue to stand directly facing the offending students and maintain your gaze. Sometimes students will try to deceive you. They may give you a smile to acknowledge that they are being observed and yet have no intention of going back to work. Without diverting your eyes directly, you should check under the offending students' desks to determine whether their knees and feet are back in the correct position for working. Unless they are, you have not accomplished the necessary task. It is wise to remember that students often play games with you. Jones likens limit setting to playing poker: Teachers increase the bet until students "fold." Teachers need to continually raise the stakes until students decline to go further. In other words, proceed through the steps of limit setting until disruptive students give in and go back to work. A rule of thumb in limit setting is to go no further than is necessary.

Step 4: Moving to the Edge of the Student's Desk.   If after hearing their names, students simply look at you and make no attempt to turn around and go to work, you should move in a relaxed fashion to the edge of the most disruptive student's desk (Figure 10.2). Move at the same pace at which you would take a stroll through your garden. Do not hurry. Keep yourself relaxed. Under no circumstances should you stop moving until you reach the student's desk. Position yourself with your legs touching the front

FIGURE 10.2
Moving to the edge of the student's desk. The teacher, at the edge of the student's desk, looks the student directly in the eye.

edge of the student's desk. While taking two relaxing breaths, look the student straight in the eye. Do not repeat the student's name, and do not repeat the class rules. Waiting at the student's desk will help you maintain your calm as well as give the student time to decide what to do. You should wait until the student goes back to work and remains working for a while.

Step 5: Moving Out.   The "moving out" phase of limit setting is just as important as the "moving in" phase. When the disruptive student has returned to work, lean over and thank the student by name. Then continue to wait in front of the desk, watching the student work a little while longer. If another student was involved, go to that student's desk and wait there. Give this second student equal time to go to work. Take two relaxing breaths and thank this student. Watch the student work for a while. Take two more relaxing breaths. At this point, you should move away slowly. Go to the student you were helping at the time of the disruption, turn and look at the students who caused the disruption, and take two more relaxing breaths. The offending students will probably look up at you and correctly ascertain that you are still monitoring their behavior. This entire procedure conveys the fact that you mean business.

Step 6: Using Palms.   Sometimes students do not respond when you stand in front of their desks. If so, Jones recommends that you lean over at the waist and, while resting your weight on one palm, give the reluctant students a prompt—either verbally (telling them exactly what you want them to do) or nonverbally (motioning with the arm and hand for them to turn around) or both. A verbal prompt should be short and direct. For example, you may say, "Turn around in your seat, and finish doing the rest of your math problems." After giving these prompts, maintain your position, leaning on your palm. Take two relaxing breaths. If the student goes back to work, watch the student for a while, still keeping your position. Take two relaxing breaths before moving to the second student's desk to repeat the process.

If the prompt does not produce the desired result, lean slowly across the student's desk and put both palms flat on the desk in such a way that you straddle the student's books and papers. Rest your weight on your palms with your elbows locked, and take two or more relaxing breaths while maintaining continuous eye contact (Figure 10.3). This position will bring you eyeball to eyeball with the student. Do not say anything. Wait for a positive work response. If the student goes back to work, watch for two more relaxing breaths, thank the student, watch for two more relaxing breaths, and then move to the next student and repeat the process. When all students are working, move out as previously described.

Sometimes during the limit-setting sequence, students will engage in various types of back talk, the purpose of which is to get control and to trap the teacher into exploring some side issue. There are several types of back talk, each of which can tempt teachers to react. Any reaction, however, just aids students in their quest for control. Jones identifies seven major types of back talk prevalent in the classroom:

1. *Feigning helplessness.* Students attempt to change the issue from discipline to instruction. Usually, they offer a pained request for help, hoping that the teacher will bite. They may say, "I don't understand this. Will you show me how to do it?" Teachers easily get sidetracked because of their commitment to help students learn. When a student professes helplessness to sidetrack you, Jones recommends that you not provide help at that time. It is better to just look at the student and wait, saying nothing. You may eventually say something like "Keep working. I'll be back in a few minutes to help you." At this point, the less you say, the better.

2. *Denying responsibility.* Students commonly profess innocence when they are caught misbehaving. They may say, "I didn't do it" or "Why are you picking on me?

FIGURE 10.3
Using palms. The teacher continues direct eye contact.

I was just sitting here." Responding to these comments only promotes conflict and further self-justification by students. Therefore, do not debate with them. Just relax, be quiet, and wait.

3. *Blaming others.* "She started it!" or "He started it!" is the usual way children blame one another. Children know that blaming one another is an effective way to get their teachers sidetracked. Teachers seem compelled to find out who started a problem so that they can punish the offender. Just remember, it does not matter who started the altercation. Knowing who initiated the disruption will not change anything. Remember, too, that students use this ploy to avoid doing their work.

4. *Accusing the teacher of professional incompetence.* Teachers have a tendency to take students' negative comments about their competency seriously. Students may say, "How am I supposed to understand? You didn't explain well enough." They may also accuse you of never making anything clear. Here again, the motive is to get you sidetracked. Students know that their teachers take these attacks seriously. It may be true that some explanation was not clear. The quality of instruction is not the issue, however. Gabbing with neighbors is not the solution to misunderstanding what is taught. Keep in mind that students will claim not to understand as an excuse to avoid responsibility.

5. *Urging the teacher to leave.* Sometimes students tell their teachers to go away:
   "OK, just leave me alone. I'll get back to work."
   "Hey, just back away from here and get out of my face. I'm going to do this."
   "I'll start doing this just as soon as you back away from here."
   "Holy cow! Get off it, would you? Back your face out of here."
   Students think that they can control a situation if they are the ones who tell others what to do. They depend on the shock value of such statements to get teachers to react to them. Obviously, teachers must avoid the temptation to react to such directions.

6. *Hurling insults.* Students are gambling for high stakes when they use insults to throw their teachers off balance. Students may insult their teachers when they feel that they have very little to lose. When they insult teachers, students may act cocky or pretend to be offended or upset:
   "Hey, who buys your clothes? I've never seen anything clash so bad."
   "Did you know hair styles like yours went out during the Civil War?"
   "Where'd you get that big wide tie? The last one of those I saw was on Nutsy Squirrel."
   "Hey, move back a little. You've got bad breath!"
   Even if you do have bad breath, you should stand your ground. Just relax and hold your position, leaning on the student's desk and looking the student straight in the eye. The issue is not whether or not you have bad breath. If you can avoid reacting, you will ultimately control the situation.

7. *Using profanity.* As a last-ditch effort to upset you, students may swear at you. Some profanity is considered mild and evokes a negligible response in most people. Some words, however, may have a tendency to provoke a reaction. If students call you names, you may feel it necessary to put them in their place. Most adults feel that young people should not be allowed to get away with name-calling. However, the purpose of profanity is to get you to react. It is better to relax, keep quiet, and wait. If you remain calm, you can control the situation and get the student

FIGURE 10.4
Camping out in front.

back on-task. You can impose an additional sanction later if you deem it necessary. As the students file out of the classroom at the end of the period, call the student by name and say that you want to speak with him or her. This action will make other students realize that they cannot get away with profanity in the classroom. Calling the student aside after class will also allow you to confront the student in private without an audience of peers. However, if the student "folds" in the face of your silence, self-control, and proximity, then detaining the student after class will probably be unnecessary.

Step 7: Camping Out in Front.   Suppose that you have completed Step 6 in the limit-setting process, using the palms, but the disruptive students continue to make excuses and blame others. Camping out in front may now be appropriate. Start from the palms position, then bend your arm until your weight is resting on your elbow. Take two relaxing breaths, look at the student with indifference, and wait (Figure 10.4). This position puts you closer to the student and improves eye contact. If the student then stops fooling around and looks at you, take two more relaxing breaths and repeat the verbal prompt to turn around and get back to work. Repeating the prompt lets the student know that you are not accepting excuses. If work is resumed, thank the student, take two more relaxing breaths, and move slowly over to the next student and repeat the same procedure.

Step 8: Camping Out From Behind.   If, while you are camping out in front of one student, another comes to the rescue by making some comment, you may need to camp out from behind. This step may be necessary if students gang up on you and need to be separated. Move between the students, turn sideways next to one student, and lean on your elbow as you did camping out in front (Figure 10.5). If the student is on your left, lean on your right elbow and look straight into the student's eyes, take two relaxing breaths, and wait. If the student talks back, wait until the student is finished and then

FIGURE 10.5
Camping out from behind.

give a prompt to return to work. Thank the student, and then move out in the prescribed way.

One of the problems often experienced by teachers in limit setting is the level of intimidation in some situations. The purpose of limit setting is for teachers to force student compliance by placing themselves increasingly closer to misbehaving students. The closer the teacher gets, the more intimidating and uncomfortable students should feel, and the more willing they should be to stop misbehaving. Unfortunately, many teachers are also intimidated by close proximity to students, particularly when their faces are close together. In addition, it is possible that a student so challenged may react violently. Teachers using this model should be prepared for this possibility. Basic procedures for dealing with violent student behaviors are discussed in Chapter 14.

Promoting Cooperation

What if limit setting doesn't work? Many teachers may be tempted to nag, threaten, or punish. These temptations should be resisted. Punishment promotes alienation. It will not solve discipline problems.

RESPONSIBILITY TRAINING

Instead of punishing, teachers can promote cooperation through responsibility training (Jones, 1987a), which induces students to demonstrate good behavior voluntarily. Students do not cooperate without a reason. They will cooperate, however, if good relationships are established and incentives provided. Jones explains that establishing good relationships with students by itself is insufficient. It is, however, necessary. An incentive system must be devised to go with it.

Technically, Jones's incentive system is based on the concept of negative reinforcement. Incentive systems usually provide positive reinforcement as a consequence of appropriate behavior; the reward follows good behavior. In a system of negative reinforcement, however, students are given their potential reward in advance. Jones calls his reward system preferred activity time (PAT). This PAT is given to the class as a whole in predetermined units (a week's worth, for example), which the students can retain by responsible learning behavior or can squander through misbehavior. When a student misbehaves, the teacher starts a timer or stopwatch. The length of time the misbehavior lasts is then subtracted from the class PAT. The stopwatch provides an exact accounting and eliminates possible controversy over how much PAT remains.

Jones also advocates that positive reinforcement in the form of bonuses be given when students conserve time. If students hurry to clean up the classroom or finish an assignment early, the teacher can reward them with additional PAT. It is wise to give students plenty of time to do their assignments so that there is ample opportunity to earn bonuses. Bonuses can also be earned, for example, if all students are in their seats when the bell rings.

To summarize, students are given PAT in advance, which they can either retain or squander. In addition, they can earn bonuses for completing tasks in less than the time allotted. A record of penalties and bonuses is kept at the teacher's desk or on the chalkboard. In operating this system, teachers should ensure that bonus opportunities more than offset opportunities for penalty. Otherwise, the system will fail.

Preferred activity time can consist of fun and games, either for educational purposes or purely for diversion. There should probably be a mix of various options. Time should be allotted for both individual and group activities. For individual activities, you might suggest that students bring games from home to play during PAT. Group activities may include team competition in any one of a number of formats. Games based on baseball, football, or basketball are very popular. In a foreign language class, for example, students on one team can reach "bases" by translating, spelling, conjugating, and using a given verb; if a mistake is made, a student on the other team can "catch" it for an "out."

Certain problems in the class can be overcome by assessing a penalty without allowing for a corresponding reward. Jones provides specific instructions on how to provide a penalty without a reward in the case of two common classroom disruptions: students asking for the hall pass to go to the restroom and students coming to class without a pencil. When a student routinely and unnecessarily interrupts instruction and asks for the hall pass to use the rest room, the teacher should readily comply with the request and then start the stopwatch. The amount of time it takes the student to go to the rest room is subtracted from the class PAT. When their PAT is thus reduced, students will begin using breaks between class periods to go to the rest room instead of asking for the hall pass during class. The age-old problem of not having a pencil can be similarly terminated. When students inform you that they have no pencil, ask whether someone has a pencil to loan and start your stopwatch. The number of pointless trips to the pencil sharpener can also be reduced. Place a can of sharpened, but short and grungy, pencils on your desk. If students need a sharpened pencil, have them retrieve one from the desk. Meanwhile, the stopwatch will run.

Other problems can also be handled with responsibility training. The technique has been successfully used with tantrum behavior, group divisiveness, short attention span, and other problems. It has also been used in a variety of school settings outside the standard classroom, such as passing in the halls, assemblies, chemistry labs, and specialized classes (gym, shop, typing, home economics). As long as the rules are known and the teacher takes away time using a stopwatch, students behave better.

OMISSION TRAINING

Occasionally, PAT is ineffective with a few students who have special problems. For example, students with emotional disabilities may be angry or hostile and continually provoke teachers and other students. Omission training may be helpful for such students. In omission training, positive reinforcement is used instead of negative reinforcement; good behavior, not bad, is timed and rewarded. The unruly student is excluded from PAT. If the student behaves well for a predetermined period of time, a bonus is received that can be shared with the whole class. Bonuses can be earned with each subsequent interval during which the student behaves properly. Four steps are followed in omission training:

1. Prevent any further confrontation by moving the student away from the rest of the class.
2. Determine a period of time—from 15 minutes to an entire day—that you believe is reasonable and appropriate for the student to behave.
3. Identify and communicate to the student the particular behavior you expect.
4. Explain the bonuses that can be earned.

Backup Systems

In rare instances, neither responsibility training nor omission training is successful. A backup system may be necessary (Jones, 1987a). Jones advocates the systematic application of negative sanctions. They are arranged hierarchically from lesser sanctions to more serious ones. Not only teachers but also administrators and parents are involved in imposing sanctions. Jones recommends that teachers manage their own backup systems as much as possible, pointing out that the participation of school administrators and parents is often unreliable. Involving parents takes time, and parents are frequently less than fully cooperative. The greatest drawback to sending students to the office is that the sheer number of students there prevents them from being effectively helped. After a trip to the office, students may return to your class more inclined to misbehave.

Several low-level sanctions can be imposed for misbehavior. They should be applied, in order, as the need arises:

1. *Warning.*   Go to the student's desk, and quietly say that you are sorry that the student has decided to continue behaving badly. Warn the student that if you return

again, the result will be serious. Maintain eye contact and a relaxed manner. If the problem persists, go to step 2.

2. *Pulling the card.*   Pull the index card with the student's name and address from the card file while the student is watching. This should be done in a relaxed manner while maintaining eye contact with the student. It will be obvious that you intend to call the student's parents or guardian if the behavior does not stop. If this measure does not take care of the problem, go to step 3.

3. *Letter home on the desk.*   Go to the student's desk, and use your palms as described in the limit-setting procedure. Breathe in a relaxed manner, and say that you are sorry that the student has continued being disruptive. Then return to your desk very slowly. When you get there, take out a pen and paper and begin to write a brief letter home. It should explicitly detail the student's inappropriate behavior. When the letter has been completed, put it in an envelope and walk back to the student's desk. Go to your palms and calmly say that the letter is to the student's parents or guardian. Inform the student that you will send it immediately unless a week passes without any repetition of the unacceptable behavior. Explain that at the end of a week, if there is no further misbehavior, the student may tear up the letter and put it in the wastebasket. The letter should be left taped to the student's desk in self contained classrooms or to the teacher's desk if students move from class to class.

If students create more trouble, the teacher may have to impose mid-level sanctions:

1. *Time-out.*   The student is removed from the activity in the classroom. Time-out usually takes place in an out-of-the-way area in the classroom, but there may also be a special room designated for time-out elsewhere in the school. Sometimes time-out can take place in another teacher's classroom.

2. *Detention after school.*   Students have to make up the time lost by goofing off.

3. *Loss of privileges.*   Students are prevented from participating in activities such as sports, plays, and contests.

4. *Parent conference.*   Disruptive students and their parents meet with you after school.

There is also a list of high-level backup sanctions. These sanctions are the school's final effort to get disruptive students to change their behavior:

1. *In-school suspension.*   Students are placed in a designated room in the school outside the regular classroom. The room is monitored, and the students' regular teachers give them regular assignments, which must be completed there.

2. *Saturday school.*   Students attend school on Saturday to make up for time lost to unexcused absences and late arrivals ("tardies").

3. *Delivering the student to a parent at work.*   The child is delivered to the parent along with a message specifying the inappropriate behavior and the conditions for readmission to school.

4. *Asking a parent to accompany the student in school.*   The parent sits with and supervises the student all during the school day.

5. *Suspension.*   Suspended students are not permitted in school for a specified period of time.

6. *Police intervention.*   Law enforcement officers can be summoned when students are involved in criminal activity such as assault, theft, or drug dealing.

7. *Expulsion.*   As a last resort, students may be expelled. Readmission after expulsion usually involves a series of meetings and approval by the board of education.

If limit setting and responsibility training are effectively implemented, it should be unnecessary to impose negative sanctions from the backup system. These sanctions should be used only as a last resort. They are generally employed by school administrators, not classroom teachers.

Preventing Discipline Problems

In the Jones model, misbehavior is prevented primarily through responsibility training. Responsibility training, which involves the use of PAT, encourages students to focus on learning, leaving less time and inclination to be disruptive. PAT, the promised reward of participating in preferred activities, provides an inducement for students to work productively. PAT is a particularly powerful means of preventing misbehavior because it capitalizes on peer pressure. Thus, the class can lose PAT when any of its members misbehave. PAT provides a strong preventive component for this model.

Problems are also prevented by arranging seating so teachers can have access to any place in the classroom quickly. The seating arrangements provide a way to more effectively implement the praise–prompt–leave technique. This technique is a prominent preventive discipline feature in the Jones model. When teachers apply it effectively, they can more readily promote continued learning by students and prevent disruptions. With the teacher making several trips to each student in the learning period, students are more able to continue to work productively.

Schoolwide Discipline

Jones considers discipline to be almost exclusively the responsibility of the classroom teacher. He recommends that students with behavior problems not be sent to the office to be dealt with by school administrators. Instead, he encourages teachers to apply the steps in his discipline approach. It is only when teachers have exhausted what they can do in the classroom that they should refer students to the office for administrative action.

Strengths and Weaknesses of the Jones Model

STRENGTHS

1. It specifies a set of steps to follow in dealing with discipline problems.
2. It tells exactly how far to go in applying discipline techniques.
3. It defines the role of the teacher as well as the role of administrators in discipline.

WEAKNESSES

1. It does not promote autonomy in students.
2. It is difficult for some teachers to apply the techniques as specified.
3. Some teachers are uncomfortable getting as physically close to students as the procedures dictate. Close physical proximity may also produce violent reactions in students, causing some parents to intervene on behalf of their children.
4. Preferred activity time may be less educational than Jones supposes.
5. Jones's insistence that instruction should be stopped when discipline problems arise is contrary to what many educators would recommend. Many classroom disruptions are encouraged when teachers terminate instruction to focus on discipline problems.
6. Allowing the misbehavior of individual students to penalize the entire class may cause some students to be overly submissive and others to rebel.
7. Jones's approach, through some of its backup systems, promotes a "tattling" relationship between teachers and parents and can stimulate hostility between parents and teachers or the school.
8. It encourages teachers to be aggressive and controlling instead of helpful and supportive.

▼ SUMMARY

Central to Jones's discipline system is the necessity of creating and teaching classroom rules to students. Students who have a role in creating classroom rules will have a greater inclination to follow them.

Control in the classroom is enhanced by proper seating arrangements. Students should be seated so that the teacher always has immediate access to the entire classroom.

Teachers ordinarily spend too much time helping just a few students, leaving the rest of the class time to invent mischief. This problem can be avoided if teachers apply the praise–prompt–leave sequence of instruction: praising students for what they have done right, prompting them on the next single step they must take to perform a task, and immediately leaving. Teachers can thereby more effectively control the entire classroom.

When discipline problems do occur, teachers must be skillful in limit setting and responsibility training. Limit setting involves a sequence of movements made by the teacher to limit disruptions by students. With this approach, teachers use their eyes as well as their physical proximity to students to deter bad behavior. The successive steps of limit setting are applied only as students fail to respond appropriately to earlier movements made by the teacher. In responsibility training, students as a group are given a quantity of PAT, which they can either keep by behaving appropriately or squander through improper behavior. Preferred activity time gives individual students and groups of students the opportunity to participate in enjoyable educational activities such as games and contests.

If these approaches to discipline fail, backup sanctions may have to be employed, the most serious of which are suspensions and expulsions.

CENTRAL IDEAS

1. Seating arrangements that allow teachers open and quick access to all their students will help them maintain control in the classroom.

2. Limit setting involves the use of nonverbal language and movements that put the teacher's eyes increasingly closer to those of the misbehaving student. Teachers should proceed through the series of limit-setting steps no further than is necessary to cause the student to behave properly.

3. Students use helplessness, denial, blame, accusations, insults, and profanity in an effort to thwart the loss of control they sense as the teacher sets limits.

4. Preferred activity time (PAT) is given to students as a negative reinforcer. They retain as much PAT as their behavior warrants, or they squander their PAT by behaving inappropriately.

5. When neither limit setting nor responsibility training is successful in curbing students' bad behavior, omission training may be initiated. In omission training, students are rewarded for exhibiting desired behavior during predetermined intervals of time.

6. If students' behavior is still unacceptable after repeated efforts to help them change, parental as well as administrative assistance may be sought in the form of parent conferences, suspension, or, as a last resort, expulsion.

▼ QUESTIONS AND ACTIVITIES

QUESTIONS TO CONSIDER

1. How is Jones's discipline approach similar to and different from behavior modification (Chapter 3)?

2. Are there inconsistencies between the procedures of limit setting and of responsibility training and the backup sanctions of Jones's model?

3. How is Jones's model different from the traditional way in which teachers apply discipline in the classroom?

4. What kind of problems might be promoted by teachers' achieving too close a physical proximity to students?

5. To what extent will the praise–prompt–leave sequence reduce student dependency?

6. How does Jones's rule-making format compare with that of Glasser (Chapter 8)? What are the likely outcomes of these two rule-making procedures in terms of expected teacher and student behavior?

CLASSROOM ACTIVITIES

1. Present a video that depicts a teacher using Jones's limit-setting techniques. Stop the video, and analyze each step in the process.

2. Have selected students demonstrate Jones's techniques for limit setting. Have the class critique them.

STUDENT APPLICATIONS

1. Practice limit setting with classmates. Concentrate on eye contact, relaxed breathing, and movement to and from a student's desk.
2. Prepare descriptions of games and activities you could use during PAT.

EXPLORE YOUR PHILOSOPHY

1. Defend or refute the assumptions that children need to be controlled and that an appropriate way to do this is through nonverbal cues that bring the teacher into closer and closer proximity to students.
2. Defend or refute the practice of pressuring students to behave by reducing the time they are allowed to spend on preferred activities.
3. Compare the principles contained in your educational philosophy with those of the Jones model. Determine consistencies and inconsistencies. Make adjustments to your philosophy as you believe appropriate.

▼REFERENCES

Evertson, C. M., & Anderson, L. M. (1979). Beginning school. *Educational Horizons, 57*, 164–168.

Jones, F. H. (1987a). *Positive classroom discipline.* New York: McGraw-Hill.

Jones, F. H. (1987b). *Positive classroom instruction.* New York: McGraw-Hill.

Kounin, J. S. (1970). *Discipline and group management in classrooms.* New York: Holt, Rinehart & Winston.

Kounin, J. S., & Gump, P. V. (1974). Signal systems of lesson settings and the task related behavior of pre school children. *Journal of Educational Psychology, 66,* 554–562.

Creating a Comprehensive Discipline Program

To determine what discipline approach to use, you must first determine your personal philosophy and values. This determination will provide guidance as you decide which of the available discipline models is most attractive. An extensive analysis of existing theories is essential in this process. If you find that you consider the available models of discipline inadequate, you may decide to create one of your own. Then, armed with a discipline approach that has been carefully analyzed and mastered, you will be much better prepared to meet the challenges of the classroom.

A good discipline program should be comprehensive. Components designed to prevent as well as correct discipline problems are essential. In addition, a comprehensive discipline program should include schoolwide applications. This unit is designed to help you make these decisions.

11

Choosing a Discipline Approach

OBJECTIVES

This chapter is designed to help you

1. Decide on a discipline approach to use in your teaching by applying your personal philosophy and values, establishing criteria, validating assumptions, and assessing the strengths and weaknesses of various discipline models.
2. Decide whether a single existing theory of discipline meets your expectations, whether a synthesis of two or more theories is more appropriate, or whether you need to create your own personal approach to discipline.
3. Decide which discipline orientation to use (theory-based, eclectic, or shifting).
4. Select an approach to discipline that both corrects and prevents discipline problems and also has applications for schoolwide discipline.

Introduction

This chapter illustrates the process of selecting an approach to discipline using the steps outlined in Chapter 2 and the information about the various discipline models presented in Chapters 3 through 10. In this chapter, a single model of discipline will be selected, and the rationale behind the selection will be explained. Chapter 12 illustrates the creation of a personal discipline approach from elements of several of the models along with additional compatible components.

Applying a Personal Discipline Philosophy

A philosophy of discipline should be consistent with your philosophy of education as well as your philosophy of life. For the purposes of illustration, let's consider a hypothetical teacher who has a discipline philosophy with the following components. Keep in mind that this is just an illustrative list. Each individual teacher will no doubt have a personal philosophy that differs to some degree from other teachers':

1. Children are born with a will to master their environment and achieve satisfaction of their basic needs.
2. The basic needs of children include self-determination, avoidance of control by others, love and acceptance, variety, and enjoyment.
3. Because of children's needs for self-determination and avoidance of control by others, discipline should provide children with opportunities to become self-governing.
4. Children can learn to be responsibly self-governed if they are given opportunities to make free choices and taught about behavioral consequences.
5. When children are allowed to be self-governing, they are less inclined to rebel and create discipline problems in school.
6. Discipline problems can thus be prevented to a great degree if children are allowed to be self-governing.
7. Children's sense of acceptance is best achieved when teachers accept them for what they are and allow them a greater degree of autonomous self-expression.
8. Discipline problems can be prevented if teachers help children satisfy their needs through acceptable means rather than allow children's disruptive behaviors to evolve.
9. Children can become responsible more readily if they learn not to give excuses and shift blame.

Behavior modification, assertive discipline, and the Jones model are all based primarily on teachers' control and therefore are the models least consistent with the preceding philosophy statements. Before being discarded, however, these models need to be evaluated in terms of how well they satisfy our hypothetical teacher's criteria and how valid their assumptions are.

Establishing Criteria

The following set of criteria will be used to evaluate the different discipline models. Criteria are not intended to be free from individual bias. They are used to make decisions that do in fact reflect personal philosophy. They help the decision maker to think clearly and consistently about choices that are made. When criteria are listed, they can be prioritized and applied to decision making more carefully. Making them public by listing them allows others to understand the individual teacher's philosophy and to determine if the criteria are consistently applied to decisions the teacher makes. Then others can also compare the criteria to their own. The following list was devised to represent the preceding philosophical statements:

A. Is the discipline model likely to help children become more self-disciplined and responsible?
B. Is it consistent with the view that children's motives are based on a self-directed effort to achieve autonomy, gain control of themselves and their environment, and achieve a high level of acceptance by others?
C. Is it helpful in promoting good self-concept in students?
D. Is it effective in promoting good classroom behavior?
E. Is it likely to help prevent discipline problems?
F. Is it consistent with an instructional program involving self-determined learning projects?
G. Can it be easily implemented?
H. Can it be readily learned?
I. Can it be applied in a schoolwide discipline program?

It should be readily apparent that criteria A and B are outgrowths of the philosophy statements. The remaining criteria deal with more practical matters. It should also be pointed out that the list of criteria is arranged in order of importance. Whether decisions are made formally or informally, they are most often based on prioritized criteria. Otherwise, less important considerations may carry undue weight in the decision-making process. Deciding the order in which to arrange criteria is a matter of personal logic. For example, one might claim that criterion A is more important than criterion B because good classroom behavior is irrelevant if it is not voluntary; therefore, the more critical outcome of schooling is for students to become responsibly self-disciplined. The other criteria can be compared in a similar fashion and their relative importance determined.

Now let's apply the criteria to the different discipline models, assigning a rating to each discipline model based on the extent to which it satisfies each criterion. The ratings are given on a scale of 1 ("does not satisfy the criterion") to 5 ("completely satisfies the criterion"). Table 11.1 shows the results of such an evaluation. Keep in mind that deciding which discipline model best satisfies the entire set of criteria is not simply a matter of adding up the values in the table. Because the criteria have different degrees of importance, they need to be weighted accordingly. How different ratings are assigned is a matter of judgment and depends on your familiarity with the models. A few examples will be given here. It would be wise for you, however, eventually to create your own set of criteria and make your own judgments about how well each model satisfies them. In preparation for doing that, it may be useful to compare the judgments made here about how well various models satisfy the criteria by contrasting it with your own. It would be helpful to compare your ratings with classmates and visualize just how individual this process is.

Reality therapy/choice theory was given a rating of 5 on criterion A because helping children become more self-disciplined is a basic principle on which the model works. Behavior modification and assertive discipline were given a rating of 1 because, although they incorporate quite different ways of controlling students, they both assume that children require the control of teachers to behave properly. Nowhere in the description of these models and their applications do self-determination and responsibility appear as factors; they are based entirely on control by the teacher. Even though responsibility is one of the expressed aims of the Jones model, in its implementation it is oriented almost entirely toward control by the teacher, so a rating of 1 was given.

TABLE 11.1
Comparison ranges of different discipline models where 1 does not satisfy the criterion
and 5 completely satisfies the criterion.

Criteria		Behavior Modification	Assertive Discipline	Transactional Analysis	Reality Therapy/ Choice Theory	Logical Consequences	Jones Model	Teacher Effectiveness Training	Judicious Discipline
A	Self-discipline	1	1	4	5	4	1	5	4
B	Gain autonomy	1	1	4	5	4	1	5	3
C	Good self-concept	2	1	5	5	5	1	5	5
D	Good classroom behavior	5	2	3	4	4	3	3	4
E	Prevent discipline problems	2	2	3	5	4	2	3	4
F	Consistent with instruction	1	1	5	5	5	1	4	4
G	Easily implemented	4	5	2	1	1	4	1	2
H	Readily learned	4	5	3	1	1	3	1	2
I	Applied schoolwide	1	4	1	3	3	1	1	5

In terms of how well they help promote good self-concept (criterion C), five of the models received a rating of 5: logical consequences, teacher effectiveness training, judicious discipline, transactional analysis, and reality therapy/choice theory. The logical consequences model is designed to help children recognize that their misbehavior is the result of behavioral mistakes they make trying to satisfy their needs. Their frustrated efforts often produce poor self-concept. Through logical consequences, children are helped to regain a greater sense of adequacy through more need-satisfying behavior. Transactional analysis gives children a way to interact with others successfully by avoiding crossed transactions and other behaviors that cause alienation. More positive interpersonal interactions promote a better self-concept. Reality therapy/choice theory fosters the development of a good self-concept by empowering children to regulate their own need-satisfying behavior. Teacher effectiveness training is designed to promote greater self-determination as well as greater personal regard. Judicious discipline helps students develop a greater sense of community and to receive protection of personal preferences and rights. This helps students validate themselves as persons.

The other models are less likely to foster good self-concept. On the surface, it may appear that behavior modification improves children's self-concept by rewarding better academic performance. However, children exposed to reinforcement programs are unlikely to achieve a sense of well-being when their behavior is being manipulated by others. They realize that their behavior is being controlled and altered because others judge it to be inadequate. Similar criticisms could be made of assertive discipline and the Jones model. They both advocate aggressive behavior by teachers and potentially abrasive teacher–student interactions. This friction is more likely to promote poor self-concept.

You will note from Table 11.1 that behavior modification and assertive discipline are ranked much better than logical consequences, transactional analysis, teacher effectiveness training, judicious discipline, and reality therapy/choice theory in terms of ease of implementation (criterion G) and ease of learning (criterion H). Learning to use assertive discipline is relatively easy, which perhaps explains its popularity to some degree. It also corresponds well with the need of many teachers and school administrators to maintain control of students. Behavior modification is a little more difficult to apply correctly. Many teachers have the habit of mistakenly reinforcing misbehavior in their effort to curtail it. Learning to reinforce good behavior and ignore misbehavior does not come naturally. It may require considerable effort and training. The greater difficulty of using logical consequences comes from the requirement that teachers discover the operative motives of children. Because children either are unaware of their motives or deliberately hide them, teachers need considerable skill in asking questions and interpreting students' nonverbal responses. Transactional analysis is even more difficult to learn and apply. Teachers have to be alert to the games students play and avoid getting involved in playing them. They must also avoid the natural tendency to express the Parent and Child ego-states and remain in the Adult. Teacher effectiveness training is difficult to implement because teachers have to become skilled in detecting students' encoded messages and in properly implementing active listening and sending properly worded I-messages. Judicious discipline requires considerable skill interacting with students as well as applying legal principles to complicated classroom behaviors and conditions. The complexity of these two approaches makes them more difficult to apply than behavior modification and assertive discipline. Reality therapy/choice theory perhaps has the highest difficulty level because teachers need a good deal of skill to interact with students who are attempting to avoid responsibility by making excuses, lying, and shifting blame. Helping children assume responsibility is understandably difficult if they have a long history of successfully avoiding it.

Once you have a fair idea of how the various discipline models satisfy the criteria, you can make a tentative decision. The data generated so far show that reality therapy/choice theory most fully satisfies the first and second criteria. Behavior modification and assertive discipline, on the other hand, are more easily implemented and learned (criteria G and H). Because a model's ease of implementation and learning are ranked as less important than its potential for helping students become responsibly self-determined, it is easy to conclude that reality therapy/choice theory should be the model selected. This conclusion would be valid if in fact reality therapy/choice theory could be implemented and learned adequately without too much difficulty. What is an acceptable level of difficulty? If the goal of helping students become more responsibly autonomous has a high enough priority, teachers may invest considerable time and effort to achieve the skill needed to apply it. However, if learning to apply reality therapy/choice theory proves to be too difficult, this approach may have to be rejected. However much individual teachers may want to use a particular approach, their ability to learn how to use it adequately is a real limiting factor.

Examine Table 11.1 again. It appears that reality therapy/choice theory satisfies the criteria best. In addition to the strengths already identified, it has higher ratings in preventing discipline problems (criterion E) and correspondence with the intended

Analyzing and rating each discipline model and its congruence with your own philosophy can help determine the criteria for a good, comprehensive discipline program.

instructional program (criterion F). Reality therapy/choice theory's closest competitors are logical consequences, teacher effectiveness training, and judicious discipline. If they could be more easily learned and implemented, they might be better choices. However, compared to reality therapy/choice theory, they are about equally difficult to learn and implement. Therefore, according to the criteria specified and the rankings given, reality therapy/choice theory is a little more desirable—if it can be learned and implemented without too much difficulty. The differences between these four models don't make one clearly superior, even if the criteria are weighted to give one more consideration than another. Other criteria may need to be generated before a more supportable decision can be made.

Identifying and Validating Assumptions

A list of assumptions is given at the beginning of each of the chapters about discipline models (Chapters 3 through 10). You were asked to think about the validity of these assumptions as you read each of the chapters. The most important assumption that must be evaluated is either that students are able to achieve an adequate level of self-regulation or that they must be controlled by their teachers. Logical consequences, teacher effectiveness training, transactional analysis, judicious discipline, and reality therapy/choice theory all assume that humans can become responsibly self-regulated. Behavior modification, assertive discipline, and the Jones model assume that they cannot. Behaviorists claim that humans are born as "blank slates," that they have no will and simply respond to reinforcing stimuli, so consequently, they are at the mercy of the environment. It is therefore necessary for teachers to create an environment that reinforces more positive behaviors in students. Otherwise, by responding to various erratic stimuli, students are likely to behave unacceptably.

To determine whether the assumption of self-regulation is valid, examine evidence from three different perspectives (experience bases): personal experience, empirical evidence, and logical exposition. You may be personally acquainted, for example, with individuals who have left well-paying jobs and accepted positions with far lower pay in an effort to achieve a greater degree of autonomy. If we consider the power money has to satisfy most of our needs, such career moves seem to support the contention that humans have a will and are not just blank slates. But how does one account for the fact that so many people seem to be conditioned by their paychecks? Because not every person can be so conditioned, it can be concluded that those who are conditioned choose to allow the conditioning.

Empirical evidence for self-regulation is hard to obtain. Behavioristic studies usually show that individuals can in fact be conditioned. Conditioning is simply a matter of finding a sufficiently powerful reinforcer. Because behaviorists believe humans have no will, they claim that humans cannot resist the reinforcer. It is true that some children who have been conditioned by rewards later refuse to do their schoolwork without rewards. This refusal, however, does not show that they are unable to resist rewards. Rather, it shows that they have made a choice to work for rewards and not to work without them.

Glasser (1984) makes a logical argument in support of self-determination by examining the behavior that might be expected in connection with some common stimuli in the environment. A red traffic light signals us to stop, and so we do. A telephone rings, and we answer it. The question is whether we just respond to these stimuli automatically or choose how we respond to them. Haven't you ever failed to answer the telephone because you were doing something more satisfying at the time? Wouldn't you run a red light if you were hurrying to take a seriously injured child to the hospital? Most people not only would run the red light but also would ignore speed limit signs along the way. No doubt you would slow down as you approached a red light, for safety's sake, but the light in and of itself would not control your behavior. You would choose how to respond to the light stimulus.

The evidence cited here shows how the validation process works. It may not, however, prove conclusively that humans are not blank slates. Other sources may present evidence to the contrary. You should consider all available evidence and decide in favor of discipline models whose assumptions are best supported by the evidence. In our example, the evidence gives greater support to those discipline models that assume human beings to be capable of responsible self-determination. The assumptions about responsible self-determination that go along with judicious discipline, transactional analysis, teacher effectiveness training, logical consequences, and reality therapy/choice theory not only satisfy the criteria specified in the example but also can be validated.

The next step is to examine conflicting assumptions of the different models. Take reality therapy/choice theory and logical consequences, for example. Both models advocate helping children satisfy their basic needs as a way of promoting good behavior. With reality therapy/choice theory, teachers can assume that nearly all students have a similar set of needs, which they must legitimately satisfy. When using logical consequences, on the other hand, teachers must determine what particular need is currently operative. Only then can they help their students more legitimately fulfill those needs. Because finding the appropriate need level is critical to this model and because the need level is not always evident, teachers must interrogate students, asking them *why* they behave as they do. Unfortunately, many students are unaware of their motives or, if they are aware, do not want to disclose them. When students are unable or unwilling to discuss their motives, need determination becomes something of a guessing game that depends extensively on the teacher's skill in diagnosing various nonverbal cues. Because of the great potential for misdiagnosis, it cannot be assumed that teachers can accurately make this determination. The implicit assumption that teachers can consistently make accurate determinations must be judged invalid. In addition, a model designed to help students achieve a greater degree of responsibility should not include procedures that run counter to this purpose. For example, the practice in logical consequences of determining students' motives by asking them *why* may encourage them to give excuses, a result that is incompatible with helping them assume responsibility for their own behavior.

Another technique used in logical consequences that may promote less responsibility development than reality therapy/choice theory is the practice of restricting misbehaving students to two behavioral options. Children who insist on leaning back in their chair may be told to choose between sitting with all four chair legs on the floor or sitting with two legs permanently raised off the floor. In the application of reality therapy/choice theory, children are asked to explore a wide range of consequences for behavior and are permitted to choose behaviors that produce more satisfying consequences. Students are thus given a greater degree of self-determination.

Consequently, our hypothetical teacher finds that an examination of the assumptions underlying each model gives the most support to reality therapy/choice theory.

Sometimes additional information about the strengths and weaknesses of different models can help in validating assumptions. Lists of such information are included near the end of each of the chapters about discipline models (Chapters 3 through 10). As you validate assumptions, you may wish to re-examine these lists.

Considering Options

In deciding on a discipline approach, you have three options from which to choose. You can

1. Use a single existing discipline model.
2. Synthesize components of different models.
3. Create your own discipline approach.

If you decide on a single model, you are using a theory-based orientation (refer to Figure 2.2), and you must carefully apply the principles of that particular theory. Our hypothetical teacher decided on a theory-based orientation.

However, after going through the decision-making process outlined in this chapter, you may find that the model you select as best is still unsatisfactory. You may then decide that you prefer to use elements of a number of models (an eclectic orientation). If you decide on an eclectic orientation, you will need to select from among the various models those elements that suit you best and recombine them into an approach suitable for disciplining a variety of different kinds of children in a variety of circumstances (Charles, 1989). Or you may adopt a shifting orientation, in which case you would select a number of models and apply them in some systematic way depending on various factors such as the degree of self-control exhibited by students. If you decide to use a shifting orientation, you will select perhaps six or eight discipline models that differ in terms of the relative amounts of control exercised by teachers and autonomy enjoyed by students. Some of the models will be based on management theories (which assume that children's development depends on external influences), some on nondirective intervention theories (which assume that children's development depends on internal influences), and others on leadership theories (which assume that children's development depends on an interaction of both internal and external influences). The model you use in the classroom at any particular time depends on how much control you need to exercise to maintain good classroom discipline. In general, you will use various techniques from the different models as the situation seems to dictate (Wolfgang & Glickman, 1980).

After examining the various options, you may prefer to create your own discipline model. Your created model should have a theory-based orientation. That is, you must first devise a set of principles on which to base your model. Next, you need to formulate procedures that put your principles of classroom discipline into practice. You will need to provide for prevention as well as correction of discipline problems. Your model should also be applicable to a schoolwide discipline program. Chapter 12 gives a detailed example of a discipline approach created from some compatible elements of several discipline models plus several new components.

Synopsis of Discipline Models

As an aid in comparing the various discipline models, the following synopsis is given:

BEHAVIOR MODIFICATION

Assumptions

1. Human beings are born as "blank slates" and are inherently incapable of self-government.
2. Human beings have no will and respond exclusively to external stimuli. Therefore, they need to be regulated by properly arranged reinforcers.

Applications

1. Define acceptable student behavior.
2. Reinforce appropriate behavior.
3. Avoid paying attention to inappropriate behavior.

Compatible Teaching Methods

1. Lectures
2. Guided discussions
3. "Cookbook" labs
4. Demonstrations
5. Programmed learning
6. Computer-assisted instruction

Use of Rules in Discipline

1. Created and enforced by the teacher
2. Connected to a reward system

Results of Misbehavior

1. Ignore unacceptable behavior.
2. Reinforce appropriate behavior.

Strengths

1. Simple to use.
2. Results are immediate.

Weaknesses

1. Intrinsic motivation is often undermined by rewards.
2. Once the reward system is instituted, students may refuse to learn without rewards.

General Insights

Teachers often ignore good behavior and pay attention to bad behavior, thus reinforcing bad behavior.

ASSERTIVE DISCIPLINE

Assumptions

1. All students can be made to behave.
2. Students must be forced to comply with rules.
3. Students cannot govern their own behavior.
4. Punishment promotes good student behavior.
5. Parents and school administrators are needed to enforce classroom rules.

Applications

1. Teachers assume an assertive relationship with students.
2. Teachers establish the rules.
3. Track misbehavior by putting students' names and checks on the chalkboard.

4. Punishment is systematically administered to offending students.
5. Appropriate student behavior is rewarded unsystematically.
6. The severity of punishment is increased if lesser punishments are ineffective.

Compatible Teaching Methods

1. Lecture
2. Guided discussion
3. "Cookbook" labs
4. Demonstrations
5. Simulation games

Use of Rules in Discipline

Rules are constructed and enforced by the teacher.

Results of Misbehavior

1. Name and checks are put on the board.
2. Punishment is applied according to a prespecified plan.

Strengths

1. It is simple to use.
2. Parents and school administrators can be involved.

Weaknesses

1. Punishment may promote rebellion.
2. Warnings may stimulate misbehavior.
3. It fails to promote self-direction.

General Insights

Involvement by parents provides increased power to discipline.

LOGICAL CONSEQUENCES

Assumptions

1. Inappropriate behavior is motivated by the needs to gain attention, experience power, exact revenge, or display inadequacy.
2. Inappropriate behavior is the result of poor choices regarding how to satisfy needs.
3. Eliminating unacceptable behavior requires that the motive behind the behavior be discovered.

Applications

1. Help students identify motives behind their behavior.
2. Help students learn to satisfy their motives legitimately.
3. Let students suffer the logical consequences of their behavior.
4. When students misbehave, two alternatives are offered to choose from to correct the problem.

Compatible Teaching Methods

1. Reflective discussions
2. Inquiry discussions
3. Exploratory discussions
4. Role playing
5. Sociodramas
6. Projects
7. Simulation games
8. Demonstrations
9. Exploratory labs

Use of Rules in Discipline

Rules are determined and enforced cooperatively by students and teachers

Results of Misbehavior

1. Choose between two alternative ways to correct behavior.
2. Explore motives.
3. Determine acceptable behavior to replace inappropriate behavior.

Strengths

1. The use of logical consequences promotes autonomy and self-regulation to some degree.
2. It prevents discipline problems.
3. It helps students satisfy their needs.

Weaknesses

1. It is hard for teachers to determine students' motives.
2. Students may be unaware of, or fail to admit, their motives.

General Insights

Students will be more willing to replace bad behavior with good behavior when they understand their motives and realize the consequences for their actions.

TRANSACTIONAL ANALYSIS

Assumptions

1. Behavior is an outgrowth of experiences stored in the subconscious mind.
2. Inappropriate behavior emanating from the Parent and Child ego-states can be regulated by the Adult ego-state.

Applications

1. Children are taught to regulate their own behavior by remaining in the Adult ego-state and not engaging in cross transactions with others.
2. Teachers regulate their own behavior through their own Adult ego-state.

Compatible Teaching Methods

1. Reflective discussions
2. Inquiry discussions
3. Exploratory discussions
4. Role playing
5. Sociodramas
6. Exploratory labs
7. Demonstrations
8. Projects
9. Simulation games

Use of Rules in Discipline

No rules are created.

Result of Misbehavior

The teacher responds from the Adult ego-state.

Strengths

1. Transactional analysis promotes self-correction.
2. It can be applied in one's personal life.

Weaknesses

1. This model doesn't apply well to nonverbal problems.
2. Teachers may have difficulty self-regulating their overactive Parent ego-state.

General Insights

All of our experience is recorded in our brains, with the subconscious mind being the repository for much of it. A good deal of our behavior is an outgrowth of these stored subconscious experiences.

TEACHER EFFECTIVENESS TRAINING

Assumptions

1. Human beings are motivated by an internal desire to be good and are capable of solving their own problems.
2. Children with behavior problems can be helped by experiencing warm and accepting relationships with others.

Applications

1. Teachers engage in active listening with their students when students own the problem.
2. Teachers send I-messages when student behavior involves a teacher-owned problem.

Compatible Teaching Methods

1. Reflective discussions
2. Inquiry discussions

3. Exploratory discussions
4. Role playing
5. Sociodramas
6. Exploratory labs
7. Demonstrations
8. Projects
9. Simulation games

Use of Rules in Discipline

No rules are used in teacher effectiveness training.

Results of Misbehavior

1. Active listening
2. Sending I-messages

Strengths

1. Teacher effectiveness training promotes autonomy and self-regulation.
2. It promotes good student–teacher relationships.
3. It helps students and teachers understand one another.

Weaknesses

1. Teachers may have difficulty engaging in active listening and sending appropriate I-messages.
2. Teachers may have a problem accepting value differences between them and their students.

General Insights

Children can solve their own problems if they are allowed to explore them without undue interference from adults.

REALITY THERAPY/CHOICE THEORY

Assumptions

1. Children are self-regulating and can learn to manage their own behavior.
2. Children will learn to behave responsibly if they are helped to examine a full range of behavioral consequences and helped to make value judgments about their behavior and its consequences.
3. Children's behavior is motivated by the needs for love, power, freedom, and fun. They choose either good or bad behavior to satisfy these needs.

Applications

1. Teachers help students examine their behavior and its consequences along with helping them to make value judgments about their behavior and its consequences. They help students change their behavior so it matches desired consequences.
2. Teachers help students satisfy their needs for love, power, freedom, and fun in positive legitimate ways.

Compatible Teaching Methods
1. Reflective discussions
2. Inquiry discussions
3. Exploratory discussions
4. Role playing
5. Sociodramas
6. Exploratory labs
7. Projects
8. Demonstrations
9. Simulation games

Rules

Rules are established cooperatively by students and teachers.

Results of Misbehavior
1. The student and the teacher explore the consequences of the student's behavior.
2. The student creates a plan to improve behavior.
3. The student suffers the logical consequences for his or her misbehavior.

Strengths
1. Reality therapy/choice theory promotes responsibility and autonomy.
2. It helps students satisfy their needs.
3. It prevents discipline problems.

Weaknesses
1. This model requires considerable training and skill.
2. Class meetings may require a lot of time.

General Insights

Student misbehavior is stimulated by excessive coercion and control. Allowing students to have control over more of what they do will help prevent most behavior problems.

JUDICIOUS DISCIPLINE

Assumptions
1. School is an appropriate place to prepare students for living in a democratic society.
2. Students can learn to responsibly use their personal freedoms as guaranteed by the Constitution.
3. Students can learn to regulate their personal behavior so that it does not violate compelling school interests.
4. Students can help create valid rules for the classroom.
5. Consequences provide a better way to improve the classroom behavior of children than punishment.

Applications
1. Teachers help students understand their rights under the Constitution as well as their responsibilities and how these interrelate to one another.
2. Teachers teach their students to see how their rights of freedom, justice, and equality apply to them in a school setting.
3. Teachers help their students learn how to help regulate the classroom so that they can acquire the skills of living democratically in the classroom as well as in society generally.

Compatible Teaching Methods
1. Reflective discussions
2. Inquiry discussions
3. Exploratory discussions
4. Role playing
5. Sociodramas
6. Exploratory labs
7. Projects
8. Demonstrations
9. Simulation games

Rules

Rules are established democratically by students and teachers.

Results of Misbehavior
1. In the classroom, a student may be brought before an appointed judicial body to hear the particulars of his or her case. Judgments would be rendered in terms of established rules. The rules of due process would be carefully adhered to.
2. If schoolwide rules are broken, a student may have to appear before a court of original jurisdiction with the option to appeal his or her case to an appellate court and then to a supreme court.

Strengths
1. Judicious discipline imitates the legal system in a democratic society. It provides students with an opportunity to participate in the legal system they will encounter after they leave school.
2. Students' rights are protected from capricious actions by teachers and administrators.
3. It has an excellent format for application to schoolwide discipline.
4. It helps students learn to balance their rights against compelling school interests.

Weaknesses
1. It takes considerable time for students to become involved in schoolwide aspects of judicious discipline.
2. The application of personal rights and compelling school interests may be confusing to students when they exit the school at graduation.

General Insights

Students will be more likely to accept as valid a discipline approach that is much like the one they will confront as citizens in our society.

THE JONES MODEL

Assumptions

1. Children have to be controlled to behave properly.
2. Teachers can achieve control through nonverbal cues and movements that bring them increasingly closer to their students.
3. Students will behave as directed in an effort to avoid having preferred activities taken from them.

Applications

1. Create seating that allows the teacher easy access to any student from anywhere in the classroom.
2. Limit the time spent helping any one student.
3. Set limits for misbehaving students by moving closer and closer to them.
4. Use preferred activity time as a negative reinforcer to encourage good class behavior.
5. Provide omission training for students with special discipline problems.
6. Use suspensions, expulsions, and so on in cases of extreme discipline problems.

Compatible Teaching Methods

1. Lecture
2. Guided discussion
3. "Cookbook" labs
4. Demonstrations
5. Simulation games

Use of Rules in Discipline

Rules are under teacher control.

Results of Misbehavior

1. Limit setting
2. Omission training
3. Suspension
4. Expulsion

Strengths

1. The Jones model specifies steps to follow.
2. It involves parents and school administrators in discipline.

Weaknesses

1. The model fails to promote self-regulation.
2. It may be too intimidating for students and teachers.

3. It may promote violent student reactions.

General Insights

Most students will stop misbehaving if sufficiently intimidated or threatened.

▼ SUMMARY

The most critical task in choosing a discipline approach is determining your personal philosophy and style of teaching—to what degree you plan to exercise control in the classroom or encourage autonomy in your students. You also need to decide whether you prefer an orientation to discipline that is theory-based, eclectic, or shifting. Criteria can then be prepared to help you choose among the various discipline models. The assumptions behind each of the models considered should then be identified and validated. The discipline model selected not only should correct discipline problems but also should prevent them and provide for schoolwide discipline. If you discover that none of the models is satisfactory, you may need to create an approach of your own. Creating your own model will most likely involve putting together some elements of two or more models plus some of your own ideas.

CENTRAL IDEAS

1. The relative amounts of control you plan to exercise in the classroom and autonomy you intend to allow your students make up the first issue that you must resolve in making a decision about what discipline approach to use.
2. Criteria are statements that provide standards of judgment for deciding between alternatives.
3. Assumptions accompany all human proposals and activities. Their validity must be determined if teachers are to avoid making poor decisions.
4. Consistency is the critical aspect of a theory-based orientation to discipline. Teachers who prefer an eclectic orientation instead use flexibility as their guiding principle.

QUESTIONS AND ACTIVITIES

QUESTIONS TO CONSIDER

1. What is the function of a personal philosophy of education?
2. What must be done to create a functional educational philosophy?
3. How can you be certain that the discipline approach you select is an appropriate one?

CLASSROOM ACTIVITIES

1. Have the class divide into groups according to the discipline approach they favor. Have each group prepare a defense for the approach they have selected and present it to the class.

STUDENT APPLICATIONS

1. Write a set of statements that reflect your personal philosophy of education. Include a statement regarding your view about the issue of teachers' control and students' autonomy. Decide which discipline orientation you prefer: theory-based, eclectic, or shifting.
2. Prepare a list of prioritized criteria. Use them to determine which of the discipline models you prefer.
3. Make a list of assumptions for each discipline model and validate them. Use this information to further clarify which discipline model is most appropriate for your use.
4. Consider the extent to which the model you favor corrects discipline problems, prevents them, and allows for schoolwide applications.
5. Make a final decision about which discipline approach you prefer. If none is satisfactory, begin assembling ideas for a discipline approach that would satisfy your expectations.

EXPLORE YOUR PHILOSOPHY

1. With a group of your peers, defend your discipline approach. Do this by showing evidence that supports your position. Data used in validating assumptions may be used in this process. Show how your discipline approach is consistent with your criteria, and justify the criteria you have chosen to use.
2. Prepare a written description of your philosophy of education and discipline that you can include in your teaching portfolio.

▼ **REFERENCES**

Charles, C. M. (1989). *Building classroom discipline: From models to practice* (3rd ed.). New York: Longman.

Glasser, W. (1984). *Control theory: A new explanation of how we control our lives.* New York: Harper & Row.

Wolfgang, C. H., & Glickman, C. D. (1980). *Solving discipline problems: Strategies for classroom teachers.* Boston: Allyn & Bacon.

12

Creating a Personal Theory of Discipline

OBJECTIVES

This chapter is designed to help you

1. Identify the components of a comprehensive discipline program and describe the relationship of these components to one another.
2. Understand how criteria are used in creating discipline procedures.
3. Specify what makes curricula relevant.
4. Explain how satisfying students' needs can reduce discipline problems.
5. Solicit valid input from students about the instructional program.
6. Involve students in creating rules and expectations.
7. Encourage useful input from students about the teacher's role in the classroom.
8. Improve students' behavior by guiding them through the process of exploring their previous commitments to the rules.
9. Improve students' behavior by guiding them through the process of exploring their intentions.
10. Avoid colluding with students who do not want to accept responsibility for their inappropriate behavior.

Introduction

Undoubtedly, the most frightening prospect for beginning teachers is the possibility that they may be unable to teach effectively because there is so much misbehavior in their classrooms. Even veteran teachers are often perplexed by discipline problems. Most teachers have no comprehensive theory of discipline to apply consistently. Instead, they commonly use various ideas about discipline picked up from disparate sources. Teacher training may not do much to alleviate this problem. Training in discipline for many teachers is often very meager, and many teachers embark on their careers without having mastered an effective approach to discipline. Instead, they are armed with a list of *dos* and *don'ts* and an almost sure inclination to react inappropriately to inflammatory situations in their classrooms. This lack of preparation will certainly magnify the difficulties experienced by first-year teachers.

This chapter is designed to help prospective teachers design their own program of discipline. As an illustration, a comprehensive discipline program will be outlined that follows a single set of principles. It is comprehensive because it will be applicable not only in the classroom, to prevent as well as to solve discipline problems, but also on a schoolwide basis. A good discipline model must have an explicit set of guidelines and accurate, predictable explanations for a wide range of human behaviors and interactions. The more a model can explain and predict, the more valuable it is. Models of this kind can be used to deal with a wider variety of school problems. They can provide a better understanding of how discipline problems develop and how they can be prevented.

Another attribute of a good discipline model is utility—the ease with which teachers can use it in the classroom. Most teachers should be able to apply a model while they are teaching, without making special adaptations. It should, in fact, be an integral part of, and be based on, the same principles as the instructional program.

An Example of a Comprehensive Discipline Program

The discipline model outlined here is based on the philosophy that students should increasingly achieve greater autonomy over what they study and how they behave in school. This approach should most appropriately be called a *synthesis*. It draws most heavily on Glasser's reality therapy/choice theory (Chapter 8); it also incorporates from transactional analysis the teacher's practice of speaking from the Adult ego-state (Chapter 6) and from behavior modification the recommendation to avoid reinforcing students' misbehavior (Chapter 3). Some new ideas are also added.

The following criteria have been established for this discipline program:

1. Provide for students' autonomy.
2. Help students learn to be increasingly responsible and self-directed in terms of both discipline and the program of studies.
3. Correspond well with the instructional program.
4. Promote good self-concept in students.
5. Develop a greater sense of cooperation among students.
6. Prevent as well as correct discipline problems.
7. Promote increased learning.
8. Help students achieve greater consistency between their intentions and their behavior.
9. Help teachers avoid collusion (collaboration between students and teachers for deceitful purposes is a common way in which discipline problems are perpetuated).
10. Promote better schoolwide discipline.

This sample discipline program is based on the following assumptions:

1. Children can learn to govern themselves autonomously.
2. Children's basic needs include love and acceptance, control, freedom, and fun.
3. Children will collude, shift the blame, lie, and otherwise try to avoid accepting responsibility unless they are taught appropriate alternatives.
4. Children's needs are met better through cooperative learning than competitive learning. Cooperative learning improves students' relationships and reduces discipline problems.
5. When children realize that their intentions differ from their behavior, they will change their behavior to conform to their intentions.
6. Children will learn to be more responsible if they are taught to apply problem-solving skills to real-life problems in an atmosphere of freedom.

The comprehensive discipline program illustrated next consists of three components: preventing discipline problems, correcting discipline problems, and schoolwide discipline. Each of these components will be discussed in detail with some examples of how teachers might enter into a dialogue with students regarding this process.

PREVENTING DISCIPLINE PROBLEMS

It is obviously wise to have a successful prevention discipline program. If discipline problems can be prevented, many of the difficulties experienced by teachers will be avoided. Discipline problems tend to escalate once they appear. In a well-conceived preventive discipline program, problems will not have a chance to grow and become increasingly difficult to overcome. A good preventive discipline program has several important characteristics. These are listed next, followed by a discussion of each:

1. It provides for students' needs (love, control, freedom, fun) in the instructional program.
2. It encourages students to communicate what they would like to learn and how they would like to learn it.
3. It involves students in establishing explicit rules and expectations.
4. It allows students to help determine the role of the teacher.
5. It fosters the establishment of good relationships between students and teachers.
6. It helps students learn how to evaluate their own academic performance.

Providing for Students' Needs.   Human needs include control, freedom, and fun along with love and acceptance (Glasser, 1998). The misbehavior of students is often an indication that one or more of these needs is not being met. Students are often unable to satisfy their needs in school. The same may be true at home or in other social settings. Because children spend so much time in school, teachers have a unique opportunity to help them more fully meet their basic needs and enjoy a more satisfying school experience. In the preventive discipline approach described here, helping students satisfy their basic needs is an important way to prevent the problem behaviors that often result when needs go unmet.

Adults usually consider children's need for control to be illegitimate. It seems presumptuous to allow students to assume control when they often seem out of control and rebellious. However, solving the problem of rebellion in students will not be achieved by restricting their behavior. Their unruliness is a product of having too few opportunities to govern themselves. This problem can be solved only by allowing students more control and responsibility, not less.

A student's need for freedom is difficult to provide for in school because students are normally assembled in large groups and expected to pursue common goals. The curriculum and the rules of behavior are usually dictated, giving students little or no leeway. These restrictions are necessary, it is believed, because students are inherently irresponsible. Teachers tend to believe that students will choose to misbehave if given the freedom to do so. However, to reduce discipline problems, teachers should avoid restricting students' options and instead help them expand their range of choices and make their choices wisely.

Students are customarily told that learning is difficult and that to be successful in school, they have to work hard. Most teachers do not believe that they have any obligation to make learning fun. In fact, teachers themselves generally consider learning to be hard work, not fun (Glasser, 1984). Yet anyone who observes young children learning in an unstructured environment must admit that they seem to be having fun. In fact, from a very young age, children seem compelled to learn and spend much of their time engaged in learning, all the while enjoying themselves immensely. Unfortunately, however, the longer students spend in school settings, the less they like learning. In fact, school can turn some children off from learning altogether (Goodlad, 1984). How can this change be explained? One major factor is that learning in school is quite different from natural learning. For one thing, students are expected to learn what is assigned instead of what they consider interesting. Strict schedules must be followed. When compared to natural learning, completing school assignments is a drudge. It does not need to be so. Learning in school can be just as exciting as learning that occurs naturally. When it is, fewer discipline problems exist. When learning is not fun, students get bored and start looking for some other activity to entertain them. Usually they misbehave. Teachers can prevent discipline problems by allowing students to pursue many of their own personal interests.

One of the prime requirements for teachers is that they love their students. If students do not feel genuinely loved and accepted, they will react negatively. Love is demonstrated through actions (pats on the back, handshakes), words (use of the student's name, compliments), and attitudes (fairness, kindness). Excessive control, anger, and cutting remarks express a lack of love and respect. Love helps prevent discipline problems; negative expressions promote them. Teachers should generally be warm and caring and positive toward their students. Some teachers stand at the door and greet their students as they come into class. Others keep a checklist to remind them to initiate positive interactions with their students. Attending students' activities and making comments about how well students perform can be a very effective way to show that you care.

Involving Students in Determining the Curriculum.   When instructors teach interesting classes, they experience fewer discipline problems. When students are not bored and when they are fully involved in learning, they devote less time to misbehavior. Greater interest can be anticipated from students if they have a significant role in deciding what they learn. If students are involved in making curriculum decisions, teachers have less difficulty in motivating them. Teachers can then capitalize on the existing legitimate interests of students rather than attempt to impose on them a predetermined program of study, however well-planned it may be.

Students' interests can be ascertained by asking them directly, observing them in unstructured situations, and encouraging them to express their likes and dislikes. During the first day or two of class, students should be asked to supply their teachers with a list of their outside interests and hobbies. These lists not only provide insight into students' personalities but also can suggest unusual learning opportunities and stimulate better student–teacher relationships.

Teachers usually do not allow students to make decisions about the curriculum. It is supposed that students have insufficient training and experience to decide these matters. In addition, it is commonly believed that students will base their choices on how easy a subject is or express interest in areas of study that have no legitimate place in school. It is true that students have a meager knowledge of most subjects and are consequently unprepared to make valid decisions about their relative importance. However, to prepare students for making wise decisions, teachers can teach them the relative significance of various alternatives.

Teachers should first undertake with their students a comprehensive examination of possible topics and then help them consider the implications associated with each topic. For example, some topics prepare students for further schooling or college, whereas others by themselves provide essential, practical knowledge. Some courses are part of a sequence and, therefore, are relevant only to those students who plan to take the advanced courses. Sometimes topics have current relevance or interest and as time passes may become less useful. Some things are important for everyone to understand; others are simply "nice to know." Armed with information such as this, students can make better choices. In the process of making their selections, students should help create a list of topics of general interest for the entire class as well as lists for individuals and small groups. In most courses, it is unnecessary for all students to study all the same topics.

According to an old adage, you can lead a horse to water, but you cannot make it drink. Likewise, you cannot force children to learn. A particular topic may be considered important by teachers, but it will be taken seriously by students only when the students themselves decide that it is important. Sometimes students may express no interest in a particular area of study because they are unaware of its relevance. Teachers need to help students put subjects in context. Once students know more about how one topic is interconnected with others, they will be better able to judge its relative value. Ironically, sometimes the very topic most resoundingly rejected by students who are given no choice is the most enthusiastically embraced by those who are allowed to choose for themselves.

Not only must students be able to make choices regarding the curriculum, but teachers must also help them obtain resources and then provide instruction that is interesting and lively. Discipline problems can be prevented to a great extent when these conditions exist. One excellent way to make the curriculum more relevant is to arrange cooperative learning experiences for students. In some types of cooperative learning, students decide what they learn and are invited to make their selections applicable to their own interests. Cooperative learning can help avoid the debilitating effects of competitive learning.

The following discussion illustrates how a teacher can involve students in determining the curriculum for a biology class. Keep in mind that this scenario is an illustration of the process teachers might use to encourage student participation in deciding on classroom learning activities. It is not an example of the complete interaction that might take place. No doubt students will raise many additional questions that need to be explored. In addition, it should be noted that the students in the example are unusually cooperative and possess greater than average insight and understanding. Also recall that this process is based on Glasser's ideas about curriculum construction as lead management might be applied in the classroom. The process would look much different if another philosophical position were applied:

Teacher   Class, over the next few days, we will be discussing our program of studies for the year. In a class such as biology, there are many different topics, some of which may be more significant or interesting to us than others. Because there are far more good topics in biology than we have time for, we will need to choose as a class what we would like to study. We will probably find that there are a number of topics we all want to investigate and others that interest only a few of us. It is perfectly all right if the entire class works on some topics and then we break into small groups to study others.

I have given each of you a sheet containing a rather long list of possible topics. At the bottom of the list are a number of blank spaces where you can write in other suggestions. We will create our program of studies from all the topics listed and put it in some reasonable sequence. Probably the first thing you need to do is to expand the list so that topics you are interested in are included. To help you look for possibilities, I have divided you into groups. At the table where each group is sitting, I have deposited a number of copies of *Scientific American, Science News,* and some other periodicals. There is also a folder containing news articles about biological subjects I have collected over the past year or two. During this class period, you are free to browse through these sources and discuss with your group the topics that seem most appealing to you. When we meet tomorrow, we will discuss your suggestions and start making decisions about our biology curriculum.

Remember, as you look for possible topics, try to judge their significance. If we are all going to take the time to study a particular topic, it should be significant as well as interesting. The significance of a topic can often be judged by whether it (1) has received much attention, (2) has important health considerations, (3) involves important ecological concerns, (4) allows active participation by class members, and (5) involves a fundamental biological topic. These criteria have been included on your sheet so that you can refer to them as needed. You should decide on the topics you prefer and arrange them in order of importance. Remember, some of you may feel strongly about a particular topic, but others may not share your interest. Take note of those topics so that they can be studied in small groups. Now let's get started. If you have questions, I will come around and try to answer them.

The teacher must decide how long this activity should last. As many class periods should be taken as students can productively use. When this phase has been completed, the process can continue.

Teacher	Each of the lists your groups have compiled has been placed on the board. Notice that the more popular topics have been listed first. Now we need to decide as a class what would be the most profitable topics to study and how to put them in the most meaningful sequence. As you look at the lists on the board, which areas of study appear to be the most important ones?
Karl	It looks to me like AIDS probably leads the list, with ecology, evolution, reproduction, and immunity all coming in a close second.
Joyce	It looks like quite a few people want to study heart attacks and strokes, too. I think they may be more interesting to the class than some of the other subjects. Maybe we can study a unit on diseases first.
Teacher	Joyce, you've made a good suggestion: grouping areas of study based on how they are related. Diseases sounds like a good grouping. Let's look at each one a bit more and decide what we may need to study as background for each of the diseases suggested so that we can get a more complete understanding of each. AIDS, of course, is caused by a virus. What areas need to be studied before an investigation of AIDS would be meaningful?
Naomi	Obviously, we need to learn about viruses, but I think we need to learn about other things like bacteria so we see how viruses compare.
Aaron	Well, if we're going to study bacteria and viruses, we probably need to learn more about cells. Viruses and bacteria are cells, aren't they?
Teacher	Well, viruses don't carry on all the functions of a cell, but they do infect cells, and therefore the study of cells would help us understand how viruses function. What do we need to learn about the function of cells?
Camille	I know there are a lot of chemical things that go on in cells. Perhaps that would help us.
Teacher	Yes, a lot of chemical reactions take place in our bodies that you will need to understand.
Verlyn	From what I read in *Science News,* some of the diseases we want to study are thought to be inherited. High cholesterol is probably an inherited problem. So are many kinds of cancer. I read somewhere they think even alcoholism and depression may have genetic origins. There are probably a lot of diseases that are inherited. Our class is particularly interested in diseases, so I think we should spend a lot of time studying genetics. We should also study bacteria and viruses a lot. I think these subjects are all related.

Teacher	How many members of the class like what has been said so far? Does anyone have an opposing view?
Roger	I am really interested in studying diseases, but if we do that, we won't have a biology course like the one they expect you to have had when you go to college. I want to make sure I get what I need to prepare me for college.
Teacher	How can we make sure we study what we are interested in and still cover the topics Roger believes will prepare us for college?
Celia	I don't know how many of you plan to go to college, but I don't. I really want to learn how to take care of myself and avoid some of these diseases. I think we can study the topics Roger is worrying about as background for studying the more interesting and important topics.
Teacher	As we go along, let's make sure we remember to look at this question. At the present time we have expressed an interest in studying diseases, particularly those aspects of disease that pertain to subjects such as cytology, or the study of cells; microbiology; chemistry; and genetics. These are all bona fide subjects in most approaches to the study of biology. Let's go on and suggest additional topics now and continue to make comparisons.

Other topics need to be dealt with in a similar manner until the entire content of the course has been outlined. Similar discussions can be held to address questions about how the various topics are to be studied, including such issues as the frequency of labs, grouping, evaluation, and field trips. The desired outcome of these discussions is that students will feel good about both the content and the form of instruction. They need to be actively involved, so that they will feel a high degree of commitment for what is proposed. This commitment gives students a greater incentive to work and teachers a more effective means of dealing with any misbehavior that arises. Students who fail to enthusiastically learn what they agree to learn can have their previous commitments brought to their attention. This eventuality should be rare if students are genuinely involved in deciding their own curriculum. Fewer discipline problems can be expected.

Involving Students in Establishing Rules and Expectations.   Once the curriculum has been agreed on, teachers should next guide their students in formulating rules. Rules are a necessary part of any successful preventive discipline program. Students need a specific understanding of what behavior is acceptable and unacceptable in the classroom. Like the curriculum, rules should be jointly established. Students' ownership of rules depends on whether or not they have genuinely helped create them. If they do not accept rules as their own, students will not feel compelled to follow them. When students have been involved in formulating rules, they can also be relied on to help enforce them. In fact, they may take care of most necessary enforcement.

A word of caution is needed when students help enforce rules. Students can sometimes become too negative and punitive. They should, therefore, be taught that because punishment has little logical connection to rule infraction, it is unacceptable. Punishment is usually applied arbitrarily and with negative emotion and should therefore be replaced with consequences. Consequences follow logically from the rules and can be interpreted by students as appropriate and fair. Students should help determine

*Discussing rules and conse-
quences is a critical aspect of
classroom discipline.*

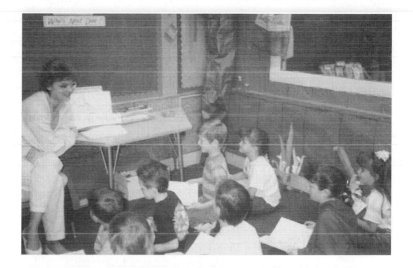

consequences. Unless they do, they will refuse to accept them, and the consequences
will fail as a deterrent to misbehavior.

The process of determining rules and consequences is illustrated in the following
discussion:

Teacher	As a class we have determined our goals and the topics we wish to study during the coming year. I personally believe the curriculum we have made will provide excellent opportunities for learning. But sometimes, as happens in almost any classroom, learning can be disrupted. As a class we need to be aware of these potential disruptions and how to prevent them. If they ever occur, we need to decide what to do about them. What kind of behavior will prevent us from achieving our learning goals?
Steve	I think talking too much is the biggest problem.
Ann	I believe the biggest problem isn't how much we talk but when we do it.
Teacher	So, Ann, what do you have to suggest about when to talk in class?
Ann	If we just talk one at a time during discussions and don't whisper to one another during lectures, things would be much better.
Rachel	Yes, and if there was no loud talking during quiet study time, we would all be able to concentrate better.
Chuck	I have a problem with that. During quiet study time I like to ask other students questions and get their help.
Tina	Well, Chuck, that can be done quietly.
Teacher	How many believe quiet conversation won't interfere with learning during quiet study time? (Most hands are raised.) I see most of you believe that it will not interfere. Let's try it for a week and then evaluate ourselves. Now, Ann suggested that just one of us talk at a time during discussions and that we refrain from talking during lectures. How do you suggest we accomplish this?

Roger	I suggest we raise our hands and have you call on us.
Elaine	I don't like that. It makes me feel like a first grader. Can't we just be sensitive to one another and then be careful not to speak when someone else is talking?
Rosanne	That doesn't work. I've been in other classes where we tried to do that. It's always too noisy. It sounds good, but it just doesn't work.
Teacher	Are there more comments about this issue? (The class is silent.) How many prefer to raise their hands during discussions? (Most hands are raised.) It looks like most of you would rather use this method. Here again, this issue can be reconsidered later if you wish. Now, in the event that any class member disturbs our learning activities by talking, what should be the consequence?
Glen	I think they should be kicked out.
Teacher	What do you mean by "kicked out"? Where would they go, and what would they do?
Glen	I haven't thought about that. I just think they shouldn't be allowed in class when they're too noisy. Couldn't we just send them to the principal's office?
Teacher	Do you think Ms. Brenchley would want to handle problems like this, problems that we as a class could handle ourselves? What could we do that would not involve the principal but would be fair and appropriate?
Dolores	Couldn't you just move the person who is talking to a new seat? In one of my other classes, the teacher did that and it worked well.
Teacher	Would you like to have your present seating be a privilege you could forfeit by talking and disturbing the class? (The students indicate general agreement.) Where would you suggest the disruptive person be seated?
Camille	I'd make them sit up by your desk.
Teacher	You have created your own rules for this class. Now it sounds like you want me to enforce them for you. Wouldn't you rather take care of these problems yourselves?
Jay	I would. I would like to have a seat designated that is right in the center of the classroom, where the person is surrounded by a discipline committee. It would be their job to make sure no more disturbances took place. If the person is still noisy, I suggest they be sent home and required to bring their parents to class and petition the discipline committee to get back into class.
Teacher	Would others like to comment about Jay's plan?
LaRetha	I think that is one of the best ideas I have ever heard. I think we should do it. We could at least try it for a while and see how we like it.
Aaron	I like it, too, but we would have to be sure the discipline committee took their responsibility seriously. Maybe we could all take turns serving on the committee. It doesn't sound like it would be much fun.

In this discussion, the teacher tries to have students consider some important points of a preventive discipline program. Other points would also be brought up and discussed.

The end product should be a few good rules, and students should have a role in enforcing these rules with appropriate consequences. The rules should be an outgrowth of the students' previously established learning goals.

Involving Students in Determining the Teacher's Role.   Once students have established classroom rules and procedures, it is appropriate to discuss the role of the teacher:

Teacher	So far we have discussed your learning goals and how you will handle disruptions. It is time to discuss some things I might do as your teacher to help your learning be more profitable. Does anyone have any suggestions?
Tina	I think we need lots of breaks from learning. I think we should have a party every Friday. (This suggestion is followed by cheers and laughter. The teacher just looks at the class and waits for additional responses.)
Renaldo	That's pretty stupid, Tina. Occasional parties are all right, but having one every Friday is a joke. You can do your partying after school.
Shon	I'd like to have parties, too. Maybe we can have one every month.
Teacher	Does anyone know the policy of the board of education regarding parties?
Jing	We all know that. We've heard it a hundred times. We are permitted one party each semester. I don't see how this discussion is related to the question you asked. Would you mind asking it again?
Teacher	I thought you might have some suggestions about things I could do to help you be more productive learners.
Karl	I like review sessions when I learn. Also, I hate surprise tests. I like to know when I'm being tested.
Terry	I agree with Karl. I also think we shouldn't have any homework over the weekends. Then we can come to school on Monday rested and ready to go to work.
Rachel	I like these suggestions. I also think we should have a better idea of what is going to be on the tests so that it isn't just a big guessing game.
Bob	I'd prefer it if we didn't have tests at all. I get so tense during tests that I can't remember anything I've studied. (Several students chime in their agreement.)
Teacher	If we didn't have tests, how could your work be evaluated and grades assigned?
Chuck	I wish we could do away with grades too. I hate them!
Naomi	Well, I like tests and grades. If you studied harder, you'd like them, too.
Teacher	Obviously, some of you like to be tested and others do not. Perhaps some of you could take tests while others had some alternative evaluation.
LaRetha	I do much better writing papers.
Karl	I would rather have oral tests.
Teacher	Now let's see what's been said so far. You have expressed a desire for various forms of evaluation. That can be arranged. You also indicated you wanted to avoid weekend homework and unannounced tests. I think these are appropriate requests. How many prefer we make these adjust-

	ments? (All the students raise their hands.) Is there anything else that you think would help you learn better?
Kulei	I would like to have more interesting lessons taught. Sometimes I really get bored in school.
Teacher	The class has already decided which topics it would like to study. Are you truly interested in learning about these topics?
Kulei	Yes, but I just want you to be a real interesting teacher.
Teacher	(To the entire class) What responsibility are you willing to assume as class members to make the lessons interesting?
Felecia	I think we should always be prepared, so that our discussions are based more on the questions students have.
Kim	I find if I have done some reading on the subject being discussed, I am interested and don't have to depend on the teacher to get me involved.
Teacher	How many would be willing to be prepared for class and come with questions to pursue in our discussions? (All the students raise their hands.) I would be willing to be as well prepared as I can be. I can't guarantee that I will always teach interesting lessons, but because you can regulate this to some extent by how involved you are in learning, perhaps everyone will be more interested and satisfied if you all search for questions you would like to have explored in class. That way the things that interest you the most can be investigated.

When students are trying to contribute suggestions about the teacher's role, they may make demands that cannot justifiably be met. Students who make these suggestions should not be humiliated or ridiculed. It is better for teachers to let other students react or to raise associated questions that need to be explored. Teachers must avoid being coercive and vetoing students' suggestions.

Fostering Good Relationships.   Whether or not teachers experience discipline problems in their classes depends to some extent on their relationships with their students. If students like their teachers, they will be less inclined to create trouble. The best relationship to establish is one of mutual respect. Such a relationship will develop when teachers help their students become more personally responsible and self-determined. If teachers are well prepared and personable in their relationships with students, avoiding all abusive behavior, they will gain more respect.

Helping Students Evaluate Their Own Work.   When teachers do all the evaluating in school, students tend to take less responsibility for their efforts and accomplishments. In fact, students develop an external locus of control when they are evaluated exclusively by teachers. An external locus of control is an outside influence to which accomplishments are attributed; success, some students believe, is the result not of effort but instead of fate or luck. Students react this way because they always have to depend on their teachers to determine the quality of their work and teachers often grade inconsistently. Helping students evaluate their own work helps them become more responsible and self-directed. The result is better discipline.

CORRECTING DISCIPLINE PROBLEMS

A comprehensive discipline program not only must prevent discipline problems but also must provide a way to correct them. The first step a teacher might take if the discipline program fails to prevent problems is to talk with misbehaving students individually. In this discussion, the teacher can help students explore the commitments they have made about their behavior and determine whether or not they intend to honor those commitments.

Exploring Commitments.   The following example is based on the principle, on which the discussion of prevention was based, that students should exercise autonomy and personal responsibility. Assume that a student named Moana talked excessively and loudly during discussions and quiet study time even though she had previously agreed not to do so. She had been subject to actions by the classroom discipline committee but had reacted by shouting to her friends across the room and ignoring the pleas of the committee to follow the class rules. When her mother came to the class to get her readmitted, Moana got into a screaming match with her, and the whole negotiation process broke down. Subsequently, this discussion took place between the teacher and the student:

Teacher	Moana, what did you do with Alice today in class during quiet study time that disturbed students around you?
Moana	I was just asking her to help me with the homework.
Teacher	What other instances are there when you have interfered with the learning of other class members by shouting to Alice and others while they were working on their projects?
Moana	I don't know.
Teacher	What about last Friday? Who were you talking loudly with just before the bell rang?
Moana	I was talking with Ralph.
Teacher	What did you agree, along with the rest of the class, about talking loudly during quiet study time?
Moana	I said I wouldn't do it, but I felt like the rest of the class was forcing me to agree to that. I really didn't accept it.
Teacher	Would you like me to write you a hall pass so that you can visit with the counselor and try to arrange to change classes? Perhaps you can find one where disruptions are more acceptable.
Moana	No. My friends are all in this class.
Teacher	What must you do so that you can remain in this class?
Moana	I guess I'll have to be more quiet during quiet study time.
Teacher	Is that what you intend to do from now on?
Moana	Yes.
Teacher	What will be the consequences if you fail to do what you stated you intended to do?
Moana	I guess I will have to find another class.

Exploring Intentions. Sometimes students will not have made commitments with other class members to refrain from certain behaviors such as talking. In these cases, students' intentions can be explored and compared with their behavior. Most students do not intend to cause trouble. It would be unusual for them to admit that they intentionally disrupted their classes. More often, they will give an excuse and claim that someone else or something else is to blame. The fact that children do not intend to cause annoyance can be used as a powerful tool in helping them behave more productively. The strategy is to have them first state their true intentions and then to compare their intentions with their behavior and its consequences. Let's observe what a teacher might say in the case of a student who talks disruptively to nearby classmates during class discussions. This discussion should take place privately, outside of class:

Teacher	Carvel, what were you doing in class today during discussion that interfered with the lesson and disturbed other students?
Carvel	I didn't do anything. I was just asking Jake something about what you said during class discussion.
Teacher	When you talk loudly with other students during discussions, what negative impact does it have on the learning of fellow classmates?
Carvel	I guess it makes it harder for some of them to learn, but sometimes I have a question I would like to ask so that I can understand better what we are talking about.
Teacher	What are your intentions about disrupting the class?
Carvel	Well, I don't mean to cause any trouble.
Teacher	You indicate you don't intend to interfere with the learning of your classmates, but when you talk out loud during discussions, what disruptive influence are you having?
Carvel	I guess I keep them from learning, but I don't really mean to do this.
Teacher	So how does your behavior compare with your intentions?
Carvel	Not very well.
Teacher	What do you need to do, then?
Carvel	I need to make sure I don't talk out in class again.
Teacher	If you did have a question, what could you do differently?
Carvel	I could present it to the entire class.

Avoiding Collusion. Sometimes students will deliberately provoke their teachers in an effort to cause a reaction, particularly when they either have failed to complete an assignment or are trying to avoid one. If students can get their teachers to react negatively, they can excuse themselves for their own failure and irresponsibility. When teachers respond negatively to students' provocations, they usually get involved in collusion. Collusion is a cooperative, but negative, exchange between individuals that allows both parties to excuse personal irresponsibility (Warner, 1980). For example, suppose that a student comes to class without completing an assignment due that day. To provoke the teacher, the student may say, "It wasn't possible to get the assignment done last night. The explanations you gave yesterday were not clear. I don't know how you could have expected us to complete the assignment with the little bit you taught us." Or the student may decide that stronger language is needed to elicit a reaction from the teacher and therefore speaks more bluntly, perhaps adding a bit of profanity: "I don't know when I've seen a stupider assignment than the one you gave us. It stunk like hell!"

Many teachers take the bait and reprimand the student for using vulgarity. If teachers sense that the assignment or their teaching is substandard, they may rise to defend the assignment the student has labeled stupid; in trying to excuse their perceived inadequacy, they end up participating in collusion. Some teachers reciprocate by calling the student stupid. Reactions such as these help students avoid accepting responsibility for their own failure. Students who claim that an assignment is bad can justify not doing it because the teacher's loss of control somehow invalidates anything the teacher requires. Students thus escape having to shoulder their academic responsibilities.

What could the teacher have said to avoid collusion when the student first started the provocation? Assume that the unfinished assignment was to solve several physics problems. The teacher could more profitably have said, "OK, let's look at the first problem." Then, addressing the provoking student directly, the teacher could have asked, "What does the first sentence of the problem say?" From here the teacher could guide the student through the problem to a successful solution and then say, "The other problems are exactly like this one. Start working on them, and see if you can finish two or three by the end of class."

The recommended reaction for the teacher in this case is to help the student do the most responsible thing, which is to solve the problem set. The teacher should not react to the student's provocation. Neither should the teacher attack the student nor accept the blame for poor teaching. None of these reactions will help students assume responsibility for themselves.

SCHOOLWIDE DISCIPLINE

It is a common practice for teachers to have the school principal deal with discipline problems they feel unable to take care of themselves. The belief that discipline problems should not interfere with the instructional program justifies this practice in part. It is hard to defend having the entire class wait while the teacher corrects the misbehavior of one student. However, when students are sent to the principal's office, the teacher may be unable to predict potential outcomes. The student may return to the classroom, but the principal may give no indication of what actions were taken. Unless teachers and administrators understand and coordinate their disciplinary measures beforehand, what is done in the principal's office may be contrary to what the teacher is trying to accomplish. It is therefore essential for administrative disciplinary actions to be consistent with discipline in the classroom. Otherwise, success will be limited. Schoolwide discipline must be based on the same principles as classroom discipline.

Two types of problems are dealt with in schoolwide discipline programs: problems in the classroom that are referred to the principal's office by teachers and problems that take place in locations other than classrooms. Discipline problems referred to the office should be coordinated by teachers and administrators. In these cases it is particularly important to maintain consistency of discipline. Otherwise, students may be sent different messages and become confused, or they may begin playing teachers and administrators against one another.

Hallways, school grounds, buses, lunchrooms, auditoriums, and gymnasiums are often sites for fights, vandalism, drug abuse, and other related problems. These problems can best be handled as part of the schoolwide discipline program. Some of these problems are serious enough to require the involvement of law enforcement officials. Fighting, vandalism, and drug abuse not only are disruptive to the functioning of the school but also may be punishable crimes. Even though a school discipline program may not itself provide for punishment, the school should not protect students from the consequences of actions that violate the law, even if such actions take place inside the school. The potential danger to other students of crimes such as drug abuse and possession of weapons may be sufficient cause to expel the guilty parties permanently.

A few years ago in an inner-city high school, there were many fights among students every day. Some of these fights involved deadly weapons. A new principal who had been assigned to the high school was determined to eliminate this problem. He decided that if any students took part in a fight, the police would be called, and the students involved would be handed over to them. They would be permanently barred from returning to school. They might attend other schools in the district, but under no circumstances would they be permitted to return to that particular high school. If they attended another high school, they had to arrange their own transportation. During the first year these procedures were implemented, there were only two fights. Obviously, students could see that no excuses would be accepted and that the administration would not back down. Actions of this kind may be necessary if discipline has deteriorated to such a point that students are endangered. In this case, the principal took it upon himself both to determine the rules and to enforce them. Ordinarily, it would be better to involve a committee of students in creating rules and the entire student body in enforcing them. When teachers and administrators make the rules, students feel less inclined to follow them.

When rules are formulated by committees of students and ratified by the entire student body, greater acceptance can be expected. Students will also be more likely to police themselves. Such involvement is consistent with the classroom discipline approach outlined in this chapter.

▼ SUMMARY

The three-part discipline program described in this chapter provides for students' self-determination and responsibility and is based on other important criteria as well. It provides an example of how you may formulate your own discipline program by borrowing some ideas from various theories and including some of your own. It describes procedures to prevent as well as correct discipline problems and includes applications for schoolwide discipline. Each of these components has been designed to be consistent with the others.

The preventive component includes the following practices:

1. Allowing students to help determine what they learn to make it more relevant to them
2. Have students help create the rules of conduct.

3. Involve students in defining the role of the teacher.
4. Improve student–teacher relationships.
5. Teach students to evaluate their own academic performance.
6. Ensure that students satisfy their needs in the school in legitimate ways.

The corrective part of the discipline program includes provisions for

1. Exploring commitments
2. Exploring intentions
3. Avoiding collusion

The schoolwide program consists of policies regarding:

1. Referring misbehaving students to the principal's office
2. Handling discipline problems in various areas of the school outside the classroom

Exploring commitments enables students to reflect on the promises they have made to classmates and to change their behavior accordingly. When students explore their intentions, they compare their actual behavior and its consequences with their intended behavior. They are then helped to alter their behavior until it fulfills their intentions. In all interactions with students, teachers must avoid collusion—interpersonal entanglements that are used by students, and sometimes by teachers, to avoid responsibility. Teachers can then assist students to become more productive and responsible.

The schoolwide discipline program is designed to deal with problems that originate in the classroom as well as those that have their origin in other school locations. If school administrators become involved in classroom discipline, their actions must be consistent with those of teachers. Students should be involved both in creating school-wide rules and in helping to enforce them.

CENTRAL IDEAS

1. All aspects of a well-organized, comprehensive discipline program should be consistent with a single set of principles.
2. Students whose needs are satisfied in the school will be less likely to rebel.
3. The relevance of the curriculum can be determined only in consultation with students.
4. Students will apply themselves more enthusiastically to their studies when they have helped determine the curriculum.
5. Students will follow rules they have helped create more readily than rules imposed on them.
6. Students are more likely to improve their behavior when they are asked to recognize and accept previously made commitments to follow rules.
7. Students often fail to realize that their behavior and its consequences are inconsistent with their intentions. When they are asked to compare their behavior and intentions, students will adjust their behavior to coincide more completely with their intentions.

QUESTIONS AND ACTIVITIES

QUESTIONS TO CONSIDER

1. What special problems are inherent in creating a schoolwide discipline program?
2. What difficulties might be encountered in creating a personal approach to discipline?
3. What does a comprehensive discipline program consist of, and how can such a program be applied consistently?

CLASSROOM ACTIVITIES

1. Have class members bring a set of criteria to class on which to base a discipline program.
2. Have small groups of students with similar criteria get together outside of class to create a description of a discipline program that is consistent with their criteria.
3. Have each of the groups present its discipline program to the entire class. After each presentation, class members can provide a critique. (Or have each group provide other class members with a written description of its discipline program a few days before the critique session so that everyone can study it and give more thoughtful responses.)

STUDENT APPLICATIONS

1. After analyzing various discipline theories and creating a list of criteria, prepare a description of a discipline approach that satisfies your criteria and that draws on various theories as well as your own ideas.

EXPLORE YOUR PHILOSOPHY

1. With a group of your peers, defend your personal discipline approach. Validate the assumptions your model is based on and how this evidence supports your model.
2. Prepare a written description of your philosophy of education and discipline that you can include in your teaching portfolio.

▼ **REFERENCES**

Glasser, W. (1984). *Control theory: A new explanation of how we control our lives.* New York: Harper & Row.

Glasser, W. (1998). *Choice theory: A new psychology of personal freedom.* New York: HarperCollins.

Goodlad, J. I. (1984). *A place called school: Prospects for the future.* New York: McGraw-Hill.

Warner, T. (1980). *Self-betrayal.* Unpublished manuscript, Brigham Young University, Department of Philosophy, Provo, UT.

U N I T

4

Classroom Management Approaches and Procedures

Classroom management procedures are an important complement to any discipline program. They contribute to an environment that enhances learning and minimizes the chance that discipline problems will occur. Teachers need to select from among the various classroom management procedures those that correspond most closely to the discipline model they use.

Any classroom management program must provide for several important factors that affect proper discipline in the classroom:

- The physical classroom environment
- The instructional program
- Teacher–student relationships

In this unit you will study the effects of the physical environment, time management, lesson management, and teacher–student relationships on the atmosphere of the classroom.

13

Classroom Management and Instruction

OBJECTIVES

This chapter is designed to help you

1. Appreciate the value of maintaining consistency between educational philosophy and the instructional program, including discipline.
2. Understand the problems created by competitive learning.
3. Understand the factors that influence motivation to learn.
4. Identify the stages students go through and the adjustments teachers must make when the classroom learning environment is changed from one that is controlled by the teacher to one that allows more freedom for students.
5. Understand the theory of multiple intelligences and the instructional strategies that are appropriate to use with the eight different intelligences.

Introduction

Teaching is one of the most complex of all human activities. It is estimated that elementary school teachers are involved in more than 500 separate exchanges with individual students during a single day (Jackson, 1968). At any given moment, teachers must choose which among many actions and interactions to give their attention to. This multiplicity makes teaching much more difficult than is commonly assumed. Doyle (1986) contends that classrooms are difficult to manage because they are multidimensional, simultaneous, and unpredictable. To complicate matters further, the classroom environment is immediate and public—that is, teachers must perform right now, right here, in full view of everyone.

Teachers must deal with many dimensions within the classroom: managing and reacting appropriately to large numbers of students, participating in daily routines and special events, and carrying out mundane tasks. Because of the number of people involved, any occasion can have multiple consequences that may require different reactions from the teacher. The behavior of any one participant has the power to influence how other participants react, and the reactions of teachers certainly influence how students behave. Many interactions in the classroom all take place at once. When teachers are engaged in instruction, they also have to keep track of time, monitor and react to students in a variety of contexts, and make last-minute changes in instructional formats and presentations, simultaneously pacing their lessons appropriately and managing students' behavior. Even in the most well-managed classroom, teachers cannot foresee or plan for every contingency. Classrooms are dynamic places. The human interactions that take place in them are often unpredictable. Teachers consequently have an enormous task in making sure that their lessons are interesting to students and that students remain involved and are not distracted.

Discipline problems are rare in classrooms in which children are involved and interested and in which they are appreciated and loved. Unfortunately, in many classrooms these conditions do not exist. In an extensive national study of schools, Goodlad found that students generally have far too few self-directed, meaningful educational experiences. In addition, he found that their learning experiences rarely go beyond mere memorization. Memorized facts are usually taught without any conceptual context, and students are seldom permitted to deepen their level of understanding by exploring the implications of important concepts or applying those concepts in real-life circumstances. Most learning does little to arouse students' curiosity or stimulate them to solve personal problems. The subject matter is ordinarily viewed by students as irrelevant to their personal struggles and development (Darling-Hammond, 1997; Goodlad, 1984).

The relevance of learning any particular subject depends on the learners. Commonly, however, students have little to say regarding their educational program. Ironically, the longer children are in school and (presumably) the more mature they become, the less they are called on to decide what they learn. Children in kindergarten have more to say about their program of studies than do high school seniors (Goodlad, 1984). It is clear that more self-determination may be kept from older students for fear that they will somehow abuse it. Yet they stand at the threshold of life, where personal decision making not only is important but absolutely essential. Where else but in school will they learn to function adequately in our complex world? How will they learn to live responsibly? These children sense their growing capacity to choose their own destiny and, therefore, assert their right to control it. Teachers need to provide students opportunities to do so (Eisner, 1992).

What can be gained by letting children make decisions about what they learn and how the classroom is managed? How can they possibly know what they should learn in school? There are two ways to answer these questions.

The first requires an examination of school practices as they currently exist. Eighty percent of what is learned in school involves rote memorization (Cunningham, 1987). This activity is of questionable value, given the fact that 65% of what is learned is forgotten in about a month (Cronback, 1965). In addition, many students refuse to memorize the information required. They do not consider such facts sufficiently useful or the competition to acquire them to be worth the effort. Without meaningful learning opportunities and the motivation to become involved, what most students learn is of low quality (Glasser, 1990). Much of the school curriculum is also out of date soon after it is taught. For example, the sum total of scientific knowledge doubles about every 5.5 years at the current rate, which is also accelerating. By the time the average medical student completes training, half of all the information acquired in medical school is obsolete (Cross, 1985). The knowledge explosion has created so much valuable information that determining what should be learned in school is, to a large extent, arbitrary. With a little coaching, students themselves can make adequate selections.

Greater personal motivation is the second reason why it is wise to let children have a significant role in deciding what they learn. Greater effort can be expected from students who are allowed to help determine their own curriculum. More learning will consequently take place. In addition to information, students must learn to make better decisions, an ability that is critical for living in our complex modern world. When children complete school, real-life situations demand responsible autonomy. How will students learn to be self-determined if during school their freedom is consistently held in check? How will they ever learn to make responsible decisions if during school they are not permitted to decide even routine matters? How will they maintain an interest in lifelong learning under such conditions? Children not only need to have the opportunity to make decisions, but they also need to be taught how to make decisions effectively. Children should be engaged in projects in which thinking and problem solving play a central part. Many complex problems confront children: dysfunctional families, peer pressure, the development of an identity, sexuality, love, acceptance. Without the help of knowledgeable and caring adults, children often turn to alcohol and other drugs to escape their problems. These problems, however, can be used as an integral part of the learning process. Sensitive teachers can assist students in developing important thinking skills in an atmosphere of freedom while at the same time helping them find valid solutions to their immediate problems. Students thus attain a growing sense of personal autonomy and thereby are empowered to make their own choices in a responsible manner. Better behavior can be expected from these students.

Consistency Between Discipline and Instructional Methods

Consistency between philosophy and practice is one of the least talked about yet most important educational considerations. Because consistency often has such a low priority, it is natural to expect inconsistency from teachers in both teaching and discipline. Maintaining consistency between various educational practices, however, has several important benefits.

First, students have an easier time interpreting expectations. If they are led to believe that they have some degree of independence and then experience excessive domination and control, they will be justifiably confused. Although students' confusion and associated dissatisfaction are not commonly considered significant, they do have a direct bearing on how successful students will be in school and how well-disciplined they will be. Preoccupation with issues of freedom and control often provides the basis for students' unrest and commonly thwarts students' learning.

A second benefit of maintaining consistency is better educational practice. When consistency is emphasized, greater effort is given to clarifying principles and applying them appropriately. If principles and practices are thought out more thoroughly, instruction is improved. In determining principles to apply in educational practice, teachers can take advantage of the careful thinking and research of others that is available in the literature.

Maintaining consistency also has a positive impact on teachers' commitment. This third benefit is perhaps the most convincing reason to support the application of educational philosophy to the development of school curricula. When teachers are committed, they are more likely to create good educational programs. Committed teachers ensure that their students are successful. Commitment comes when teachers determine for themselves the principles they will apply in their teaching.

The instructional methods teachers use should be based on their educational philosophy. Generally, the methods selected and the way they are applied depend on the relative autonomy a particular teacher provides students. Some methods can readily be applied regardless of the autonomy orientation of one's teaching philosophy. Others are less adaptable to variations in philosophy. For example, an English teacher may assign students to read a novel or write a paper. If autonomy is emphasized, students would be able to select the novel they read or decide on the topic for their paper and the format to use in writing it. Teachers who exercise more control would probably assign the entire class the same book to read as well as a particular topic for their paper. The book would likely be analyzed with criteria specified by the teacher, and the format for the paper would also have to follow specified teacher expectations. If consistency were desired, structured teachers would use behavior modification, assertive discipline, or the Jones model for their discipline program. More autonomy-oriented teachers would be more comfortable using teacher effectiveness training, transactional analysis, judicious discipline, reality therapy/choice theory, or logical consequences.

Cooperative Versus Competitive Learning

One of the most critical decisions teachers make is whether they will provide their students cooperative learning opportunities or use traditional competitive learning methods. The decision to use cooperative or competitive learning depends on whether freedom or control is emphasized. This question also forms the basis on which to decide the kind of discipline to be used. When education is based on the principle of autonomy, cooperative learning can be incorporated in the instructional program, and a discipline approach such as logical consequences, transactional analysis, or reality therapy/choice theory can be used. When control by the teacher is emphasized, competitive learning along with behavior modification or assertive discipline can be employed.

In competitive learning, students usually work independently and then take competitive examinations for their grades. Because the number of high grades is often limited, only a few students can obtain them. This scarcity encourages students to look out for their own interests and to avoid helping their peers. In some instances, students sabotage the efforts of one another for the sake of grades.

The most telling attribute of competition is that some students must fail so that others can succeed. This seems quite all right in America, where competition has become almost a state religion. To question the appropriateness of competition is viewed as suspiciously un-American by many (Kohn, 1992, p. 2). Competition comes in a variety of forms. Some competitions, like college admissions, do not require participants to interact. They may not even be aware of one another. Others, like war and tennis, require interaction. In tennis, success depends on the player's ability to hit the ball so that the opponent is unable to return it. Each player tries to best the opponent by forcing him or her to make errors. In golf or beauty contests, participants may be aware of one another, but their competition is not interactive.

Sometimes competition occurs without our even being aware of it initially. Perhaps the most extreme case of this is when students are ranked and placed on the basis of their grades or test scores without even being aware such placements are competitive. In some cases, students are very much aware that their academic success depends on not only their own good performance but also their classmates' low performance. They realize that grade distribution is regulated by a "normal" bell-shaped curve. There are a limited number of high grades and an equal number of low or failing grades. The knowledge that personal academic success depends on the failure of others has stimulated some students to interfere in devious ways with the successful achievement of their peers. Removing critical study materials from the library and cheating on tests are common tactics to raise one's grades relative to classmates.

A number of myths regarding competition are generally accepted in our society. They include the following:

1. Competition is an unavoidable fact of life. It is part of human nature.
2. Competition motivates us to do our best. We would cease being productive if we didn't compete.
3. Contests provide the best, if not the only, way to have a good time.
4. Competition builds character and promotes self-confidence.

Contrary to the preceding myths, the majority of human activity in all societies is not competitive but cooperative. This cooperative attribute has been found even among toddlers and infants (Yarrow, Scott, & Waxler, 1973). Not even natural selection requires competition; on the contrary, it discourages it. Survival demands that individuals work with rather than against one another. Whatever competition does exist is superficial and superimposed on an essential, mutual interdependence. A growing number of anthropologists are concluding that cooperation—not brain size or the use of tools, and certainly not aggressiveness—defined the first humans (Kohn, 1992, p. 34).

In addition to not being inherent in humans, competition is not much of a motivator—a myth that is deeply imbedded in the schools. Cooperation is a better motivator, as demonstrated in a meta-analysis completed by D. W. Johnson, Maruyama, Johnson, Nelson, and Skoin (1981). They reviewed 122 studies from 1924 to 1980 and found that in 65 studies cooperation promoted higher achievement than competition. Only 8 studies favored competition, while in 36 studies no differences were found.

It appears that, at least in sport, competition should promote better performance levels. Actually, the pursuit of victory reduces the level of performance in sport. Apparently, concern about winning distracts the competitor's attention from achieving excellence (W. D. Johnson, 1979, p. 446).

The idea that competition provides the best way to enjoy yourself is another myth accepted at face value. Winners may experience enjoyment, but losers seldom do. Humans are more likely to gain enjoyment out of play than competition. Play is voluntary and is chosen because it is pleasing. Play is something we like to do for its own sake. The end result is of little consequence. Competition, on the other hand, focuses on outcomes and strips many activities of their zest.

Some activities have both cooperative and competitive components. Football, as well as some kinds of cooperative learning models, like team games and tournaments, have both elements. In these team activities, participants are led to accept the value and naturalness of having adversarial relationships. They conclude that cooperation is used only as a means to achieve victory. In the process, participants commonly see hostility and even aggression as legitimate. They also learn to accept conformity and authoritarianism. The usual display of dislike for rival teams in sport is evidence of this. The same hostility has been found among participants in cooperative learning where team members cooperate with one another but compete against other teams.

The idea that competition builds character and self-confidence has long been accepted. However, competitiveness is really a deficit-motivated trait. Being an outstanding performer in some activity can be something we choose to do, but outperforming others is experienced as something we have to do to validate ourselves. Self-esteem is at stake. Low self-esteem appears to be the root of competition in many cases. In competition participants find a way to satisfy an aching need to prove themselves and an approved mechanism for doing so at other people's expense. However, good psychological health requires one to think good of oneself regardless of what happens in life. In competition, unfortunately, one's self-esteem depends on the uncertain outcome of the contest, making self-esteem conditional. It should be noted that competitions are usually public events, thus accentuating the necessity of winning and the terror of losing. Ironically, winning doesn't necessarily provide comfort for the victor. Winning is not permanent. There is always the next competitive event where the necessity of having to prove oneself continues. Under these conditions, it is no wonder that competitors experience little sense of personal control (Kohn, 1992, pp. 99–105).

The true value of competition can be seriously questioned. Keep in mind that it is responsible for illegalities in political campaigns, scientific fraud, corporate deceptions, the use of performance-enhancing drugs in sport, as well as a plethora of cheating strategies in the classroom. Cooperation, in contrast, has far more favorable effects on individual and group productivity, individual learning, social relations, self-esteem, attitudes, and a sense of responsibility to other group members. This has been established by hundreds of studies despite the widely held ideology about the relative benefits of competition (Kohn, 1992, p. 162).

Cooperative learning makes the success of each student dependent on the achievement of group members. Group members are encouraged to cooperate rather than compete. All cooperative learning approaches encourage group interdependence. In some instances, the learning program is regulated so that students can learn what they need to know only from one of their peers. In other cases, students cannot complete their learning projects without help from others. In some cooperative learning approaches, the grade given to individual group members is a group average; this method of assigning grades, of course, is supposed to stimulate group cooperation and achievement. Students exercise varying amounts of autonomy in deciding what they will learn. Some approaches give students a choice about the nature and pace of what they learn. Students may even decide when and how they are evaluated in some cases.

For example, in Jigsaw II each member of the group becomes an expert in a particular assigned topic as members of an expert group. They then teach their own group. Individual test scores are added together to form a team score (Slavin, 1986, 1995). With Original Jigsaw each team member becomes skilled in different sections of an assigned topic and thus is the only possessor of unique information. This creates greater intragroup dependence (Aronson, Blaney, Stephan, Sikes, & Snapp, 1978). In Co-op Co-op cooperative learning, group members select a topic from among several presented. The topic is divided into components with each group member researching and reporting to the group on one of them. A total group presentation is then made to the class (Kagan, 1985). Both Student Teams Achievement Divisions (STAD) and Teams-Games-Tournaments (TGT) focus on the mastery of teacher presented material. Group members help one another master the material. Individual achievements are included in a group score. With STAD, evaluation is in a regular paper and pencil format. With TGT a tournament is held, with students answering questions orally. Question difficulty is adjusted to reflect the previous performance of team members (Slavin, 1986, 1995).

All of the preceding cooperative learning groups are organized heterogeneously in terms of gender, achievement levels, race, and other relevant factors. However, Student-Directed Cooperative Learning allows for students to determine both group membership as well as the topics each group studies. No restrictions are placed on the topics selected as long as they are appropriate for the particular course of study (Edwards, 1996).

Motivating Student Learning

Motivation refers to the initiation, direction, intensity, and persistence of behavior, particularly goal-directed behavior. Little children seem to be perpetually in a quest to learn about their environment and put it to their use. Once children are in school, the intensity of their desire to learn wanes and continues to do so as long as they remain in school. In addition children in the early years of school show more positive self-concepts and higher success expectations. Younger children also tend to be motivated more intrinsically. The longer they are in school, the more motivation shifts to extrinsic forms like grades (Brophy, 1998).

Most contemporary views of student motivation focus on its cognitive and goal-oriented features. From this perspective human motivation is a personal, internal phenomenon. This represents a significant departure from earlier beliefs, which emphasized behavioral theory. In the behavioral view humans are depicted as relatively passive except in response to reinforcers that satisfy basic drives or needs. Behaviorists believe appropriate behavior has to be shaped through systematic application of reinforcers made contingent on the desired behavior. At the present time cognitive models of motivation have gained in prominence and place more emphasis on learners' subjective needs and goals. These models include reinforcement as a component but portray it as mediated by the individual. In other words, students have control over their behavior, which can be influenced to some degree by external rewards.

Need theories were the first to emerge as alternatives to behavioristic thinking. In this view, motivation is a matter of inborn, universal needs. These include physiological needs, safety needs, love needs, esteem needs, and needs for self-actualization and function in a hierarchy with the first on the list having to be satisfied before the next becomes active (Maslow, 1962). Now theorists talk more about goals than needs. There is greater acknowledgment that humans are more proactive in deciding what they want to do and why they want to do it. Goals actively sought include the following:

1. Affective goals: entertainment, tranquility, happiness, pleasurable bodily sensations, and physical well-being
2. Cognitive goals: exploration to satisfy one's curiosity, attaining understanding, engaging in intellectual creativity, and maintaining positive self-evaluations
3. Subjective organization goals: unity (experiencing a spiritual sense of harmony or oneness with people, nature, or a greater power) and transcendence (experiencing optimal or extraordinary states of functioning that go beyond ordinary experience)
4. Self-assertive social relationship goals: experiencing a sense of individuality, self-determination, superiority (in comparisons with others), and resource acquisition (obtaining material and social support from others)
5. Integrative social relationship goals: belongingness, social responsibility (meeting one's ethical and social obligations), equity (promoting fairness and justice), and resource provision (giving material and social support to others)
6. Task goals: mastery, task creativity, management (handling everyday tasks with organization and efficiency), material gain, and safety (Ford, 1992)

When classroom motivation efforts focus on student goals, teachers emphasize supportive relationships and collaborative learning arrangements for students. Students are encouraged to adopt learning goals and are persuaded to focus their energies on learning without becoming distracted by fear of embarrassment and failure or resentment for being assigned tasks that they view as pointless or inappropriate.

The shift from behavioristic theories to personal goal-directed ones is perhaps best documented in the current emphasis on theories of intrinsic motivation. These theories emphasize free choice and behavior that is an outgrowth of curiosity, spontaneity, and personal interests. No separate motivating consequences are needed. Spontaneous interest and enjoyment in an experience are sufficient to drive learning. From this perspective, motivation depends on satisfying three innate psychological needs: *competence* (developing and exercising skills for manipulating and controlling the environment), *autonomy* (self-determination in deciding what to do and how to do it), and *relatedness* (affiliation with others through prosocial relationships). This means that students are inherently motivated to desire connections to others, to function effectively, and to feel a sense of personal control and initiative while doing so (Deci & Ryan, 1985, 1991).

Some theorists believe that to capitalize on intrinsic motivation students must be able to freely select their own learning activities. Others point out that self-selection has more application in play or recreation activities than in work or learning activities. Even when students are intrinsically motivated to learn, their learning usually features leisurely explorations to satisfy curiosity rather than sustained efforts to achieve critical learning objectives. In addition, even when intrinsically motivated learning is goal oriented, it tends to require special conditions rarely present in the classroom (Brophy, 1998). The counterargument made is that learning that is self-regulated *is* the play and recreation of humans and that learning conditions can and should be created in schools that are free of the impediments that deter intrinsic motivation. The controlled management of student learning is precisely why students are not motivated to learn and do not feel responsible for the quality of their school work (Glasser, 1998).

HELPING FAILURE-PRONE STUDENTS LEARN

Students lack motivation to learn for various reasons. In some cases they may have limited ability and experience difficulty keeping up and consequently develop chronically low expectations while desensitizing themselves to failure. Others develop learned helplessness from attributing their performance to low ability. A third group of students who have a lot of difficulty are those who are obsessed with the need to protect their self-worth and who thus focus on performance goals rather than learning goals.

Teachers can help students overcome preoccupation about self-worth by helping students recognize their own abilities.

Low achievers can be helped by first individualizing activities and assignments. With greater individualization, the difficulty level of tasks can be reduced. Multisensory input sources can be used rather than expecting students to get information from a single source like the textbook. Once the strongest learning modality of these children is recognized, more learning activities can be cast in ways to emphasize their strengths. Learning activities can also emphasize personal interests and be kept within an appropriate range of the student's ability.

Low achievers can also be helped by structuring learning tasks more carefully. This may involve repeating instructions, modeling the task, providing detailed instructions regarding what must be done, explicitly stating the desired level of accomplishment, and setting time limits within which the work must be completed. Teachers can also provide task assistance or tutoring. This might be done either by the teacher, an aide, or a classmate. The help given might include rephrasing questions and providing hints, giving praise, requiring revisions of unacceptable work, and promoting relationships between low achievers and their more able peers. Finally, teachers can try to maintain motivation by providing encouragement, promoting realistic goal setting, informing parents of their children's successes, using performance contracts, and grading students in terms of their improvement rather than making comparisons between them and the rest of the class (McIntyre, 1989).

Unlike low achievers, who commonly fail despite how hard they try, students with learned helplessness fail because they don't try. Learned helplessness can be found among students at all levels of academic ability. These children have low initial success expectancies, give up quickly when encountering difficulty, attribute success to luck, and have low estimates about future achievements. Learned helplessness is especially likely to occur in classrooms where the teacher uses controlling rather than autonomy-supporting teaching and learning strategies and where students have been taught to accept an extrinsic motivational orientation (Boggiano et al., 1992).

It is suggested that teachers help students overcome failure syndrome problems by practicing the following:

1. Guarantee that students experience success regularly, provide them recognition for real effort, and show appreciation for their progress.
2. Project positive expectations.
3. Emphasize personal causation in students' learning by allowing them to plan and set goals, make choices, and use self-evaluation procedures to check their progress.
4. Provide activities that help students appreciate their positive qualities.
5. Promote positive recognition from peers (Wlodkowski, 1978).

Children with learned helplessness also benefit from attribution retraining. This consists of providing a planned series of experiences, couched within an achievement context in which modeling, socialization, practice, and feedback are used to teach them (1) to concentrate on what they try to learn without worrying about failing, (2) to deal with mistakes by retracing their steps to find where they slipped up and by analyzing the problem to find a more reasonable approach, and (3) to attribute their failures to insufficient effort, lack of information, or use of ineffective strategies rather than lack of ability (Craske, 1985). These efforts are necessary because success alone is not enough.

Even a steady diet of success will not change an established pattern of learned help-lessness. Rather, students should experience controlled exposure to failure. Only in this way can they eventually conclude that their successes are not exclusively due to luck and that failure can be avoided through constant, steady effort (Brophy, 1998).

Students who experience a preoccupation with their self-worth focus their attention on performance goals instead of learning goals. The most powerful strategies for dealing with these problems emphasize prevention rather than cures. Covington (1992) recommends the following six strategies:

1. Arrange engaging assignments for students that appeal to their curiosity and personal interests and that provide challenging yet manageable goals. Let students have a choice in what they do and some control of the level of challenge they accept.
2. Arrange a reward system that allows all students to receive the desired rewards. Reward students for setting meaningful goals, posing challenging questions, and working to satisfy their curiosity rather than reinforcing them for various performances.
3. Help students make a connection between their efforts and achievements. Help them set realistic goals and develop confidence in reaching them.
4. Help students learn to take pride in personal accomplishments and their developing expertise, and to minimize the attention given to competition and social comparisons. Help them achieve a feeling of self-worth through their achievement efforts.
5. Promote positive beliefs about ability. Help them see that their intelligence is not a given amount, but that they can increase it with effort and learning.
6. The teacher should emphasize the teacher's role as a resource person not an authority figure.

INTRINSIC MOTIVATION

Until recently, motivation theorists generally depicted intrinsic motivation and extrinsic motivation as incompatible opposites and cautioned teachers against using extrinsic reinforcers lest they erode their students' intrinsic motivation to learn. Now it is conceded that extrinsic incentives can be used in ways that do not undermine intrinsic motivation. However, there is still a preference for using intrinsic motivation (Brophy, 1998). Intrinsically motivated actions are performed out of interest and require no external prods, promises, or threats. These actions are expressed as wholly self-determined and emanate from a personal sense of self. They are pursued when students feel free from external pressures (Deci & Ryan, 1991, 1994). Extrinsically motivated tasks, on the other hand, are usually performed with incentives or other external pressures. To make it seem like teacher expectations have at least some self-determined components, Deci and Ryan (1994) suggest three strategies: (1) provide students with meaningful rationales that enable them to understand the purpose of a learning activity and its importance to them personally; (2) acknowledge students' feelings when asking them to do something they don't want to do; and (3) use a teaching style that emphasizes choice rather than control.

Deci and Ryan (1994) advocate movement along a continuum from external regulation, which involves rewards, pressures, or constraints, to a point of integrated regulation where students are mostly self-determined. Often, autonomy is seen as individuals regulating their own behavior without regard for others. However, along with autonomy, students need to develop a sense of competence and relatedness. This makes learning in a community essential. In a learning community, students act under the influence of others and in the process modify personal desires to fit others' expectations as long as adjustments are not excessive. In this way students are able to achieve autonomy along with a true sense of connection within the learning community.

Brophy (1998) makes a distinction between motivation to learn and intrinsic motivation. *Motivation to learn* involves students' tendencies to find academic activities meaningful and profitable while trying to get the benefit from them that teachers intend. This is a cognitive response in contrast to the more affective response involved with intrinsic motivation. Motivation to learn, therefore, involves attempts by students to make sense of learning activities, understand related knowledge, and master the skills promoted. Thus students can be motivated to learn from an activity whether or not they find its content interesting or its processes enjoyable. They may not be able to choose the activity, but they can get involved and achieve a sense of understanding and accomplishment. This assumes that the kind of activity provided has the potential to satisfy these ends. The activity must have inherent value that students are able to adopt and willingly pursue. Even then, some students may choose not to become involved. This is because the very act of choosing has enormous reinforcing properties. Students may actively learn things they choose but reject the very same activities when they are chosen by the teacher.

Self-regulated learning is the highest form of cognitive engagement in the classroom. It involves active learning in which students assume responsibility for motivating themselves to learn with understanding. This should be the ultimate goal of all motivational efforts in school (Rohrkemper & Carno, 1988). This kind of learning is promoted when teachers encourage both intrinsic motivation and motivation to learn. It occurs when teachers provide a variety of learning activities and frequently offer students choices to accommodate their individual preferences and interests. Both student–teacher and student–student discussions are featured in this kind of learning, as is a focus on in-depth study of topics that develop increased understanding of important, meaningful information. Learning communities, in which student autonomy is promoted, add to self-regulated learning.

Multiple Intelligences

During the first years of life, children become proficient in their native language, singing songs, riding bikes, dancing, organizing their belongings, throwing and catching balls, along with dozens of other skills. In addition, they develop powerful theories of how the world works and how their own minds work. This they do with little formal tutelage. These very young children, who readily master symbol systems like language and art forms like music as well as developing complex theories of the universe and intricate theories of the mind, often experience the greatest difficulties learning what they are taught in school (Gardner, 1991).

Not all children experience the same kind of learning difficulties when they enter school. Although certain features do characterize the learning of the vast majority of students, recent cognitive research documents the extent to which students possess different kinds of minds and therefore learn, remember, perform, and understand in different ways. These different ways are referred to by Gardner (1991) as *multiple intelligences*. There are eight distinct ways of knowing and representing the world; each is an intelligence unto itself with its own unique rules, codes, and symbols. Various learners operate out of different intelligences and consequently approach problems and learning in different ways. Each person has a different mix of these intelligences with the tendency to have a predominating learning orientation. The following are the eight intelligences identified by Gardner along with descriptions of how they can be focused on in a variety of classroom settings (Campbell, Campbell, & Dickinson, 1999):

1. *Bodily-kinesthetic*:   Creating and understanding meaning through movement. Common activities that apply to this kind of learning include drama, role playing, simulations, dancing, games, demonstrations, physical exercises and sports, and field trips. Many of these activities can be applied in various kinds of classrooms. A person who has been educated kinesthetically has body awareness, space awareness, tactile discriminating ability, grace and coordination, mastery of nonverbal communication, authentic acting ability, a flair for the creative and dramatic in various artistic expressions, the ability to make appropriate physical movements in a variety of games and sporting activities, and the ability to use various kinds of manipulatives.

2. *Linguistic*:   Creating and understanding meaning through language. Stories or poetry renditions often serve as a good way to focus the development of these skills. These can be modeled by the teacher, and stories in particular can be used to introduce the content of various subjects. Storytelling is also a good way to illustrate the dimensions of various cultures, as is role playing. Linguistic development occurs when students compare their own ideas to those they listen to and attempt to draw conclusions and formulate questions for further study and consideration. It also helps to routinely examine what they hear in terms of its appropriateness, soundness, and how well it relates to their lives.

3. *Logical-mathematical*:   Using highly organized, logical and rule-based systems to create and understand meaning. This involves the creation of and understanding of number systems. To help students engage in logical-mathematical thinking, teachers should (1) use diverse questioning strategies, (2) pose open-ended problems for students to solve, (3) have students construct models of key concepts, (4) have students predict and verify logical outcomes, (5) have students discern patterns and connections in diverse phenomena, (6) ask students to justify their statements or opinions, and (7) provide students opportunities for observation and investigation.

One of the best ways to help students think logically is to have them engage in inquiry activities. In a science class, for example, they might observe some phenomenon, think up questions regarding their observation, and devise experiments to find answers to their questions. Questioning strategies that engage students in higher-level thinking are also useful tools for encouraging logical thought. Students can also be asked to discern patterns or break codes. Patterns are evident in nearly all traditional subjects. In the life sciences, patterns of plant and animal interactions are observed in the various ecosystems. In art, patterns are apparent in the history of painting, and in the structure of novels, poetry, and music composition. Patterns also occur in mathematical models, architecture, clothing designs, and the characteristics of various elements and compounds in chemistry.

4. *Visual-spatial*:   Creating and understanding meaning through visual and spatial symbols and conceptions. All classrooms have potential for the use of visual-spatial learning. To encourage this kind of learning, the teacher should provide a variety of tools and materials that students can use to create objects and displays of various kinds. Creations could include flow charts representing complex concepts, visual outlines of stories that students are composing, and concept maps representing the relationships between interrelated ideas.

In a science classroom, students might be asked to create a model for a cell with all its organelles. In math, children might be taught fractions by having them cut pieces of paper into relative parts. In learning language arts, students might create puppets, paint murals and backdrops, as well as illustrate literature through construction of storyboards.

5. *Musical*:   Creating and understanding meaning through musical symbols. Skills in this domain include composing and performing all kinds of music as well as being expert in musical criticism. The stage between age 4 and 6 appears to be a critical period for development of sensitivity to sound and pitch. During this time a rich musical environment can provide the foundation for later musical development. Music is an aural language in which the three basic components of pitch, rhythm, and timbre can be arranged in countless combinations and give rise to a remarkable variety of musical sounds. Because of the strong connection between music and emotions, a positive emotional environment can be created in the classroom conducive to learning. Music can be used to heighten the suspense, sadness, tragedy, or joy of stories from literature and history. Humorous songs can add zest and warmth to most any classroom.

Music in education involves not only listening and performing but composing. In listening, students' attention might be focused on the thoughts and images music evokes along with the feelings. Students might also be asked to listen for techniques the composer used to create a particular effect and then explain the effects of particular pieces of music in creating feelings and images. In playing music, students might be asked to incorporate some emotion or feeling and then poll classmates to determine if the identified emotion was successfully stimulated. Students can compose music for a variety of purposes. They might create background music, music that is an integral part of a play, music to generate or enhance emotions, or music to help in memorizing important conceptual information.

6. *Interpersonal*:   Creating and obtaining meaning through the social world. This involves skill in understanding society and its problems and processes and the procedures that promote group work. One of the needed skills is the ability to manage conflict. Students must be helped to understand that conflict can be dealt with by making sure that individual needs are being met, that power is equitably distributed, that communication is effective, that values and priorities are considered and properly addressed in activities and deliberations, that perceptions of situations vary from per-

son to person, and that learning approaches and personalities differ and can have enhancing or denigrating effects on group processes. Learning about and appreciating diverse points of view are critical aspects of promoting interpersonal intelligence. Working on projects alongside members of various age groups, classes, and racial groups can help develop this appreciation.

7. *Intrapersonal*:   Creating and understanding meaning through intrapersonal symbols. Intrapersonal intelligence involves self-reflection philosophically, psychologically, and religiously. To develop the capacity for self-reflection, children need to be taught higher-level thinking skills. These skills need to be taught in connection with an understanding of emotions and feelings. Emotions need to be understood and expressed in ways that promote a sense of well-being. Greater intellectual capacity is also necessary in understanding values and building a viable value system. Students should understand how their personal preferences and values must be consistent with social expectations and standards. The development of an integrated personality depends on a full understanding of self and self-expression that is consistent with important societal morals and ideals.

Goals and ambitions along with self-reflection can be expressed in journal writing. Students can be encouraged to explore their own identities through writing that explores self-awareness, self-acceptance, self-actualization, and self-disclosure. They might write about what they have gained from life experiences, from interactions with others, from their views of the world, and from images of the persons they want to be compared with who they currently believe they are. They could also write regarding what they believe are their strengths, what they are trying to live up to, the changes they find they have to cope with, and some things in life they may have to live without and what they believe the result of this will be. They might also be asked to reflect on their own level of self-esteem and how this could be improved.

8. *Naturalist*:   Using the natural world as the means for creating and understanding meaning. This kind of learning focuses on the ability to make meaningful distinctions in the natural world and to visualize patterns and relationships between plants and animals (Carreiro, 1998; Gardner, 1993).

The essential capacities of this intelligence include observing, reflecting, making connections, classifying, integrating, and communicating perceptions of the natural and the man-made world. To encourage the development of naturalist intelligence, teachers might have students make and record observations, conduct research, and formulate theories that explain how they interpret their research. Themes for study might include interdependence, change, adaptation, balance, resources, diversity, competition, collaboration, interrelationships, cycles, patterns, and populations.

Classrooms filled with tools for observation like microscopes and telescopes along with plenty of reference materials, laboratory facilities, and specimens of various kinds provide a way for students with naturalistic intelligence to access the naturalistic curriculum. Schools might also have outdoor arboreta, ponds, and other outdoor facilities for more naturalistic orientations for the study of plants and animals. These facilities provide a way for children to sharpen their observation skills and to observe plants and animals in a more realistic environment. These as well as other settings made accessible through field trips can help children hone their ability to perceive relationships, collect specimens, do naturalistic studies, and come to understand the interdependence of the earth's flora and fauna.

▼ SUMMARY

Few students feel sufficiently successful in competitive classrooms. All students would like to get As, but As seem to be reserved for just a successful few. Often, patterns of success or failure are established early in life before various skills have had a chance to mature. In some cases, children enter school already able to do some of the things school is designed to teach. Some children, for example, already know how to read and are immediately singled out by teachers and reinforced. The early ability to achieve what teachers are looking for is a good guarantee of continued success. The sooner children show promise, the more likely they will be to garner a disproportionate amount of recognition by the teacher. As these children go through school, the achievement gap between them and their "less able peers" gradually widens.

Cooperative learning provides hope for altering this unhappy situation. It provides a way for students to assert themselves without the discomfort of always being compared with their peers and found lacking. Properly organized cooperative learning can help all children experience success and feel more accepted in school. Classrooms thus become more exciting places to learn because students have greater control over what they learn and because the atmosphere in which learning takes place is more fun. In cooperative learning programs, teachers can capitalize on the motivation students already have for learning by involving them in decisions about what they learn and then allowing them to pursue their own interests in their own style.

Students will also establish better relationships with their peers and learn how to get along more successfully with them. When children report what they consider to be their most significant school experiences, they rarely tell of something they have done alone. More often, they report experiences involving others, such as winning a basketball game or participating in a school play. Almost never do they report receiving an A or completing a difficult assignment for a class as their "moment of glory" (Slavin, 1986). Succeeding in group activities is far more exhilarating than solitary success. It is apparently more satisfying to succeed when it involves helping others become successful as well. Unfortunately, most cooperative experiences in school are confined to physical education classes and extracurricular activities. Rarely do students have these experiences in academics.

Cooperative learning holds the promise of making school more satisfying and exciting and at the same time improving the achievement levels of all students. It precludes the causes of discipline problems associated with the competitive classroom, so many classroom disruptions may never materialize. In addition, when group support is elicited, many potential problems can be prevented, and those problems that do arise can be solved much more easily. Cooperative learning is likely to be more fulfilling than regular competitive learning because cooperative learning can better provide the diversity and self-determination necessary to satisfy students' varied needs (Savage, 1991).

Competition may have debilitating effects on students. Grading provides competition at its worst because only a limited number of students can obtain high grades. Competition promotes poor self-concept and low productivity. Cooperation provides a better format for success in society than competition.

Theories of motivation have changed from having a behavioristic orientation to one of students' being goal directed. Children are intrinsically motivated to satisfy affective, cognitive, social, and task goals. In school, though it is preferred that intrinsic motivation provide the direction for learning, educators may feel that students should pursue goals they specify. Extrinsic reinforcement could then be employed to encourage learning.

Some students are motivated to succeed, while others are motivated to avoid failure. Students who are motivated to learn pursue learning with vigor, while those motivated to avoid failure need their teachers to help them believe that they can have control over their successes and that effort can increase their chances of learning effectively. The establishment of learning communities in the classroom often provides a more attractive learning environment for less successful students.

It has been found that children learn in different ways. Gardner (1991) has identified eight intelligences that influence how children approach problems and process information. Traditional schools cater to just a few of these, leaving some children with little means for school success. Learning activities need to be devised from various perspectives to ensure all students can use their most adept learning modality.

CENTRAL IDEAS

1. When educational practice is consistent with educational theory,
    a. Students will be better able to interpret expectations.
    b. The instructional program will be improved.
    c. Teachers will increase their commitment.
2. Competitive learning limits students' success and promotes poor self-concept.
3. Human motivation is primarily an internal phenomenon that is directed toward individual goals. Individuals seek affective, cognitive, social, as well as task-oriented goals.
4. Motivation depends on satisfying the needs of competence, autonomy, and relatedness. Thus students are inherently motivated to desire connections to others, to function effectively, and to feel a sense of personal control and initiative while doing so.
5. Instead of being motivated to learn, some children are motivated to avoid failure. Their primary concern is to preserve their reputation and a sense of well-being. This deflects their learning orientation from feeling personally capable of succeeding if they give enough effort to believing their intelligence is set and that they have no control over their success. Achievement is greater when children attribute their performance to internal, controllable causes rather than to external, uncontrollable ones.

6. The most powerful strategies for dealing with students' preoccupation with self-worth emphasize prevention rather than cures. They involve providing choices for students that cater to their curiosity, helping students see connections between their efforts and achievements, helping students take pride in personal accomplishments, and helping students see that their intelligence can be increased through effort and learning.
7. Each person has a different mix of eight basic intelligences. They include: bodily-kinesthetic, linguistic, logical-mathematical, visual-spatial, musical, interpersonal, intrapersonal, and naturalist.
8. Teachers can capitalize on the inherent interests of students by allowing them to choose what they learn. If teachers alone determine the curriculum, they have to motivate students to learn what they otherwise would not or what they may initially refuse to learn.
9. It is a myth that competition is natural, motivates us to do our best, provides pleasure, and builds character.

▼ QUESTIONS AND ACTIVITIES

QUESTIONS TO CONSIDER

1. What kinds of curricula are most appropriately used with cooperative learning?
2. How can the theory of multiple intelligences be applied to the subject you plan to teach?
3. What is the function of self-determination in classroom learning?
4. How can intrinsic motivation be emphasized in your classroom?

CLASSROOM ACTIVITIES

1. Divide the class into teams of four members each. Have each group member learn one of the following topics from Chapter 13 and teach it to group members:
   a. Consistency between discipline and instructional methods
   b. Cooperative learning
   c. Motivation
   d. Multiple intelligences

STUDENT APPLICATIONS

1. Assume you have a class with some students who have learned helplessness and others who are poor learners, along with students with a variety of abilities and interests. Organize a series of lessons that take into account appropriate motivation strategies and cater to multiple intelligences.

EXPLORE YOUR PHILOSOPHY

1. Determine the extent to which cooperative learning is consistent with your philosophy of education.
2. Explore the implications for various teaching strategies in terms of motivation. Decide what strategies you plan to use.
3. Examine your philosophy of teaching in terms of multiple intelligences. Decide how you will acknowledge multiple intelligences in your teaching.

▼ REFERENCES

Aronson, E., Blaney, E., Stephan, C., Sikes, J., & Snapp, M. (1978). *The jigsaw classroom.* Beverly Hills, CA: Sage Publications.

Boggiano, A., Shields, A., Barrett, M., Kellam, T., Thompson, E., Simons, J., & Katz, P. (1992). Helplessness deficits in students: The role of motivational orientation. *Motivation and Emotion, 16,* 271–296.

Brophy, J. (1998). *Motivating students to learn.* Boston: McGraw-Hill.

Campbell, L., Campbell, B., & Dickinson, D. (1999). *Teaching and learning through multiple intelligences* (2nd ed.). Boston: Allyn & Bacon.

Carreiro, P. (1998). *Tales of thinking: Multiple intelligences in the classroom.* York, Maine: Stenhouse Publishers.

Covington, M. (1992). *Making the grade: A self-worth perspective on motivation and school reform.* Cambridge: Cambridge University Press.

Craske, M. (1985). Improving persistence through observational learning and attribution retraining. *British Journal of Educational Psychology, 55,* 138–147.

Cronback, L. (1965). *Educational psychology.* New York: Harcourt, Brace and World.

Cross, K. P. (1985). The rising tide of school reform. *Phi Delta Kappan, 66,* 167–173.

Cunningham, R. T. (1987). What kind of question is that? In W. W. Wilen (Ed.), *Questions, questioning techniques, and effective teaching* (pp. 67–94). Washington, DC: National Education Association.

Darling-Hammond, L. (1997). *The right to learn: A blueprint for creating schools that work.* San Francisco: Jossey-Bass.

Deci, E., & Ryan, R. (1985). *Intrinsic motivation and self-determination in human behavior.* New York: Plenum.

Deci, E., & Ryan, R. (1991). A motivational approach to self: Integration in personality. In R. Dienstbier (Ed.) *Nebraska symposium on motivation. Vol. 38, Perspectives on motivation* (pp. 237–288). Lincoln: University of Nebraska Press.

Deci, E., & Ryan, R. (1994). Promoting self-determined education. *Scandinavian Journal of Educational Research, 38,* 3–14.

Doyle, W. (1986). Classroom organization and management. In M. C. Wittrock (Ed.), *Handbook of research on teaching* (3rd ed., pp. 392–431). New York: Macmillan.

Edwards, C. H. (1996). A naturalistic study of student directed cooperative learning. *Oklahoma Association for Supervision and Curriculum Development Journal, 8*(1), 25–30.

Eisner, E. W. (1992). The federal reforms of schools: Looking for the silver bullet. *Phi Delta Kappan, 73*(9), 722–723.

Ford, M. (1992). *Motivating humans: Goals, emotions, and personal agency beliefs.* Newbury Park, CA: Sage.

Gardner, H. (1983). *Frames of the mind: The theory of multiple intelligences.* New York: Basic Books.

Gardner, H. (1991). *The unschooled mind; How children think and how schools should teach.* New York: Basic Books.

Gardner, H. (1993). *Multiple intelligences: The theory in practice—A reader.* New York: Basic Books.

Glasser, W. (1984). *Control theory: A new explanation of how we control our lives.* New York: Harper & Row.

Glasser, W. (1990). *The quality school.* New York: Harper & Row.

Glasser, W. (1998). *Choice theory: A new psychology of personal freedom.* New York: HarperCollins.

Goodlad, J. I. (1984). *A place called school.* New York: McGraw-Hill.

Jackson, P. (1968). *Life in classrooms.* New York: Holt, Rinehart & Winston.

Johnson, D. W., Maruyama, G., Johnson, R., Nelson, D., & Skoin, L. (1981). Effects of cooperative and individual goal structures on achievement: A meta-analysis. *Psychological Bulletin, 89,* 47–62.

Johnson, W. D. (1979). From here to 2000. In Eitzen, D. S. (Ed.), *Sport and contemporary society: An anthology* (p. 446). New York: St. Martin's.

Kagan, S. (1985). *Cooperative learning resources for teachers.* Riverside: University of California, Department of Psychology.

Kohn, A. (1992). *No contest: The case against competition.* Boston: Houghton Mifflin.

McIntyre, T. (1989). *A resource book for remediating common behavior and learning problems.* Boston: Allyn & Bacon.

Maslow, A. (1962). *Toward a psychology of being.* Princeton, NJ: VanNostrand.

Rohrkemper, R., & Carno, L. (1988). Success and failure on classroom tasks: Adaptive learning and classroom teaching. *Elementary School Journal, 88,* 297–318.

Savage, T. V. (1991). *Discipline for self-control.* Upper Saddle River, NJ: Prentice Hall.

Slavin, R. (1986). *Using student team learning* (3rd ed.). Baltimore: Johns Hopkins Team Learning Project, Center for Research on Elementary and Middle Schools.

Slavin, R. (1995). *Cooperative learning* (2nd ed.). Boston: Allyn & Bacon.

Wlodkowski, R. (1978). *Motivation and teaching; A practical guide.* Washington, DC: National Education Association.

Yarrow, M. R., Scott, P. M., & Waxler, C. Z. (1973). Learning concern for others. *Developmental Psychology, 8,* 240–260.

14

Classroom Management and Teacher–Student Relationships

OBJECTIVES

This chapter is designed to help you

1. Improve your relationships with students and thereby improve classroom discipline.
2. Understand how students' self-concept problems are promoted in the school.
3. Explain what teachers can do to keep their students from developing poor self-concepts.
4. Affirm diversity in culture and language, and provide instruction for minority students that increases the chances of success in school for them and for all students.
5. Understand the nature of gender bias and how to eliminate this problem from school learning materials as well as from teaching practices.
6. Understand the problems faced by exceptional students and how to help them have more successful school experiences.
7. Understand the nature of religious differences and how to deal with school problems having religious implications.
8. Deal with violence in the schools.

Introduction

▼   Cheryl took her seat next to the window and immediately began talking with Lois about the previous night's basketball game. Cheryl was a drummer in the marching band, and Lois was in the color guard. Their conversation centered on half-time activities. Cheryl wanted to know whether Lois had seen Blair at the game, but before Lois could answer, Ms. Cherrington called the class to order. Cheryl muttered to Lois under her breath, "I don't feel like being in class today." Lois nodded in agreement as she crossed her arms on her desk and laid her head on them.

As Ms. Cherrington began the lecture, Cheryl found her mind wandering back to Genene's performance at the game. Genene was one of Ms. Cherrington's "pets." Cheryl laughed quietly and then muttered to herself, "Genene, you can never remember anything. Why can't you, for once, get through a routine without messing up?" She laughed again, loudly enough this time to be heard by those around her, and they turned to see what was so funny. Ms. Cherrington tapped her desk with her pencil to direct the attention of the class to the front of the room. "Who can remember the definition of a simile?" she asked, ignoring the disruption. The students turned back around in their seats as Ms. Cherrington went on with the lesson. Cheryl was still unable to concentrate, however, and her mind soon wandered again. This time she began beating her pencil on her desk as though she were playing an imaginary snare drum. Ms. Cherrington continued to talk as she walked down the aisle past Cheryl's desk. As she went by, she calmly took Cheryl's pencil from her hand and laid it quietly on the desk. She then continued on to the back of the room. "I'm going to ask a very important question about similes," she said, "and I want Allen, Ruth, David, Cheryl, Blaine, and Claron to be prepared to answer it." She paused a moment. "What effect do similes have when you use them in stories?" She paused again and then asked, "Blaine, can you tell us?" Blaine just shook his head. "Cheryl, do you have an answer?"

"I guess they help add life to the story," responded Cheryl.

"Yes, you're right, similes often do add life to stories," said Ms. Cherrington. "Can you think of an example of a simile from the story we read yesterday in class and explain what its effect was?"

Ms. Cherrington was obviously trying to get Cheryl involved in the lesson without causing her any embarrassment. When her classmates turned to look at her, Ms. Cherrington skillfully redirected their attention. Obviously sensing that Cheryl was having trouble concentrating, she tried to bring her back to the matter at hand without putting her on the spot. Teachers like Ms. Cherrington are greatly appreciated by students not only because they avoid embarrassing their students but also because they seem genuinely to care about them.

Successful teachers have good relationships with their students. Good relationships not only lay the groundwork for students' learning, but they are also the keystone of good discipline. Many discipline problems may be prevented because teachers have good relationships with their students and teach interesting and relevant lessons. Positive teacher–student relationships have been shown to produce more positive responses by students in school (Aspy & Roebuck, 1977) as well as higher academic achievement (Brophy & Evertson, 1976). High-achieving students are much more likely than low-achieving students to believe that their teachers approve of them (Morrison & McIntyre, 1969). This perception is consistent with the fact that many teachers favor high achievers (Allington, 1991). Student–teacher relationships also depend on gender and race. Students receive notably different opportunities in classrooms as a function of their gender (M. Sadker, Sadker, & Klein, 1991). In science classes, for example, M. Jones and Wheatley (1990) found that male students receive more positive and negative contact than female students. With regard to race, Leacock (1969) found that teachers generally rated black students as less favorable than white students and showed particular hostility and rejection toward the brightest black students. This is the reverse of the way white students are treated by their teachers. Black male students generally experience a higher rate of rejection than black female students (Ross & Jackson, 1991).

Improving Student–Teacher Relationships

Some teachers do not realize that learning and discipline can be appreciably improved by creating better teacher–student relationships; many of them therefore do not actively work on improving relationships with their students. Some teachers are afraid to encourage personal friendships with students, fearing loss of control in their classrooms. However, being warm and friendly with students actually promotes more positive student behavior.

ASSESSING ATTITUDES

One of the first things teachers might do to improve relationships with students is assess their own attitudes and behaviors toward students. They should ask themselves questions such as

- Am I courteous toward students?
- Do I listen carefully to students' questions and requests?
- Do I listen to students and respect their opinions?
- Do I control my temper when students behave improperly?
- Do I like to be with students?
- Do I treat students fairly?

It is also helpful to discover the attitudes of students toward teachers and the subjects they teach. Teachers should ask students such questions as

- How relevant are the topics covered in this class?
- What topics do you like the most?
- What topics do you like the least?
- Do you believe that the teacher likes you?
- Does the teacher take the time necessary to help you understand difficult concepts?
- Does the teacher treat you courteously?
- Does the teacher have any distracting habits?
- Does the teacher listen to suggestions made by students?
- Do students' needs and interests receive the teacher's attention?

IMPROVING COMMUNICATION SKILLS

Teachers' communication skills are a critical factor in creating and maintaining good student–teacher relationships. Good communication usually helps establish a warmer and more friendly atmosphere in the classroom. Communication involves sending as well as receiving messages.

Sending Messages.   We all send messages, both verbally and nonverbally, but we are generally less aware of the nonverbal than of the verbal messages. However, our nonverbal messages are often very powerful and may even distort the accompanying verbal meaning. Children often become adept at reading the nonverbal messages of their teachers. Children often discover through experience that nonverbal cues are more dependable than verbal information. For example, a teacher who claims to care for students may have a tone of voice or mannerisms that contradict the verbal message. Voice inflections can convey the message that teachers consider students to be dumb or smart, manageable or rebellious, cooperative or antagonistic (V. F. Jones & Jones, 1986). Teachers need to make their nonverbal messages congruent with their verbal ones. Students with behavior problems often experience difficulty interpreting nonverbal cues. These students may mistake a friendly gesture for a hostile one and react negatively (P. J. Cooper & Simonds, 1999).

Teachers can improve relationships with their students by not making coercive demands and by letting students feel that the classroom belongs to them as well as to the teacher. Teachers often insist that students comply with their demands unquestioningly. Students are told where they may sit, what they should learn, when they must submit papers and other work, when they can go to the bathroom, and so on. Some of these demands may be helpful, but others are made exclusively for the convenience of teachers. Sometimes demands are made simply to control. Consequently, students are made to feel that the classroom belongs to the teacher. Teacher–student relationships can be improved if teachers help students realize that they share the classroom and can help determine procedures that are necessary for successful learning there. Active listening and appropriately constructed I-messages can go a long way in maintaining good student–teacher relationships (see Chapter 7).

Teachers need to speak courteously to their students. Commonly used expressions such as *thank you, please,* and *excuse me* are absolutely essential. Courteous teachers not only enhance relationships with students, but they also serve as important role models. Many children speak rudely and even abusively to one another and to adults. They need to realize that such mistreatment interferes with the relationships they wish to establish.

Teachers should be genuinely concerned for their students. They need to find out about the activities of their students outside of class and show an interest in what they are doing. In some cases, teachers will find common hobbies and activities that can establish closer relationships with some students.

There are critical stumbling blocks to effective communication. First is the assumption that the personal needs, desires, and beliefs of others are the same as our own. Second, expressions in one language may carry meanings that can be confusing when translated into a different language. Third, misinterpretation or mistransmission of nonverbal messages may send incorrect or confusing information. Fourth, preconceptions and stereotypes may keep us from being objective. Fifth, premature judgments about others' actions or statements bias our view and shut down communication before it starts (P. J. Cooper & Simonds, 1999). Effective communication with students depends on avoiding these problems.

Receiving Messages.   Effective communication also involves receiving messages. Teachers can communicate genuine interest simply by paying attention to their students, maintaining eye contact, and listening carefully to what they say. Listening skills are extremely important to teachers because they help students feel significant, accepted, and respected. Teachers who listen effectively can help students clarify their feelings and resolve personal conflicts. Unfortunately, some teachers listen halfheartedly to their students and provide superficial answers to students' questions, particularly questions that involve emotions. Rather than try to understand the emotions being expressed, many teachers try to sidestep the situation, often by suggesting that students have little reason to be emotional. Teachers thus avoid having to deal with the discomfort they feel when faced with students' emotions (Ginott, 1971). Teachers who are rated high in effectiveness in coping with problem students are generally more successful dealing with both hostile, aggressive students as well as those who are shy and inhibited (Brophy & McCaslin, 1992). These teachers deal with aggressive behavior by demanding that disruptive students curb their unacceptable behavior and are prepared to back up these demands forcefully. In dealing with more shy students, these teachers hold private talks with them and involve them in special activities or assignments in an effort to draw them out and to minimize stress and embarrassment for them (Brophy & McCaslin, 1992).

As teachers listen to their students, they should give their undivided attention and in an empathetic and nonjudgmental manner seek to understand what is said. With such teachers, students learn (1) that their feelings are acceptable, (2) that their feelings can be expressed openly, and (3) that they can clarify and come to understand feelings that are at first confusing and frightening (V. F. Jones & Jones, 1986). This assurance reduces the tension and anxiety associated with emotions and also increases the chances that their expression will be productive. When feelings are not dealt with openly, they often are expressed in the form of anger, vandalism, or truancy.

Self-Concept and Discipline

The relationships that teachers establish with their students influence the development of students' self-concept, which in turn affects discipline in the classroom. Students with a poor self-concept not only fail to perform well in school, they are also more likely to display unacceptable behavior (Bandura, 1989; Purkey, 1970). Teachers often claim that students who do not perform well are simply unmotivated, that some students just do not want to learn anything. However, students are in fact never unmotivated (Covington & Beery, 1976). They may not be motivated to do what teachers want, but it can never truly be said that they are unmotivated. When students are required to learn what they have no interest in learning, they often do not apply themselves and fail as a result (Deci & Porac, 1978).

In school, one's success or failure depends primarily on test performance. This preoccupation with performance begins surprisingly early in children's school careers. Schools are particularly adept at teaching children, at a very young age, that achievement determines their relative position among their peers. Before children have spent much time in kindergarten, they already are aware of the place they occupy. They can tell you the brightest and dullest of their classmates with comparative ease and often point out this fact with relish (Weiner & Peter, 1973). In the beginning school years, academic performance is influenced primarily by learning readiness. Children whose parents emphasize reading and other school-related tasks, rather than those unrelated to school structure and school achievement, enter school far better prepared to succeed than those whose early experiences fail to promote these skills. As children move through the school system, differences in their performance become more pronounced and visible (Katz & Zigler, 1967). These differences are emphasized by the grades they receive. Special privileges are reserved for children who are academically achieving. This emphasis on schoolwork tends to reinforce the self-concept of students. Some children who experience initial success will continue to do so, and children who are unsuccessful at first will continue to follow a pattern of failure (Dweck & Reppucci, 1973).

Parents too usually place considerable importance on school success, so children are often under pressure from both the school and their parents to be high achievers. If children are low achievers, their self-worth is threatened. Some fear that if they fail in school, they will not be worthy of love and approval. This fear is not unfounded. In our society, human worth tends to be equated with achievement. In practice, people are considered to be only as good as their socially valued achievements (Covington & Beery, 1976). The feelings of inferiority that accompany failure can cause lifelong problems.

Schools, however, allow the possibility of success for only a fraction of the student population. These are the students who get the As and Bs. To some degree, most other students feel a sense of failure (Levine, 1988). The possibility of failure is a constant threat to these students. When they do fail, they may attribute their failure to an innate lack of ability (Dweck, 1991, p. 203; Weiner & Kukla, 1970).

The threat of failure and its attendant lack of self-worth are difficult for children to accept. In their anguish and frustration, some may resort to defense mechanisms. Children employ at least two strategies for maintaining a sense of self-worth when they believe that their chances of academic success are low: avoidance and overstriving.

AVOIDANCE

Sometimes children decide that if they cannot be sure of succeeding, they can at least protect their dignity by orchestrating their own failure (Aronson & Carlsmith, 1962). They accept the premise that they are prone to fail, but they attempt to reject the implication that their failure stems from inability. To avoid this implication, children may arrange circumstances so that their failure can be blamed on something other than a lack of ability. They rationalize that their failure is not an indication of their potential and therefore is not a real measure of their worth. These children become expert at keeping their actual ability a secret (Covington & Beery, 1976). They hide their competence by not performing and not participating. Such students are sometimes referred to as underachievers. They make a virtue of failure to do work that, they claim, is unimportant.

In addition to nonparticipation, failure-avoiding children use other techniques to protect themselves from feelings of unworthiness. They come late to class, claim not to have heard what the assignment was, feign illness, pretend to be busy, and daydream. Because there are usually strong sanctions for not trying, these children often combine nonparticipation with false effort (Birney, Burdick, & Teevan, 1969). If children appear to be making an effort, we usually forgive their lack of productivity because as a culture we value "trying." To convince teachers that they are really doing their best, these children feign attention during class discussions, giving the outward appearance of thinking or adopting quizzical expressions. These efforts are deceptive because the students are not really trying to succeed, only trying to avoid failure. This deception involves a balancing act for students. They must calculate correctly to escape punishment and at the same time avoid putting forth too much effort. They do not believe that they could succeed if they really tried. If they should study hard and still do poorly, they could no longer blame failure on lack of participation. Instead, their ability could be called into question. They therefore try to protect themselves from discovery. When children count their success only in terms of avoiding failure, their learning is impeded. When learning is limited by lack of involvement and deception, the result is detachment, apathy, and passivity. These children may become disenchanted with school and often spend their time being disruptive.

In trying to avoid failure, some children attempt to maintain a sense of personal worth by establishing impossibly high goals for themselves. Teachers are often inclined to hold high expectations for their classes, so they unwittingly collude with these students by supporting their impossible goals, virtually ensuring that they will fail. The children can then claim that their failure to achieve such high goals reveals very little about their ability. If the standards are sufficiently high, their failure seems comparatively small. If only the most able students can reach such goals, then these children cannot be blamed for their failure to achieve them (Covington & Beery, 1976).

Setting goals too low is another technique of failure-avoiding children. They like to achieve easily attainable goals for the same reason that they pretend to work for unreachable goals—neither failing at a difficult task nor succeeding at an easy one reveals much about their real ability. Both approaches help children avoid having to demonstrate what they really can do. These children know that the level of success they are striving for is not real. However, it is a level at which they feel they can at least appear to be successful. They commonly announce their low expectations publicly. In doing so, they have the added advantage of appearing modest (Birney et al., 1969). No one can accuse them of bragging.

Such children know that they can achieve at a higher level. They consequently do not find satisfaction in their performance. Their self-respect is an illusion. However, they prefer this illusion to the possibility of disclosing their presumed lack of ability by doing their best and failing.

OVERSTRIVING

Overstriving is another tactic used by children to maintain their self-respect (Martire, 1956). These children try to escape failure through hard work. Instead of working for success, however, they are working against failure (Dweck & Elliott, 1983). Like underachieving children, overstriving children have the devastating belief that the sole measure of self-worth is school achievement (Covington & Beery, 1976). And like under-achievers, they constantly try to fulfill the role they have created for themselves. They too may be plagued by the ultrahigh standards they set. The interesting thing about overstrivers is that they get high grades. They appear successful. However, their success is a burden. With each new achievement comes the need for increased performance to reach the next level of accomplishment. Therefore, achievement becomes successively more elusive, requiring an ever-increasing level of effort (Jackson, 1968). Sometimes these children learn to fear success as much as they do failure because it signals yet another escalation of self-imposed demands. Still, they continue to strive until little additional improvement is possible (H. Cooper, 1979). Often the pressure these children experience is intensified by teachers who encourage them to keep striving. They are told that they can be even more successful by trying harder. Teachers have no reason to doubt the value of this admonition. They have verified it repeatedly in the past. When the pressure mounts, however, these children come to loathe failure. They never view failure as simply part of the learning process, a stepping stone to ultimate success. Instead, they interpret it as evidence of their worthlessness. School, therefore, becomes a place of conflict for the overstriver. On the one hand, there is cause for optimism because of past successes. On the other hand is the ever-present specter of failure created by the escalation of demands.

Helping Children Improve Self-Concept

Improving children's self-esteem is not an easy task. A poor self-concept is resistant to change. Once children establish a poor concept of themselves, they tend to retain this negative perspective (S. C. Jones, 1973). Sometimes these negative views are unintentionally strengthened by actions taken to help children overcome self-concept problems. For example, it is commonly believed that students' negative self-concepts can be overcome if the children are given the opportunity to experience success. It seems logical that if the original difficulty is the lack of success, then providing success experiences should rectify the problem. Teachers assume that once children get a taste of success, they will continue to seek it.

However, failure-avoiding students are largely unresponsive to success. Indeed, they appear almost calculating in their rejection of potential success experiences provided for them (Aronson & Carlsmith, 1962). Once they see themselves as failures, success loses its reward value. Success is not expected, so when it does occur, they believe it to be a consequence of luck or fate instead of effort. What many teachers fail to realize is that success-oriented children attribute success to ability and failure to lack of proper effort, whereas failure-prone children attribute their failure to lack of ability and whatever success they may occasionally achieve to the momentary generosity of teachers and others, lucky guessing, or unusually easy tasks (Weiner & Kukla, 1970). But in reality, although they may try to hide it, these children are aware that their lack of success can be attributed to themselves. Teachers who try to entice such children to try harder to succeed fail to realize that these students cannot afford to believe that success comes from their efforts or abilities. To accept such a thought would undermine their sense of well-being. If they continue to believe that their success occurs because of luck, then their lack of success does not have to be attributed to inability.

Failure-prone students believe that if they experience success, teachers and parents will expect them to continue being successful. However, children with low self-esteem feel unable to meet such an expectation, particularly when they believe that their success has been achieved through luck anyway. These children want to be successful, but they fear that if they evidence limited success, they will be obliged to repeat it on demand. Feeling unable to do so, they frequently act counterproductively to keep success from happening. They sabotage their own work when they find themselves in danger of succeeding (Aronson & Carlsmith, 1962).

What can be done about this problem? The most obvious and necessary measure to take is to adjust the present competitive system in school (D. W. Johnson & Johnson, 1989). The disabling effects of competition are certain (Kohn, 1992). Because of these effects, many students experience poor academic performance and consequently suffer low self-esteem. The long-term effects are enormous. When children are evaluated exclusively by their teachers, they usually conclude that teachers are the only source of valid assessment. Because the evaluations of various teachers are rarely equivalent, students may learn that their grades depend more on luck than effort (Weiner & Kukla, 1970). One solution to this problem is to allow students to do more self-assessment. When children learn to evaluate their own performance, they no longer have to depend solely on an outside source of affirmation, and they develop a more realistic and honest image of themselves (Farr & Tone, 1994). Self-assessment can also provide more consistency in grading and thus reduce the variability inherent in the evaluations given by different teachers.

Self-assessment can be fraught with difficulties. These problems are usually in consequence of students' previous experiences where teachers exclusively evaluate their academic work. Students themselves are rarely given an opportunity to evaluate their school performances. They, therefore, become conditioned to their teachers' evaluations, and out of fear of failure, develop various coping strategies like believing luck not effort is responsible for success. Before students can validly evaluate their own work, they need considerable experience making these judgments while receiving mentoring from their teachers. Otherwise, their lack of experience and various biases will invalidate the assessments they make. Students need to learn how to evaluate their work in ways that are not a threat to their egos but that represent a valid assessment of what they have accomplished. To achieve this, students should be given experiences comparing their work with other similar efforts that have explicit statements of evaluation and criteria attached. These evaluations should consist of clearly written explanations of the evaluation, and how the student work being evaluated satisfies given criteria. Students also need to be exposed to work that exceeds the quality ordinarily expected of students. This way, students can learn to make judgments of their work in terms of reasonable expectations but can also visualize higher-quality work they may strive to accomplish. They also need to be taught the basis on which judgment criteria are created and how these are applied in making evaluations. Students particularly need to evaluate their work in terms of the improvements they are able to make. In the beginning, a good deal of coaching will be needed to help them to make the necessary discriminations.

Teachers can also help by reducing the level of control they exercise over students and by helping students develop an intrinsic motivational orientation. Failure syndrome problems are developed through social mechanisms centered around experiences with failure. Most children begin school with enthusiasm, but many soon experience anxiety-provoking and psychologically threatening conditions. These occur when teachers control through monitored performances, comparative grades, and public exposure of failures. These control measures and extrinsic motivational strategies constitute a threat to the academic performance of many students (Boggiano et al., 1992).

Students who believe that their efforts influence their performance are said to have an internal locus of control. Individuals who believe that what happens to them is a matter of luck or fate have an external locus of control. People with an internal locus of control are more likely to accept responsibility for what they do. Those with an external locus of control are more likely to display helplessness, avoiding blame by giving excuses and lying. They are also much more likely to misbehave and to make excuses for their bad behavior. To help children become more internally controlled, teachers need to show them (1) how consequences relate to their actions, (2) how outcomes can be predicted based on personal actions, and (3) how choosing and planning can result in desired outcomes (Curwin & Mendler, 1988).

Overstriving students must learn to focus on success rather than on fear of failure. The first step is for teachers to stop insisting that overstriving students can and ought to improve themselves by trying harder. These children also need to realize that failure is not a permanent condition. They must understand that incorrect responses can be changed and improvements made without leaving an indelible mark. Mistakes should be viewed as stepping stones to future learning rather than immutable consequences (Brophy, 1998).

Cultural Diversity and Interpersonal Relationships

Cultural differences—such as socioeconomic status, ethnicity, gender, language, exceptionality, or religion—are involved in numerous discipline problems experienced by teachers. In modern society, it is increasingly typical to have children from different cultural backgrounds in the same classroom. In fact demographers tell us that by the year 2020 one of every three people in the United States will be what we now refer to as a minority (Sobol, 1990). To effectively work with such diverse student populations, teachers must teach their students that all people have similar needs, desires, and problems, but they have diverse ways of satisfying their desires and solving their problems. The assumption is that when students realize that people who behave differently are actually the same, they will have more respect for the differences between people (Grossman, 1995). Teachers must learn to deal with a variety of cultures and help children from these cultures face the problems of everyday life, especially in school. Teachers must take into account differences in cultural norms and learning styles along with specific language problems. Teachers must learn to monitor their own behavior to be sure that they do not model prejudiced attitudes and behavior. Necessary changes in the attitudes and behaviors can be expected to require significant time and effort (Grossman, 1995).

Over the years, government and school officials have sought to assimilate minorities into the dominant American culture. In addition, solutions have been sought to eliminate biasing school practices that have adverse effects on children as a result of race, social class, gender, and exceptionality. The American commitment to equal opportunity is presumed to be the primary force behind these efforts. Various laws have been passed in an effort to achieve these ends:

- Title VII of the Civil Rights Bill, which prohibits discrimination based on race, color, national origin, or gender
- Title IX of the 1972 Education Amendments, which prohibits denial of full participation in all educational programs and activities on the basis of gender
- Public Law 94-142, the Individuals With Disabilities Education Act, which mandates educating children with disabilities to the maximum extent possible in the least restrictive environment
- The Bilingual Education Act of 1988, which provides that limited English-proficient students may be instructed bilingually for 3 years and up to 5 years if needed to bridge the transition from their native language to English
- The Equal Educational Opportunities Act of 1972, which indicates that no state can deny equal educational opportunity to an individual by failure of an educational agency to take appropriate action to overcome language barriers that impede equal participation by its students in its instructional program

Cultural differences can lead to misunderstandings between teachers and their students.

- The McKinney Homeless Assistance Act, which provides educational programs for homeless and runaway children without requiring proof of residency
- *Plyler v. Doe* (1982), which guarantees the rights of undocumented immigrants to a free public education
- The Americans With Disabilities Act, which is designed to end discrimination against individuals with disabilities
- The Civil Rights Act of 1964, which was enacted to end discrimination against minorities
- Section 504 of the Vocational Rehabilitation Act Amendments of 1973, which prohibits exclusion from programs solely on the basis of one's disability

Despite these efforts, only limited assimilation has been achieved, and only marginal improvements have been made in eliminating bias. This is in part due to prejudice but is also due to the many subtle ways in which bias operates in society. In addition, because of the cultural segregation in the United States, many citizens are unaware of cultural norms different from their own. Lacking the insights necessary to understand and accept other cultures, many people act suspiciously and aggressively toward their fellow Americans.

Though these laws and legal decisions seem appropriate to protect the rights of minorities, there have been backlashes regarding certain of these guaranteed rights. For example, Proposition 187, which was passed on the election ballot in the 1994 election in California, specifically denied welfare, health care, and public education to undocumented immigrants. It is claimed that the state could no longer finance these services to illegal immigrants because of the enormous influx of these people during recent years. It is anticipated there will be a protracted legal battle regarding the constitutionality of Proposition 187. In the meantime there appears to have been an increase in racial incidents involving citizens who have been enraged by the issue.

ASSIMILATION VERSUS CULTURAL PLURALISM

Assimilation is a process where groups either adopt or change the dominant culture. The cultural patterns that distinguish the different groups either disappear, or the distinctive patterns of groups become part of the dominant culture, or a combination of the two occurs (Gollnick & Chinn, 1994). Assimilation develops through stages in which the new cultural group (1) adjusts its cultural patterns to be more consistent with the dominant group; (2) develops significant large-scale relationships with the dominate group; (3) intermarries fully with the dominant group; (4) loses its sense of identity as separate from the dominant group; (5) encounters no discrimination; (6) doesn't experience prejudiced attitudes; and (7) is not involved in power struggles and value incompatibilities with the dominant group.

The first stage in the process of assimilation is *acculturation*. In this stage, the cultural patterns of the dominant group are adopted by the new or oppressed group. The speed of this process varies, depending on how isolated and segregated a particular group is. For example, because Native Americans have been isolated on reservations, their acculturation has been very slow. Groups who are discriminated against for various reasons (race or religion for example) may also find the acculturation process very slow (Gordon, 1964).

A more advanced stage of assimilation is referred to as *structural assimilation*. This occurs when different groups share primary group relationships such as membership in the same cliques and social clubs. Limited structural assimilation has occurred in the United States, except for white Protestant immigrants from northern and western Europe. Other groups have given up their own cultures and languages and have come to behave like the dominant culture, at least publicly, but this has not guaranteed acceptance by the dominant culture (Gollnick & Chinn, 1994). Assimilation efforts by educators and others might be one reason for the difficulty experienced at integrating the school curriculum with ethnic content and moving away from Eurocentric school patterns. An assimilationist ideology makes it difficult for educators to acquire a commitment to making the curriculum multicultural (Banks, 1993).

Different theories have been developed about how assimilation takes place. One of these, the Anglo-conformity theory, holds that an individual's ancestral culture is renounced in favor of the behavior and values of the Anglo-Saxon core group (Nieto, 1992). This theory is the one that is frequently accepted and on which most school practices are based. A second theory, the "melting pot" theory, contends that disparate cultures from all over the world could be assembled in "America's divinely inspired crucible" and somehow merge into a single, unique American culture to which all cultural groups would contribute. This admixture has never occurred. Instead, the specific cultural contributions of the various groups have been limited by the dominant culture (Gordon, 1964).

In reality, neither the melting pot theory nor the Anglo-conformity theory successfully accounts for what has taken place in America. Cultural pluralism provides a better explanation: Enough subsocietal separation has been maintained to guarantee the continuance of various ethnic cultural traditions and the perpetuation of various subgroups without interfering with the operation of general American civic life. When minorities are not assimilated into the dominant American culture, they tend to maintain their own ethnic communities and participate peripherally in the larger cultural life in which they have been denied full membership (Gollnick & Chinn, 1994).

Probably the best explanation of what has happened in the United States in terms of inculturation is the modified cultural pluralism theory. According to this view, assimilation and pluralism are ongoing processes. In practical terms cultural diversity should be accommodated in public education, and interactions of individuals from different cultural groups supported. In the classical theory of cultural pluralism, group autonomy depends on the maintenance of rigid group boundaries. This separation minimizes the influence society at large will have over group members. In the modified version, however, groups continue to retain elements of their own culture but take on certain aspects of majority culture. When applied to schools, modified cultural pluralism advocates different emphases depending on circumstances. When group maintenance and support are of primary concern, schools tend to be segregated both in terms of students and teachers. The emphasis is on community control, native language instruction, and a curriculum strong in ethnic studies. On the other hand, when the goal is to achieve a better balance between the dominant culture and ethnic attachments, similarities as well as differences are integrated and highlighted. The curriculum focuses on the national identity and interests while at the same time valuing cultural diversity and pluralistic perspectives. This approach usually emphasizes integration of students and staff, equal educational opportunity, and a curriculum sensitive to individual and group needs (Hernandez, 1989).

SOCIAL CLASS

Generally, there are two views regarding class structure in the United States with two significantly different beliefs about the possibility of achieving equity and advancing one's position socially and economically. The first of these accepts the reality of social classes but supports the idea that individuals can move to a higher class if they work hard enough. In this view there is an inherent struggle between those who control most of the resources and those who are oppressed. The oppressed are usually believed to be inferior, and their hardships are blamed on their lack of middle-class values and behaviors. A society based on this class system ensures that the ablest and most meritorious, ambitious, hard-working, and talented individuals achieve the highest levels in society. Popular stories abound regarding individuals who have risen above their poor circumstances to achieve notoriety and wealth. From this perspective, affirmative action should be discouraged. It is thought to be alien to democratic principles and encourages mediocrity.

The second view of social class is that a few families and individuals own and control corporations, banks, and other means of gaining wealth. These few comprise the privileged upper class. Those who sell their labor to make a living make up the other classes. Inequality is acknowledged, but it is not explained in terms of class differences and conflicts. Instead, the existence of classes is a function of low motivation and inability. Consequently, it is the individual's fault for not moving up the class ladder. This phenomenon is often called "blaming the victim." In this view, most people are caught in the socioeconomic strata into which they were born, and the politicoeconomic system ensures that they will remain there. Equality cannot be achieved from this perspective through providing oppressed group members an equal chance. Instead, equal results must somehow be guaranteed. Affirmative action has a significant role in achieving the desired goals. Equity is judged to have occurred if equal results are achieved in school dropout rates, college attendance and graduation, and access to high-paying jobs (Gollnick & Chinn, 1994).

Some people have been successful in raising their class status. It is claimed that this has come about as a result of their own ingenuity and efforts. Others seem unable to improve their position in life no matter what they do. There appears to be no simple explanation for this disparity. Some just seem able to compete in society better than others. It seems self-evident that people who have wealth and power would try to maintain their advantageous position. Not only would they protect their own wealth and position in life, but they would also ensure that their children enjoy it as well. This is done ordinarily by occupying important positions on boards that determine state and local policies, on boards of colleges and universities, and on corporation boards. By controlling policies that can influence their investments, they are able to protect their interests (Parenti, 1988).

Economic inequality is most pronounced among African Americans, Hispanic Americans, and Native Americans in the United States, with Native Americans suffering the most poverty. Many social reformers, educators, and parents believe that education can be used as a powerful device for achieving social change and reducing poverty. In keeping with this belief, the federal government has initiated various educational programs (e.g., Head Start, Upward Bound, Title I, Job Corps, Neighborhood Youth Corps) to help eliminate the disparity between classes and to raise economic levels for impoverished people. Unfortunately, the intended goals of improving income equity and eliminating poverty, despite participation in these programs by disadvantaged individuals, has not been realized. Some have come to believe that schools, rather than being an agent for social reform and improvement, are a mechanism for inculcating the values and developing the skills necessary for maintaining the current socioeconomic and political systems (Gollnick & Chinn, 1994).

The continuation of the present socioeconomic order is supported in some ways that have a benign appearance but that have devastating consequences for lower-class children. For example, Rist (1970) found that children were categorized into reading and mathematics groups as early as the eighth day of school and that these groupings were made according to nonacademic factors. Children in more advanced groups came to school in clean clothes, interacted with the teacher more successfully, were more verbal, used standard English, and came from more socioeconomically advantaged families.

Lower-class children receive a lower-quality education. They are provided less effective learning experiences than their more advantaged counterparts. They miss out on learning that involves critical thinking. Instead, they are given compensatory education, which is essentially remedial. It is assumed that these children do not learn as quickly and cannot understand difficult concepts. They also have fewer opportunities to engage in creative thinking and instead participate in recitation activities and structured writing experiences (Gamoran & Berends, 1987).

One of the major educational practices that adversely affects lower-class children is tracking. Tracking involves assigning children to specific classes according to test scores, socioeconomic status, and teacher grades and recommendations. Once tracking occurs, students get locked into a group with common expectations. "High-ability" groups have high expectations, while "low-ability" groups are generally considered unable. Lower-track students get feedback from teachers as well as their peers that they are dumb and that little can be expected from them (Banks & Banks, 1989).

What should be done to provide lower-class children an appropriate educational experience? Teachers need to present these children with opportunities to acquire the knowledge and to develop the skills that can be used to overcome their poverty. Approaches must be used that are the same as those used for gifted students (Wheelock, 1992). Teachers must also systematically evaluate their interactions with students to determine if they are giving some students a disproportionate amount of their time and expecting lower-class students to respond in less sophisticated ways. Educators must also become aware of personal prejudices and understand how these are reflected in their classroom behavior. Students need to be taught about the class struggle in this country and to understand the nature and causes of inequity. The curriculum should not reflect only middle-class America. Students need to see some of their own cultural experiences manifested in what they learn. Children should understand that all persons do not share equally in material wealth but that everyone has the potential to improve their situation.

ETHNIC DIVERSITY

The United States is reportedly composed of at least 276 different ethnic groups, including 170 different Native American groups (Gollnick & Chinn, 1994). One's ethnic identity as an American is based on national origin, religion, and race. Ethnic identity continues with individuals even though they may have emigrated from their country of origin and taken up residence elsewhere. It is common for those who emigrate to adopt some of the culture of the dominant society in their new location while retaining some of the cultural uniqueness of their national origin. Ethnic groupings are usually considered in a general sense. The usual breakdown is Europeans, Asian Americans, African Americans, Hispanic Americans, and Native Americans. However, this provides a much too superficial view of cultural diversity to be helpful. Not all Hispanic peoples, for example, are sufficiently alike culturally to fit into a single category. Mexican Americans, Puerto Ricans, Spanish Americans, and Cuban Americans have very different backgrounds and experiences. Even inhabitants of different countries in South and Central America cannot be treated as though they are from a single culture. Each of these countries has a different history, involving different political and economic pressures and concerns, and each has developed different customs in a variety of social interactions. Even languages differ, Portuguese versus Spanish, for example, along with local idioms. People of these countries may have shared a common national origin, but over the years they have developed their own cultures (Omi & Winant, 1986).

African Americans, on the other hand, are tied together by race and common heritage. Their skin color ranges from very light to very dark. Thus, their skin color does not define them. Their identification is based, in part, on sharing a common national origin. More importantly, they have become a single ethnic group because they share a common history, language, economic life, and culture, which has developed over four centuries of living in the United States. Race, nevertheless, remains a central part of their identity (Appiah, 1990). This is in contrast to blacks who have recently immigrated. They identify themselves with other specific ethnic groups, like Puerto Rican, or Nigerian American, or West Indian.

Historically, race has been important in this country only because it allowed the dominant culture to single out certain groups as inferior and thus as eligible for discriminatory treatment. The existence of many ethnic groups within a particular race has not been considered important. However, from an educational standpoint, each ethnic group along with its unique culture must be understood and responded to appropriately by teachers.

Ethnic groups other than the dominant Western European group usually are accorded minority status. Most minority groups experience a wide range of discriminatory treatments and develop attitudes and behaviors that oppose those of the dominate group. Others who cross the boundaries into the dominant group may experience both internal opposition or identity problems and external opposition or peer and community pressures (Ogbu, 1988, p. 176).

Some members of minority groups grow up in ethnic enclaves, not in multiethnic communities. Chinatown, Little Italy, Harlem, and Little Saigon are examples of ethnic enclaves in some of the nation's larger cities. Children who grow up in these environments may become culturally encapsulated. Most of their primary relationships and many of their secondary relationships are with members of their own ethnic group. They may be unaware of other cultures and find difficulty living with those who speak different languages, eat different foods, and value things that their own ethnic group does not value. Unlike their white counterparts, most minority peoples are eventually forced out of their ethnic encapsulation to achieve economic mobility. These individuals may form secondary relationships with members of other ethnic groups with whom they work but rarely with members of the dominant culture (Gollnick & Chinn, 1994).

As a result of prejudice, members of oppressed groups are commonly discriminated against, even though they may strive to be assimilated by the dominant culture. They may eventually share the same cultural characteristics of the dominant culture but be denied full access to the economic, political, and social spheres of the dominant group. When ethnic minorities reject the culture of their own group to assimilate into the culture of the dominant group, and when the dominant group denies assimilation, some of these individuals become suspended between two cultural groups. They belong to neither group and develop self-identity problems. Educators must be aware of this. They must also learn that members of the same ethnic group are products of their own experiences and, therefore, may not fit a stereotypical definition of a particular ethnic group. For example, families who emigrated from Vietnam in the early 1970s were predominantly from the wealthy and professional middle classes. In the mid- to late 1970s, Vietnamese immigrants came mostly from peasant and rural backgrounds. Unfortunately, some educators have come to expect the same academic performance from all Asian Americans in the schools. Miscalculation of this kind can be avoided if teachers become more familiar with various microcultures (Gollnick & Chinn, 1994).

Ethnic group membership has a significant impact on students' perceptions of themselves as well as their school experiences. Because the environment of the school is so incongruent with the cultural experiences of many students, teachers need to make modifications that provide more hospitable and comfortable conditions in which to learn. An environment must be created in which students can learn to participate in the dominant society while maintaining distinct ethnic identities if they choose. Students who are members of the dominant culture need experiences that acquaint them with the cultures of their minority classmates.

Each cultural group within the school should enjoy sufficient status that group members do not feel inclined to oppose teachers and the educational program. Patterns of resistance and opposition are common reactions when minority students are subordinated in the school. This opposition often takes the form of breaking school rules and norms, belittling academic achievement, and valuing manual over mental work (Ogbu, 1988; Solomon, 1988).

Sometimes, understanding very subtle differences between cultural expressions can help immensely. For example, African American adults seldom ask questions that require their children to state something that the children realize adults already know. Instead, they are asked to talk about things of which adults are unaware. However, teachers commonly ask questions regarding topics they obviously know more about than their students. African American students are often puzzled by this, particularly in the early grades. In addition, African American adults usually ask questions regarding children's experiences, while teachers ask about things outside children's experiences. Children are thus unprepared to make intelligent responses. Finally, African American parents issue direct orders to their children and give specific directions regarding what they want them to do. European American teachers are usually more indirect. They may say, "Why don't you do such and such?" African American students take these indirect instructions as suggestions rather than expectations (Brice-Heath, 1982, p. 163).

Native Americans also find themselves in cultural conflict when they enter the schools. For example, to Native Americans, exactness of time is generally of little importance. In the dominant Western European (Anglo) culture, time is of the utmost importance, and punctuality is considered a virtue if not a necessity. Native Americans hold that because the future is uncertain, preparing for unknown eventualities is an inappropriate activity and an unhealthy approach to living. European Americans put money into insurance, fret over savings and investments, and do many other things that make little sense to Native Americans. Native Americans value patience. One's ability to wait is important. Western European culture admires quick action more than patience. In school, teachers often value punctuality, while actions taken to enforce it may seem alien to Native American students. Furthermore, teachers may view Native American children to be slow and dull and in need of encouragement to take action more quickly than the children are inclined.

Native Americans believe in achieving a balance with nature. Consequently, they pay attention to nature's signals and adapt themselves accordingly. The Anglo culture, however, constantly searches for new ways to control and master the elements around them and tends to indiscriminately consume the earth's resources with no thought of adverse affects. For Native Americans, getting along with nature means more than not misusing the earth. They believe that the Great Spirit is in all things and therefore all things deserve respect. Native American children may find the emphasis on consumption to be offensive, making it hard for them to respect those from the Anglo culture who promote these ideas.

Individual freedom is greatly prized among Native American peoples. However, from their viewpoint, freedom means the right to make an appropriate choice. Above all else, appropriate choices are those that enable the group to survive. Even so, no one in the group has the right to force the choice of another individual. Traditional Native American government was a true democracy, with a provision that those who did not agree with the decisions made were free to leave the group. They did not have overall leaders. Leadership depended on the situation and on the talent of the individuals involved. One person might be the best at hunting, another at making war. Even in war, no one was forced to participate. If someone wanted to get up a raiding party, only those who chose to go went along. In Anglo society, leadership is often inherited or granted rather than earned. Once the group has voted, all members are expected to comply with group wishes. Those who do not want to go to war, for example, are conscripted. This attitude underlies our two-party system of government. The losing party is still active in government, but those who win govern. It is common for unsuccessful candidates for political office to concede their loss and voice support for the winner. This attitude is deeply ingrained in Anglo culture. Native American children may find some difficulty accepting such expectations and find themselves in conflict with their teachers and peers (Bennett, 1986).

Immigrant and refugee students may require special attention. Too often, they do not receive the help they need to overcome the culture shock experienced when entering the new and strange environment of the school. As a result, they may react angrily and aggressively or become sullen, depressed, or withdrawn. This is particularly true of children who have never attended school before because they come from rural areas, internment camps, or cultures that have no written language (Grossman, 1995).

Though individuals have various common attributes by right of belonging to the same ethnic group, they also have significant differences due to the socioeconomic class and gender to which they belong. All of these factors interact to produce a disparity among individuals. Teachers must understand that each student brings to the classroom a personal reality that is based on a complex, dynamic, and unique blend resulting from the interaction of race, gender, class, as well as personal characteristics (Hernandez, 1989).

LANGUAGE AND COMMUNICATION STYLE

Mismatches between students' and teachers' communication styles can adversely affect student–teacher relationships and impair students' learning. For example, because of their lack of awareness, teachers may mistakenly believe students are expressing shyness, insecurity, or disrespect when they are not. Students may be unable to distinguish when their teachers are serious and when they are joking.

The communications styles of Hispanic Americans and some Asian and Pacific American groups are more formal than either European Americans or African Americans. Also, African Americans tend to be more passionate when they express their feelings, while European Americans value coolheadedness. European Americans prefer direct communications. They like straightforward expressions. Many Asian peoples shun frankness. They may even employ the services of a mediator in communicating with a teacher rather than approaching the teacher directly (Howells & Sarabia, 1978).

Cultures vary considerably in the extent to which honest expressions are acceptable. It may be more important to avoid disagreement and conflict or personal responsibility than to be perfectly honest. With Cambodians, Laotians, or Vietnamese, for example, the essential question is not whether a statement is true or false, but rather its intention. Does it facilitate interpersonal harmony? Does it indicate a wish to change the subject? These are far more important considerations (Nguyen, 1984). Out of respect, some Native Americans will tell others what they want to hear, never believing that their words are untruthful. They will also avoid telling someone what they believe that person does not want to hear. Some Native Americans have a custom of giving away all of one's possessions to honor someone else. Paradoxically, giving or sharing with the idea of getting honor in return destroys the essence of sharing. For this reason, when someone does something for you out of kindness, without being asked, it is very rude to thank the person. This is tantamount to paying for generosity (Bennett, 1986).

Different cultures also vary in how they respond to guilt or accusations. European Americans trend to express guilt by lowering their eyes and avoiding eye contact. When they are falsely accused, they may issue vigorous denials. African Americans, on the other hand, lower their eyes as a sign of respect, not as an admission of guilt. In addition they do not feel the same need to proclaim their innocence by making emotional statements. Southern European cultures and some Latin American groups may be voracious in expressing their emotions (Grossman, 1995). Eye contact is also differentially used by various cultures in expressing defiance or submissiveness. European Americans typically express defiance with a silent stare. African Americans roll their eyes, while many Asian and Pacific Americans force a smile (K. R. Johnson, 1971). European Americans expect direct eye contact as a sign of respect and submission. African Americans, Asian and Pacific Americans, and Hispanic Americans typically avert their eyes to show submissiveness (Grossman, 1995).

In some cultures, Mexican American, for example, sensitivity to others' needs is so paramount that it is unnecessary for individuals to directly express the need for help. Children in these cultures are accustomed to having others notice when they need help. Help is provided without having to ask for it. This behavior is likely to provoke a rebuke from European American teachers who expect students to ask for help when they need it.

Admitting errors and mistakes is more actively avoided in some cultures than others. European Americans have expressions that help them avoid responsibility. For example, when a person breaks a glass, saying "The glass broke" implies no clumsiness of the person who dropped it. In Spanish-speaking countries, greater efforts are made to avoid blame. In fact, they may find it difficult to make an expression in English that keeps them from feeling guilty for mistakes (Jaramillo, 1973). European American teachers are inclined to place blame and expect children to admit wrongdoing.

What should be said when a person is unwilling or unable to do something? The Japanese will find a way to avoid saying "no" directly. With their cultural emphasis on harmony and respect, they rarely contradict another person. Even when the situation involves nothing personal, considerable effort is generally made to avoid "no" responses. Hispanics also try to avoid direct argument or contradiction. To them, these actions are rude and disrespectful. On the surface, they may appear agreeable and take their time expressing their genuine opinion as tactfully as they can (Grossman, 1995).

In some cultures, physical contact is used to communicate. Hispanics, for example, show affection and acceptance through touching. Friends may kiss when they meet, and Hispanic males may hug or pat each other on the back. It is also common for them to touch one another while conversing. Lack of touching communicates unacceptance (Grossman, 1984). Children from some cultures, Hawaiians, for example, will lay a friendly hand on an adult they are trying to communicate with in lieu of making a verbal approach. European American teachers may find this uncomfortable and misinterpret the students' intentions. The resultant interaction may leave the teacher feeling encroached on, while the child may feel rejected or ignored. One part of the body for which Hawaiians have a taboo against touching is the head. In contrast, patting a child's head or tousling their hair is one of the few touching gestures that is natural and comfortable for European American adults. Hawaiians react negatively to head touching. Their emotions range from vague feelings of discomfort to resentment, anger, or feelings of physical violation (Grossman, 1995).

Children from the Hispanic community encounter a unique set of language problems in the classroom (Ramirez & Price-Williams, 1976). It is understandably hard for children who do not understand the dominant language to succeed in school. However, even after Hispanic children gain some facility with the language, they continue to experience difficulty with "voice" as they try to communicate and understand. Voice refers to the influence of the community and culture on the understandings and thought processes of its members. Even though Hispanic children may use the English language in what they believe to be its proper form, their understanding of word meanings reflects the culture they have grown up in rather than the dominant Anglo culture. For example, in a study by Walsh (1991), Puerto Rican children asked to respond to the English word *respect* most often spoke of concrete relationships with authority figures:

> Respect is if the teacher say to you shut up, you have to respect. The same thing with your parents, the teacher, the pastor; if they say to you, you have to respect.

> When my mother talk to me, I don't talk back. . . . When she hit me, I go to my bed and I let my mouth shut as I should because if I'm smart to her, she will smack me.

The same kinds of definitions were also obtained in Puerto Rican children's responses to the Spanish word *respeto*. However, Anglo children made no such direct reference to the sense of authority and honor for their elders when they were asked to respond to the word respect. Instead, their responses were less subservient:

> Like you don't do anything bad to it or bother it.

> Having manners.

Several Anglo children even described the word respect broadly as treatment due them or attention they could count on:

> Respect is when like your mother respects you and stuff, she takes care of you.

> Like when you go to your aunt's house you expect her to respect you.

The Hispanic children had not adopted an Anglo-like voice when speaking English or defining English words. This, of course, is contrary to the way humans learn. Their use of English appeared to be an extension of the Hispanic voice they had already established.

It is generally thought that once children learn to speak English, they also think in English. It is also assumed that children learn not only to speak English words but also to grasp their significance, use, and contextual appropriateness in varying situations. However, in children for whom English is a second language, the native tongue appears to exert a continued and significant influence. The predominance of a culturally based perspective on meaning is generally ignored by English-speaking teachers and school officials. Unfortunately, teachers who fail to understand the cultural voice in which Hispanic children speak find the responses of these children garbled, bothersome, and exasperating. When these children discover that their teachers do not understand, some of them react negatively, not only to their teachers but also to the whole educational process and to the entire culture and language the teachers represent. Some even reject their own culture (Christian, 1978).

For many Hispanic children, the school produces discord between the home and school. It places the cultural norms of the majority in opposition to the sociocultural and linguistic realities of these children. The school thus invalidates the inner voice that had previously defined the children's existence. As a result, the children internalize pieces of reality from two opposing worlds and in the process lose their sense of direction and identity. They may devalue their own cultural heritage and language and at the same time feel rejected by the dominant American culture.

The feelings of inadequacy that are outgrowths of these conditions are often amplified in the interactions of minority children with peers from the dominant culture. At the same time that minority students are learning to disparage their own language, culture, and social group, majority students are also thinking negatively about them. Majority students often believe that Anglo culture and language are superior to that of minorities. Such beliefs form the basis for perpetuating inequities in school, in the workplace, and in other areas of society (Wilkins, 1995).

Curriculum and Instruction for Minority Students

Effectiveness in multicultural classroom depends on the teachers' ability to relate content to the cultural backgrounds of their students. Teaching that ignores student behavior norms and communication patterns provokes student resistance to learning. Learning is greatly enhanced when teachers create (1) a learning atmosphere in which their students feel respected and connected to them, (2) a favorable disposition toward the learning experiences through personal relevance and choice, (3) challenging, thoughtful learning experiences that include student perspectives and values, and (4) an understanding that students are effective in learning something they value (Wlodkowski & Ginsberg, 1995). The curriculum of the public schools should include material about various minority groups. The history of these groups can be discussed, along with the contributions their members have made in the world. Textbooks, however, commonly ignore the contributions of minorities and focus almost exclusively on the accomplishments of Anglo community members. Individuals from the different minorities have indeed made significant contributions to American life in nearly all its aspects. Recognition of this fact can give minority students some sense not only of their collective American identity but also of their particular ethnic heritage. Ethnic studies should not be confined to special courses. These courses are taken primarily by the members of the particular ethnic group studied. Instead, material currently covered in ethnic studies needs to become part of the general curriculum. A multicultural curriculum not only would benefit minority students, it would provide all students multiple perspectives and help them become more informed regarding history. A more unbiased understanding of history and a greater understanding of cultural differences can help all children live more successfully in our diverse society.

General emphasis on bilingualism is another significant way to provide a better learning environment for minority children and help all components of diverse American culture be more accepting of cultural differences. Although it has one of the most diverse populations in the world, the United States is one of the more parochial, even paranoid, nations as far as bilingualism is concerned (Walsh, 1991). In America, the English language is considered the norm; learning other languages is thought to be unnecessary, wasteful, divisive, or unpatriotic. Bilingualism is usually associated with minority status and with an inability or an unwillingness to be assimilated. The possibility that English could fruitfully coexist with other languages is considered impossible. In most other nations, however, knowing a second—or even a third—language is a prerequisite for active societal involvement and for daily communication, both public and private. In such countries, bilingualism is promoted and supported by the state and its public institutions (Walsh, 1991).

It is important that teachers provide all children, particularly minority children, learning experiences that suit their learning styles. Both ethnicity and socioeconomic status appear to be important factors in learning style differences. Most minority students tend to be field-sensitive learners: They prefer that teachers use more personal, conversational techniques and provide instruction in groups where social interactions are prevalent. Anglo and Asian American children may find field-independent teaching more to their liking, a teaching style that capitalizes on students' inclination to achieve at a high level and compete among themselves. Unfortunately, finding out that minority children favor one kind of learning has encouraged educators to overprescribe this category of learning for all members of the group. This is an oversimplification. Educators must remember that not all European Americans are field independent and not all minorities are field sensitive. This kind of approach tends to dichotomize learning. It is doubtful that a process as complex as learning can be characterized in this way, when as many as 14 different learning styles have been identified by various theorists (Nieto, 1992).

Many minority children can be motivated to learn in a cooperative learning environment (Slavin, 1983). In fact many minority students have backgrounds that have taught them that the way to survive and thrive in the world is to work together for shared goals (Vasquez, 1988). However, the orientation of most traditional classrooms in America emphasizes competition and individual achievement exclusively. These demands can be stressful for all children whose learning style doesn't fit the norm. Cooperative learning has been shown to make phenomenal improvements in relationships among members of different ethnic groups in desegregated schools. After the introduction of cooperative learning, race tends to be eliminated as a criterion for friendship among participants. In addition, students who participate in cooperative learning reach higher levels of achievement. They also engage in less off-task behavior and create fewer discipline problems (Slavin, 1986).

Role playing is also an effective method of teaching minority children, particularly Puerto Rican students. Students are asked to take a dramatic role, portraying another person as they believe that particular person would have acted. Attitudes and values can be explored more dramatically and validly in this way. This approach first and foremost allows minority students to construct, assume control over, and then take ownership of the curriculum. It also helps them to become more attentive to the various voices in the classroom and to recognize differences and similarities among them. It gives them a sense of worth about themselves and their culture and language and an ability to recognize the sources of tension and pressure around them and how to diffuse or lessen them (Walsh, 1991).

The cultural pluralism ideology focuses on the need to provide students experiences specific to their culture. Students are encouraged to learn how to succeed within their own ethnic groups. This is in opposition to the assimilationist ideology, which strives to integrate all ethnic groups into a common culture. Neither of these can successfully guide effective teaching. Teachers need to embrace an ideology that reflects both of these positions and yet avoids extremes. Pluralism-assimilationist ideology meets these criteria. This position assumes that while the ethnic group and the ethnic community are very important in the socialization of group members, individuals are strongly influenced by the common dominant culture during socialization. In addition, even if they live in and never leave their ethnic community or enclave, group members still live within a larger society that touches them socioeconomically and in other ways (Banks, 1977).

Eliminating Gender Bias

Gender bias is a significant problem for children of all ethnic backgrounds. This is because of the traditional role expectations ordinarily associated with gender. Throughout history, the roles of men and women have been specifically defined and enforced through subtle as well as more explicit social actions. The assignment of roles was based in part on the physical makeup of the sexes. Men, on the whole, were better equipped for hunting. Women, who alone were able to bear children, began to tend to responsibilities closer to home. Because of the roles they occupied, women eventually were considered physically and intellectually inferior to men. If necessary, this could be enforced through the power positions ordinarily held by men. Ultimately, women came to be thought of as incapable of performing professional and administrative work and were denied access to manual labor that required significant strength. In recent years, this view has begun to change. Many jobs that formerly required greater physical strength now can be performed by anyone having the skill to operate labor-saving equipment. Women have also shown sufficient intellectual capacity to do things that formerly were denied them.

Although they are sufficiently capable intellectually, women in the work force still find themselves employed at lower-paying jobs with less responsibility than men. Often, the differences in work opportunities and pay are a function of prejudice. Even though women make up an increasing percentage of the work force, and are often responsible for running a household by themselves, they tend to be compensated as though they have a lesser responsibility as breadwinners. Sometimes, the low-paying jobs taken by women are those they have selected and for which they have prepared themselves. Traditionally, the positions of elementary school teacher, nurse, and secretary are filled by women. Women are less frequently involved in higher-paying and more prestigious jobs in medicine, law, and science. Why do women select lower-paying, less prestigious jobs? Obviously a number of factors are involved, but one primary influence is cultural bias and its perpetuation in the schools. From the time children are very young, they are provided with gender roles and encouraged to follow them. The messages of parents and others in each child's environment have a virtually irreversible effect on the child's gender identity (Strickland, 1995).

If women identify with the roles provided for them, they often accept lower expectations for themselves. For example, although there is some improvement in math education (Backes, 1994), women are taught, subliminally and sometimes overtly, that they are somehow less capable than men of doing science. Some consequently devalue their own potential and assume that a man's career has greater importance than their own. Even when women can freely choose what to do in life, their choice is shaped by the existing social structure with all its expectations. This constraint is learned early and reinforced by most societal institutions. The outcome is that men perform the important functions in society and women are relegated to a supporting role (Weiler, 1988).

The schools generally perpetuate gender bias. In textbooks, for example, girls are seen as stereotypes—playing with dolls, giving tea parties, or working in the kitchen. They are frightened of animals and loud noises, ask the advice of others, and seek assistance in solving problems. Girls are often depicted as passive spectators, usually watching boys actively participate. In contrast, boys are shown engaged in important activities that prepare them for important careers. They save girls and mothers from danger. They solve problems and are sufficiently ingenious and creative to find the answers by themselves. Boys in textbooks are almost always shown being active—swimming, running, riding bicycles, playing ball, or unraveling mysteries (Gollnick, Sadker, & Sadker, 1982). Pictures of adults in various occupations are likewise biased. Textbook occupations for women are usually very limited.

In a study reported in 1975, women in textbooks most often were shown in service occupations such as cafeteria worker, cashier, cleaning professional, dressmaker, librarian, nurse, teacher, or telephone operator. Occasionally, a female physician was shown. Men were found working in about six times as many different occupations as women (Women on Words and Images, 1975).

Over the past two or three decades, some improvements have been made regarding male and female stereotyping in textbooks and other school materials. However, the problem still generally persists. This is true even though gender roles are gradually changing. Gender roles continue to be projected stereotypically in the socialization process as well as various media. This socialization process begins at home and is reinforced in the school and society. Now in addition to books and magazines, television has become a great perpetuator of gender stereotyping (Gollnick & Chinn, 1994).

Interactions between teachers and students in the classroom are also biased. Boys are spoken to more frequently than girls in most science classes and are asked more higher-order questions (Becker, 1981). Boys are also praised more for the quality of their work, whereas girls are praised for being neat. Teachers tend to give boys instructions on how to complete their science projects; they are more likely to show girls how to actually do the project or even to do it for them. In addition, boys receive more attention in the classroom than girls in the form of praise, criticism, remediation, and expressions of acceptance (D. Sadker & Sadker, 1985). Teachers also rarely wait more than 5 seconds for student responses after asking questions. They also rarely call on nonvolunteers. Both these behaviors favor male participation (Lundeberg, 1997). In the early grades the school curriculum is somewhat biased in favor of girls. Girls are generally better prepared than boys for learning activities such as reading and writing, which are focused on in the early grades. Later there is a decided bias in favor of boys. While girls prefer learning activities that incorporate relationships and cooperation, along with emphasizing caring, later there is more stress on competition, justice, objectivity, and self-interest. What is needed is a pedagogy that encourages more interaction, feeling, and democratic dynamics (Scering, 1997).

Teachers must recognize and avoid these double standards so that their female students can participate fully in the classroom and prepare for a greater variety of occupational possibilities. Textbooks need to show girls and women in more challenging and prestigious roles. The curriculum should include contributions made by women and introduce students to the writings of both women and men. These measures and others may help to begin eliminating the gender bias so prevalent in the schools.

Exceptionality

The Individuals With Disabilities Education Act of 1990 (IDEA), formerly the Education for All Handicapped Children Act of 1975, provides that children with disabilities must be given a free appropriate public education with the least restrictive environment (LRE). This implies that to the greatest extent possible, all children, regardless of learning difficulties, should be educated with their peers. A centralized special education environment is considered only when the severity of the disability is such that the use of supplementary aids and services in the regular classroom is insufficient to help a child progress. If a child fails to benefit academically by inclusion in the regular classroom, or is so disruptive that the education of others is impaired, or when costs are so significant they will have a negative effect on other students, it is generally appropriate to educate the child in a special education classroom.

The term *inclusion* is not mentioned in the law, but it is used to refer to placing children with disabilities in integrated classrooms for the full day. Mainstreaming, another term used to describe placement of disabled children, refers to integrating these children for only a portion of the day. This may be during only those portions of the day when nonacademic subjects are being taught. Inclusion provides for students with disabilities to be taught in the regular classroom of their home school, with their age mates, for the full day with support services provided within the classroom.

The Supreme Court has not ruled on the LRE provision of IDEA, although it appears destined to do so in the future. Lower courts, however, have made decisions supporting both inclusion as well as special placements. This, of course, poses some problems, because the lower courts have limited jurisdictions; their decisions are binding only in the states within that particular jurisdiction. Controversies regarding inclusion, therefore, have not been resolved nationwide, but some idea regarding the current status of the issue can be gleaned from various decisions rendered in federal district courts as well as federal circuit courts of appeal. Courts have ruled that students with disabilities need not be placed in their neighborhood schools as long as such children are mainstreamed with nonhandicapped students as much as possible (Gillette v. Fairland Board of Education, 1991). School officials must assess whether placement in the regular classroom will benefit the child, not be disruptive to the learning of other students, and be cost-effective (Devries v. Fairfax County School Board, 1989; Roncker v. Walter, 1983). Courts have ruled that the burden is on the school district to rebut IDEA's strong preference for mainstreaming.

The American Federation of Teachers (AFT) has called for a moratorium on the placement of disabled children in the regular classroom, while educators review how to more effectively deal with such placements. Their position is supported by the results of a study that found that three fourths of regular classroom teachers object to schools' adopting a full-inclusion policy. Teachers feel unprepared to implement the policy fully. The National Education Association (NEA) has taken the more moderate view of supporting inclusion, if in fact regular classroom teachers are prepared to help children with disabilities. The NEA contends that support for inclusion depends on teachers' receiving appropriate training, being allowed additional time to plan for teaching disabled students, and having class sizes reduced when disabled students are present (McCarthy, 1994).

Regular classroom teachers have insufficient training in working effectively with students with disabilities. In addition, knowledge is limited regarding how to productively help these children within the context of the regular classroom without adversely affecting the learning of other students. Strategies for implementing the IDEA are yet to be created and tested sufficiently. Meanwhile, the law has been implemented, with conflicts and problems being left to the courts to resolve.

Religious Diversity and the Schools

Religious differences can be very problematic for teachers. In one community, teachers may be expected to expose their students to many different perspectives, while in another, a good deal of censorship may be experienced. This is complicated by the fact that teachers themselves may have their own religious beliefs or strong opinions about the role of including religious perspectives in school.

Even though many communities have a large cross section of different religious denominations, some regions of this country have large majorities of one religious persuasion or another. In the Southeast, for example, students may come from conservative Southern Baptist or Pentecostal families. These religious congregations may be opposed to sex education and other value-laden subjects and carefully scrutinize textbooks and other educational materials to ensure the content is sufficiently consistent with their beliefs. In inner-city schools of the East Coast, an entirely different problem may exist. Because many different denominations are likely present, teachers may have considerable difficulty avoiding conflicts when there are so many different viewpoints and expectations. In Utah many communities are dominated by members of the Church of Jesus Christ of Latter-day Saints (Mormons). Mormons typically are involved in church activities on week nights as well as on Sunday. In addition, many serve in lay leadership positions in the Church. At the same time, they may hold responsible positions in business, civic, and various service institutions. Although religion is not taught as part of the school curriculum, Mormon values and attitudes are reflected in school practices. Many children receive religious instruction during the school day in Mormon seminaries located adjacent to schools. Day-to-day activities of Mormons are governed by such practices as sexual morality, not smoking, and refraining from drinking alcoholic beverages, tea, and coffee. Obvious difficulties are possible for teachers who stray too far from accepted norms.

Some of the problems educators may have to confront that have religious connections include prayer in the school; the celebration of Christmas and Easter; and teaching sex education, evolution, values clarification, and secular humanism. Conflicts may also occur if a religious community expects teachers to include instruction that centers on particular values and character development. There may be significant differences in what is considered appropriate by various religious groups as well as between teachers and these groups. Teachers must be aware of the attitudes and practices of churches in the community that have a particular interest in whether or not these topics are included in the curriculum. Religious groups have considerable influence in communities. They commonly take an active role in censoring undesirable educational materials. These groups may be offended by materials judged to be disrespectful of authority and religion, destructive of religious values, obscene, pornographic, unpatriotic, or in violation of individual and family privacy rights (Gollnick & Chinn, 1994). Educators should avoid putting the school in conflict with the religious values and mores of the community.

America has a long tradition of religious freedom. Many groups came to this country as a result of religious persecution with the hope of finding a place where religion could be practiced unobstructed. Despite this, conflicts often arose between these early sects. Since these less tolerant beginnings, religious pluralism has been fostered, and a rapid accommodation of many American religious denominations toward mainstream acceptability and respectability has occurred. A few exceptions include Jehovah's Witnesses, Seventh-Day Adventists, Christian Scientists, Children of God, and the Unification Church. These churches, which have attempted to maintain their historic distinctiveness, have been victims of harassment by members of mainstream religious groups (Gollnick & Chinn, 1994). The beliefs of some of these religious groups that have been particularly troublesome include not honoring the flag and denying blood transfusions and other medical attention to children who are sick or dying. Teachers need to be aware of potential problems and conflicts and try to limit their deleterious effects in the school.

Some religious groups have a liberal orientation, while others are conservative. These differences need to be taken into account in understanding religious behavior. Liberal Protestant groups, for example, have tried to rethink Christianity in forms that are meaningful for a world dominated by science and rapid change. They emphasize the right of individuals to determine for themselves what to believe. They believe that authority emanates from personal religious life rather than dogmatic church pronouncements or strict Bible interpretations. Many liberal Protestants reject the traditional emphasis on the supernatural events recorded in the Bible and stress human dignity.

Church members commonly participate in social action programs, because they believe that individuals become what they are as a result of their environment, over which they have little control (Gollnick & Chinn, 1994). Conservatives, on the other hand, believe in the Bible as the exact word of God, in the reality of supernatural phenomena, and in the return of Jesus in bodily form during the Second Coming. These groups emphasize personal morality rather than social ethics (Woodward, Barnes, & Lisle, 1977). These contrasting beliefs form the basis for conflicts and misunderstandings.

Most churches have been persecuted during some part of their history. Schools should play a significant role in making students aware of the history of religious persecution and in helping students define a role for themselves that can help eliminate religious prejudice and discrimination. Schools should also be places where students' religious views are respected and where children can be free of persecution. Teachers need to be sensitive about what they say regarding religions so that no religion is belittled.

Dealing With Student Violence

There is little question that violence among children is a serious problem in America. This problem has been addressed repeatedly since the 1940s, but emphasis has increased as a result of an alarming increase in child homicide. Every year since 1950, the number of children killed by guns has doubled. Currently, homicide is the third leading cause of death of all children between the ages of 5 and 14 and the second leading cause of death for all youth between the ages of 10 and 24. It is the leading cause of death among African Americans of both sexes between the ages of 15 and 34 (Sautter, 1995).

Because of the apparent magnitude of the problem of violence, it is tempting to believe that youth crime is at an all-time high. In reality, the youth crime, in both gross numbers and percentages of all crime, peaked in the mid-1970s and has fallen off since. For example, in 1975 total arrests for youth 18 years and under rose to an all-time high of 2,078,459. This constituted 26% of all arrests. By 1980 arrests for this age group fell to 2,025,713, or 20% of all arrests. By 1990 the total was 1,754,542, or 15% of all arrests. Arrests for robbery, assault, and drug-related offenses have all decreased. However, arrests for murder have steadily increased from a low of 1,578 in 1975 to a peak of 2,829 in 1992. While total crime statistics show a decrease, extreme violence has nearly doubled in less than two decades (Sautter, 1995).

Although crime among youth under 18 generally has decreased, the problem of school violence has worsened. Ironically, over 3 million assorted crimes—about 11% of all crimes—occur each year in America's 85,000 public schools, compared to just 1 million crimes committed in the workplace. The figures would probably show an even greater contrast if all school crimes were reported. However, many are treated as school discipline problems and go unreported. It is sobering to learn that 22% of inner-city boys own guns. Nine percent of eighth graders carry a gun, knife, or club to school at least once a month. Overall, students carry 270,000 guns to school each day. On any given day, 160,000 students stay home because of fear of violence in or on the way to school (Sautter, 1995). The increase in severity of crimes committed by school-aged children has greatly impacted the schools. Instead of teaching children better social manners, or separating students involved in fisticuffs, as was the case some years ago, school personnel find themselves confiscating drugs and guns.

Despite efforts to manage violence and to eliminate lethal weapons in schools, there have been a number of unfortunate incidents of students' slaying fellow students. For example, at Columbine High School in Littleton, Colorado, during the spring of 1999, student perpetrators managed to bring a large number of explosives and guns into the school and use them to murder their classmates. Questions arise, of course, regarding what might have led to such a tragedy. Some point to the psychological impact students have on one another and how ridicule and rejection may have precipitated the disaster, and how teachers and administrators, as well as parents, should have noticed various tell-tale behaviors that might have alerted school personnel to anticipate this catastrophe. Proponents of gun regulation simply point to the necessity of stricter gun laws. Law enforcement personnel indicate that tighter security may have averted these events. Unfortunately, these solutions only help to a degree and ignore underlying problems. Violence management along with more security and regulation may help to some extent. However, more fundamental causes need to be addressed. The nature and structure of schools may perhaps be faulted. Some students may feel overwhelmed by the curriculum and achievement expectations or by how student behavior is managed. Large school size and resultant feelings of anonymity may also be contributors. The Columbine High School tragedy has no doubt provided a few answers and has stimulated greater urgency to solve this perplexity.

The American Psychological Association (APA) (1993) reports that the most critical developmental predictor of a child's involvement in violence is a history of previous violence. This suggests that early childhood intervention is essential to future crime reduction in the schools. The APA also reports that violence is related to crimes witnessed on television and in the home, in addition to a lack of supervision by adults. These and a host of other probable causative factors need to be addressed by society generally. Unfortunately, schools have traditionally had very little direct influence on some of these problems. Schools, therefore, need new strategies to deal with these problems in a way for which they are best equipped. One thing schools can do is to eliminate factors that promote a milieu of aggression in the school environment. The APA (1993) has indicated that imposition of behavioral routines and forced conformity, along with poor building designs and excessive crowding, promote violence in schools.

These problems can and should be addressed immediately. Students can be more involved in regulating themselves in school activities. Students who have greater autonomy along with requisite responsibility can be expected to be less disruptive and violent. Appropriate adult supervision and reduction of overcrowding will require even more time and commitment. Perhaps greater financial outlays need to be made for these problem-prevention strategies than for the solutions inherent in current crime legislation, which primarily puts more police officers on the streets and increases the number of prisons. Similar legislation has been enacted in the recent past with little appreciable positive impact.

Children who manifest aggressive tendencies need to be identified early and given special treatment. Commonly, these are children who have little self-control and deal with conflict and frustration by breaking things and hurting others. Identification needs to be done when children are in preschool, Head Start programs, and early elementary school, before aggressive behavior has an opportunity to become well developed. Schools may need to employ the assistance of psychologists and social workers to help with these children.

It is generally recommended that violence reduction curricula be created for children of all ages. Some programs have been established with limited success. Such programs may be criticized because they take time that is usually devoted to studying traditional subjects. Until the threat of violence in the schools is reduced, however, it will be necessary to devote some time to this important topic. Some strategies that have been suggested include cooperative learning and promotion of positive ethnic identity and sense of belonging through exposure to various cultural activities. Other programs focus on conflict resolution and conflict management. In these programs, children are trained as mediators, who then mediate everyday disputes among their peers.

Conflict resolution training is now mandated in the state of Illinois. Other states have funded violence prevention education and promoted the creation of appropriate curricula. One program is designed to teach a think-first model of violence reduction. In this program, students go through the following four steps:

1. *Keeping cool.*   In this phase, students deal with the issue of being hotheaded versus coolheaded. They learn that being coolheaded has peer acceptance and that they can remain coolheaded in conflict situations.
2. *Sizing up the situation.*   Violent children automatically define problems in hostile ways. They treat other people as adversaries when it is unwarranted. They need to see problems in less violent terms and realize that the way they define problems influences the way they choose to solve them. These skills are taught to children in this phase.
3. *Thinking it through.*   Children, particularly violent ones, rarely think of the consequences of their actions. They need to be taught to routinely examine the consequences of all their choices, so that the outcomes desired and the ones realized are the same. Children need to consider long-range goals and compare these to the consequences of their immediate behavior. This way their lives will be purposeful and their behavior regulated in terms of their desires and needs.
4. *Doing the right thing.*   Children are taught to pick responses that are most likely to help them solve their problems nonviolently. It has been found that most children want to associate with individuals who solve their problems in this way. Because it makes sense to children to solve their problems without violence, teachers can successfully teach their students conflict resolution skills (Sautter, 1995).

Based on its research, the APA (1993) recommends that the programs chosen to reduce violence be based on an understanding of developmental and sociocultural risk factors that lead to antisocial behavior and that they include theory-based intervention strategies with known effectiveness in changing behavior. These programs should have well-tested designs and should be validated through objective measurement techniques. Care should be taken because some programs are not effective. Good programs have a home-visit component and begin at the earliest level of schooling. They also promote social and cognitive skills including perspective taking, alternative solution generation, self-esteem enhancement, peer negotiation skills, problem-solving training, and anger management. It is recommended that programs focus attention not only on children already exhibiting violent behavior but also on a more general audience.

A comprehensive plan to end school violence should involve not only teachers and school administrators but also the entire community, including students themselves. It should address violence problems as they exist in a particular community. A comprehensive plan should include early identification of violent children and their immediate treatment by competent professionals. Each child needs frequent contact with an adult mentor who can help the child make successful connections to the society at large. After-school alternatives, supervised by adults, should be available for children who have nowhere else to go but to spend time with their peers. These activities may be particularly useful if they are tied directly to classroom activities.

MANAGING STUDENT ASSAULTS AND FIGHTS

School personnel are periodically required to terminate fights between students or to protect themselves or others from personal injury by student attacks. Taking the proper action is important both from a safety and legal point of view. From a legal standpoint, teachers operate to some degree in loco parentis, or in the place of the parents. At one time, this meant that teachers were authorized to terminate any behavior by students judged to be inappropriate. At the present time, teachers have less latitude in correcting student misconduct, which is due to a greater current emphasis on student rights. In the past, students were denied certain rights guaranteed other citizens. For example, citizens are protected from unwarranted searches, whereas principals could search students' lockers without regard to fundamental rights.

Teachers must also comply with the rule of reason in dealing with various aspects of the classroom, including student misconduct. According to the rule of reason, teachers must act as any prudent adult would when confronted with dangerous or potentially dangerous situations. Teachers can be held liable, for example, if they fail to take action to ensure the safety of their students by securing a cabinet that stores dangerous chemicals or by failing to properly supervise students who are using power tools in a wood shop. They may also be considered negligent if they knowingly let students bring dangerous weapons or drugs into the classroom. Ordinarily, teachers would not be required to search their students for suspected weapons or to take weapons from them. They would, however, be expected to report the presence of weapons to school authorities.

Teachers may sometimes find themselves in confrontational situations with students who do not have lethal weapons. A student may be doing something that is either annoying or dangerous to themselves or others. Suppose a student named Blake picked up a meter stick from the desk of Ms. Dawson, his teacher, and then walked around the class hitting his classmates on the head.

Ms. Dawson	Blake, stop! You could hurt someone. Return the meter stick to my desk and take your seat.
Blake	*(Holds the meter stick in his hand and glares at Ms. Dawson, then continues hitting his peers on the head.)*

Ms. Dawson	*(Moves to a position between Blake and the next student Blake apparently intends to hit. She turns her body at an angle to Blake with her right foot pointing directly at him and her left foot orientated at a 45 degree angle. She avoids squaring her shoulders with Blake in order not to provoke him further and holds out her right hand with the palm up.)* Blake, you must either put the meter stick on my desk or hand it to me.
Blake	*(Screams)* The hell with you! Get away from me! Don't you touch me!
Ms. Dawson	*(After a short pause, Ms. Dawson walks up to Blake, still holding out her hand and maintaining a nonconfrontational stance.)* Blake, stop. Put the meter stick on the desk, or hand it to me. Otherwise I will have to take it from you.
Blake	*(Blake appears very distraught. He faces Ms. Dawson and then angrily rushes her with the meter stick held high above him, obviously with the intention of hitting her over the head with it.)* Damn you! You bitch! I'll get you!
Ms. Dawson	*(Steps toward Blake and catches his wrist with her right hand before he can bring the meter stick down across her head. She then steps behind Blake, and placing her left hand in the "V" between his right arm and rib cage, pushes down, while at the same time turning Blake's wrist in a clockwise direction. She continues to apply this restraining technique until Blake's head is below his waistline. She then positions her left foot in front of Blake and between his two feet, thus preventing him from walking out of the restraining hold. In this position Blake is unable to hit or kick her. Ms. Dawson applies just enough pressure to keep Blake restrained but not to hurt him.)* Blake, I can see that you are very angry. I am not going to hurt you, and I am not going to let you hurt me. You are safe. I will not hurt you.
Blake	*(Blake tries to kick at Ms. Dawson but finds himself unable to do so.)* Damn you! Damn you! Damn you! Let go of me! Stop it! You bitch! You're going to be sorry if you don't let me go!
Ms. Dawson	*(Ms. Dawson continues to hold Blake while at the same time talking to him in quiet tones.)* I'm not going to hurt you Blake. You are safe. I will not hurt you.
Blake	*(Blake appears to calm down a bit, so Ms. Dawson releases him and steps back three or four paces and watches him. Blake looks up and glares at her and starts cursing while making his way toward her office in the back of the room.)* I told you I would get you, you bitch! *(Blake then steps into Ms. Dawson's office and scoops a pile of books from her desk to the floor and turns and looks at her defiantly.)*
Ms. Dawson	*(Ms. Dawson just looks at Blake in a calm manner. She observes that some of his resolve for revenge appears to be dissipating. She walks a little closer to him and invites him to sit down on a chair. With a little "huffing and puffing" he does. Ms. Dawson pulls up a chair 5 or 6 feet away. She continues to appear calm and is careful not to invade Blake's personal space.)* Blake, you really seem unhappy this afternoon. Tell me what is bothering you.

Ms. Dawson then engaged in active listening while Blake explained how the other students in school taunted and tormented him without mercy. He had taken all he could handle in the hallway that day. So when he entered class, he picked up the meter stick and began striking some of them. Luckily, Ms. Dawson acted before Blake's rage escalated to an uncontrollable state. Her manner was firm, but at the same time calm and reassuring. Applying this strategy, she was able to calm Blake down sufficiently. After she released him, she let him continue to "blow off steam." She made no comments about Blake's foul language, even though it was directed at her. Making an issue about his cursing she knew would only inflame him more.

After discovering the cause of Blake's outburst, Ms. Dawson could have engaged in problem solving with him. This involves (1) defining the problem, (2) creating possible solutions, (3) evaluating the solutions, (4) deciding which solution to apply, (5) implementing the solution, and (6) evaluating the solution. This way, problems can be solved before they escalate. If the problem had involved conditions that exist beyond the classroom, problem solving may not have been appropriate. Active listening would be a preferred alternative (see Chapter 7).

If Ms. Dawson had decided Blake was too difficult to handle on her own, she may have sent to the office or to an adjoining classroom for assistance. If two people were required to subdue Blake, the other person would have used the same strategy used by Ms. Dawson, except on the opposite side. If it was necessary to remove Blake from the classroom, Ms. Dawson, on his right, would have grasped his right wrist with her right hand and then wrapped her left arm under her right arm and around to where she could grasp her own right wrist. The other person would take a similar stance on the other side of Blake. He could have been safely and securely moved in this manner.

Experts recognize deepening levels of crisis in violent assaults by students (Wolfgang, 1995). The first stage is simply a potential crisis. In this case, students will appear frustrated and ready to explode. They may clench their fists and pace. Their gaze is also uncharacteristic. They may either avert their eyes or glare at you. In this stage, a student may be rational enough to respond positively to the teacher's talk. Redirect the student away from social interaction with other students, and give him or her plenty of personal space. Make as few demands as possible, and listen to what the student says.

The second stage is referred to as the developing crisis stage and is characterized by the student's attempting to achieve and maintain power over the teacher or peers. The student usually screams and threatens others, calling them names and swearing. At this point, teachers should position themselves in a nonthreatening way and let the student vent his or her aggression. Teachers should not react to verbal assaults and name-calling. Teachers commonly believe their primary responsibility is to "save face" in these circumstances. Reacting to these verbal outbursts, however, will only escalate aggression. If the aggression turns to defiance, the teacher should quietly inform the student of possible consequences, promise safety, and then give the student time and space to vent frustration without physical intervention. The teacher can deliver I-messages (see Chapter 7).

Imminent crisis is the third stage. In this case, the student assaults either the teacher or peers. The student becomes revengeful and irrational and strikes out by hitting, throwing, biting, or choking. In response to physical assault, teachers should first protect themselves. Kicks and thrown objects should be deflected if possible. If a child succeeds in getting his or her hands around your neck, respond by standing erect, thrusting both arms upright above your head, stepping back one step to put the student off balance, and turning suddenly to the right or left. If he bites you, do not pull away. Instead, place your free open hand between the child's nose and his upper lip and vibrate your hand up and down with sufficient force that the child will release you. If a child grabs your hair, clasp his hand and push it hard against your head while at the same time turning toward the student and bending your upper body down at about a 45 degree angle. His wrist will be bent back enough to cause him to lose the strength of his grip. The student may then need to be restrained in the manner previously described and transported to another location.

The final stage is achievement of equilibrium. Here, students gain a sense of composure after being out of control. They should be encouraged to talk about the situation while the teacher actively listens. The teacher should reaffirm a positive relation with students at this point (Wolfgang, 1995).

The popular press occasionally reports that the quick response of teachers has substantially reduced injury to students from individuals firing assault weapons on school grounds. Teachers have also been reported to have subdued weapon-wielding assailants, thus protecting their students from injury and even death. When weapons are used threateningly, it is usually best not to challenge the individual yourself. Ordinarily, it is more appropriate to send for help, if possible. If security personnel are present, and it is reasonable to do so, they should be summoned immediately. If an assailant is firing a weapon, children should be instructed to lie flat on the ground or dive for shelter if it is available.

A single teacher should not ordinarily try to break up a fight alone, whether or not weapons are present. If the offending students do have weapons, security personnel or school administrators should be called immediately. If the fight does not involve weapons, a teacher in an adjoining classroom may be summoned, or someone may be sent to alert school officials.

With violence becoming more common in the schools, teachers need to prepare themselves to deal with it. They should be on the lookout for the presence of weapons and drugs and take quick and decisive action to limit the impact of violence in their classrooms. Students who are present during violent outbursts need to be protected by school personnel. They also need special help once the offending students are subdued. Some children may be terrified after witnessing an assault. Others may simply be amused. It would be well, once the assault is under control, to allow class members to process what they witnessed to be certain they make proper judgments both about the threatening behavior of their classmates and the appropriateness of your actions. Children need to feel that the teacher's actions were an effort to control the irrational students' outbursts and to ensure the safety of both the offending students and classmates.

Zero-tolerance measures have been established in some schools when it comes to drugs and weapons. The Gun-Free Schools Act (20 U.S.C. Section 8921), which was enacted in 1994, compels all states who receive federal funds to pass laws requiring school officials to expel for 1 year any student who brings a gun to school. Modifications are allowed on a case by case basis. In addition, states are permitted to expand their laws to include more than guns. Ohio, for example, allows expulsion of students who bring knives to school. Congress has also passed the Jeffords Amendment, which provides that a student with a disability who brings a firearm to school may be removed to an alternative placement for up to 45 days while a change in placement is arranged (Kelly, 1998).

▼ **SUMMARY**

Good discipline depends to a great extent on how successful teachers are in relating to their students. Teachers who have fostered good teacher–student relationships have fewer discipline problems. Several significant factors can promote better teacher–student relationships. The first is good communication skills. Communication involves both sending and receiving messages. Students need to receive messages that they are cared for and appreciated. They need to express their feelings to understanding teachers who take the time necessary to help them analyze their feelings.

A second factor is autonomy. Student–teacher relationships are greatly enhanced when students feel free to make important decisions and when they are taught how to make their own decisions responsibly. Students' needs can more appropriately be met when they have a significant role in deciding what they will do in school.

Good self-concept is perhaps the most important factor in developing student–teacher relationships and in promoting achievement and good discipline. The role of the teacher in encouraging the development of students' self-concept is strategic. Teachers who provide more opportunities for students to cooperate instead of compete in the classroom will foster more learning and reduce the incidence of poor self-concept and discipline problems.

Teachers must learn to interact successfully with children of different classes, religions, and cultures as well as to help exceptional children. Failure to do so can significantly diminish the effectiveness of their teaching. Teachers must also avoid gender bias if they want all their students to have a full range of possibilities in their lives.

Schools are increasingly violent. These problems need to be addressed in school programs that help children deal with their anger. Teachers need to know how to handle violent outbursts by their students and to react to the presence of weapons in the school.

CENTRAL IDEAS

1. Improving student–teacher relationships will improve classroom discipline.
2. Good student–teacher relationships are built on effective communication, which allows students to feel accepted and important.
3. Teachers create discipline problems by promoting poor self-concept development among their students.
4. Failure-prone students have developed elaborate schemes to get through school without exposing their true ability to public scrutiny. They arrange their own failure, which is more acceptable to them than trying their best and failing.
5. Overstriving students are driven to succeed to prevent the possibility of failure. Teachers unintentionally raise the specter of failure for them by continually expecting more of them.

6. Rather than provide success experiences for failure-prone students, teachers need to help them learn how to evaluate their own performances.
7. Cooperative learning may be a useful way to help overstriving students reduce their unreasonable expectations of themselves.
8. Teachers can more effectively help students of different classes and ethnic groups by understanding their cultures and language.
9. Teachers can help children from different ethnic groups by providing cooperative learning opportunities for them and by engaging them in role playing.
10. Teachers can enhance the potential of all their students by eliminating gender bias from their classrooms.
11. Teachers must learn to take their students' religion into account in what and how they teach.
12. Exceptional children usually receive the best education in the least restrictive environment in the regular classroom.
13. Teachers can use specific moves and holds designed to control and transport violent students and to protect teachers from attack and injury.

▼ QUESTIONS AND ACTIVITIES

QUESTIONS TO CONSIDER

1. What can be done to ensure that students' developing self-esteem is not adversely affected in the schools?
2. What decisions are typically made at school in which students could take part?
3. What can teachers do to improve their communication skills in school?
4. What specific changes in curriculum and instruction will help minority students and female students achieve recognition and acceptance as well as academic success?

CLASSROOM ACTIVITIES

Break the class into groups of three students. Have one student act as a student, the second as the teacher, and the third as an observer.

1. Use role playing to simulate the following situations, which ensue when the student makes the indicated remark. In each situation, make sure that the student has in mind an underlying emotion that is not explicitly stated.
    a. "I hate you and I hate your class! How did you ever become a teacher?"
    b. "I'm not learning anything in this class."
    c. "This class is too hard. There is way too much homework."
2. Have the teacher in each group help the student prepare a solution for the following problems. Have them prepare a set of assumptions and criteria, which they then will apply in solving the problem.

a. Whether to study a unit on practical chemistry or take a more theoretical approach
b. What to do when a girlfriend or boyfriend you have gone steady with for a year decides to end the relationship

STUDENT APPLICATIONS

1. Prepare a description of how in your own teaching you might avoid the devastating effects school often has on students' self-concepts. Include provisions for dealing with special problems posed by differences in ethnicity, economic class, and gender.
2. Practice the holds and moves designed to protect you from attack by students and to safely transport a violent student.

EXPLORE YOUR PHILOSOPHY

1. Prepare a plan to improve student–teacher relationships that is consistent with your philosophy of education. Take into account racial characteristics of your students as well as gender.
2. Prepare a plan for dealing with students who manifest extreme discipline problems.
3. Prepare a plan to effectively communicate with your students. Keep in mind the specific differences you are likely to find among the students you teach.

▼ REFERENCES

Allington, R. (1991). Children who find learning to read difficult: School responses to diversity. In E. Hiebert (Ed.), *Literacy for a diverse society* (pp. 237–252). New York: Teachers College Press.

American Psychological Association. (1993). *Violence and youth* (Vol. 1). Washington, DC: American Psychological Association.

Appiah, A. (1990). *Early African-American classics*. New York: Bantam.

Aronson, E., & Carlsmith, J. M. (1962). Performance expectancy as a determinant of actual performance. *Journal of Abnormal and Social Psychology, 65,* 178–182.

Aspy, D., & Roebuck, R. (1977). *Kids don't learn from people they don't like*. Amherst, MA: Human Resources Development Press.

Backes, J. S. (1994, February). Bridging the gender gap: Self-concept in the middle grades. *Schools in the Middle,* 19–23.

Bandura, A. (1989). Human agency and social cognitive theory. *American Psychologist, 44,* 1175–1184.

Banks, J. A. (1977). The implications of multicultural education for teacher education. In F. H. Kassen & D. M. Gollnick (Eds.), *Pluralism and the American teacher: Issues and case studies* (pp. 1–30). Washington, DC: American Association of Colleges for Teacher Education.

Banks, J. A. (1993). Approaches to multicultural curriculum reform. In J. A. Banks & C. A. M. Banks (Eds.), *Multicultural education: Issues and perspectives* (2nd ed., pp. 195–214). Boston: Allyn & Bacon.

Banks, J. A., & Banks, C. A. M. (1989). *Multicultural education: Issues and perspectives*. Boston: Allyn & Bacon.

Becker, J. R. (1981). Differential treatment of females and males in mathematical classes. *Journal of Research in Mathematical Education, 12,* 40–53.

Bennett, C. I. (1986). *Comprehensive multicultural education: Theory and practice.* Boston: Allyn & Bacon.

Birney, R. C., Burdick, H., & Teevan, R. C. (1969). *Fear of failure.* New York: Van Nostrand.

Boggiano, A., Shields, A., Barrett, M., Kellam, T., Thompson, E., Simmons, J., & Katz, P. (1992). Helplessness deficits in students: The role of motivational orientation. *Motivation and Emotion, 16,* 271–296.

Brice-Heath, S. (1982). Questioning at home and at school: A comparative study. In G. Spindler (Ed.), *Doing ethnography: Educational anthropology in action* (p. 173). New York: Holt, Rinehart & Winston.

Brophy, J. (1998). *Motivating students to learn.* Boston: McGraw-Hill.

Brophy, J., & Evertson, C. (1976). *Learning from teaching: A developmental perspective.* Boston: Allyn & Bacon.

Brophy, J., & McCaslin, M. (1992). Teachers' reports of how they perceive and cope with problem students. *Elementary School Journal, 93,* 3–68.

Christian, C. C. (1978). The acculturation of the bilingual child. In F. Cordasco (Ed.), *Bilingualism and the bilingual child* (pp. 160–165). New York: Arno Press.

Cooper, H. (1979). Pygmalion grows up: A model for teachers expectations communication and performance influence. *Review of Educational Research, 49,* 389–410.

Cooper, P. J., & Simonds, C. (1999). *Communications for the classroom teacher* (6th Ed.). Boston: Allyn & Bacon.

Covington, M. V., & Beery, R. G. (1976). *Self worth and school learning.* New York: Holt, Rinehart & Winston.

Curwin, R. L., & Mendler, A. N. (1988). *Discipline with dignity.* Washington, DC: Association for Supervision and Curriculum Development.

Deci, E. L., & Porac, J. (1978). Cognitive evaluation theory and the study of human motivation. In M. L. Lepper & D. Greene (Eds.), *The hidden cost of rewards: New perspectives on the psychology of human motivation.* Hillsdale, NJ: Erlbaum.

Devries v. Fairfax County School Board, 882 F.2d 876 (4th cir. 1989).

Dweck, C. (1991). Self-theories and goals: Their role in motivation, personality and development. In R. Dienstbier (Ed.), *Perspectives on motivation: Nebraska symposium on motivation 1990* (Vol. 38, pp. 199–235). Lincoln, NE: University of Nebraska Press.

Dweck, C., & Elliott, E. (1983). Achievement motivation. In P. Mussen (Ed.), *Handbook of child psychology. Volume IV: Socialization personality and social development* (4th ed.). New York: Wiley.

Dweck, C. S., & Reppucci, N. D. (1973). Learned helplessness and reinforcement responsibility in children. *Journal of Personality and Social Psychology, 25,* 109–116.

Farr, R. C., & Tone, B. (1994). Portfolio and performance assessment: Helping students evaluate their progress as readers and writers. In *Growing up to meet your needs.* New York: Harcourt Brace College.

Gamoran, A., & Berends, M. (1987). The effects of stratification in secondary schools: Synthesis of survey and ethnographic research. *Review of Educational Research, 57*(4), 415–435.

Gillette v. Fairland Board of Education, 1991; A.W. v. Northwest R-1 School District., 813 F.2d 158 (8th Cir. 1987), cert. denied, U.S. 847 (1987).

Ginott, H. (1971). *Teacher and child.* New York: Macmillan.

Gollnick, D. M., & Chinn, P. C. (1994). *Multicultural education in a pluralistic society* (4th ed.). Upper Saddle River, NJ: Merrill/Prentice Hall.

Gollnick, D. M., Sadker, M., & Sadker, D. (1982). Beyond the Dick and Jane syndrome: Confronting sex bias in instructional materials. In M. Sadker & D. Sadker (Eds.), *Sex equity handbook for schools* (pp. 60–95). New York: Longman.

Gordon, M. M. (1964). *Assimilation in American life: The role of race, religion and national origins.* New York: Oxford University Press.

Grossman, H. (1984). *Educating Hispanic students: Cultural implications for instruction, classroom management, counseling, and assessment.* Springville, IL: Charles C. Thomas.

Grossman, H. (1995). *Teaching in a diverse society.* Boston: Allyn & Bacon.

Hernandez, H. (1989). *Multicultural education: A teacher's guide to contents and process.* Upper Saddle River, NJ: Merrill/Prentice Hall.

Howells, G. N., & Sarabia, I. B. (1978). Education and the Filipino child. *Integrated Education, 16*(2), 17–20.

Jackson, D. W. (1968). *Life in classrooms.* New York: Holt, Rinehart & Winston.

Jaramillo, M. L. (1973, November). *Cautions when working with the culturally different child.* Paper presented at the Teacher Corps Associates conference, Madison, WI.

Johnson, D. W., & Johnson, R. (1989). *Cooperation and competition: Theory and research.* Edina, MN: Interaction Book Company.

Johnson, K. R. (1971). Black kinetics: Some nonverbal communication patterns in the Black culture. *Florida Reporter, 57,* 17–20.

Jones, M., & Wheatley, J. (1990). Gender differences in student–teacher interaction. *Journal of Research in Science Teaching, 27,* 861–874.

Jones, S. C. (1973). Self- and interpersonal evaluations: Esteem theories versus consistency theories. *Psychological Bulletin, 79,* 185–199.

Jones, V. F., & Jones, L. S. (1986). *Comprehensive classroom management* (2nd ed.). Boston: Allyn & Bacon.

Katz, P., & Zigler, E. (1967). Self-image disparity: A development approach. *Journal of Personality and Social Psychology, 5,* 186–195.

Kelly, E. B. (1998). *Legal basics: A handbook for educators.* Bloomington, IN: Phi Delta Kappa Educational Foundation.

Kohn, A. (1992). *No contest: The case against competition.* Boston: Houghton Mifflin.

Leacock, E. (1969). *Teaching and learning in city schools.* New York: Basic Books

Levine, D. U. (1988). Teaching thinking to at-risk students: Generalizations and speculation. In B. Z. Presseisen (Ed.), *At-risk students and thinking: Perspectives from research* (pp. 117–137). Washington, DC: National Education Association and Research for Better Schools.

Lundeberg, M. A. (1997). You guys are overreacting: Teaching prospective teachers about subtle gender bias. *Journal of Teacher Education, 48*(1), 55–60.

McCarthy, M. M. (1994, November). *Research Bulletin,* No. 13. Bloomington, IN: Phi Delta Kappa, Center for Evaluation, Development and Research.

Martire, J. G. (1956). Relationships between the self-concept and differences in the strength and generality of achievement motivation. *Journal of Personality, 24,* 364–375.

Morrison, A., & McIntyre, D. (1969). *Teachers and teaching.* Baltimore: Penguin.

Nguyen, L. D. (1984, March). *Indochinese cross-cultural adjustments and communication.* Paper presented at the annual meeting of the Teachers of English to Speakers of Other Languages, Houston, TX.

Nieto, S. (1992). *Affirming diversity: The sociopolitical context of multicultural education.* New York: Longman.

Ogbu, J. (1988). Class stratification, racial stratification, and schooling. In L. Weis (Ed.), *Class, race and gender in American education* (pp. 176–177). Albany, NY: State University of New York Press.

Omi, M., & Winant, H. (1986). *Racial formation in the United States: From the 1960s to the 1980s.* New York: Routledge & Kegan Paul.

Parenti, M. (1988). *Democracy for the few* (5th ed.). New York: St. Martins Press.

Plyler v. Doe, 457 U.S. 202 (1982).

Purkey, W. W. (1970). *Self-concept and school achievement.* Upper Saddle River, NJ: Prentice Hall.

Ramirez, M., & Price-Williams, D. R. (1976). Achievement motivation in children of three ethnic groups in the United States. *Journal of Cross-Cultural Psychology, 7,* 49–60.

Rist, R. C. (1970). Student social class and teacher expectations: The self-fulfilling prophesy in ghetto education. *Harvard Educational Review, 40*(3), 70–110.

Roncker v. Walter, 700 F.2d 1058 (6th cir. 1983), cert. denied, 464 U.S. 864 (1983).

Ross, S. I., & Jackson, J. M. (1991). Teachers' expectations for black males' and black females' academic achievement. *Personality and Social Psychology Bulletin, 17,* 78–82.

Sadker, D., & Sadker, M. (1985). Is the O.K. classroom O.K.? *Phi Delta Kappan, 55,* 358–361.

Sadker, M., Sadker, D., & Klein, S. (1991). The issues of gender in elementary and secondary education. In G. Grant (Ed.), *Review of research in education* (Vol. 17, pp. 269–334). Washington, DC: American Educational Research Association.

Sautter, R. C. (1995). Standing up to violence: Kappan special report. *Phi Delta Kappan, 76,* K1–K12.

Scering, G. E. S. (1997). Themes of a critical/feminist pedagogy: Teacher education for democracy. *Journal of Teacher Education, 48*(1), 62–67.

Slavin, R. (1983). *Cooperative learning.* New York: Longman.

Slavin, R. (1986). *Using student team learning* (3rd ed.). Baltimore: Johns Hopkins Team Learning Project, Center for Research on Elementary and Middle Schools.

Sobol, T. (1990). Understanding diversity. *Educational Leadership, 48*(3), 27–30.

Solomon, R. P. (1988). Black cultural forms in schools: A cross national comparison. In L. Weis (Ed.), *Class, race, and gender in American education* (pp. 249–265). Albany, NY: State University of New York Press.

Strickland, B. R. (1995, January). Research on sexual orientation and human development: A commentary. *Developmental Psychology, 31,* 137–140.

Vasquez, J. A. (1988). Contexts of learning for minority students. *The Educational Forum, 52*(3), 243–252.

Walsh, C. E. (1991). *Pedagogy and the struggle for voice: Issues of language, power and school for Puerto Ricans.* New York: Bergin and Garvey.

Weiler, K. (1988). *Women teaching for change: Gender, class and power.* South Hadley, MA: Bergin and Garvey.

Weiner, B., & Kukla, A. (1970). An attributional analysis of achievement motivation. *Journal of Personality and Social Psychology, 15,* 1–20.

Weiner, B., & Peter, N. V. (1973). A cognitive-developmental analysis of achievement and moral judgments. *Developmental Psychology, 9,* 290–309.

Wheelock, A. (1992). The case for untracking. *Educational Leadership, 50*(2), 6–10.

Wilkins, R. (1995, October). The Brown decision: Dream deferred, not defeated. *The Education Digest, 61,* 19–23.

Wlodkowski, R. J., & Ginsberg, M. B. (1995). A framework for culturally responsive teaching. *Educational Leadership, 53*(1), 17–21.

Wolfgang, C. H. (1995). *Solving discipline problems: Methods and models for today's teachers.* Boston: Allyn & Bacon.

Women on Words and Images. (1975). *Dick and Jane as victims: Sex stereotyping in children's readers.* Princeton, NJ: Author.

Woodward, K. L., Barnes, J., & Lisle, L. (1977). Born again! In H. L. Marx, Jr. (Ed.), *Religions in America.* New York: Wilson.

15

Managing the Classroom

OBJECTIVES

This chapter is designed to help you

1. Begin the school year in a way that will help promote better classroom management.
2. Learn how to become better acquainted with students and thereby enhance teacher–student relationships.
3. Manage time and establish classroom routines that contribute positively to classroom management.
4. Use the skills necessary to increase the amount of time students remain on-task.
5. Arrange the physical environment of the classroom so that it enhances learning and helps prevent discipline problems.
6. Understand how to manage the classroom when student self-direction is emphasized.
7. Learn how to enlist the help of parents in promoting students' best interests in school.

Introduction

▼ When the bell rang, a few students were at their desks while others milled around the classroom socializing with their friends. Several students were in the hall outside the classroom door trying to juggle a kick-sack with their feet. Mr. Orme called for attention and implored the students out in the hall to come in before they were marked tardy. Mr. Orme's request had little effect, so he began to call out the names of students who were not in their seats. When someone failed to answer, Mr. Orme made inquiries about why that student was not in class. When he was satisfied that he had an accurate record of attendance, he hung the office notification form on a nail by the door. Some students were still out of their seats when he announced that he was going to pick up the previous night's homework. He made his way slowly around the room while students shuffled through their notes trying to find the requisite assignments. After he had finished collecting all the homework, he took a pile of papers from his desk and began handing them out one by one, calling out individual students' names as he did so. When this task was completed, Mr. Orme announced that the class would start Chapter 12 that day and asked how many students had remembered to bring their books. This question was met with groans and requests to retrieve books from hall lockers. Mr. Orme confessed that starting Chapter 12 was a change from what had been previously assigned, but he maintained that students should bring their books to class routinely anyway. This pronouncement was followed by a long lecture about responsibility. All the while, students continued to talk in various places around the classroom. Fifteen minutes of class time had now passed, and the day's lesson had still not begun. Strain showed plainly on Mr. Orme's face, and his voice registered his anger. Finally, in frustration he sent three students to the principal's office as a warning to the rest of the class to settle down and go to work.

This example illustrates the difficulty teachers experience when they fail to properly manage time in their classrooms. Many discipline problems can be avoided by properly managing the classroom environment and timing various classroom events so that students are meaningfully involved in learning. Without realizing it, Mr. Orme himself exacerbated the discipline problems by not getting his class immediately involved in productive work and by not using economical procedures for taking roll and passing out and receiving class assignments. Mr. Orme could have omitted the lecture on responsibility and the referral of students to the principal's office had he been better organized beforehand and created various routines to handle the day-to-day classroom operations efficiently and effectively. Unfortunately, poor handling of classroom routines not only takes up valuable instruction time, but it also encourages students to misbehave. Most teachers are unaware of the extraordinary amount of instructional opportunity lost as a consequence of poor time management. In one study, it was discovered that 57% of an instructional hour was taken up by in-class and out-of-class distractions such as announcements

Poor management skills can lead to significant classroom disruptions.

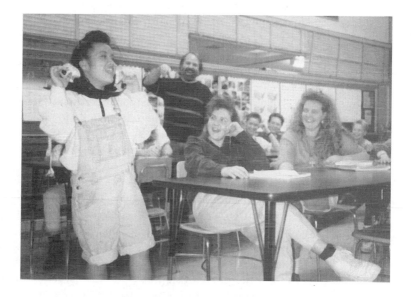

and various other intrusions. Additional time was lost because of poor attention that was due to ineffective management skills. On the average, only 19 minutes and 48 seconds of an entire instructional hour was effectively used for learning (Latham, 1985).

Beginning the Year

Getting off on the right foot with a class can make a big difference in the entire year. Some tasks and behaviors unquestionably should be avoided. Other activities can greatly enhance learning and help prevent discipline problems. Perhaps the most important day of the school year is the first one. Teachers ordinarily use this time to pass out books and take care of other essential business. However, other activities should take precedence over these business matters during the first few days. The first day is a particularly good time for teachers and students to get acquainted and for students to learn about one another.

GETTING ACQUAINTED

Students can get acquainted with their teachers in several different ways. For example, teachers may teach their best lesson on the first day of class. Students can thus get a fairly good idea of what they may reasonably expect from their teachers. Another way for teachers to introduce themselves to students is to give some type of performance or display of their talents. Art teachers can paint or draw a portrait of one of their students while other students watch; they can also place examples of their artwork around the room. Music teachers may give a concert, either vocal or instrumental, or teach students some entertaining songs. Drama teachers can do a reading from a play, enlisting the help of more experienced students to help demonstrate the kinds of skills new students might be expected to acquire. Science teachers may talk about their own research with their students. English teachers may share examples of their writing. The purpose of these first-day activities is to help students gain a perception of their teachers as acceptable human beings with talents and skills, including considerable teaching ability. Students should conclude that they will have a very enjoyable experience spending a year with their teachers.

Many teachers find it useful to have their students get acquainted with one another, particularly when they plan to have students working together in groups. Sometimes teachers invite students to play get-acquainted games or tell the class something about themselves. One teacher has been successful in getting to know her students by having them break into pairs and talk to each other extensively about themselves; then one member of the pair tells the rest of the class about the other.

Another teacher plays a game called Passing a Face. Students are arranged in groups of about 10 students. One member of each group is instructed to make a face at another person in the group. This individual then tries to alter the facial expression slightly before passing it on to the next person. This progression goes on until the last person makes a face at the person who started the game. The teacher can join in this game, too. After it has been completed, questions can be asked about the experience: "How did you feel while you were playing the game?" "What was difficult about the game?" "Whose expression did you like the best?" Games of this kind help break the ice and reduce the natural uneasiness students may feel as they begin a school year. Such games also help students see their teachers as human beings (Lemlech, 1988).

Some teachers have their students divide into groups to write a class song. This assignment can take the form of a contest: The winning composition will be the theme song for the class. The song may then be sung on various occasions throughout the year.

Teachers obviously need to know the names of their students. Students also need to know one another's names. Sometimes students are already well acquainted with one another. At other times, such as the beginning of junior high or high school, they may have many unfamiliar classmates. One way to practice names is to arrange the class in a long line around the room. If the name of the first person in the line is John, he simply announces that fact to the person next to him. Ruth, the next person in the line, points at John and says, "Your name is John, my name is Ruth." This procedure is continued until the last person in the line has named herself or himself; then that person must name all the other students in the line. After this first round, the person at the back of the line goes to the front, and the whole procedure is repeated. The game continues until all the students and the teacher can name everyone in class. (Teachers may also want to employ a seating chart for a few weeks until they are sure that they know every student's name.)

Getting to know students is more than learning names. Teachers also need to become familiar with their students' likes and dislikes, favorite activities, and learning preferences. One way to obtain such information is to ask each student to fill out a card and list hobbies, school activities, interests, work experience, and so forth. This information may help teachers better understand their students and can stimulate class participation and the development of better student–teacher relationships. In the case of students at the secondary level, it is also important to know whether they plan to attend college after graduation and what vocational plans they have. This information is helpful to teachers in determining the kinds of experiences students in their class will benefit from most.

Teachers also need to communicate whatever expectations they may have. Students need to know such things as whether homework will be assigned on weekends, whether unannounced quizzes will be given, whether reports will be oral or written, whether the format of the class is primarily lecture or discussion or independent study, whether there will be group projects, how much reading will be expected, and how they will be evaluated. Students need to know what to expect from their teachers and how it will contribute to their education.

ESTABLISHING RULES

Rules need to be established in every classroom. If they are not, misbehavior can be anticipated. Although rules are essential, they do not necessarily have to be determined exclusively by the teacher. Students can be significantly involved in determining rules as well as consequences for rule infractions. This activity is one of the single most important goals to accomplish during the first few days of class. It is probably a good idea to take care of this important task soon after you have given your students some idea of what to expect from you as a teacher. Rules may require several days to establish if students are involved. Otherwise, one class period may be all that is necessary. Whichever approach you choose, it is wise to post the rules and provide a copy to each student. Some teachers even send a copy of the rules home to parents.

If teachers decide to allow students to help determine rules, it is important to let them know that the rules they make must reflect the more general rules that have been established by the school or school district. For example, if the school has a rule against gum chewing, the class should not be allowed to make an exception. Teachers may also want to temper the consequences students decide to impose on those who break the rules. Some of these consequences may not be in the best interest of students and their learning. Others may even create legal problems for the school.

Time Management

Managing time in the classroom to keep students on-task is an important factor in maintaining good discipline. One problem teachers face is that of determining how much time they will allot for each of the planned classroom learning activities. Sometimes teachers make this decision in terms of their own interests. They make little effort to determine either the interests of their students or the amount of instruction time appropriate to their students' current level of proficiency. Teachers must balance the curriculum to meet the diverse needs and interests of students. Teachers, of course, have a professional and ethical obligation to teach those subjects and concepts their students need most. Taking into account students' interests and needs, teachers must ask themselves what learners need to know and how much time will be required for them to achieve an acceptable level of competence. How much time can be profitably spent on different topics without contributing unnecessarily to the boredom of students who have only a marginal interest in the subject? This decision is almost always a judgment call for teachers. The only rule of thumb is that as much time should be taken as students need in order to benefit most from the activities.

After time has been allocated for various topics of study, teachers must concern themselves with making sure that students remain engaged and on-task. Keeping students on-task is not just a matter of making sure that they are working; they must be meaningfully involved in learning. Therefore, so-called busywork should be avoided. The only sure way to avoid giving busywork is to be sure that students are consulted about what they learn. In addition, students should experience a reasonable level of success. Unsuccessful students will not remain on-task for long. Their minds will wander, and what they decide to put effort into will in all likelihood create discipline problems.

ESTABLISHING ROUTINES

One essential time management task is the establishment of classroom routines. Tasks such as taking attendance, making announcements, distributing materials, and collecting students' work need to be turned into routines so that they do not waste time or cause disruptions. Ways also need to be devised for moving from one activity to another and for deciding what to do when students need to go to the office, get something from their locker, or take a rest room break. All these activities can be handled with a routine that does not take the time or the attention of the teacher away from the instructional process.

A lot of time is commonly wasted at the beginning of a class period or school day. Ordinarily, teachers use this time to take attendance, collect homework, deal with absences from the previous day, get a lunch count, and make announcements. In many schools, announcements are confined to the first and last period of the day; in others, interruptions can be expected over the public address system at any time during the day. It is far better to be able to anticipate those times when announcements will be made and plan accordingly.

The other housekeeping duties that ordinarily take place at the beginning of a period also have to be routinized. Assigning students as helpers to handle routine tasks allows the teacher to spend the time making sure that class members start their work and are not involved in disruptions. Another effective way of handling housekeeping routines is to do them during class activities that are scheduled to begin as soon as students arrive. If these activities are designed to start as soon as the bell rings, or even before, less time will be lost and fewer discipline problems will develop. Students may be routinely directed to attend to instructions on the chalkboard or overhead projector screen. These instructions may inform them to review some material, begin working on an advance organizer for the current lesson, solve a puzzle, or engage in some enjoyable activity. While students are working, the teacher and student helpers can complete the various administrative tasks.

One helpful routine is to have students place their homework and other assignments in appropriately marked baskets located near the door. The teacher then does not have to deal with this daily chore. Corrected papers and tests can also be distributed in a similar manner. In some cases, students have small mailboxes into which teachers can put all materials that are to be returned to them. If this approach is impossible, the aid of student helpers may be enlisted to pass out papers at the beginning of class, especially if the teacher wants to go over the material during class. If mailboxes are used to distribute materials, thought should be given to their location. It is unwise to place them where students have to line up to retrieve their materials.

Activities such as going to the rest room, using the pencil sharpener or drinking fountain, going to learning centers, using computers, working on projects with other students, and going to the library, the cafeteria, the main office, the nurse, or the counselor all require the establishment of routines. In most schools, movement in the hallways during class time is carefully regulated. Students are generally not allowed in the hall without permission. Teachers need to create a system so that they do not have to respond endlessly to students' requests to be excused from class. In many classrooms, a hall pass is provided for this purpose. Rather than sign individual passes, teachers may direct students to take turns using a single hall pass as necessary to conduct their business outside the classroom. This routine allows students to regulate themselves unobtrusively. The one problem that may occur is that a few students will monopolize the hall pass. But this problem can also be regulated by students. A hall pass monitor can be assigned to check the frequency and duration of hall pass use. In this way fairness can be achieved without excessive intervention by the teacher.

MAKING CLEAR ASSIGNMENTS

The way in which teachers make assignments also has the potential for wasting time and promoting discipline problems. Nearly all teachers have had the experience of making assignments, only to receive a request a moment later to repeat them. Sometimes several students will make this request for each assignment. Nevertheless, it is not uncommon to discover the next day that one or more students misunderstood the assignment. Repeating instructions for assignments several times should be avoided. In the first place, some students use this ritual as a way to manipulate their teachers. Second, those students who understood the assignment the first time are understandably bored and perplexed by repeated explanations. Some teachers solve the problem by writing assignments on the board or passing out an assignment sheet to each student. Some use overhead transparencies. Others post long-term assignments on the bulletin board. Many teachers, however, make the mistake of giving all assignments orally. Unfortunately, oral assignments are easily misinterpreted and forgotten. If children are unprepared or complete their assignments inappropriately, they can always claim that they did what they thought you said. Written instruction helps prevent this problem. Probably the most effective method of making assignments is to provide students with written instructions along with verbal explanations. With this method, most misinterpretations can be corrected immediately. Many children have a difficult time understanding and following written instructions without verbal explanations. Yet they need written instructions to refer to later, in case they forget something. If after giving verbal and written instructions, the teacher requests one or two students to explain what they think the assignment is, any lingering confusion can be cleared up. This process is markedly different from the practice of some teachers who say to their students, "I'm only going to give this assignment once. If you don't get it, that's tough."

DISTRIBUTING MATERIALS

Slowdowns and disruptions can also be caused by the inefficient distribution of learning materials. Most classrooms have large supplies of books and magazines, art supplies, and laboratory and audiovisual aids of various kinds. These instructional materials often need to be passed out or collected sometime during the class period. This distribution can waste time and create disruptions. To avoid such aggravation, the materials should be strategically located so that their distribution creates as few problems as possible. Procedures for distribution should be established. For example, if reference books need to be passed out, book monitors can be selected to supply them for the students in their row. This procedure helps teachers avoid the congestion and potential scuffling that may occur when the entire class tries to retrieve or return their books at the same time.

ENDING THE LESSON

Most teachers have experienced the inevitable book closing and paper rustling that occurs just before the bell rings as students ready themselves to leave the classroom. This flurry of activity prompts many teachers to cut short their lessons and to mumble last-minute instructions, which few students hear. This transition too can be more effectively managed with the establishment of a routine all students understand and are willing to follow. This time should be used productively by the teacher. Perhaps it can be a time when lesson objectives are reviewed and last-minute instructions for assignments are given. Students can be informed that if they work until told to stop, they will be dismissed on time. Teachers should then make sure to finish with all instructional activities before the bell rings. If this procedure is routinely followed, students will not feel compelled to provide cues to teachers that it is time to start winding up the lesson.

Pacing

If students are to learn effectively, learning activities must be appropriately paced. However, pacing is a very difficult and complex task. Because students have different learning needs and interests as well as abilities, there is a wide variation in the time it takes them to understand what is being taught or to complete assignments. Some students are able to grasp a concept or master a skill quickly, whereas others are unable to learn it at all in the time allotted. If it is not necessary for students to learn the same things in about the same length of time—for example, if instruction is individualized and self-paced—this diversity poses no problem. If, however, all students need to learn the same material at the same time, pacing is critical.

One method teachers can use to gauge instruction is to find several students in the class, a reference group, who can provide them cues about the appropriateness of the classroom pace. This reference group can be asked questions about the concepts being taught; from their responses, teachers can make judgments about the general level of understanding. They can also observe various nonverbal cues. Teachers may look for puzzled expressions on the faces of specified students. If high-achieving students look puzzled, the teacher knows that nearly the whole class is likely to be lost. Boredom can also give an indication of poor pacing. The pace is usually too slow when a significant proportion of the class starts looking out the windows, thumbing through their books, or poking and talking to one another.

The question is, What is an appropriate pace? If you go too slow, the more able students get bored. If you go too fast, the less able members of the class get lost. How do you please the most students—or displease the fewest? Savage (1991) recommends choosing a pace that is appropriate for about 75% of the class. This pace, he explains, will be a bit slow for the more able learners, but it will keep the lesson moving along and provide success for a majority of the students. Students who are unable to keep pace will require some additional help. Perhaps periods of time could be set aside specifically for this group. If time is reserved for some students, teachers should be careful not to stereotype them. Their lack of success is probably a result of self-concept problems that developed in other classrooms where their inabilities received too much attention.

Maximizing On-Task Behavior

As Kounin (1970) and his colleagues found out, it is far easier to prevent discipline problems than to deal with them once they occur. Successful classroom managers, they found, used several strategies to ensure students' continued involvement in instructional activities. Successful teachers were better prepared and organized and able to guide their students smoothly through their learning activities. These teachers also had a greater awareness of what was happening in the classroom and could communicate this awareness to their students. These teachers were better able to teach interesting, stimulating lessons and to employ techniques that individualized instruction and appealed to the interests of students. Most of these strategies encouraged students to stay on-task and become productive learners.

Several well-documented practices can be used to maximize on-task behavior, and these are discussed next.

STIMULATING STUDENTS' INTEREST

Maximizing on-task behavior depends on maintaining students' attention. One way to maintain students' attention is to use the introduction to a lesson to stimulate their interest and get them involved. Start the lesson with a highly motivating activity. Often, lessons create interest and help maintain students' on-task behavior if they begin with an overview of how the topic is related to issues the children consider important. Waiting to start a lesson until such distractions as extra books, papers, and toys have been removed and everyone is paying attention also promotes on-task behavior.

Another way to maintain students' attention is to ask them questions. In a question-and-answer session, teachers should ask the question before calling on a student to answer it. Students who answer questions should be selected at random so that they do not know when they will be expected to make a response. It is also wise for teachers to wait a few seconds after asking a question and getting no response before calling on another student or answering the question themselves. Often students pretend not to know the answer if they realize that the teacher habitually waits only a very short time before asking other students to answer the question. A pause of at least 5 seconds after asking a question should be routine. A pause of as much as 10 seconds may sometimes be appropriate. Incredibly, the average time teachers wait for students to respond to their questions is a mere 0.9 second (Rowe, 1974).

Another way to maintain students' attention is to ask them to respond to their classmates' answers. In the typical classroom, students believe that the only worthwhile information is that provided by the teacher. Students' responses are considered unimportant, especially for test purposes. It would be rare, but very worthwhile, for students to record the responses made by classmates in their notes.

Students' attention can be expected to improve if teachers avoid mimicry, the practice of parroting back a student's response and following it with a short reinforcing statement. Typically, a teacher–student interchange begins when the teacher asks a question. The student gives a response, which the teacher mimics and then reinforces. For example, the teacher may ask, "What is 2 times 2?" The student responds, "4." The teacher says, "4. That's correct. Good response." Ordinarily, most student–teacher recitation sessions consist mainly of numerous repetitions of this question-response-acknowledgment cycle. Research has demonstrated that this pattern greatly reduces inquiry by students in the classroom. In addition, the length and quality of students' responses are greatly reduced (Edwards, 1980).

GUIDING STUDENTS' LEARNING

Effective seat work is an essential ingredient in keeping students on-task. It is easy for children to get distracted once seat work begins, often because they have made poor transitions from preceding learning activities and seat work. To make transitions properly, students must know precisely what to do and must have the necessary materials readily available. Once students begin their work, it is critical to monitor them.

Students sometimes fail to work consistently on an assignment until it is completed because they have no clear concept of how their work is related to previous learning, what procedures they should follow in completing the work, or how it will be evaluated. Teachers should give instructions that tell students exactly what they will be doing and how this activity relates to what they have done before. Students also need to know how to obtain assistance, what to do when the work is completed, and how much time the learning activity is likely to take. In addition, students need to know that they will be held accountable for the quality of their work.

To remain on-task, students need to know how they are doing. They need immediate and specific feedback about how they are performing so that they can make quick adjustments. The teacher needs to provide students with the information they need to continue their work successfully. One mistake teachers often make is spending too much time with too few students. Jones (1987) indicates that when teachers supervise seat work, they ordinarily ask students where they are having difficulty. They then proceed to show students where they are making mistakes. This process takes so much time that teachers do not get around to all students who need help. Jones recommends that each of these help sessions be shortened. He suggests that teachers avoid lengthy explanations; instead, they should give students a short prompt to help them solve the next part of the problem they are working on and then move on to the next student. In this way teachers are able to get around the room and help more students, thus keeping the entire class working. Otherwise, students tend to become distracted.

MINIMIZING DISRUPTIONS

Students find it difficult to remain on-task if their teachers handle class disruptions ineffectively. Teachers need to demonstrate "withitness" in their classrooms—knowing what is going on in the classroom at all times. They also must know how to target the most disruptive behaviors first and use proper timing in correcting them. If teachers are late in making their desists or focus attention on less serious problems before solving more significant ones, they will be unable to maintain proper classroom control. In addition, they must be able to demonstrate skill in "overlapping"—handling several situations simultaneously. A teacher may, for example, have to redirect one student while continuing to help another solve a problem (Kounin, 1970).

Managing the Physical Environment

Research has shown that the physical arrangement of classrooms contributes to the amount of learning that takes place in them. Furniture must be arranged to accommodate the instructional program. Consequently, the physical arrangement of the classroom must be flexible enough so that adjustments can be made for individual work, group work, and total-class activities. Space must be properly arranged to accommodate the traffic patterns of the teacher and students. Classrooms not only should be functional; they should also be aesthetically pleasing and comfortable.

THE ACTION ZONE

Adams and Biddle (1970) found that when classrooms were arranged with the students' desks in rows, the front and center of the classroom constituted an "action zone," where greater student–teacher interaction took place and where students were more successful academically. They found that students sitting in the action zone participated more in class, demonstrated better on-task behavior, had better attitudes, and attained higher achievement levels. Students who sat outside the action zone had lower self-esteem and felt threatened by proximity to the teacher. By sitting in the periphery, they succeeded in getting called on less often, thus reducing their risk of failure. Teachers tended to monitor them less frequently and allowed them to be less involved in all class activity. Some evidence indicates that students with a poor self-concept can have more positive experiences when they are assigned seats in the action zone (Dykman & Reis, 1979). Students who have difficulty staying on-task may also benefit from being in the action zone. Because students who are in the action zone receive more constructive feedback and have higher achievement levels, they experience greater feelings of competence and attain more intellectual growth.

Because the action zone is defined by proximity to the teacher, it can be changed at will by the teacher. When the seating is properly arranged, teachers can shift the action zone to almost any place in the classroom. Teachers therefore need to arrange the seating in such a way that they can decide at any time which class members to include in the action zone. Shifting the action zone should entail no more than a quick movement by the teacher to a different location in the room.

STUDENTS' SEATING

How students' desks are arranged is important not only to the movement of the teacher through the classroom but also to the creation of specific learning configurations. There is no one best way to arrange students' seating. Different seating arrangements influence behavior in different ways. It is the teacher's task to ensure that the seating arrangement employed provides optimum conditions for the kind of learning intended. Desk arrangements provide the major framework for shaping student–teacher interactions and the learning that results.

Weinstein (1979) indicates that organizing desks such that student-to-student interaction is limited to two or three students leads to higher on-task behavior, less off-task movement, and less loud talking. According to Rosenfield, Lambert, and Black (1985), students maintained greater on-task behavior and paid closer attention in discussions when they were seated in a circular pattern. However, more students also spoke out of turn. Obviously, sitting in a circle enhances students' spontaneity. Students seated in rows, on the other hand, were more likely to withdraw from discussions and engage in more off-task behavior. Students arranged in clusters were less spontaneous than those arranged in circles, but they still maintained a good deal of on-task behavior.

Teachers should create seating arrangements that correspond to their instructional intentions. If, for example, they wish to limit students' interaction and promote independent work, seating by rows would be appropriate. If they want students to initiate discussion, a circle arrangement would be best. Clusters may be the arrangement of choice when ordered participation is desired.

Good and Brophy (1986) report that students in a fourth-grade classroom who were seated at rectangular tables to do a creative writing assignment experienced difficulty in completing the assignment. Apparently, it was hard for children to work on an independent assignment when every time they raised their heads they were looking into the eyes of their peers. This arrangement facilitated discussion, but it greatly inhibited the actual writing process.

Glasser (1977) made a study of the physical design of open classrooms. He found that classroom boundaries were necessary for students to engage in activities without interfering with one another. Teachers may find it necessary to partition off areas of their classrooms to serve different purposes. Book shelves and filing cabinets are useful for this purpose, as are movable dividers. Figure 15.1 illustrates an elementary classroom designed for different types of work, partitioned off to provide some degree of privacy. Notice that the teacher's desk is located where all areas of the classroom can be simultaneously monitored. Conceivably, some students could finish assigned seat work while others engage in laboratory work, do small-group work, watch films, or read. This arrangement provides the kind of flexibility necessary to accommodate the needs of students and the instructional strategies of teachers.

CLASSROOM ENVIRONMENT

Classrooms should be exciting, comfortable places. No classroom should be ugly or forbidding. Instead, the classroom environment should produce feelings of security and warmth. Because the classroom environment has a direct impact on children, the teacher has the important responsibility of creating pleasant surroundings that emphasize learning. According to Weinstein (1979), studies have shown that as the quality of the classroom environment deteriorates, teachers become more controlling and less friendly and sensitive. Students become correspondingly less involved and engage in more conflicts with peers. Students in unattractive classrooms experience more feelings of fatigue and discontent.

What can teachers do to improve the learning environment? Providing more comfortable furniture is one thing that may be done. A couple of overstuffed armchairs and a few beanbag chairs appropriately placed would help. Some reading lamps and live plants and pictures can also make the classroom more comfortable. Bulletin boards on which questions to be investigated are posted provide intellectual stimulation. Books and magazines can be placed in strategic places in the room as well. Books discarded by local libraries can be picked up for a few pennies. Many of these books are still valuable and can serve as additional learning resources for students.

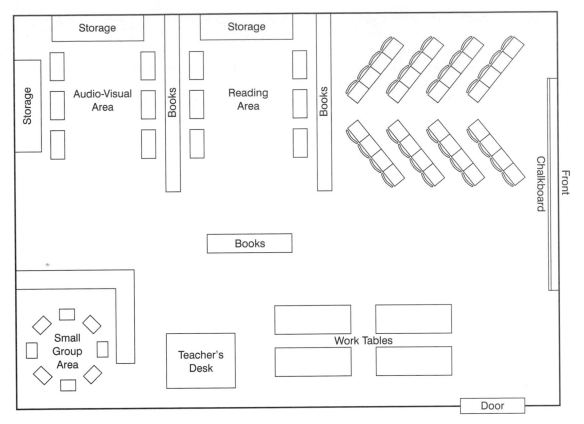

FIGURE 15.1
A flexible classroom arrangement.

Creating efficient traffic patterns is also a critical factor in arranging classroom furniture. Jones (1987) suggests several arrangements that allow teachers easy, quick access to all areas of the classroom (see Figure 10.1). Teachers need to be able to move from one location to another without having to retrace their steps or move around various obstacles.

The location of the teacher's desk is also a consideration. In many classrooms, the teacher's desk is located at the front of the room. However, this is probably the worst possible location (Savage, 1991). A much more suitable location is a corner in or near the back of the room. Here teachers can conduct business with individual students in greater privacy, and students can share their feelings with teachers with less risk of embarrassment. In addition, if the teacher is in the back of the room, students are less aware of when they are being closely monitored. More on-task behavior can be expected under these conditions.

Background music can also improve classroom ambience. Soft music in the background can aid learning and may even improve academic performance (Charles, 1983).

Music can be used to create a sense of relaxation and to block out various distractions. It can also be used to create a learning set—that is, classroom conditions arranged in such a way that students want to begin learning immediately. One elementary teacher used a piece of music called "Popcorn" to enhance a lesson on poetry. While the children were out for recess, this enterprising professional placed three or four popcorn poppers around the room. Just as the children were coming in from recess, the poppers began emitting an unmistakable sound and an irresistible aroma. Meanwhile, "Popcorn" played softly in the background. As the students took their seats, they were instructed to go to work immediately writing a poem about popcorn. As they worked, their little bodies moved with the music while their teacher moved around the room depositing little piles of popcorn on their desks. The children's poems were so extraordinary that the teacher's eyes filled with tears as she read them.

Classroom Empowerment

The classroom management procedures outlined in this chapter are consistent with teacher-directed instruction, but some are incompatible with student-directed learning and discipline. For example, the procedures for promoting on-task behavior are generally designed to help students focus on teacher-assigned activities. Teachers who emphasize student-directed learning and discipline have different management problems that require a different set of management techniques. These techniques consist of ways to empower students to regulate their own classroom activities responsibly.

One of the central problems in classroom management is eliminating wasted time. The solution to this problem in teacher-directed learning is to motivate students and then carefully direct their learning. With self-directed learning, however, student interests take precedence over teacher objectives and control. In this case, the teacher tries to determine what student interests are and then provide ways for them to pursue their interests rather than attempting to motivate them to do what the teacher has planned. Once learning has begun, the teacher needs to visit with students periodically to ask questions about the work they are doing and the progress they are making, to clarify concerns, and to remove roadblocks. The teacher may also need to provide additional resources and encouragement so learning can proceed unimpeded. Occasionally the teacher may need to question students to determine if they are indeed learning responsibly.

Learning in the classroom may include whole-class experiences, small-group activities, or individual learning. Students can decide on the kind of learning configuration they prefer by examining their goals and deciding which learning tasks lend themselves to whole-class learning and those best learned in other configurations.

Once class members have a good idea of what they desire to focus their time and energy on, and how they wish to do it, it is imperative that these desires be clarified and written down. Students should be polled to determine if they have sufficient commitment to the learning goals to vigorously pursue them. This interaction should be followed up by additional meetings to ensure that learning goals continue to hold student interest or if they should be modified in some way. It is wise to conduct these classroom meetings on a regular basis so that students can anticipate them. Also, in the event problems arise, the teacher can indicate to students that they will be addressed in the next meeting. The focus of these meetings should be on clarification of the learning expectations and a recommitment by students to conscientiously pursue them.

It is likely that teachers will need to occasionally provide students instruction regarding their role in self-directed learning and self-governance. Many students will have had more experience with teacher-directed learning and find it difficult to adjust to radically different classroom management conditions. Unless students have a thorough understanding of how to manage their own learning, and have made a firm commitment to do so responsibly, this learning approach will have limited success. In self-governing environments, misunderstandings may occur that need to be quickly resolved. Again these should be part of the agenda in periodic classroom meetings.

With self-directed learning, satisfying student needs becomes paramount. Before they will pursue learning activities with enthusiasm, students want to feel that these experiences will satisfy their needs. The needs, and the extent to which they are being satisfied by current learning activities, can be explored during classroom meetings, and necessary adjustments made so students do feel satisfied.

In self-directed learning, teachers may experience difficulty providing the learning resources their students need. Every effort should be made to have the materials on hand, or to have determined in advance where materials may be obtained. In some cases, the items students want may be inaccessible or too expensive. Sometimes access to appropriate materials and equipment can be arranged through parents or nearby universities. Special arrangements may need to be made for students to visit locations outside the school to get the necessary materials and equipment. In school, students may need access to laboratories or study areas at times outside regular classroom hours. Procedures need to be created to give them the access they need.

The way in which students are evaluated, or asked to demonstrate their learning, needs to be managed. In some cases, projects may be housed in the student's home, or in a laboratory or some other setting outside the school, making them difficult to examine. Also, some students will desire to make presentations to the class on their projects. Time constraints and conflicts, arranging for equipment, and other related factors should be attended to in scheduling classroom presentations and in making assessments of student work.

Parent Involvement

Epstein (1987) has identified five major types of parent involvement that influence the quality of children's experience in the schools. They follow:

1. The basic obligation of parents to address the health and safety concerns of their children. Many parents lack the necessary parenting and child-rearing skills to properly prepare their children for school. They need to be taught the special skills necessary to supervise, discipline, and guide their children at each age level and to

build positive home conditions that support school learning and appropriate school behavior of their children.

2. There must be adequate communications between the home and school about school programs and children's progress. The means of communication must provide the most effective way of communicating accurately and positively with parents.

3. Parents should be involved in school affairs as volunteers in a variety of ways. They may be asked to assist teachers, administrators, and children in the classroom. They need to support a wide variety of student activities in addition to classroom experiences.

4. Parents must learn how to provide their children with the help they need at home to effectively complete homework assignments and to work cooperatively with teachers in coordinating the work done at school as well.

5. Parents need to be involved in school governance. They need to take decision-making roles in advisory councils or other committees or groups at the school, district, or state level. They have a significant role to perform in monitoring the schools and making recommendations for improvement.

PARENTING AND CHILD-REARING RESPONSIBILITIES

In some cases parents of preschool children are still in school themselves. The potential for neglect is pronounced in these cases. In addition many parents have a desire to be good parents but lack the necessary skills. In some cases this lack leads to various kinds of abuse, which eventually may limit the children's ability to learn effectively. States who have taken Epstein's (1991) recommendations seriously have initiated programs to provide training for parents. Notable examples include California (Solomon, 1991) and Illinois (Chapman, 1991). In these states, as well as a few others, parents are given training in how to raise children with a positive self-concept as well as how to help their children better prepare for school.

COMMUNICATIONS

Parent–teacher conferences have been the mainstay of programs to enlist parent cooperation in the schools. Ordinarily these take place once or twice a year. However, parents commonly express discomfort with these sessions because of their formality. Parents are dissatisfied because school people tend to be too businesslike, too patronizing, and too much inclined to talk down to them (Lindle, 1989). Parents prefer school relationships where their opinions are valued and their involvement in solving problems is sought.

Parents appreciate teachers and administrators who keep them appraised of situations involving their children. They prefer to be alerted regarding potential problems rather than learning hours later of negative incidents involving their children. Parents prefer less formal relationships with teachers and more regular and frequent contacts by them. It would be well if these contacts involved positive school happenings as well as problems. Many parents have learned that the only time they receive calls from the school is when their child is in trouble.

Parent–teacher conferences should not focus exclusively on academic performance. Social and psychological adjustments should also be explored. Parents should learn how well their child relates to other children, whether he or she participates in classroom activities enthusiastically, and the extent of growth in a variety of intellectual capacities. It would be wise for teachers to keep anecdotal records of their students' activities along with examples of their work. A portfolio assembled by each student is an excellent starting point for a teacher–parent discussion. The following four steps are useful in conducting parent–teacher conferences:

1. *Build rapport.* Establish a comfortable relationship by making parents feel welcome and at ease. Create an informal atmosphere by engaging in small talk about some neutral topic.
2. *Obtain information.* The success of this will depend on how good a listener the teacher is. One good approach is to ask parents to express how they believe their child feels about the class. Negative or emotionally laden questions should be avoided. Teachers are better able to give a valid report of a child's success in school once they get a better idea of the home background. They can also get insight about parents' expectations.
3. *Provide information.* Start by offering suggestions for how to enhance the student's learning. Statements regarding the child's progress can then be reviewed. Make every effort to ensure parents that you will act upon their concerns in helping their child make progress at school.
4. *Follow-up strategies.* Toward the end of the conference, review the major points of the meeting and mention any unresolved issues that may need additional discussion or action. If additional conferences are needed, they can be scheduled at this time. Contact parents within 2 weeks of the conference. If the conference went well, a simple thank-you note is sufficient. If additional consultation is needed, this can be arranged. If problems were experienced in the conference, this contact will help re-establish friendly relations (Wolf & Stephens, 1989).

Communication between the school and parents has also been enhanced with new technology. Computers along with answering machines have provided daily access to the school by parents and by teachers to their students' homes. Technology has also been used to provide parents with assistance in working with their children on homework assignments.

To encourage more effective communication between the home and school, some districts have established Parent Centers. Centers are staffed by parents who have students in school and provide a place where other parents can drop in to express their concerns, get information about school programs, or engage in informal conversations. Home Visitor programs have also been established to aid school–home communications. Home visitors call on families who may have little or no contact with the school due to work schedules or other constraints. They provide information to families about school expectations, the curriculum, rules, and requirements. They also dispense advice and materials on how family members can help children with their schoolwork (Davies, 1991).

VOLUNTEERS

One way to promote greater parent involvement is to have them serve as volunteers. There are at least three categories of experiences that parent volunteers can provide the schools: (1) skills in hobbies and crafts, (2) direct knowledge and experience in occupations, and (3) appreciation of, knowledge of, or skills in many aspects of different cultures. Regarding hobbies and crafts, parents can be asked to provide displays, do demonstrations, or teach students how to engage in the particular hobby. In providing information about occupations, volunteers can show examples of a typical day at work, explain the skills needed and levels of training required for a particular occupation, explain the pros and cons of going into a particular field, and indicate the possibilities of employment and potential salaries. If parents have spent time in foreign countries, they will be particularly helpful in explaining the history, geography, customs, art, music, and political life of these countries (Hunter, 1989).

One commonly untapped source of school volunteers is senior citizens. Senior citizens are an important resource given the fact that the pool of parent volunteers has shrunk over the last few years. More and more schools are discovering the wealth of experience and expertise available in senior citizens (Armengol, 1992). The Salt Lake City School District recruits and trains older adults to become involved in classrooms with such activities as story reading, field trips, tutoring, arts and crafts, and sports. Many of these volunteers work in resource rooms with special education students (Salt Lake City School District, 1992). Older volunteers can enliven a classroom by offering new and unique perspectives on a variety of topics. One side benefit is that such intergenerational programs can fill an important gap left by the decline of the extended family. Senior volunteers often serve as surrogate grandparents. Their involvement can help dispel negative stereotypes that youth and older adults may have about each other (Matters, 1990).

SCHOOL GOVERNANCE AND PARENTAL DECISION MAKING

Parents should be involved in governance, decision making, and advocacy, including participation in parent–teacher organizations and in various decision-making and advisory roles (Epstein, 1991). There is no better way to promote genuine involvement than to share decision-making responsibilities. People find it hard to get enthusiastically involved when their input is neither valued nor sought. Involving parents holds the potential for infusing school decision making with new insights and concerns. It also provides a means to energize the community in promoting school programs, funding, and policy development. Schools need the creativity, resourcefulness, and ingenuity of all stakeholders, be they administrators, teachers, nonprofessional staff, parents, students, or other community members. Such involvement energizes and affirms people and challenges them to contribute their energy and ideas to a commonly pursued enterprise. One benefit that can be accrued from parent involvement is the ability of parents to focus on the most critical point of schooling, that their children receive a good education. Hopefully, with input from parents, some of the educational practices that have become entrenched in the schools can be examined and appropriate changes made (Jennings, 1989).

▼ SUMMARY

Successful classroom management can go a long way toward preventing discipline problems. It is far better to prevent discipline problems than to solve them once they occur. Effective classroom management begins on the first day of class. Because good first impressions are so important, teachers may plan to teach their best lesson of the year on that day. Afterward, classroom rules should be established. Then teachers and students can take part in get-acquainted activities. Teachers need to know the names of their students and get some idea of their interests and favorite extracurricular activities. All this groundwork needs to be laid before such mundane tasks as passing out books are undertaken.

A critical part of classroom management is time management, the establishment of routines that economize classroom operations. Better discipline can be expected when books and papers are passed out and collected efficiently.

Children need to make the best use of their time and maintain their concentration on learning if they are to achieve the most from their school experiences. The more time spent studying, the greater the potential for learning. Time on-task can be enhanced by maintaining students' attention, giving clear instructions, presenting stimulating lesson introductions, making proper use of questioning strategies, carefully monitoring students' seat work, providing timely and specific feedback, and managing disruptions effectively.

The physical environment of the classroom contributes a great deal to students' comfort and learning. The arrangement of students' seating should allow teachers to move the action zone wherever they desire. It should also help teachers maintain control. Different seating arrangements should be used depending on the kind of learning activity. The classroom can be made more pleasant for students with the addition of comfortable furniture, better lighting, more interesting bulletin boards, supplementary learning materials, and other amenities. Improving the classroom environment will improve students' learning.

When student-directed learning is emphasized, student interests take precedence over time management. The teacher's role changes from managing behavior to encouraging students to manage their own behavior. Satisfying student needs becomes paramount, and supplying them with materials exceeds dispensing information in importance.

Students benefit extensively from parent involvement. Parents need to know how to prepare their children for school, communicate effectively with the school regarding their children's educational progress, work effectively with their children on their homework, and become involved in school governance to ensure quality education for their children.

CENTRAL IDEAS

1. The first day of class is usually the most important day of the school year. It should be filled with learning activities that promote a positive image of the teacher.

2. To properly manage a classroom, teachers need to know their students well not only their names but also their interests and favorite activities. Teachers can use this information to foster more positive relationships with their students.

3. All classrooms need rules. Students may or may not be involved in determining the rules. Students should help make the rules if the goal of the teacher is to help them become more self-governing.

4. If students are engaged in common learning experiences, teachers need to properly pace instruction so that the greatest number of students receive the greatest benefit. Instruction that is given at too slow a pace bores the more able students, and the less able students become lost when the pace of instruction is too fast. Teachers must try to find a pace that accommodates both groups.

5. Classroom routines such as collecting and passing out papers must be managed so that little time is lost and students do not become distracted.

6. Proper classroom management involves keeping students on-task. When students are allowed to be distracted, discipline problems occur.

7. Seating in the classroom should provide maximum flexibility for teachers. They should be able to move quickly to any place in the classroom to maintain control or adjust learning conditions.

8. The environment in the classroom does make a difference in the achievement as well as the comfort of students.

9. Schools can be made more effective by creating a positive ethos, monitoring and regulating classroom climate, formulating clearly understood goals, promoting effective teaching and leadership, promoting effective communication, involving teachers and students in leadership and decision making, providing positive incentives, and establishing good order and discipline.

10. When self-directed learning is emphasized, management involves helping students learn more responsibly. The teachers' role is to promote student interests, supply materials, and carefully monitor student progress.

11. Parents need to be committed to their children's education. This involves properly preparing their children for school, communicating productively with the school, working effectively with children on their homework, and becoming involved in school governance.

▼ QUESTIONS AND ACTIVITIES

QUESTIONS TO CONSIDER

1. What issues need to be resolved in creating classroom rules?
2. How can teachers get the resources they need to create a stimulating and comfortable atmosphere in their classrooms?
3. How can teachers involve parents productively in school affairs that include their children?

4. How does the teacher's management role change depending on whether student self-direction is emphasized or not?

CLASSROOM ACTIVITIES

1. Have the class develop a list of routines for managing the various tasks and conditions in classrooms that can become management problems.
2. Create a diagram of a classroom. Have students position various items of furniture in appropriate places to enhance learning and provide proper classroom control.

STUDENT APPLICATIONS

1. Create a comprehensive statement about how you can become an effective classroom manager. Discuss what you could do during the first few days of class to improve student–teacher relationships and to provide an image of yourself as a competent teacher.
2. Explain what you plan to do about classroom rules. Outline the routines you plan to use in managing your class. Sketch some furniture arrangements you would like to have in your classroom. Describe the ways in which you could make your classroom environment more comfortable and conducive to learning.

EXPLORE YOUR PHILOSOPHY

Examine your classroom management plan along with your philosophy, and decide if they are consistent with one another. Make adjustments to your plan as necessary.

▼ REFERENCES

Adams, R. S., & Biddle, B. J. (1970). *Realities of teaching: Exploration with videotape.* New York: Holt, Rinehart & Winston.

Armengol, R. (1992). Getting older and getting better. *Phi Delta Kappan, 73*(6), 467–470.

Chapman, W. (1991). The Illinois experience: State grants to improve schools through parent involvement. *Phi Delta Kappan, 72*(5), 355–358.

Charles, C. (1983). *Elementary classroom management.* New York: Longman.

Davies, D. (1991). Schools reaching out: Family, school and community partnerships for student success. *Phi Delta Kappan, 72*(5), 376–382.

Dykman, B., & Reis, H. (1979). Personality correlates of classroom seating position. *Journal of Educational Psychology, 71,* 346–354.

Edwards, C. H. (1980). The relationship between type of teacher reinforcement and student inquiry behavior in science. *Journal of Research in Science Teaching, 17,* 337–341.

Epstein, J. L. (1987). What principals should know about parent involvement. *Principal, 66*(3), 6–9.

Epstein, J. L. (1991). Paths to partnerships; What we can learn from federal, state, district, and school initiatives. *Phi Delta Kappan, 72*(5), 345–349.

Glasser, W. (1977). Ten steps in good discipline. *Today's Education, 66*(4), 61–63.

Good, T. L., & Brophy, J. E. (1986). *Educational psychology* (3rd ed.). New York: Longman.

Hunter, M. (1989). Join the "par-aide" in education. *Educational Leadership, 47*(2), 36–41.

Jennings, W. B. (1989). How to organize successful parent advisory committees. *Educational Leadership, 47*(2), 42–45

Jones, F. H. (1987). *Positive classroom instruction.* New York: McGraw-Hill.

Kounin, J. S. (1970). *Discipline and group management in classrooms.* New York: Holt, Rinehart & Winston.

Latham, G. (1985, November 7). *Defining time in a school setting.* Presentation to PDK/UASCD Conference, Salt Lake City, UT.

Lemlech, J. K. (1988). *Classroom management: Methods and techniques for elementary and secondary teachers.* New York: Longman.

Lindle, J. C. (1989). What do parents want from principals and teachers? *Educational Leadership, 47*(2), 12–14.

Matters, L. (1990). *Intergenerational relations: Older adults and youth.* Columbia, MO: Center on Rural Elderly.

Rosenfield, P., Lambert, N., & Black, H. (1985). Desk arrangement effects on pupil classroom behavior. *Journal of Educational Psychology, 77,* 101–108.

Rowe, M. B. (1974). Reflections on wait-time: Some methodological questions. *Journal of Research in Science Teaching, 11,* 263–279.

Salt Lake City School District. (1992). *SMILES (Senior Motivators in Learning and Educational Services).* Unpublished manuscript. (ERIC Document Reproduction Service No. ED 346 983)

Savage, T. V. (1991). *Discipline for self-control.* Englewood Cliffs, NJ: Prentice Hall.

Solomon, Z. P. (1991). California's policy on parent involvement: state leadership for local initiatives. *Phi Delta Kappan, 72* (5), 359–362.

Weinstein, C. (1979). The physical environment of the school: A review of the research. *Review of Educational Research, 49,* 577–610.

Wolf, J. S.,& Stephens, T. M. (1989). Parent/teacher conferences: Finding a common ground. *Educational Leadership, 47*(2), 28–31.

Index